CO-AWX-306

After
Jews AND Arabs

After
Jews and Arabs

REMAKING LEVANTINE CULTURE

Ammiel Alcalay

University of Minnesota Press

Minneapolis

London

Published by the University of Minnesota Press
2037 University Avenue Southeast, Minneapolis, MN 55414
Printed in the United States of America on acid-free paper

Library of Congress Cataloging-in-Publication Data

Alcalay, Ammiel.
    After Jews and Arabs : remaking Levantine culture / Ammiel Alcalay.
        p.   cm.
    Includes bibliographical references (p.) and index.
    ISBN 0-8166-2154-3 (hc). — ISBN 0-8166-2155-1 (pb)
    1. Jews—Civilization—Arab influences.   2. Jewish-Arab relations.   3. Israel—Intellectual life.   4. Sephardim—Intellectual life.   5. Jews, Oriental—Israel—Intellectual life. 6. Middle Eastern literature—History and criticism.   7. Jewish literature—Middle East—History and criticism.   8. Israeli literature—History and criticism.   I. Title.
    DS113.A398   1993
    305.892'4—dc20   92-19124
                                                                                                          CIP

The University of Minnesota is an
equal-opportunity educator and employer.

To the memory of Dr. Lily Moed

When the LORD your God brings you to the land you are about to invade and occupy, and He dislodges many nations before you—the Hittites, Girgashites, Amorites, Canaanites, Perizzites, Hivites, and Jebusites, seven nations much larger than you—and the LORD your God delivers them to you and you defeat them, you must doom them to destruction: grant them no terms and give them no quarter. . . . The LORD said to Moses: You are soon to lie with your fathers. The people will thereupon go astray after the alien gods in their midst, in the land which they are about to enter; they will forsake me and break My covenant which I made with them. . . . Therefore, write down this poem and teach it to the people of Israel, put it in their mouths, in order that this poem may be My witness against the people of Israel. . . . This poem shall confront them as a witness, since it will never be lost from the mouth of their offspring.

Deuteronomy 7:1–3; 31:16, 21

It is easy to say: My homeland is where I was born. But you have returned to the place of your birth and found nothing. What does this mean? It is easy to say: My homeland is the land where I shall die. But you can die anywhere. Possibly you will die on the border between two countries. . . . You abandon the past when you write a history of it. Make amends with your past, date your wounds and your estrangement.

Mahmoud Darwish

Contents

Acknowledgments

The kind of endeavor this book represents is, almost by definition, a collective one. The insights I have been able to gain rest on the tradition of generations of great scholars, writers, and thinkers. There are a number of departed for whom, or at least so I had hoped, this book would have been meaningful. I think particularly of the late Dan Pagis, whom I had the priviledge of knowing and studying with in Jerusalem. I also think of the late S. D. Goitein, truly a giant in the field of Mediterranean studies, but someone who always found the time to answer a query. And the death, too, of Edmond Jabès has left a great void in our sense of memory and exile, in our connections between the old Levantine world and its new diasporas. The more recent death of a dear friend, Edouard Roditi, whose global presence harked back to a different sense of time and place, marks another, even more immediate, loss. An ancient Chinese proverb warns us against living in "interesting times." Yet it seems as if, indeed, we have been condemned to live in *very* interesting times. It was in such a time, in Jerusalem, that I met Lily Moed, to whose memory this book is dedicated. To all who had the pleasure of knowing and working with her — as a friend, teacher, advocate, or activist — her joy, compassion, and constant sense of humor are irreplaceable. She was certainly both a presence and an example for me throughout my work on this book.

There are so many to thank for their help and support. Beginning at the CUNY Graduate Center, I would like to thank Allen Mandelbaum for his generosity and human presence; such an acknowledgment cannot even begin to recount the traditions he has been instrumental in passing on to me and other students and colleagues whose spirit he has embraced. I would also like to thank Burton Pike for his continued clarity and sense of perspective; Frederick Goldin, for his wisdom and uncanny ability to ask the essential questions; Angus Fletcher, for many, many hours of informed conversation, in its most stimulating form. I thank Edward Said for an early reading and Omar Addi for his friendship and assistance. Thanks to the Hacham, Rabbi Salomon Gaon, for his encouragement and support; to David Shasha, for the intensity and precision of his thought; to Gordon Piltch and Rabbi José Faur.

I would also like to mention the late Robert Gilleece of the CUNY Graduate Center Financial Aid Office without whose ingenuity I might never have gotten so far. I was also fortunate enough to be the recipient of a number of awards and grants without which completion of research for this project would have been much more difficult than it was: the Newstead Memorial Competition and the Newstead Dissertation Award from the CUNY Graduate Center, in the memory of Dr. Helaine Newstead, distinguished professor of English and comparative literature; the Fulbright Predoctoral Research Grant, and the National Foundation for Jewish Culture Doctoral Fellowship. My gratitude for these awards, and for the people who supported my nomination, is genuinely heartfelt; as the Talmud says, "If there is no flour, there can be no *Torah*."

Along the routes toward knowledge and understanding, there are many incarnations: for their examples of clarity and precision in writing and teaching, I would like to thank Vincent Ferrini, Gilbert Sorrentino, and Toby Olson. In France, I thank Jacques Hassoun for his continuing exchange and Shmuel Trigano for the enormous contributions he has made to consolidating Sephardic thought. In the Levant itself, I would like to thank Sasson Somekh of Tel Aviv University for his constant help and generosity; Nissim Rejwan, for opening his door to my initial inquiries many years ago and for keeping that door open; and Shime'on Ballas of Haifa University, for his personal attention and public courage. At Hebrew University, I would like to thank Isaac Benabou, Albert Arazi, Shmuel Moreh, Meir Bar-Asher, and Shlomo Elbaz; also Ephraim Hazzan at Bar Ilan University, for persevering to open up the field of Hebrew literature, and T. Carmi at Hebrew Union College, for his work and generosity. I would like to thank Itshak Betsalel and the staff at the Ben Zvi Institute in Jerusalem; Rabbi Aharon Singer, for his openness and support in times of adversity; and Dr. Amnon Orent, for his assistance over the years. Many thanks are due to my dear friends Simon Lichman, Jill Magen, Carol Spencer, Carol Ann Bernheim, Esther Merzel, Kathy Bergen, David Neuhaus, Mahmoud Hawari, Roland Rance, and Kamilia Bishara for talking, thinking, reading, listening, and being there; and also to Shelley Elkayam, Tikva Levi, Eli Hamo, Sami Chetrit, Avi Bardugo, Dudi Mahleb, and Charlie Abutbul, for allowing me to share their energy and enthusiasm in efforts to affect true change. Many thanks to Shlomo Swirski for his support and the integrity of his endeavors. Thanks also to Mrs. Hava Eliachar for giving me access to a world long gone; and to Eva Weintraub for entrusting me with the task of making the important works of Jacqueline Kahanoff known to a larger audience. Many, many thanks to Mr. Aziz Yifrah, an encyclopedic source of knowledge on Middle Eastern music, in whose shop I spent many hours talking and listening. Thanks to the staffs at the Arab Studies Society, particularly Ghada as-Shammali, and the Palestine Human Rights Information Center in East Jerusalem, particularly Samir Abu-Shakrah, from whose sources I learned so much. Thanks also to the Alternative Information Center in West Jerusalem for help and hospitality in providing a forum during frustrating times. Thanks also are due to David Hamou, Erez Bitton, and Michel Elial, also for providing a forum in their respective journals, *Another Newspaper, Aperion,* and *Levant.* Thanks to Daniel Elazar for providing me with desk space for a period at his Jerusalem Center and to Moshe Shaul at the Judeo-Spanish section of Israel Radio for his friendship and help in providing access to sources. Finally, to all the residents of Rehov Korazin in Nahlaot, Jerusalem, who sometimes kept me from working and other times inspired me further.

Back in the "west," my work met quite a bit of resistance along the way. I would like to give thanks to the faithful, those who believed in and supported my work at various stages: to Frankie Westbrook, for trying; Barbara Harlow, for continued enthusiasm; Ella Shohat, for her suggestions; to Joan Dayan, Victor Perera, Anton Shammas, Susan Einbinder, Kamal Boullata, Lilly Farhoud, Yerah Gover, and David Jacobson, for their constant and unequivocal support; and also to Joelle Bahloul, Jacob Bender, Hannah Davis, Joe Stork of *Middle East Report,* and Nadine L. McGann of *Afterimage.* Finally, I would like to express my deep gratitude to Biodun Iginla at the University of Minnesota Press for immediately believing in my work and thank the staff at the press for making the production of this book such a pleasurable experience. Thanks also to Ann Klefstad, for her excellent emendations and suggestions.

At Queens College, I find myself in what seems to be a fairly unusual situation. I have had the good fortune of being able to work on very contemporary Hebrew texts with large groups of students who are either Israeli or come from an Israeli background, and I can only hope that I have taught them as much as I have learned from them. In particular, I would like to thank Orit Redl, Galia Barkai, Svia Finkelman, Avital Kordova, Avraham Dory, Yoram Solomon, Nahum Khaziev, Avi Weinberg, and Ronit Ben-Naeh for their originality and intelligence. Many thanks also for the continued support of my colleagues at Queens: Joel Lidov, Jerry Acker, Susan Spectorsky, Elisheva Carlebach, Emanuel Goldsmith, Ali Ahmed, Jose Kozer, Tom Byrd, and Jack Reilly.

I am sure there are many others whose help along the way was essential; please accept my apologies if I have failed to mention you. And finally, many thanks to Klara and Aram, my truest readers in the largest sense of that term.

Introduction

Charting the Terrain

> The only thing that begins by reflecting itself is history. And this fold, this furrow, is the Jew. The Jew who elects writing which elects the Jew . . .
>
> Jacques Derrida

> . . . *difficulty of being a Jew, which coincides with the difficulty of writing: for Judaism and writing are but the same waiting, the same hope, the same depletion.*
>
> Edmond Jabès[1]

I. People of the Book

The modern myth of the Jew as pariah, outsider and wanderer has, ironically enough, been translated into the postmodern myth of the Jew as "other," an other that collapses into the equation: writing = Jew = Book. By what sleight of hand? Metaphor? Metaphysics? Such an exclusive address (whether it is an open or a closed book) ultimately obscures the necessity of mapping out a space in which the Jew *was* native, not a stranger but an absolute inhabitant of time and place. The urgency of reiterating not only the memory but the possibility of such a world can be felt most acutely now, upon the present scene, where the political context of "the people of the Book" has undergone a radical transformation while the terms used to record and interpret their history and culture have not only remained static but even regressed into a kind of fixed, iconic solidity.

Writing and reading — interpretation — no matter where, have a lot to do with the unearthing, the grasp, the mastery of and giving over to both presences and absences: reading as recovery and relapse; the ink of writing as lifeblood, animator, nourishment — the book as fertile ground nurtured by ink. But the "furrow," the "fold" that may be both "history" and the "Jew," runs the risk of diffusion, dispersion, and, finally, inertia. Like anything that looms large in a people's memory, this field can become muddy, and these furrows turn to drainage ditches that empty out into a stillborn swamp, final resting place for what is allowed to go unquestioned, uninterpreted, and unrelated to social fact or present circumstance. Paradoxically, the movement of memory too often reappears in the form of inert, unyielding images: resilient and indelible, their clarity

1

is blinding. In his *Commentary on the Mishnah*, also known as *The Eight Chapters*, Maimonides wrote:

> One action may resemble another action, so that the two actions are thought to be identical even though they are not. For example, consider three dark places: the sun shines upon one of them, and it is illumined; the moon rises over the second place, and it is illumined; a lamp is lit in the third place, and it is illumined. Light is found in each one of them, but the reason for the first light and its cause is the sun, the cause of the second is the moon, and the cause of the third is fire. . . . There is no notion common to all of them except through equivocation. Grasp this notion, for it is extraordinarily marvelous.[2]

History, with its rigid paradigms of order, comes to shore up the insecure ramparts of a failing memory.[3] Untangling the strands of the past--or submitting to their confusing but exhilarating intricacy— cannot simply be an act of recognition, of fitting events into fixed patterns, of just seeing the light. It must begin, rather, by apprehending the sources of light and the present objects they shade or illuminate, and follow with an active, incessant engagement in the process of naming and renaming, covering and uncovering, consuming and producing new relations, investigating hierarchies of power and effect: distilling light into sun, moon, and fire. Just as maps interpret and redefine terrain in the image of their makers, readings can yield both past and prospective orders: in the Crimean port of Theodosia, not far (in mind) "from Smyrna and Baghdad," Osip Mandelstam wrote of a "bookish earth" and dreamt of a place that, within the inherited wisdom of its people, embodied an allegiance to words. Sentenced to internal exile, Mandelstam placed the form of his vision and the memory of his biblical ancestry in a Mediterranean world in which Spain and, even more specifically, Andalusia was central: sowing dormant seeds, he unearthed his own genealogy.[4]

II. Double Standards

Putting aside any nostalgic yearning for an idealized past, some of the qualities of this vision *can* be located in time and space. To say that Jews have inhabited this part of the world—the ancient Near East, the Fertile Crescent, the world of classical antiquity, various Islamic empires, the Middle East, the Levant, or whatever else it has been or might be called—is a truism, a fact that remains indisputable. Yet, for the uninitiated, access to more than the barest veneer of this world is fraught with obstacles. The legacy of hierarchical thinking clearly remains with us: we have not yet fully cast off the residue gathered by such amorphous concepts as the "rise" and "fall" of civilizations—concepts laced with bias, impoverished by lack of access to antithetical knowledge and self-serving fabrications of "other" "realities." In her *Before European Hegemony*, Janet Abu-Lughod notes: "In the course of history, some nations, or at least groups within them, have gained relative power vis-à-vis others and have occasionally succeeded in setting the terms of their interactions with subordinates, whether by means of direct rule (empires), indirect supervision (what we today term neocolonialism), or through unequal influence on the internal policies of others (hegemony)."[5]

Hand in hand with European military, technological, financial, and political predominance has come the institutionalized transmission of European culture. The excising of references to the Levant, with its common and uncommon, Semitic and non-Semitic past (Hebrew, Arabic, and African; Persian and Turkish; Zoroastrian and Manichaean; Islamic and Judaic), from most if not all standardized versions of the European curriculum has made myths of European superiority and self-containment that much harder to dislodge. Conventional patterns and hierarchies for thinking about or studying Western civilization and European culture (Greece, Rome, medieval Christendom, Renaissance, baroque, the Enlightenment, and the industrial age, followed by various "posts") have left little room for such densely overlapping matters. These would include not only the diverse development of cultures within an Arabic or Islamic context, but the crucial roles of Arabs and Jews as active participants in the formation of "European" culture on European soil. As Maria Rosa Menocal cogently puts it:

> The crystallization of the concept of Europeanness and its ancestry was largely spun out in the nineteenth century, and it played a critical role at this moment of high-pitched awareness of the particularity and superiority of Europe that came with the imperial and colonial experience and the post-Romantic experience with the Orient. This experience certainly helped sharpen the perception not only of European community and continuity but also its difference from others, or from the Other. It was an Other (and the Arab world was one of its principal manifestations) that Europe was by its own standards bringing out of the darkness and civilizing, at least as far as that was possible for those who were not European in the first place.
>
> Thus was eliminated the possibility that the Middle Ages might be portrayed as a historical period in which a substantial part of culture and learning was based in a radically different foreign culture. To view an Arabic-Islamic component, even in its European manifestations, as positive and essential would have been unimaginable, and it would remain so as long as the views and scholarship molded in that period

continued to inform our education. The proposition that the Arab world had played a critical role in the making of the modern West, from the vantage point of the late nineteenth century and the better part of this century, is in clear and flagrant contradiction of cultural ideology. It is unimaginable in the context of the readily observable phenomenon that was institutionalized as an essential element of European ideology and that has remained so in many instances to this day: cultural supremacy over the Arab world.[6]

This consolidation of nationalist ideology—so deeply ingrained as to simply appear normal—is exacerbated within the context of Jewish discourse where, in many cases, one standard applies to "us" and another to "them." The particular circumstances of modern Jewish existence imbue this legacy of supremacy with deeply disturbing contradictions that are often manipulated to produce or legitimize very concrete cultural and political consequences. Yosef Hayim Yerushalmi's profound ruminations on history and memory include this passage:

> Today Jewry lives a bifurcated life. As a result of emancipation in the diaspora and national sovereignty in Israel Jews have fully reentered the mainstream of history, and yet their perception of how they got there and where they are is most often more mythical than real. Myth and memory condition action. There are myths that are life-sustaining and deserve to be reinterpreted for our age. There are some that lead astray and must be redefined. Others are dangerous and must be exposed.[7]

The results and implications of such dichotomies are manifold. A representative example can be seen in the work of Norman Stillman, whose work has become authoritative on the history of non-European Jews. In his latest and most significant work to date, *The Jews of Arab Lands in Modern Times*, he can state without irony that Jewish communities in the Arab world go back "before the great Islamic conquests of the seventh century, before most of what today are called the Arab countries had any Arabs."[8] This astonishingly static view achieves a number of things in a remarkably condensed form. To begin with, the history of the "Jews" (since the formation of this entity as a national and religious community predates that of Islam) is granted a privileged—if not exclusive—sense of legitimacy. "Arabs," "Arab countries" and "Islam" are presented in an amalgam that cannot help but be confusing and therefore somehow impure. The assumptions underlying such a statement seem to imply that only recognizable modern nation-state categories render peoples into historical entities. This precise formulation, one should not forget, has been one of the primary means of delegitimizing Palestinian claims to a homeland. The more disturbing aspects, however, only appear as history unfolds. In recounting the period of the demise of Jewish communities in Arab countries, Stillman notes:

> By the late 1930s, tensions between Jews and the surrounding
> population were mounting everywhere in the Arab world. During the
> last two years leading up to the Second World War, there was a rash of
> sabotage incidents aimed at Jewish private and communal property in
> Iraq, Syria, Lebanon, and, for the first time, Egypt. The primary factor
> was the conflict in Palestine, which between 1936 and 1939 had
> degenerated into an open rebellion against the British mandate and the
> Zionist enterprise.[9]

While there is nothing untrue about this statement, the very concrete effects of Zionist policies in Palestine and their further consequences for the region are simply left unexamined throughout his analysis of this crucial period. On one hand, Jews are granted historical legitimacy through the premises upon which their relations to others (in this specific case, the others are Muslims or Arabs) are based; on the other hand, when push comes to shove, Jews are acted *upon* without being granted the qualities of agency or responsibility. This double standard reaches to the heart of Yerushalmi's contention and courses throughout much of contemporary Jewish discourse. The gaps and silences are enough, for they are buttressed by so much else that is left unsaid, left to the designs of the "natural" order of "languages of containment" that "abbreviate the human" to the point of rendering certain things so unlikely as to be unthinkable.[10]

III. Crossing Borders

Misconceptions as to the extent or possibility of physical, intellectual, and spiritual mobility in times more or less remote from ours make it hard to envision a world in which passage was neither exotic nor indifferently equivocal. Writing, even more than other forms, has suffered the consequences. From the medieval period, to give an obvious example, the texts of Aquinas, Dante, and Chaucer are likely to be assigned to students, but seldom are they even made aware of the existence of Maimonides, Averroës, Rumi, Ibn Arabi, al-Harizi, al-Ma'ari or Rabi'a. Yet there can be no question that the texts of these and other Arabs, Jews, and Persians were *constant* presences—sometimes illuminating, sometimes daunting—for the Christian writers whose works constitute the standard curriculum of the European cultural heritage:

> General anthologies of European medieval literature do not, as a matter
> of course, include examples of literature written in Arabic or Hebrew,
> nor do they even, in many cases, acknowledge or discuss its existence as

part of the general historical background. Courses on medieval literature, with few exceptions, perform the same excision. Even the very definition of what is "Spanish" literature that is implicit in the structure of courses and histories and anthologies of the literature systematically excludes what was written in Arabic and Hebrew at the same time as what was written in the Romance vernaculars. . . . In the often daunting inventory of languages deemed necessary tools for a medievalist, Arabic rarely figures. The respective bodies of literature are shelved in different sections of our libraries, are studied by different scholars, and are taught in different departments, even though in some cases they may come from the same place and time.[11]

The efforts of scholars working in highly specialized fields are, as a rule, not absorbed into the general curriculum. The minimal list of exceptions only bears this out. The texts they have laboriously unearthed and interpreted are usually relegated to that state of limbo labeled "influential." As such they are either held in disdain or respected from a great distance but seldom read, studied, or taken seriously into account as part of the enormously complex amalgam of interacting texts that helped form European thought and went to make up the body of extant world literature. Menocal discusses this in writing on a very "influential" text, the *Disciplina Clericalis*, written by a Jewish convert to Christianity educated in the Arabic tradition:

It is misleading, in such a context, to forget that it is al-Andalus and the general Arabic intellectual prominence in Europe that are directly associated with texts such as these. They are the *direct* source, that which brought such stories to the attention of the rest of Europe and with which such a collection would be identified by all other Europeans— Europeans who, unlike the modern scholar, might find it quite difficult to distinguish between the Persian and the Arabic source in such texts and would distinguish poorly, if at all, between the religious traditions of Maimonides and Avicenna.[12]

For medievalists or students of comparative literature, this continuing controversy regarding either Arabic or Hebrew "influence" on the early Romance lyric and European narrative is one of the only cracks in the ideological ramparts through which at least some of the light of al-Andalus can filter in. While some scholars have set the stage for a thorough reassessment of conventional patterns of study, their influence has not yet been felt strongly enough to place, for example, the corpus of early and late medieval Arabic and Hebrew writing within the context of a still very Levantine Europe, whose contours would run from the troubadours to Rimbaud and beyond into the colonial period.[13] Such inclusion would certainly both enrich and change the way we think about standard authors such as Chaucer, Dante, Petrarch, Boccaccio, or Cervantes; books like *Sir Gawain and the Green Knight*, *The Pearl*, or *The Book of Good Love*; movements like the *dolce stil novo*, the English courtiers and metaphysicals, or forms like the romance lyric and the picaresque narrative, to mention only some. It would, as well, bring our relatively parochial twentieth-century sense of this time much closer to what was embodied by the people of that time. Over and above exploring the more marginal sphere of the influence of Arabic and Hebrew forms on European works such a shift would also mean looking at how "the centrality of the European-Arabic world and its multiple manifestations may be embodied and reflected"[14] in the texts that we have unequivocally come to consider "ours."

At the same time, scholarly work is not by any means exempt from the ideological constructs and prejudices that form a good part of our cultural heritage:

> Modern civilization's myriad pretensions to objectivity have unfortunately tended to obscure the fact that much of our writing of history is as much a myth-making activity as that of more primitive societies. We often regard tribal histories or ancient myths that do not cloak themselves in such pretensions as less objective than our own. We are prone to forget that history is written by the victors and serves to ratify and glorify their ascendency—and we forget how many tracks are covered in the process. The writing of literary history, the close and often indispensable ancillary of general history, is preoccupied with the myths of our intellectual and artistic heredity, and it, too, tells those stories we want to hear, chooses the most illustrious parentage possible, and canonizes family trees that mesh with the most cherished notions we hold about our parentage.[15]

Again, as Menocal points out, the very assumption that Arabic and Romance culture are so distant they must somehow be bridged—even by scholars trying to prove connections—is itself an entirely ideological construct that would have made very little sense to a twelfth-century Parisian, a seventeenth-century Venetian, or even an early-twentieth-century Syrian. In other words, the very idea of these kinds of interconnections and interactions must first be deemed *possible* before we can even begin to hope that they will enter into a revised curriculum and exert some influence on our interpretations of the past.[16] At the same time, such revisions should not be carried out merely for the sake of replacing one standard with another, albeit more inclusive standard. The intent, rather, should be toward further eroding the claims of *any* kind of exclusivity. In going back to the medieval and thinking about the suppression of its heterogeneity, it is most instructive to note the different structural relationships governing that world, as Janet Abu-Lughod does here:

> The "modern" world system that emerged in the centuries following the sixteenth gradually became organized hierarchically according to different modes of production (capitalist, semifeudal, and precapitalist) that were roughly coterminous with a specific geographic distribution: a capitalist *core hegemon* located in northwest Europe, an agrarian semiperiphery geographically concentrated in eastern and southern Europe, and a periphery, located everywhere else . . . the world system of the thirteenth century was organized on very different principles. Rather than a single hegemon, there were a number of coexisting "core" powers that, via both conflictual and cooperative relations, became increasingly integrated over the course of the thirteenth and the first half of the fourteenth century. Since the system was *not hierarchical*, in the sense that no single hegemon dictated the terms of production and trade to others, no geographic entity could be said to be located at *the* center. Rather, cores, semiperipheries, and peripheries (and undoubtedly some intermediate categories as well) were found at a number of places around the globe.[17]

IV. Europe and the Middle East

The closer we come to the present, the more tense potential relations, exclusions, and absences get. Efforts to keep the "East" east and the "West" west are loaded with volatile political, social, and ideological implications. While these are never absent from the medieval period, their import there is simply less immediate and more restricted. At the same time, connections between historical misrepresentations of the past and those of the present are never spurious. Due to a lack of either direct or colonial involvement, this phenomenon is even more pronounced in America than, for example, Spain, France, or England. Very little material is available in the United States to fill the "middle ground" of cultural space. On one end, the highly specialized and often very technical realm of scholarly knowledge seldom filters through to either the general or literate public; on the other, the highly circumscribed litany of standard images of Arabs, Islam, the Middle East (and, by extension, Jews of non-European origin) made available through the mass media simply tends to stifle further inquiry.[18] The circular nature of this conundrum is evident: in order to combat commonly accepted stereotypes and biases, one must begin researching them. Many of the sources available, however, are often so highly specialized or written from such a partisan point of view that they appear all but inaccessible to a general reader. The sporadic, market-oriented nature of literary translation from languages outside the immediate realm of the "developed," more familiar world only adds to the difficulties a nonspecialist faces in trying to gain access to cultures whose images are bandied about indiscriminately but whose textures remain elusive.

Naturally, every culture mirrors its own image of itself quite accurately through the kinds of foreign culture made accessible within it. Despite the seemingly happenstance nature of this process—involving monetary and technical restraints as well as more or less informed publishers and translators—the possible space of reception is always paved by culturally sanctioned imagery and discourse involving a diverse range of conscious decisions, motives, and circumstances. It is only in the last few years, for instance, that literary translations of contemporary (for want of a better or more accurate term) Middle Eastern works have begun to appear with greater frequency in the United States, but even here, the atmosphere is tinged with provincial bias. In a review, for instance, of Abdelrahman Munif's *Cities of Salt*, undisputably a landmark of contemporary Arabic prose, John Updike wrote: "It is unfortunate, given the epic potential of his topic, that Mr. Munif, a Saudi born in Jordan, appears to be . . . insufficiently Westernized to produce a narrative that feels much like what we call a novel."[19]

Another more recent and telling example of how general assumptions and prejudices not only diminish but even cut off the possibility of receptive space can be seen in the Associated Press obituary of the monumental Egyptian writer Yusuf Idris. In the space of four short paragraphs, the Associated Press managed to mention Idris's alleged "anti-Israel" views twice. Nowhere are we told what those words might mean, and in what context such views might have been held. Instead, "anti-Israel" becomes a code word implying that Idris is somehow not one of "us." Nowhere are we given an indication of the magnitude and scope of Idris's art. His work, translated into 24 languages, is admired by readers throughout the world—not just the "many Arab writers and critics" mentioned in the obituary.[20] It is misrepresentations such as this that have kept Idris and other Arab writers off the lists of major American publishers.

While a major work like Tayib Saleh's *Season of Migration to the North* appeared in Britain in 1976, the American edition only came out in 1989. Nor is this an exceptional case. Even where American publishers and the American market are extremely responsive, as in the translation of contemporary Israeli writing (where the books of popular authors almost appear simultaneously in Hebrew and English), there is a marked tendency *not* to translate work emerging from a Levantine or Arabic milieu unless, as in the case of *Arabesques* by Anton Shammas, it corresponds (through no fault of its own) to particular perceptions.[21] Thus, for example, *Refuge*, a novel by Sami Mikhael, an extremely popular and highly regarded Israeli writer originally from Iraq, only appeared in 1988, 11 years after its original Hebrew publication. Again, much of this seems to have to do with the range of expectations that an audience has constructed or that has been constructed for it. The work of Mikhael, which deals in a highly personal way with the complex relations between Jews and Arabs within the Communist Party in both Iraq and Israel, may simply have seemed so unlikely as to appear fantastic to an audience weaned on certain assumptions. In this case, reality itself, and the breakdown of a consensus of imagery resulting from changing perceptions of that reality, helped pave the way for at least the partial (since it was not published by a major press and has yet to appear in paperback) acceptance of such a book. Yet this too is an isolated case, an exception to the rule that proves just how stringent the rules are.

The works of many other Jewish writers, thinkers, and historical figures from the Arab world and the Levant remain inaccessible in English, despite the enormous resources, clearly defined market and wide-open space of reception available for works of Jewish interest. Deemed marginal in relation to the central narrative of modern Jewish history as it has been interpreted and appropriated, at least in this country (and by proxy through the influence American Jewish discourse exerts over the rest of the Jewish world), the testament and experience of these writers remains poised, like parts of messages left in many bottles, all waiting to be found and put together.

The examples abound: a major figure like Eliyahu Eliachar (a witness, participant, and astute observer who lived through the Ottoman, British mandatory, and Israeli state periods), in addition to not being translated, is not even mentioned, for example, in Stillman's *The Jews of Arab Lands in Modern Times*. The important work of Ya'aquob Yehoshua, particularly his six-volume *Childhood in Old Jerusalem*, has not appeared in English translation. The exuberant and carnivalesque work of Albert Cohen (a Sephardic equivalent of Isaac Bashevis Singer), though once translated, remains out of print. The French works of Shmuel Trigano, perhaps the most important contemporary Jewish thinker after Emmanuel Lévinas, have not been translated into *either* English or Hebrew. The work of Jacqueline Kahanoff, an Egyptian who studied in New York before moving to Beersheba, ironically remains in print only in Hebrew, despite the fact that she wrote in English. Shime'on Ballas, an important Israeli novelist and scholar of Arabic literature originally from Baghdad and now living in Tel Aviv, depicts a milieu even more unimaginable to conventional expectations than that of Sami Mikhael. From his first novel, *The Transit*

Camp (1964), to his most recent, *The Other One* (1991), Ballas has forged a possibility unusual for Hebrew fiction, that of the internal exile attempting to reenact the political complexities of a surrounding world that has been declared forbidden territory. Another younger untranslated playwright and novelist, Yitshak Gormezano Goren, has also depicted a world beyond the reach of constructed assumptions about Jewish life in the Arab world. His novels, set in Alexandria and then Israel, dissect the dissolution of Jewish middle-class life in Egypt and the resultant shock of running aground in the promised land. The work of Samir Naqqash remains, perhaps, the most difficult to classify and the least accessible. Also from Baghdad (like Shime'on Ballas and Sami Mikhael), Naqqash refused to make the transition from Arabic to Hebrew. The only important Jewish writer still writing in Arabic (though one can only hope not the last), Naqqash's work is better known and more available in Cairo and Morocco than Tel Aviv or New York. The recalcitrant response to such work is due, in part, to the very fact that the experience of these writers—transformed into art—disrupts many of the convenient assumptions about the world they come from as well as about the ability of "natives" to speak for themselves.

The different dimensions of receptive space available to works from the Levant in different places can be instructive. In England, many of the more negative aspects of institutional Orientalism have provided precisely the foundations upon which a greater interest in contemporary Arabic and Middle Eastern culture can be sustained. Regardless of the often devastating colonial circumstances involved with their transmission, a large body of classical texts had entered the consciousness of English writing and had somewhat prepared the ground for a further, more critically attentive reception of writing emerging from those distant, certainly distorted, but not wholly unfamiliar cultures. Add to this the large expatriate community of Middle Eastern writers, journalists, publishers, and visual artists (with political and human rights groups, a lively press, publishing houses, readings, art exhibits, and other cultural activities), and the climate is entirely different from that prevailing in the United States. Lacking such a context, a certain literary activism is needed in order to effect changes in the habits of American publishers, who bypass the large amount of Middle Eastern writing already made available through British presses.

Spain presents another situation. There, despite official suppression for many centuries, the Arab, Islamic, and Jewish presence has permeated the culture in both the public and private spheres, in language and architecture, form and memory. In the academic realm, the fact that scholarly battles are often waged over the matter with great fervor indicates the high stakes involved in a historical revision that would finally have to acknowledge the Arab presence as more than just a 700-year aberration. At the same time, Spain does not really have the problem of losing the middle ground between the scholarly and the popular, since so many aspects of the culture have been touched and affected. The popularity of Lorca, with his Andalusian themes, as well as the continued presence of musical forms so obviously connected to an "impure" past, are evidence of this. Yet it is no accident that the work of Juan Goytisolo, whose trilogy (*Scenes of Identity*, *Count Julian*, and *Juan the Landless*), which actually ends in Arabic and represents a frontal, unrelenting attack on official Spanish culture, was banned in Spain for many years. This "return of the repressed" is analogous to the situation prevailing in France, where such confrontations and transformations have taken place on an even greater and more momentous scale.

At a time of growing anti-Arab and anti-Jewish sentiments and actions in France (with some 250 Arabs killed in vigilante-style attacks since 1985, as well as the chilling desecration of Jewish graveyards and corpses in May 1990), the awarding of the prestigious Prix Goncourt in 1987 to Tahar Ben Jelloun, a Moroccan writer living in France, is not without significance. Despite the long-standing tradition of exiled francophone writing in France (the negritude movement, with writers such as Aimé Césaire or Léopold Senghor; North Africans such as Kateb Yacine, Driss Chraibi, Mohammed Dib, Taos Amrouche, Albert Memmi, or Albert Camus), it was the first time the prize had been given to a North African.

Yet the story of French culture during (and even a decade prior to) this period of intolerance has been primarily the story of formerly colonized peoples, particularly North African Arabs and Jews, as well as Africans and Caribbeans, recreating France in their own image. This has been true in literary and academic discourse through the work of writers such as Jacques Derrida, Edmond Jabès, Assia Djebar, Hélène Cixous, Abdelwahab Medeb, Abdelkabir Khatibi, Jacques Hassoun, Abdellatif Laabi, Adonis, and Shmuel Trigano, to mention only some of the more prominent figures, as well as in more popular cultural expressions such as film, music, and grass-roots political movements such as SOS Against Racism.[22] Ironically, current conditions in France present the opportunity for a revival of true anti-Semitism, one that—like the Inquisition—doesn't distinguish between Jews and Arabs. In this there would be very little deviation from the context of a long tradition of standard European education and ideology. The cultural/historical fates of Maimonides and Averroës bear more than some similarity to this phenomenon:

As Spaniards they were denied their birthright, their nationality, by latter-day Spaniards, for whom Christianity was a requirement for citizenship, even retrospectively. Brilliant, luminous stars in their own lifetimes and in the times and events of Europe for years to come, they were eventually neglected and forgotten (or misnamed) because they did not fit into the established norms of our prestigious European ancestry, an ancestry by and large as cleansed of Jews and Arabs as Spain had tried to be in the sixteenth century.[23]

V. Language and Cultural Difference

Few fields are currently more in vogue than that of multiculturalism and cultural diversity. This *inter*-linguistic, *inter*-cultural phenomenon is a process transpiring in many places and on many levels. On the literary plane, the critic Homi K. Bhabha has pointed to such writing (using Salman Rushdie as a paradigm) as constituting an innovative and original genre, "the new Metropolitan, or post-colonial work."[24] The use of such terminology, however, can obscure and collapse some of the real issues still at stake. To speak of a "post-colonial" culture—no matter what kind of intellectual gymnastics are involved and despite the term's reference to an accepted historical process—obscures the fact that people are still colonized, albeit in new and different ways. To speak of cultural diversity and to point to significant changes in many areas of the curriculum obscures the fact that often such changes only catalogue choice representatives of diversity without questioning the very structures to which they have been delegated, as Trinh Minh-ha makes clear:

> Multiculturalism does not lead us very far if it remains a question of difference only between one culture and another. Differences should also be understood within the same culture, just as multiculturalism as an explicit condition of our times exists within every self. Intercultural, intersubjective, interdisciplinary. These are some of the keywords that keep on circulating in artistic and educational as well as political mileux. To cut across boundaries and borderlines is to live aloud the malaise of categories and labels; it is to resist simplistic attempts at classifying, to resist the comfort of belonging to a classification, and of producing *classifiable* works. Interdisciplinary is, for example, not just a question of putting several fields together, so that individuals can share their specialized knowledge and converse with one another within their expertise. It is to create in sharing a field that belongs to no one, not even to those who create it. What is at stake, therefore, in this inter-creation is the very notion of *specialization* and of *expertise*, of *discipline* and *professionalism*. To identify oneself with a position of specialized knowledge, to see oneself as an expert or as an authority on certain

matters, even and especially on artistic matters is to give up all attempts at understanding relations in the game of power.[25]

Contemporary American writing — as well as its reception and further academic positioning — can also be instructive: the work of Maxine Hong Kingston, Toni Morrison, or Leslie Marmon Silko (among others); the rereading of Zora Neale Hurston, Langston Hughes, or James Baldwin; and the (re)discovery of the slave narrative all constitute instances of historical revision and reinscription from a variety of ethnic, racial, sexual, and class perspectives. Yet as laudable as this thrust toward pluralism appears, it may also be just a bit too early to celebrate the disruption of the canon and the dawning of a new, more equitable order. Charles Bernstein notes that the exclusion goes deeper:

> My problem is not the introduction of radical alternatives to parochial and racist reading habits engendered by the educational system and the media but that these alternatives are often ameliorative rather than politically or aesthetically exploratory. I see too great a continuum from "diversity" back to New Critical and liberal democratic concepts of a common readership that often — certainly not always — have the effect of transforming unresolved ideological divisions and antagonisms into packaged tours of the local color of gender, race, sexuality, ethnicity, region, nation, class, even historical period: where each group or community or period is expected to come up with — or have appointed for them — representative figures who we all can know about.
>
> This process, more than not, presupposes a common standard of aesthetic judgement or implicitly aims to erect a new common standard. In this context, diversity can be a way of restoring a highly idealized conception of a unified American culture that effectively quiets dissent.[26]

This categorization (some would call it ghettoization), which comes from being placed in an order that is "politically correct" in only the most superficial ways, confronts individual artists (not to mention communities or peoples) with particularly thorny problems.[27] As Zora Neale Hurston already wrote in "How It Feels to Be Colored Me": "It is thrilling to think — to know that for any act of mine, I shall get twice as much praise or twice as much blame."[28] The already laboriously fought-for space of expression becomes even more circumscribed. (As Tillie Olsen put it: "Circumstances, time, development of craft — but beyond that: how much conviction as to the importance of what one has to say, one's right to say it. And the will, the measureless store of belief in oneself to be able to come to, cleave to, find the form for one's own life comprehensions.")[29] And as Sami Mikhael writes:

But how to convey the truth about your life, your experience, about things the way they really happened, of the situation as it was, without hurting the pride of your fellow immigrants, without deepening the feeling of inferiority on one side, as it were, and encouraging the feeling of superiority on the other side? This problem still haunts me. To this day I feel I'm walking a very thin line when dealing with this subject, and so far I can't say I have found a solution to my own satisfaction.[30]

Contradictory personal and formal concerns are often held in abeyance as the cultural worker — finally empowered to tell the tribe's story, to revise history and express its undeniable rage and frustration — finds him- or herself more and more beholden to a "tribe" that may only exist in the minds of conference organizers. As Trinh Minh-ha writes in "Difference: 'A Special Third World Women Issue' ":

With a kind of perverted logic, they work toward your erasure while urging you to keep your way of life and ethnic values *within the borders of your homelands*. This is called the policy of "separate development" in apartheid language. . . . To persuade you that your past and cultural heritage are doomed to eventual extinction and thereby keeping you occupied with the Savior's concern, inauthenticity is condemned as a *loss of origins* and a whitening (or faking) of non-Western values. Being easily offended in your elusive identity and reviving readily an old, racial charge, you immediately react when such guilt-instilling accusations are leveled at you and are thus led to stand in need of defending that very ethnic part of yourself that for years has made you and your ancestors the objects of execration. Today planned authenticity is rife. . . . We no longer wish to erase your difference, we demand, on the contrary, that you remember and assert it. At least to a certain extent.[31]

Writers thus categorized as "others" must constantly remain alert to the implications and contexts of both exclusion *and* inclusion. They must continually devise new ways of thinking and acting, speaking and keeping silent, to avoid fulfilling the sterile role of either "heroic artist" or "unspoiled native" within the parameters of what James Scully defines as "bourgeois freedom":

However bourgeois freedom may be fantasized, it presumes that each person is self-constituted as an individual subject. An indivisible subject that is socially buffeted, perhaps, but not socially constituted. The fantasy is not without consequence. It demands that freedom be conceived as a property rather than a quality. Bourgeois "freedom" produces unfreedom as surely as bourgeois wealth expropriates wealth and well-being, so to produce the poverty it needs in order to exist. . . . "Freedom" and "poetry" are not transcendent categories. They are historically conditioned and are bound, however loosely or complexly, into social power. Each is as implicated in the web of social relations and values as we ourselves are. The power to call "poetry" poetry, or to enforce a literary canon by means of publishing corporations and hegemonic academic institutions—the power to make an ideological, historically specific designation seem natural and therefore universal—is one with the power, say, to pass off "human rights" as human rights. It is the power to present a class-serving projection as a class-transcendent fact or revelation.[32]

For writers who see literature as an arena of struggle or resistance, these "projections," transcendent "facts," and "revelations" must be confronted beyond the minimal space that has now been allotted, as Trinh Minh-ha acutely implies, within "special categories" such as "third world women," which remain as technical, recondite, and determined as the other categories to which these new ones were supposed to serve as an antidote. The distribution, then, of such "conflicts" in areas where the stakes are relatively low, between categories such as "Third World women" or "Chicanas" or "African-Americans" and "everyone else" must, at best, remain a mixed blessing. To begin with, the circumscription of "others" who must always strive to assimilate, explain themselves to or be different from the dominant and assumed category of everyone else (themselves an extreme minority), simply perpetuates the very structures that define possible modes of discourse. But an even deeper part of the problem has to do with the systemic nature of these structures and the extent to which they have been internalized, as Erica Hunt has described:

> The languages used to preserve domination are complex and sometimes contradictory. Much of how they operate to anesthetize desire and resistance is invisible; they are wedded to our common sense; they are formulaic without being intrusive, entirely natural—"no marks on the body at all."
>
> These languages contain us, and we are simultaneously bearers of the codes of containment. . . . The codes and mediations that sustain the status quo abbreviate the human in order to fit us into structures of production. There is a place for everyone, even the subordinate, if they know their place.[33]

These languages of containment, once proposed, remain a determining factor in the very definition of the categories themselves, particularly in groups that have been defined—and then sometimes come to define themselves—according to dominant and dominating standards:

Long treatment as an undifferentiated mass of other by the dominant
class fosters collective identity and forms of resistance. In a sense, then,
oppositional groupings, be they based on class, race, gender or critical
outlook, have traditionally been dependent, in part, on external
definition by the dominant group—the perceived hostility of the
dominant class shapes the bonds of opposition. And that quasidependent
quality extends even further: we get stuck with the old codes even as we
try to negate them. We experience acute difference: autonomy without
self-determination and group identity without group empowerment.[34]

The consequences of such dichotomies are considerable, both in formal
terms as well as in how writers position themselves in relation to their
ostensible "subject" matter. In many parts of the world, the most fundamental literary material is thrown into relief: the question of language itself, *which* language a writer can or needs to use, becomes a central concern. According to Samir Naqqash:

Language is the most important form of communicating with people.
Communication is the basic objective of the writer. Language is the raw
material and the writer's expressive power and energy is in proportion
to his grasp of the raw material.[35]

Outside of highly specialized studies, this is an issue that gets short shrift
except at certain crucial junctures (junctures, that is, that are crucial to the
dominant culture) such as the break from Latin to the vernacular in medieval Europe. Yet many—one could even venture to say most—texts
and cultures are informed by the particular conundrum in which contemporary "others," "minorities," or formerly subjected peoples now find
themselves. To conceptualize literary history otherwise is simply to perpetuate a "conventional poetics" that, as Erica Hunt writes,

might also be construed as the way ideology, "master narratives," are
threaded into the text, in content and in genre. . . . The affinities and
subordination are familiar—and familial—linked traceably to the way
the social body is organized. Notions of character as a predictable and
consistent identity, of plot as a problem of credibility, and theme as an
elaboration of a controlling idea: all these mirror official ideology's
predilection for finding and supplying, if necessary, the appropriate
authority. Social life is reduced once again to a few great men or a
narrow set of perceptions and strategies stripping the innovative of its
power.[36]

Taking language choice as just one fundamental nexus of intersecting
and sometimes contradictory possibilities, the maintenance of the "conventional poetics" of "master narratives" becomes almost impossible

when examined in the light of historically specific instances of literary contexts. Examples are numerous, likely and unlikely, more or less obvious. Charles Bernstein, for instance, argues convincingly that the centrality of linguistic concerns in American modernism, and much of its innovative energy, comes from the fact that many writers falling under this rubric were *not* native English speakers, something that allowed for a certain fluidity and willingness to experiment with "correct" and learned forms:

> The immigrants of 1880 to 1900 radically subverted the language environment of the Northeast and Midwest as non-English speakers began to settle here at an almost geometrically escalating rate. By 1900, according to Peter Quartermain's assessment, about one-quarter of the white U.S. population either did not speak English or learned it as a second language. . . . As Quartermain documents, Stein, Williams, and Zukofsky—three poets who created a ground for twentieth-century poetry—all learned English as a second language. Zukofsky grew up in a Yiddish-speaking New York neighborhood, while Williams probably learned Spanish and English simultaneously. Stein's family moved to Vienna before she was one, where she had a Czech tutor and a Hungarian governess and probably spoke her first words in German; from four to six, she lived in Paris; the family then moved to Oakland. Stein spent her adult life listening to and speaking French while writing English.[37]

Conversely, loyalty to the mother tongue often marginalizes writers: Yiddish modernism, Chicano/Chicana writing in America, *The Songs of Gold Mountain* or the remarkable works of Asian American masters such as Taro Yashima, are perfect cases in point. These writers or movements are, however, often only marginalized within the terms of dominant literary history or discourse. At a time when William Carlos Williams could barely get published, the poetry of writers like A. Leyeles, Jacob Glatshteyn, and Moyshe-Leyb Halpern—nurtured by the full range of European modernism, Russian Futurism and Acmeism, as well as American Objectivism—appeared in the Yiddish press, with a circulation, at its height, of up to 700,000.[38] Similarly, as the late Arturo Islas has noted, Chicano and Chicana writers usually gain recognition in America long after their intimate and long involvement with Latin American literature, a tradition that has itself entered the discourse of North American literary history only belatedly.[39]

The question of language choice, as the body of this work will further examine, has been crucial in the Levant from the formation of classical Arabic culture to the present. The use of different languages for different audiences (as in the texts of Maimonides or Yehuda Halevi); the vast enlargement of the parameters of Arabic through the territorial, political, and religious victories of Islam (the fact that many of the greatest writers of Arabic were not Arabs, but subject peoples who had assimilated into the dominant culture) — these are just two instances of this phenomenon. As far as Jews are concerned, we constantly need to be reminded — given the often pejorative and politically loaded context of presentation — that, as Norman Stillman points out, "Among the three major Jewish languages of the post-Talmudic period (that is, Judeo-Arabic, Yiddish, and Ladino), Judeo-Arabic holds a place of special significance. It has had the longest recorded history — from the ninth century to the present. It has had the widest geographical diffusion — extending across three continents during the Middle Ages. And finally, it was the medium of expression during one of the foremost periods of Jewish cultural and intellectual creativity."[40]

The language question also informs and serves as a constant backdrop to contemporary writing in the Levant. Issues such as the marginalization of Jews writing Arabic after the mass immigration to Israel of the 1950s, examined later in the work of Samir Naqqash and others; the colonial and "postcolonial" rift between native and foreign languages, particularly in the struggle between North African francophone and Arabic writing; and current theoretical and practical debates taking place as to how a culture can best be served once it has been internally or externally exiled, pervade the formation of contemporary Middle Eastern literatures.[41]

These internal debates, choices, and conflicts — as well as the larger contexts in which they transpire and evolve — affect not just the material base of the literature in question, the language itself, but also the uses to which language is put. Again the "native" is caught in the binds of representation, and flight comes in forms of subversion, refusal, attack, irony, imitation, mockery, and invention as diverse as the writers themselves, strategies that sometimes go against the grain of already established "representatives."[42] For many writers that have come to be categorized as "minorities," "others," or simply belonging to the "third world," cultural activity is socially based and politically motivated. Refusal to be defined by others also means refusal to be subjected by others. In coining the term "resistance literature," for example, the Palestinian writer and activist Ghassan Kanafani explicitly connected his academic research to the liberation movement of his people, with no disclaimers concerning "scientific objectivity." As he put it, "There are those who can bring to a given topic a completely critical capacity. This is not the case for us, however, who are a part of the very question of resistance."[43] Such a stance rejects not only the reservations carved out of dominant discourse but the very divisive terms and conditions of that discourse it-self, for this kind of writing constantly "produces historical specificity arrived at through personal social struggle."[44] The concept of "resistance literature" is also very different from that of "engaged" writing in Euro-pean discourse precisely because it does not privilege (thus reduce) liter-ature to a circumscribed activity within which one can either be engaged or disengaged. Rather, it assumes writing or any other cultural activity to simply be one part of the greater subjective reality. While literature emerging from such conditions and making such claims often seems un-concerned with aesthetics, the hypersensitivity to both language choice and language usage contradict this. In fact, it is in language, with its em-bedded assumptions, its inclusions and exclusions, as well as its modes of categorizing not just thought but the possibility of certain thoughts, that such writing makes its finest distinctions, as in Roque Dalton's fre-quently quoted "Ars Poetica 1974":

> Poetry
> Forgive me for having helped you understand
> you're not made of words alone.[45]

Such a doubly responsible sense of language may be the only one worth striving for. As Claire Gebeyli, a Lebanese writer, put it: "Of what use is the pen if it forgets to press down on people's breasts? If the words that it pours forth are mere particles sewn and resewn on the body of lan-guage?"[46]

Maintaining the "necessary illusions" (to use Noam Chomsky's apt phrase), in which activities can be circumscribed and ladled out in rations of significance and insignificance, where aesthetics and politics are made out to be a contradiction in terms and people can be categorized in order to dilute their impact on changing accepted structures of power (whether these be cultural, political, economic, or social), ultimately means, again, to "abbreviate the human,"[47] to cynically diminish human potential and agency in the world. Short-circuiting the real connections that do exist between works and the world, besides trivializing the concrete social for-mation of a culture, shrinks even further the already shrunken space of reception left between highly specialized forms of knowledge and more accessible or available forms. The actual consequences of this process for particular cultures, societies, and people are not negligible.

VI. Nativity and Exile

To come full circle: the space of that "bookish earth," with the Mediter-ranean as its focal point, has been a site of Jewish creativity and culture since, to use a hackneyed phrase, time immemorial. It is a truism, as well, to say that "Jews" and "Arabs," however amorphously those terms have and continue to be deployed, inhabited this space—along with many other peoples—together. This is not to imply that these groups lived in some complete and idealized harmony throughout the ages—no groups ever have—but that they recognized each other, implicitly and explicitly. Despite the very distinct elements pertaining to this particular community, one can get some sense of the depth of traditional Jewish/ Arab communal recognition in the following description of Jerba given by Abraham Udovitch and Lucette Valensi, a sense often missing in contemporary scholarship:

> There is no single generalization or rule which could serve to characterize the whole range of social and economic contacts between Jerban Jews and Jerban Muslims. Each circumstance between them has its own movable boundaries in which elements of friendship and hostility, confidence and suspicion, collaboration and competition are intermingled in varying proportions. In the market, the notion which governs commerce between Jews and Muslims is that of *haqq al-yahud*, a concept which has many meanings and uses, but which translated literally means "the law, the justice, the honesty of the Jews . . . " It is not surprising to find this quality invoked by the Jews themselves. But it is also invoked by Muslims as a password to cut short bargaining or other negotiations concerning the price or quality of an object. Concluding a discussion with the invocation of haqq al-yahud is equivalent to giving an oath. The Jewish jeweler places his honesty, his reputation, his reliability on the line—that is, all the qualities which form the basis of his relationship with his clients. But, this is more than a personal engagement; it is, at the same time, that of the group to which the jeweler belongs. Beyond the single moral quality of honesty—individual and collective—there is also the reference to respect for the law. Put in another way, since the *ahl al-kitab* [people of the book] are people of the law, one can deal with them.[48]

With the formation of classical Andalusian culture in tenth century Spain, and its subsequent influence throughout the Levant writ large (which would include present-day Portugal, Spain, southern France and Italy, the Balkans, Greece, Turkey, Iran, Iraq, Yemen, Syria, Lebanon, Cyprus, Israel/Palestine, Egypt, Morocco, Tunisia, Algeria, Libya, and even parts of West Africa and India), Jewish creativity also extended itself, sometimes following, sometimes leading. This remains true right up until the full or partial dissolution of these Sephardic, Levantine, Ottoman, Arab, and Persian Jewish communities and their massive transfer to Israel in the 1950s.

The cultural and textual legacy of this time and space is overwhelming, even to the erudite. As Haim Schirmann, one of the great scholars of Hebrew poetry (only one facet, albeit an important one, of what remains), once remarked, the mandatory equipment for the exegete embarking on this voyage includes "a knowledge of many subsidiary subjects, such as history, bibliography, paleography, linguistics, and liturgy . . . several languages — e.g., Aramaic, Syriac, Byzantine Greek, Latin, Arabic, Spanish, Italian, and Provençal — and the closer we approach our own time, the more languages are required".[49] Despite the fact that a vast amount of scholarly work has and continues to be undertaken, thousands of manuscripts — not only of poetry — remain scattered, unedited or indecipherable. The sheer number of books written is overwhelming; although it is, again, in many ways an exceptional case, a look at the situation in Jerba can give us some sense of the importance of writing for Jewish communities in the Levant:

> Over the past hundred years, the Jewish community of this island has produced close to five hundred published books. Because of the informal, disorganized nature of this activity, the exact number is nearly impossible to establish and it might, in reality, be much higher. These are published books and the figure does not include works still in manuscript form. . . . In addition to books, for two decades, beginning in the mid-30s, there were between three and five monthly journals published and written in Jerba. . . . These data would be of little significance or interest if it were not for the fact that the community we are talking about numbered, for most of this period, between 2000 and 3000 people; that for only a brief period in the 1940s and early 1950s did it approach 5,000 souls, and that, until recently, none of its women could read or write. Furthermore, this is a community in which 90 percent of the males earn their livelihood by the sweat of their brow. . . . This impressive level of literary productivity is unusual, and, with the exception of such specialized communities as academia, may be unprecedented.[50]

At the same time, due to the massive variety of material that *does* exist, scholars have tended to work in very particular and specialized areas. Inevitably, this has resulted in the kinds of gaps between diverse forms of knowledge described earlier. In addition to these more technical reasons, the subordination of writing to other concerns — philosophical, religious, political, philological, or anthropological — has effectively stifled the possibility of these Levantine texts entering a common literary vocabulary. A good example of this is the subordination of Hebrew language study at its inception in Europe to theology, relegating much rabbinic writing, such as textual commentary, to the field of religious polemic rather than literary criticism, poetics, or linguistics. Beyond all of this, the fundamental problem is not technical, in the form of even more stringent textual and linguistic requirements, but conceptual:

> What is required, is considerably more difficult and challenging, the alteration of our attitudes toward European literary history (and thus, in considerable measure, toward ourselves). With this done, and with a vision of Arabic and Hebrew, Morisco and Mozarabic, as central rather than peripheral, the amount of material available even to the scholar with no knowledge of Arabic becomes exceedingly rich, and the number of future generations who would accept that Arabic and Hebrew are important reading languages . . . would subsequently increase as a matter of course. . . . The more difficult, and essential of the tasks is that of considering the validity of the views we hold, understanding their ideological bases, and readjusting them if they are found wanting.[51]

For contemporary Jewish literary history, a number of other particular problems—over and above those that have already been touched on—also exist. Difficulties are often found in trying to fully reconcile writing that emerges from a religious environment with writing that doesn't. Stress is thus put on the division between something conceived of as "tradition," a hermetically sealed area cut off from the "worldly" concerns of other writers, and the "perils" of attraction to that worldliness that is secretly admired and often considered or assumed to be superior to "tradition." This self-imposed bind can isolate and diminish the fuller possibilities of the writing itself, particularly if it has been produced under the different assumptions framing less familiar cultural configurations. The relocation of the central focus of Jewish life back within the heart of the Levantine and Arab world, and the creation of a distinctly new nationality through whose filter the past is constantly being reinterpreted, problematizes many of the prevalent divisions and suppositions regarding the study and categorization of "Jewish" texts.

These texts, along with the materials, intentions and aspirations of the culture, like those of any other, have been transmitted and interpreted in very different ways at different times. For the last hundred years, the protracted conflict between Zionism and Palestinian nationalism has retroactively affected, in one way or another, most historical, cultural, political, and social discourse on Arabs and Jews in general. The success of Zionism as a movement for the "liberation" of the Jews has almost been taken as a truism, whether or not its ideology is taken to a logical conclusion by those subscribing to or accepting such a presupposition. One is hard put to find, regardless of political persuasion or stance, formulations of Jewish history and culture that do not take at least some of the assumptions of Zionist ideology at face value. It is almost inconceivable, for instance, to conjure up a world in which the Holy Land was just another stop on a familiar and well-traveled route, not the longed-for and mythified ideal "solution" for the Jewish "problem." Eliyahu Eliachar has written that

> the Land of Israel is a small portion of a region in which many peoples dwell, most of them having one faith, and a strong desire to be united. Our land has *never* been a limited geographical unit: it was and still is at the crossroads of East and West, between Egypt, Assyria and Babylonia in the past. Today, our country is the one entity restricting the will towards unity held as an ideal by other Arab configurations.[52]

Geographic and conceptual reductionism, along with hostility and ignorance of the region, have characterized the tone of prevailing Jewish discourse and practice since the arrival of Eastern European settlers in the promised land. In Eliachar's words:

> The biggest mistake of the Zionist movement was that we disregarded the fact that our country does not exist on a solitary, unsettled and uninhabited island, with other peoples—primarily Arabs—in its environs. The further I went into investigating the issue, as well as being a full participant in the events taking place in the Land of Israel for over fifty years following the "numbered" immigrations—as well as those prior—a film of errors passes before me, filled with the inability to take into account the inhabitants that have lived in our land for hundreds of years—not just the Arabs but, to my regret, the Jews as well. . . . In particular one must point out, with great sorrow, the contempt for our neighbors held by a good portion of Israeli citizens. This contempt is a result, primarily, from Jewish-Israeli arrogance whose roots can be found in misleading information, lack of knowledge, lack of contact, and a lack of cultural familiarity. Certainly there are exceptions to the rule, but they only prove the rule. Anything that has been done by institutions relating to this issue—whether governmental, the Jewish Agency, or on a private level—to inform public opinion regarding our neighbors, is worthless when looked at against the obligation and necessity that should be imposed upon every Israeli citizen to become familiar with the surroundings we have planted ourselves in. Alienation will take its vengeance on us.[53]

Nor has this critique only come from native Jews; though, as Eliachar points out, exceptions have been few, one can get some sense of the extent of this neglect through the following comments of Lova Eliav, a principal figure of the Labor Movement and not one to speak outside of the consensus of terminology regarding Jews from Arab countries: "First, we snatched from them the valuable treasure that they brought with them—Arabic. We, the Ashkenazim, have been carried away by a wave of condescension and arrogance towards the Arab world . . . we have made Arabic and Arab culture something hateful and despicable."[54]

While Israel maintains its centrality as the major component of Jewish identity in the diaspora, the majority of Israelis—Jews from the Islamic world—find themselves farther and farther from any reconciliation with that space of origin, not to mention a just place in their own country. They remain possessed, to repeat Erica Hunt's phrase, of "group identity without group empowerment."[55] This is expressed from the head to the heart to the feet of the social body through what the Israeli sociologist Shlomo Swirski calls "the ethnic division of labor." The Israel Swirski describes is a far cry from the country that has come to be known through the Hebrew novels that are translated into English and the images that appear in the American or European media:

> In the development towns, workers with fifteen, twenty, twenty-five years' seniority are thrown into the street with no options; women from the slums and development towns work in electronics factories, and receive less than a living wage; workers are exposed to companies which have acquired great experience of exploiting and oppressing workers in Hong Kong, Malaysia, Argentina and Brazil; boys and girls absorb the humiliating lesson that they are "not equal" and must choose between life on the stupefying production line and an exhausting, and generally hopeless, upward climb. . . . Local labor contractors press for unions, but most of them surrender because of instructions and pressure from above. Workers in factories threatened with closure barricade themselves in and fight the police and the hired thugs. . . . Their exploits are covered on the inside pages of the newspapers, in the crime and riots columns, because the media shows up only when they overturn tables, and thus again and again present them as "primitives," lacking a "discussion culture."[56]

These divisions, Swirski points out, are "reproduced by an ideological apparatus that presents the low social, political and economic standing of the Orientals as a result not of the class nature of Israeli society but of the fact that they come from non-modern and culturally backward societies."[57] This formulation explicitly clarifies the enormous contradictions that such social and cultural situations entail. While discrete parts of a lost culture are painstakingly preserved in forms that are all but inaccessible to people locked out of the power structure, this very culture is presented as precisely the reason for this same group's low status. At the same time, economic and cultural dependency—on America, in this case—firmly dictates which options are open to whom. This relationship can be traced with some precision simply by looking at imports and exports, which retain their class orientation in either direction. Some examples of this, besides the issue of translated literary texts already touched upon, would include the following: the "high" and "low" American culture imported into Israel (programs featuring visiting writers at the American Cultural Center for a highly select audience versus reruns of *Dynasty* for the working class; the export of specialized workers—such as academics or scientists—on contract to American institutions, as against the massive economic and highly uncertain immigration of less skilled working-class Israelis).

The situation previously described by Trinh Minh-ha, with its jargon of authenticity and separate development that "with a kind of perverted logic works toward your erasure" in order to "abbreviate the human," takes on specific constituents:

> In Israel, the Jewish labourer is Oriental despite the fact that he was
> born to parents who in all likelihood were not employed as labourers in
> their countries of origin, and who probably would not have become
> labourers if they continued living in them—and he, therefore, attributes
> the fact that he is a labourer to the fact of his being an Oriental in Israel.
> He is Oriental because whatever he does, his social status is presented as
> the product of attributes unique to Orientals—large families, low
> educational level, origin in an underdeveloped country, and the like. He
> is Oriental because he is accustomed to finding—and expects to find—
> Orientals in positions similar to his own, and Ashkenazim above him.
> He is Oriental because, in his contacts with the system, he feels a sense
> of alienation, for he does not meet the symbols and configurations he
> has grown up with. He is Oriental because, when he finally makes it, he
> is not treated simply as an individual, valued for what he is and what he
> does, but also as a representative of his "race"—the ethnic group as a
> whole.[58]

This constant referral back to the "race" and its "cultural backwardness" makes it evident that, in addition to struggling for social equality, such groups also imagine and enact a poetics of resistance. This poetics works to salvage the past from highly specialized but inaccessible categorization as well as from vulgar and rationalized reduction in the service of cultural hegemony. For some, at its most extreme, it means accepting the fact that "return" might simply mark the beginning of a new exile, as in Albert Suissa's powerful new novel, *The Bound*:

> The old people aroused a feeling of sorrow in Mister Fazuelo. They

seemed to him like plucked chickens, desecrated. He knew most of
them, and even some from "there," according to their ancestral names.
Empty heads, laid between their shoulders, limp as the hands across
their knees or over their bags of food. Stunned, still unable to digest
authority with no king, naive to the point of stupidity. The world
turned upside down. Some of them even get hit by their kids, still
stretching out in bed at this hour. He didn't see them at synagogue, woe
unto them, desecrators of the Sabbath. A fading generation, and the one
after is destroying itself beneath it. Exile! There is no other path. Exile
in the Holy Land itself. At a time of dispersion one must congregate.[59]

VII. Reimagining History

Human history is no one else's; its shape and bent literally determine our
future, through images and stereotypes, fears and hopes, textbooks and
policies, realms and relations fertile with new union, creativity, and
power, and through those that are dismissed out of hand, not even
deemed imaginable. What I am attempting in this book is to shed some
light on a realm that, at least during the past century, has remained a well-
guarded bastion of experts. I have tried to chip away at the walls, to illuminate those dark confines deemed too complex or exotic for the uninitiated to enter.

My work here does not, by any means, even pretend to be a comprehensive history of the life and culture of Jews in the Levant. Its underlying themes, rather, are threefold: first, to examine the relationships between Jews and Arabs on the literary, cultural, historical, social, and
political planes as seen through paradigmatic historical moments and encounters. Next, to delve into the relationship of the Jew to the Arab
within him- or herself. And, finally, to chart the relationship of the native
Jew to a native space, namely the Levant, a notion so foreign to the modern dogma of the Jew as eternal stranger that it might appear almost unthinkable. In addition to these more particular aims, the book also serves
as an introduction to literatures, particularly Levantine Hebrew and Arabic, that have not received much critical attention in English within the
context of contemporary theoretical discourse. Beyond the text itself, the
range covered is meant to give readers a sense of just how much writing
from the Levant's various periods and cultures is available in English or
other European languages, and just how uncritical it is not to take it into
account by reorienting one's own referential parameters.

The space of this Levant writ large—as I have chosen to present it—is
framed by two blocks of time, limit points on either side. The first takes
the roughly sixty-year period from the 1930s to the present, a time in
which most of the elements of the conflict in Palestine had taken on fairly

rigid characteristics. Not to hold the most current manifestations of Jewish/Arab relations (the double transfer of Jews out of the Arab world and Arabs out of Palestine, along with the present site of the Palestinian uprising in the disputed lands of Palestine and Israel) as the clearest lens through which any productive interpretations of the past have to be refracted, seems to me at best disingenuous. The other limit point ranges between the appearance of Sa'adia Gaon's Arabic translation of the Bible and the appearance of Arabic meters, forms, and themes in the tenth-century Hebrew poetry of his student Dunash Ben Labrat. These two literary events also limn the sweeping social and economic changes brought about by what the great historian S. D. Goitein called "the great bourgeois revolution" of the ninth century; it was then that the long process transforming the Jews from a primarily agricultural to a primarily urban people had reached its final stage.

By sticking to these two points—marked specifically on one end (in approximately 965) by the appearance of Dunash's famous wine song (the first secular Hebrew poem), and on the other by the appearance (in 1951) of the Yemenite laments (poems written in the transit camps of Israel that tragically usher in the new class and ethnic divisions that would come to characterize life in Israel for Jews of the Levant)—I have suggested a time span within whose limits (with some befores and afters) a certain fluidity exists. This fluidity does not signal an ahistorical aversion to the specificities of time and place, but is an attempt (within a very broad framework) to mirror the conditions of space, at least as I have interpreted and presented them, in the Levant. My sole justification for this is decidedly historical: Jews lived and traveled, settled down and created from one end of this realm to the other throughout the roughly thousand-year period in question.

Within this time and space, my central concern has been to trace the development and erosion of the qualities of mobility, diversity, autonomy, and translatability possessed by the Jews of the Levant for such a long time. The index to the deep erosion of these qualities is, of course, unequivocal: most of the Jewish communities of the Levant simply no longer exist. Those that do are but shadows of their former selves. The deeply tragic nature and complex human consequences of this fact, it seems to me, cannot be overstated and are most vividly illustrated by the effects of the harsh socialization process undergone by what have now come to be called Oriental Jews in Israel. This too is a theme coursing throughout the book. In a caustic, bitter poem that indicts this process while reclaiming autonomous space through the very pointed subversion of standard linguistic and symbolic counters, the young Israeli poet Sami Shalom Chetrit speaks for both a generation and a class:

Don't touch my wounds!
They're mine, like my Lord you uprooted with such fervor.
Like my innocent love that you mocked, they're mine.
They're mine like my mother's suffocated songs.
They're mine like the downcast eyes of my elders
before the almighty savior king in khaki shorts.
They're mine, like all the prisoners of Zion
from the jails of Beersheba to Tel Mond.
They're mine like my brothers strung out on white powder
like their spirits sold out to the blue and the white.
They're mine like this importunate land.
They're mine, like the compassionate Eastern sun.

Don't touch my wounds.
Don't come to me now to "rescue us from shame."
Save yourselves.
I am my wound and my wound is mine
and what could be sweeter than this pain
to the very end
to every primitive beat
what could be more pulsating than this pain
to the very end
to every African drum
what could be more uplifting than this pain
to the very end
like the wailing of my failed mothers
what is more right than this pain
to the very end
like the whispered psalms of my fathers
what could be more twisting
to the very end
than the ascending scales of Eastern voices
grating in your terror-stricken ears [60]

Here Chetrit takes the syntax of the Song of Songs ("I am my beloved's, and my beloved is mine. . . . How fair is thy love, my sister, my bride! How much better is thy love than wine") to very different ends. The sense of comparison, of textual, spiritual, and communal ideals become literalized: "prisoners of Zion" (also with its veiled reference to "prisoners of hope," a standard trope of medieval Hebrew poetry), have become the inmates of Israeli prisons, over 90 percent of whom are the descendants of Jews from Arab countries. In addition, Chetrit redeploys the most jingoistic and pejorative references of official Zionist discourse (as in Ben-Gurion's comparison of the Jews from Arab countries to "blacks who were taken over to America as plantation slaves"),[61] into a different context of solidarity and identity. Unlike the Israeli poets of the previous generation, Chetrit doesn't go back to the biblical text or to classical references to stress his ambivalence in relation to them; rather, he shows how deep the chasm is between the ethical and aesthetic ideals of that world and the present reality.

Such unequivocal assertions of power on the part of "others" — if not ignored — are usually ascribed to "anger" or "frustration" within the terms of the dominant discourse. Yet, when such projects are undertaken from the inside out, laying bare connections between the past and the present through the particular uses and channeling of language that has circumscribed thought and action, they become much more difficult to accommodate. For the "West," itself a construct, the "Arab" largely remains an enigma, ruled by primal and unfamiliar forces, operating through a crude and ultimately inscrutable logic. Nor has the non-European Jew fared much better, accruing a similar set of characteristics though to a slightly lesser degree. Being, for some reason, more familiar (however he or she might be referred to: as Asian, African, Oriental, Arab, Mediterranean, Levantine, Indian, Persian, Georgian, Kurdish, Falasha, or, to use a Yiddish phrase once popular in Israel, *schvartze hayas* — black animal), the non-European Jew can still be reformed, given the right circumstances, to become one of "us." While seeming to be polemic, these are simply the givens of much academic and popular discourse, examples of which abound at all levels. In a litany of truisms, Ella Shohat comprehensively catalogues the operating assumptions within which Israel's majority has been described and circumscribed:

> According to that mythic discourse, European Zionism "saved"
> Sephardi Jews from the harsh rule of their Arab "captors." It took them
> out of "primitive conditions" of poverty and superstition and ushered
> them gently into a modern Western society characterized by "humane
> values," values with which they were but vaguely and erratically
> familiar due to the "Levantine environments" from which they came.
> Within Israel, of course, they have suffered the problem of "the gap";
> not simply that between their standard of living and that of European
> Jews, but also that due to their "incomplete integration" into Israeli
> liberalism and prosperity, handicapped as they have been by their
> Oriental, illiterate, despotic, sexist, and generally pre-modern formation
> in their lands of origin, as well as by their propensity for generating
> large families. The political establishment, the welfare institutions, and
> the educational system, according to this discourse, have done all in
> their power to "reduce the gap" by initiating the Oriental Jew into the
> ways of a "civilized, modern society." At the same time, intermarriage
> is proceeding apace and the Sephardim have won new appreciation for

their "traditional cultural values," for their folkloric music, rich cuisine, and warm hospitality. A serious problem persists, however. Due to their inadequate education and "lack of experience with democracy," the Jews of Asia and Africa tend to be extremely conservative, even reactionary, and religiously fanatic, in contrast to the liberal, secular, and educated European Jews. Anti-Socialist, they form the base of support for the right-wing parties. Given their "cruel experience in Arab lands," furthermore, they tend to be "Arab-haters," and in this sense they have been an "obstacle to peace," preventing the efforts of the "Peace Camp" to make a "reasonable settlement" with the Arabs.[62]

Shohat goes on to illustrate each of these categories with quotes from politicians and intellectuals spanning the range of liberal to reactionary over the past forty-odd years. These include such choice characterizations as people whose "primitivism is at a peak, whose level of knowledge is one of virtually absolute ignorance, and, worse, who have little talent for understanding anything intellectual." Such people are "only slightly better than the level of the Arabs, Negroes and Berbers"; they "lack roots in Judaism, as they are totally subordinated to the play of savage and primitive instincts," and display "chronic laziness and hatred for work." These Jews are always identified with negatively characterized Arabs and the fearful specter of sinking into the inferiority of the surrounding world: "We do not want Israelis to become Arabs. We are duty bound to fight against the spirit of the Levant, which corrupts individuals and societies." As Abba Eban, a figure instrumental in conveying a certain image of Israel through his statesmanship, writing, and historical productions for television, put it, "the object should be to infuse the Sephardim with an Occidental spirit, rather than allow them to drag us into an unnatural Orientalism. . . . One of the great apprehensions which afflict us . . . is the danger lest the predominance of immigrants of Oriental origin force Israel to equalize its cultural level with that of the neighboring world."[63]

One could go on and on, even into the metaphysical realm, as described in Kalman Katznelson's notorious *The Ashkenazi Revolution*. After defining the Jews as a "congregation of peoples," Katznelson goes on to discuss why the Ashkenazi "people" or "nation" are superior:

Ashkenazi rule over the Afro-Asiatic Jewish peoples and over the other non-Ashkenazi peoples continues even in the State of Israel. This Ashkenazi control is not the fruit of the means and tools at its disposal, but the result of Ashkenazi control over time. We are in control of the dimension of time in the State of Israel and due to this, by default, we control everything subject to this dimension—in other words— *everything*. The tools and the means that are in our hands are nothing but the result and the product of our control over modern time, since modern tools and means can only be created through authoritarian power over modern time and through coordination with that time. *The non-Ashkenazi peoples in the State of Israel* do not possess their own time. Or, at any rate, very little time. Because their time is dead. These peoples live within the cycle of Ashkenazi time, through the power and by the right of Ashkenazi time. We offer them—every hour and every minute—their portion of vital time, and through this power, we control them. If the State of Israel were an enormous experimental laboratory, of the kind used in the research of natural phenomena, and if all the Ashkenazim were removed and replaced with an equal number of non-Ashkenazim, the State of Israel would be conquered by the Arab states within a few hours. . . . We have undertaken tremendous efforts to destroy the gap [between Ashkenazim and non-Ashkenazim]. But the results are meager. After eighty years of educational and social work we are at the point where we have not even begun to struggle with the environmental and hereditary factors that form the basis of this failure. There is no possibility of closing the gap completely. Even those Ashkenazim who believe in closing the gap speak of an extended process lasting hundreds of years. However, the Sephardo-Oriental movement for equality refuses to wait. It asks us to close the gap with the speed that environmental improvement projects—such as the draining of lake Hula, or the construction of big buildings—are undertaken. If we sincerely would like to close the gap within the space of one or two generations, there is only one way: we must descend, deteriorate most surprisingly. We must cease reading serious books, abbreviate our studies, and drastically reduce the number of Ashkenazi children going into secondary school and then on to the universities. Perhaps we should also begin to play the game of *sheshbesh* [backgammon] or other Oriental games of similar kind and type. This is the only realistic way for us to achieve equality quickly with the Sephardo-Orientals. If we refuse to follow this path, then we must tell the Sephardo-Orientals the truth. We must tell them that only a few of them, primarily those of the Ladino Jews, have the chance of reaching our cultural level, and that the gap between us and the great mass of Sephardo-Orientals will be fixed firmly until the end of days.[64]

This remarkable text (characterized by Eliachar in a letter to Ben-Gurion as "written by a Jewish Nazi who, to my regret, only echoes what many good people in our nation think, even if they dare not put it to paper")[65] speaks for itself. It is, however, particularly ironic that Katznelson chose the draining of the Hula swamps as an example for his great natural laboratory, for it was precisely Jews from Arab countries living in the transit camps who carried out this project at subsistence wages. Rather than think such attitudes are a thing of the past, the current mass immigration of Jews from the Soviet Union has simply revived these briefly dormant concerns in just as blatant and virulent forms.[66] Given the open fissure that the Palestinian uprising has wedged into both Israeli society and world public opinion, this discourse has possibly become even more desperate to stake some claims on "truths" that have lost even the spurious validity they had once tried to project.

Despite this, I do not intend this work to be about victors and victims: to pit a powerless and gnawed-at "East" against a voracious "West" with its consuming imagery, energy, and capital is to propose an argument as blind in its reliance on essence as the one it purportedly was trying to topple. And despite what seems like a time of chaos and catastrophe, in a crowded space of ever-dwindling resources, increased debt, and other more ancient and insidious forms of oppression, an innovative, powerful, and hopeful culture is being produced in the Levant. The Palestinian poet Walid Khazindar writes in "At Least":

> If you would smash the glass against the wall
> if you would wake anyone you please, now at two in the morning,
> if you would just say what you wrote yesterday, secretly, on the
>   cigarette box,
> "It has rained, spring has come
> and the murdered man is still lying in the garden"—
> if only you would do something, friend:
> cut something down with your scythe, fling dust around!
> Because when you sit like that at the edge of your sofa,
> hands between your knees,
> after your fourth glass, saying nothing,
> I feel a jar breaking inside me.[67]

This proverbial jar has broken in the form of the Palestinian uprising, a phenomenon that has profoundly affected the relationship of Jews and Arabs as well as the possibilities for social and political change throughout the Arab world, despite the shocking wounds wrought by the Gulf War. The deep scars that young Palestinians (the only contemporary Arabs to have access and contact with Jews) are sure to carry from the constant brutalization they face makes the need to stake claims on a past that offers possibility instead of closure both urgent and necessary. This also signals an effort to move beyond the critique of institutional Orientalism and into an examination of how cultures produce *themselves* within the conditions in which they happen to exist and evolve. The model, then, is an ecological one. By reclaiming and recycling antithetical episodes that can perforate circumscribed versions of history and serve to inform a forward-looking future, the shards of so many shattered jars can begin to move out of museums or libraries and back into use as containers that hold nourishment for the social body *and* the body politic. Given the fact that this work encompasses an enormous variety and range of texts that have been studied by many scholars with great labor and dedication, there may be more than a few rough shards left. Despite the geographical and chronological span I have chosen to work with, this study seems, in many ways, like a preface. Many of the texts I cite are paradigmatic. Behind, to the sides, over and above are many more waiting to be unearthed and put back into circulation. An extensive bibliography tracing this context (with writers from all periods, anthologies, literary background, poetics; sources on the history, politics, religions, societies, cultures, and thought of the region) could not, finally, be included for practical reasons. My use of existing sources has been pragmatic. Whenever possible, I have used material available in English, despite obstacles. Often the issues were technical, as in my use of Reichert's translation of al-Harizi's *Tahkemoni*. Despite idiosyncracies, this translation *still* makes a seminal text available. Sometimes, considerations were historical, as in my reliance on Miriam Cooke's *War's Other Voices*. Despite the fact that many of the writers examined were quite critical of the parameters set up by Cooke (also furthering debate among Arab intellectuals—women and men—on Western feminist approaches to their culture), her work remains one of the only sources for English readers to get a sense of the achievement of women's writing in Lebanon. To embrace the intricacies of all these circumstances is a daunting task.

In my efforts to contextualize, many writers receive only the briefest attention—Elias Canetti and Naguib Mahfouz, for example. Others are not even brought up. I think here, to mention only some from the modern period, of the North African writers Albert Memmi and Edmond El Maleh, the Yemenite writer Shoshannah Shababo, the Greek singer Rosa Eskenazi, and the Turkish singer and composer Isak El-Gazi. There are many others, in every period discussed. The same is true for vast areas of creative endeavor and social history: rabbinic responsa, for example, or the response of a figure such as the former Moroccan political prisoner Abraham Serfaty to questions posed by competing ideologies, so crucial—not only for Jews—in the twentieth century. Broader, underlying issues (the influence of Africa in the formation of Arabic and Moorish culture, for example) are not even touched on. Nevertheless, I have tried to make each section suggestive of a whole range of possible research and discovery. I can only hope that those who find things of value here and go on to investigate them further will refine and improve upon my preliminary conjectures.

Chapter 1

Discontinued Lines: Drafts for an Itinerary

I. Militant Archeology: Dispossessing Native Jews

The "old" Levantine world coincides with but is not exclusive to Islamic rule. Although its central source of nourishment remains the fertile symbiosis of Arabic, Jewish, and Romance culture created in the Western Caliphate of Spain from the tenth to the thirteenth centuries and known as the Golden Age, the culture formed there also refers back to Baghdad and the Eastern Caliphate. This culture, in turn, refers back to its roots, connections and conflicts with Persia, Byzantium, the remnants of the Hellenic world and the ancient Near East. Prospective as well, it survives the Inquisition to go forward and feed Europe, to enrich and stabilize the Ottoman Empire, to collude and collide with the Enlightenment before crashing head-on into the European powers and colonialism. From there, it emerges fragmented and uncertain, oddly bereft of its own nativity, arbitrarily cut up into radically revised national units, constructs as synthetic, if not more so, as Mandelstam's own elected affinities. These units went along with what Timothy Mitchell has called "the machinery of truth" that distinguished the colonial reordering of the world:

> Colonialism was distinguished by its power of representation, whose paradigm was the architecture of the colonial city but whose effects extended themselves at every level. It was distinguished not just by representation's extent, however, but by the very technique. The order and certainty of colonialism was the order of the exhibition, the certainty of representation itself. . . . Modern politics was to reside within a reality effect, a technique of certainty, order and truth, by which the world seemed absolutely divided into self and other, into things themselves and their plan, into bodies and minds, into the material and the conceptual.[1]

Despite the severity of this encroachment, the dense and intricate interconnectedness of the Levantine world—its conceptual and concrete, though not necessarily political, unity and texture—remained remarkably intact, particularly for the Jews, well into the twentieth century. Although by no means always smooth or uniform, the identical geographical space of this world both sustained and outlasted a variety of ruling, administrative, and ideological orders. This was achieved through communal and familial ties, along with an international network of trade and

35

communications (often intertwined through economically advantageous marriages linking and expanding family and business conglomerates), all bound together and woven through by educational, religious, and intellectual authorities, traditions, and institutions. The early and decisive formation and structuring of these orders and connections, "the displacement of the center of gravity of Judaism from the frontiers of Persia to the Western Mediterranean" did not come about through "the internal social or ideological logic of Judaism";[2] it came about, rather, through the expanded frontiers—physical, social, and intellectual—forged by Islam:

> With the great Arab conquests following the rise of Islam, which converted all the countries between Spain and Persia into a single territory dominated by the new religion, and soon after by the Arabic language as well, the majority of the Jewish people of that time came under Arab rule. Thus began the long and great period of Jewish-Arab symbiosis. . . . At the time of the Muslim-Arab conquest, the majority of the Jews were still engaged in agriculture and manual labor. . . . The Jewish people, too, more or less, disappeared as an agricultural people during the seventh and eighth centuries, but, unlike other ancient populations, returned to life as a nation of merchants and artisans. This transformation was due to the great "bourgeois revolution" of the ninth century. Due to this revolution, the civilization of the Middle East during early medieval times was characterized by its commerce, industry, and bureaucratic organization, at a time when Western Europe was mainly agricultural and dominated by knights and feudal lords. The Jews took their full share in this great Middle Eastern mercantile civilization, in particular from the tenth to the thirteenth centuries; and it was at that time and in that part of the world that Judaism itself received its final shape.[3]

The journey leading from this period to the only other subsequent period imbued with such unequivocal and far-reaching significance for Jews of the region is indeed long, intricate, and relentlessly complex. More than simply a movement through space, it involves the replacement of religious, communal, and cultural affiliations by a national entity as the focus of world Jewish life. In the years between 1948 and the late 1950s, roughly half a million Jews from Asia and Africa immigrated to the new state of Israel, only to undergo a proletarianization process directly opposite to that of the urbanization and upward mobility of the ninth century.[4]

As made evident in the introduction, even naming these "natives" accurately is problematic. Are they Asian, African, North African, Middle Eastern, Turko-Iranian, "Sephardo-Oriental" (to use Katznelson's quaint appellation), Sephardi, Arab, non-Western, Eastern, or even, as they have been pejoratively labeled in official Israeli terminology, "children of the Oriental ethnic groups"? Every category seems to come at the expense of another, either leaving something out or succumbing to a negative definition that presupposes one group to be the standard of measurement or all groups to be in possession of some common, primordial "essence." As Ilan Halevi notes, "these vaguenesses of vocabulary, reservations and obstructions reflect in reality the shifting character of the barriers themselves, and the fact that the language is not ready for the social reordering that is underway."[5]

No matter how diverse or connected these communities might have been in the old world, their radical displacement and realignment in the new order meant that they would share a common fate, albeit one with entirely different, unfamiliar, and externally imposed elements binding them together. People from places as various as Marrakesh, Baghdad, Aden, and Isfahan all found themselves dispossessed in the promised land. No matter to what extent current Israeli discourse assumes it has put the transit camp period under its belt (so to speak — as if it has been thoroughly assimilated and absorbed with the iconic image of immigrants being sprayed with DDT), the explication of the human cost of those years has not yet begun; even less examined is the densely symbiotic relationship between the oppression of dispossessed Jews in Europe and the policies of empowered Jews in Palestine and Israel:

> We were wearing our Sabbath clothing. We thought as the plane landed that Israel would welcome us warmly. But goodness, how wrong we were! When the plane had landed at Lod airport, a worker approached us and sprayed us all over with DDT, as if we were lice-infested. What sort of welcome was that? We felt they were spitting in our faces. When we disembarked from the plane, they herded us into a train, which was so crowded that we were stepping on each other and our fine clothes were dirtied. My husband was crying and so was I. Then the children started crying and our sobs went up to heaven and cast a pall over the train. Since it was a freight carriage it had no electric light, but as it sped along we thought of the death trains which had taken European Jews to the Nazi camps. Finally we reached the "Sha'ar Ha'aliya" camp and we were taken in with other families, then they wrote down our names and "gave" us new Hebrew names. "Said" became "Hayyim," "Su'ad" became "Tamar" and I was renamed "Ahuva" and so on. . . . Sha'ar Ha'aliya Camp had been a British army detention centre before it had become an immigration camp. The Israeli security authorities had reinforced the camp's security by doubling the height of barbed wire around it and installing a direct telephone link to the Israeli police in Haifa port. There was a police force of sixty constables, four sergeants

and an officer to supervise the immigrants, who were housed in tents or tin-roofed barracks. . . . As I wandered amongst these tents, an elderly Iraqi waylaid me. "I have just one question," he said. "Are we immigrants or prisoners of war?" My tongue was tied and I could not reply.[6]

Now the only communities left in that ancient world (many with histories going back as far as the Babylonian exile in 586 B.C.) are in North Africa, Turkey, Iran, and Syria, with only a handful of Jews remaining in other countries such as Yemen and Egypt. A fraction of their original size and distinction, all told these communities number about 60,000 or 70,000, according to recent estimates. Those who didn't come to Israel settled primarily in France, England, North and South America, following the immigration patterns of their respective compatriots. Those from Asia Minor, for example, arrived in the Pacific Northwest with other Greek refugees after the turn of the century. Jews from Syria and Lebanon settled in Brooklyn and Latin America in the same waves that brought Christians and Muslims to seek their fortunes in the New World after the great famine at the turn of the century and the destruction and havoc wrought by the breakup of the Ottoman Empire and the First World War; those from Cairo and Alexandria joined Greek, Armenian, and other foreign nationals also forced to start new lives in various diasporas; those from Algeria, Tunis, and Morocco found themselves in a very familiar milieu with other North African emigrés in Paris and Montreal.

While those with the means or luck to reach Europe or the New World were able, for the most part, to maintain or successfully strive toward the same economic, educational, and cultural standards that would have been expected of them in their countries of origin, the situation in Israel was, to say the least, somewhat different.[7] Heirs to a truly astounding diversity of experience and culture (manifested in the unbroken Hebrew textual tradition whose works span the generic gamut while adding new ones, as well as in innumerable writings in at least twenty other languages, not to mention the vast storehouse of native and hybrid musical and artistic styles and conventions), these Jews found themselves succinctly dismissed, in Ben-Gurion's infamous phrase, as "human dust"; raw material to be remolded into the idealized forms acceptable to the new state's professed European/Socialist ideology.[8] The "socialists," however, turned out to be the owners, while the "Europeans" turned out to be Poles, Russians, and others from beyond the pale of settlement who had never reconciled themselves with their own marginality in relation to a glorified "West."

The prevailing terms of complete economic and cultural hegemony on the part of a particular sector of Eastern European and Russian Jews put the new (often unwilling and certainly bewildered) immigrant/refugees into a state of radical alienation and displacement, despite the fact of their citizenship. The crucial factors, however, delineating the terms of this imbalance find their roots at the very beginnings of the Zionist movement and throughout the prestate period in the ongoing and intertwined struggles over control of the educational system, the voting system, and the labor unions. With the breakup of the Ottoman Empire, representatives of the Zionist parties turned their attention to the capitals of Europe; Eliachar wrote of this turning to the "West":

> During the days of the Ottoman Empire, leaders of the Zionist
> movement were accustomed to take counsel with Sephardic leaders in
> the Land of Israel. After the British occupation, this practice ceased,
> particularly as the Anglo-Saxon and Eastern European basis of those
> parties increased. Apparently, their reasoning went like this: since
> authority has passed from Turkey to Britain then the authority of the
> Sephardic Jewish leadership has also passed on to Anglo-Saxon, Eastern
> European and Western European Jewry. Their opinion, due to the fact
> that they were the "haves," was also quite antagonistic. . . . Since the
> British occupation, the Sephardim were swept into the corner. They
> have been overlooked, as if they had never existed.[9]

Complaints by Middle Eastern Jews of neglect at the hands of Zionist party officials were legion, despite the fact that the Jews of the region contributed inordinately more money for the realization of projects in Palestine, per capita, than did Eastern European Jews. Stillman, for instance, notes that when Yehezqel Gurgie Shem Tov, a wealthy Jew from Basra, "donated all of his property, estimated at 140,000 pounds sterling, to the Jewish National Fund, the Zionist Organization in London did not even send him a letter until prodded by Dr. Ariel Bension."[10] Sometimes, these contributions sent clear political messages that could not have been greeted with much enthusiasm; Sir Ellie Kadoorie of Hong Kong (the major contributor for the building of Hebrew University), for example, contributed 150,000 Palestinian pounds to build two agricultural schools, one for Jews and one for Palestinians.

But the arrival at a consensus among opposing factions in the years of institution building—the forming of the state—determined the nature of the state as well as the final exclusion of native Jews from any significant roles in policy-making bodies, as Shlomo Swirski has noted:

> People from different movements who, during the Old Yishuv period
> and under the British Mandate, fought with each other, now became the

rulers of a self–governing state bureaucracy. This position of authority— whether composed of coalition or opposition members—slowly produced a sense of kinship and identical interests between the diverse streams, if not internally then at least externally—in terms of the Arab minority, whom everyone perceived as a threat, and also towards the Oriental Jews whom everyone perceived as different and as cultural outsiders. Alongside the continuing internal battles there now appeared a common stand of "sovereign responsibility" directed to the outside; this expressed itself, for example, in the complete repudiation of any kind of organization based on ethnic or national background.[11]

One can add the obvious here: *except* in the case of the major parties themselves, which were almost exclusively Ashkenazi. One of the key processes limiting the possibility of any encroachment upon the hegemony of Ashkenazi-dominated parties was the successful undoing— through party-affiliated schools—of the separate prestate Sephardi educational system. Contrary to the prevailing mythology, the educational status of Levantine Jews, both in Palestine and in the Arab and Mediterranean world, was much higher then than during the state period. In fact, studies have shown that the grandparents of Oriental Israeli high-school students reached higher levels of formal education in their "primitive" countries of origin than their grandchildren in the technologically advanced and Western-oriented state of Israel. During the crucial formative years of the 1950s, for example, as many as 60 percent of the transit-camp children did not attend school.[12] Rather than being a new development, this was simply a process that had begun earlier, which was described so poignantly by Eliachar in his important document, "The Problem of Education and the Street Children," published in English and presented to a Mandatory committee in 1945:

It is important to note that the extant conditions in the country prior to World War I were much more advantageous for our children. This is because it was not acceptable at that time to divide education up according to party affiliation. The Alliance schools, the Ezra schools, the Hebrew schools and the Talmud Torah academies were in competition with each other to provide all of our children with a practically free education. . . . Presently different investigations have come to the conclusion that the number of children among Oriental Jews who either do not attend school or have only attended school briefly reach into the tens of thousands. . . . Thousands of children have been abandoned to the streets and a portion of them turn into criminals from a young age. . . . This troubling situation, in our opinion, stems from the following: (a) because there is no law for compulsory free education; and (b) because the existing educational system does not fit the needs of our children and, moreover, it seems as if not much importance is given to those learning in our schools. . . . But the problem is not exclusively financial. The energy expended to eradicate conflicts and differences of opinion resulting from the constantly changing demands presented by different party-affiliated bodies adds another obstacle because no time is actually left for the division of Hebrew education to deal with the role it has been created to fulfill, namely, education.[13]

In fact, it was the party system, with the strength of its consensus and common interests, that managed to overpower the two last prestate systemic challenges initiated by veteran Sephardim, and to insure that system's predominance over future immigrants. Both of these challenges — the attempt to create a separate Sephardi labor movement and the 1945 Sephardi boycott of the Zionist party elections — proved to be failures, coming too late to influence the fixed and highly developed party structures that had evolved since the turn of the century. Eliachar, whose testimony regarding this crucial period is still among the most vivid, saw both defeats as decisive attacks on the possibility of developing truly democratic institutions in the state-to-be. In terms of the labor-union movement, he had already long ago pointed out the dangers of "Hebrew labor" as a major point of friction between Jews and Arabs, particularly when seen against the tragic consequences of the First World War for neighboring Syria and Lebanon, where one out of every four people had died or been killed, often through starvation. But he also saw that the party-affiliated labor unions, like the educational system, had become the opposite of what they were supposed to be; in an article called "Why a Sephardi Workers' Union," printed in 1941, Eliachar recorded his criticisms:

> The concern of the heads of labor organizations, such as they were, in the Yishuv of that time, was to become a political/class movement without a worry for workers and laborers who did not have the privilege up to that point of becoming educated to understand the worth of such an organization and sign on as part of the rank and file. Not to mention that in the first organizations of workers there was a kind of special selection to bolster the political/class values espoused by the leadership. In addition, the "lumpen-proletariat" was not recognized by the Yishuv as an element worthy of support or integration into the new workers' organizations.[14]

At the bottom of all these processes lay the nonrepresentational party-bloc voting system, a problem that still impedes the effective functioning of the Israeli government. Again, Eliachar felt that the root of societal divisions, inequalities, and conflicts stemmed from "the will to maintain an ethnic hegemony over both the management and the material means donated by Jews of the diaspora for strengthening settlement in the Land of Israel."[15]

Regarding the new immigrants of the 1950s, denigrated and stigmatized for their primarily Arabic, Levantine, Turkish, or Persian culture, language and communal structure became the primary targets at which the darts of socialization were aimed. Housing, naturally, was the most efficient way of tackling both "problems." By scattering immigrants along the borders, two birds were killed with one stone: as a buffer zone for continuing acts of resistance by exiled Palestinians, these Jews could be initiated into the state's rites of power, suspicion, and fear regarding the Arabs. Naim Giladi recalls his experience of this strategy:

> Along with other new Iraqi immigrants we were put in a *maabara*, transit camp, near Askallan which is now Ashkelon. We slept in tents, we had nothing, and we were supposed to wait until we were sent to places where we would get jobs. Later, a group of Romanian immigrants was put in the same camp: but for them wooden huts were built, with windows and doors. The group of young Iraqis to which I belonged sent a delegation to the authorities, that is, to the official of the Jewish Agency who ran the camp, to complain about this discriminatory treatment. We were told the Romanians came from a country where it was very cold, and they could not bear the climate like us who were used to the great heat of Mesopotamia. We agreed. Nevertheless, when our first winter in this country came, thinking we were going to die of cold, we went back to see the official, who sent us away.
>
> Then, the Iraqis in the camp threw stones at the Romanians' windows, and several important figures in the Jewish Agency came to calm us down. They said to us in substance: "Be patient: soon we shall drive the Arabs out of Majdal and you will be able to have their houses."
>
> For us this was a shock. Majdal was a nearby little town, and we knew nothing of its inhabitants. One night, five or six of us crossed the barbed wire that surrounded Majdal to go and speak to the inhabitants, to see who they were, and why they wanted to drive them out. Talking to them, we discovered that they were very peaceful people, very hospitably disposed towards us, and ready to behave as loyal citizens of the state that had just been founded.[16]

In addition to playing this role in securing the border, the new immigrants were used as an alternative source of cheap labor. This practice dates back to the early waves of Yemenite immigrants "who were known for their diligence, their ability to 'get along on very little,' and were considered 'similar to Arabs.' "[17] Early reports about the Yemenites were filled with enthusiasm; as *Ha-Ahdut,* an early Zionist paper, put it in 1909, "There is no doubt that we need a foundation of Yemenite workers. They are simple workers, who work naturally and without shame, without philosophy and without singing. Mister Marx is not in his pocket and not in his brain. Probably the Yemenite Jew will remain in the same condition as he is today: wild and barbaric. The Yemenites are on the same level as the Arab farmers. Only the Yemenites can take the place of the Arabs." On an official level, many Zionist leaders were captivated by the "advantages" this new labor force offered; as Ben-Gurion noted in 1911, "We need people who are born workers. We have to pay attention to the local element, the Oriental Jews, both the Yemenite and the Sephardic. Their standard of living and their needs are lower than the European workers. They will be able to compete successfully with the Arab workers." Others, like Dr. Arthur Ruppin and Dr. Yaakov Tehon, saw even further; as Tehon observed in 1908, "If we could only make the Yemenite families stay in our settlements permanently. By doing this we can have their women and girls work in our houses, instead of the Arab women who work in most every house, and for such a high salary."[18] Thus another line of confrontation—one that remains volatile to this day—was opened up. The progressive entrenchment of the Oriental Jewish population within confrontational settings—particularly in the military and security services following 1967—served another, extremely useful purpose:

> For Ashkenazi commanders and administrators, viewing the Orientals as they carried out the tasks assigned to them from above, it was convenient to attribute the latter's conscientiousness to "hatred of the Arabs." Such a stance enabled them to present themselves as having a higher order of humanity than their underlings and as having a monopoly on humane feelings and lofty ideals. It also allowed them to ignore the fact that they were the ones in charge of the policy of control and expropriation.[19]

This highly imbalanced encounter between the newcomers and the veterans saw the breakup of families and communities, with all their old allegiances, due to a complete dependency on a system in which practically all forms of expression and exchange were tied to Zionist party-based institutions. Ties to language and native culture dissipated as "absorption" into a distinctly new but not yet very clearly delineated national identity began. That most ironic of all prophecies (the only place in the biblical text where Sepharad, that site-to-be of Arabic/Hebrew symbiosis, is mentioned) had come true, in spades: "And the exiles of Jerusalem, who are in Sepharad, shall occupy the cities of the Negev."[20]

Which is precisely, almost to the letter, as it happened. The memory of Jerusalem (however faded for some) and the legal, liturgical, poetic, and mystical texts written in or emerging from Sepharad/al-Andalus (whether ritually practiced or not) still formed (in conjunction with modern French, English, Italian, Persian, Turkish, or Arabic education) the semiotic parameters, if not the basis, of much of the "exiled" "native's" broader cultural boundaries. The new curriculum, however, based itself on a combination of nineteenth-century Russian, Eastern European, and Hebrew Enlightenment ideology and texts, along with the narrowest mode of Ashkenazi religious culture. Political life was monolithically paternalistic and party-oriented while the cities of the Negev were little more than border outposts or cynical company towns, to which people were dispatched in what ended up being a singularly one-way trip.[21]

Here, though, "one must be careful not to reduce this movement to a single pattern, or this problematic to a single and contingent event. The Jews of the Arab countries did not spontaneously uproot themselves from the world where they had lived for centuries moved solely by their own will, and without heartbreaks: the double pressure, both repulsion and attraction, of the changing Arab society in which they were living, and the alluring devices used by the Zionists already established in Palestine, played a decisive role in this self-extraction."[22] The background to this mass exodus stretches back at least a hundred years to the colonial presence in the region and the varying forms of competitive protectionism offered the peoples of the Book, both Jews and Christians:

> Non-Muslims also began during the last century eagerly to avail themselves of the benefits of a modern European education provided by the various cultural and religious missionaries who flocked into the Middle East and North Africa. For the Jews, the Alliance Israelite Universelle became the chief provider of modern education in the major towns and cities of most Arab countries from the 1860s onward. French, rather than Arabic or Turkish, became the primary language of high culture for thousands upon thousands of Jews. The Alliance gave its pupils more than an education. It gave them a new self-image, created new expectations within them, and helped to arouse a sense of international Jewish solidarity. It also produced cadres of westernized native Jews who now had a distinct advantage of opportunity over the largely uneducated Muslim masses as the Islamic world was drawn ineluctably into the modern world economic system. Together with the rapidly evolving native Christians who benefited from missionary schools, Jews came to have a place in the economic life of the Middle East and North Africa that was far out of proportion to their numbers or their social status in the general population. Their foreign ties, Western acculturation, and economic success were deeply resented by

the Muslim Arab majority. This conspicuous overachievement by some Jews and Christians would contribute to their undoing as a group in the twentieth century with the rise of nationalism in the Arab world.[23]

This passage leaves out several crucial factors: the rise of Zionism, for example, as part of the undoing of Arab Jewish communities; the fact that "international Jewish solidarity" within the Oriental communities was not a function of the Alliance sytem but had always existed on a religious, cultural, institutional, and economic basis; and the extent to which Jewish communities were composed of differing strata, some rooted almost exclusively in Arabic culture, others who managed to bridge a number of cultures, and yet others who were more Western-oriented. It nevertheless goes some way to outline the background of the demise of Arab Jewish communities. Unquestionably, though, the inroads, conflicts, and pressures superimposed by colonial rule upset the traditional forms of confessional autonomy and went into creating "an unequal process which linked the Jewry of the Mediterranean Islamic countries to the movement of European expansion, and detached it from the fate of the Arab peoples."[24] While this may have been particularly true in countries such as Tunisia, Algeria, and Egypt, the situation in Morocco, for example, was quite different. There it was the Moroccan king himself who offered protection to the Jews, even in defiance of the Vichy regime.

In Iraq, on the other hand, the situation was defined by its own unique history. Thoroughly assimilated into Arab society while retaining their distinct identity, Jews did not act out premonitions of impending doom (despite the virulent and devastating anti–Jewish violence of 1941, which was ignited by social unrest, nurtured by British nonintervention, and fueled by struggles between Axis collaborators, deposed rulers, and up-and-coming opportunists). This is borne out by the fact that "even after the proclamation of Israeli statehood in 1948, new schools were still under construction—out of nine schools established by the community after Iraqi independence, six were built in the 1940s, including two in 1948-49."[25] In his memoirs, the Baghdad-born journalist, literary critic, and historian Nissim Rejwan recalls life at the time among a circle of friends who frequented the Al-Rabita bookshop where he worked and which prided itself on carrying "the last word in literary fashion—in poetry the works of T. S. Eliot, Ezra Pound, Auden, MacNeice, Spender, Barker, Edwin Muir; in fiction the works of Joyce, Kafka, Mann, Koestler, Orwell, Greene, Warren, Trilling, and Bellow—not to speak of the host of little magazines fashionable at the time—*Partisan Review, Sewanee Review, Kenyon Review, Hudson Review,* and *Politics* from the United States,

Horizon, Scrutiny, Cornhill, Life and Letters, and *Polemic* from Britain."
Without idealizing the very real conflicts that did exist, Rejwan remembers that "as a matter of fact, all the seemingly world-shaking events of
the times—the United Nations Partition Plan for Palestine, the Ports-
mouth Treaty between Iraq and Britain and the popular convulsion in the
streets of Baghdad which came in its wake, the dispatch of an army to
Palestine and its defeat there at the hands of 'the zionist bandits,' and the
wave of persecution and harrassments to which the Jews of Iraq were
subjected subsequently—all these and many more developments occurred without relations between Jews and non-Jews in our circle being
the least affected."[26]

A survey of Rejwan's own book reviews written for the English-
language *Iraq Times* in the late 1940s also goes against the grain of many
historical renderings of this time of "crisis," renderings in which much
simply falls through the cracks. In these reviews we can see, for instance,
Rejwan defending the aesthetic methods of the likes of Virginia Woolf,
D. H. Lawrence, Elizabeth Bowen, and James Joyce against the reservations of a crotchety British critic or discussing the work of Henry Miller
in the context of idealized images of American life:

> In the minds of most people the word America is generally associated
> with everything that is accomplished, grand, and enjoyable in this
> world. For them, it is, first of all, the land where they make "the
> pictures," where such blessed souls as Greer Garson, Ingrid Bergman,
> Clark Gable and Robert Taylor live, make love and use new dress- and
> hair-fashions every day. It is the place where a workman, a salesman or
> a clerk can afford to drive his own car; where a newsboy can be a
> Henry Ford, a manicurist, a Hollywood star and anyone a President by
> sheer hard work and perseverance: where, in short, everyone is happy,
> enjoying himself and "swell" . . . But there are other people who would
> complain that there are other, more important things than these, to
> them, superficial and outward features. There is the human aspect, the
> problem of living happily and satisfactorily. In the midst of so much
> regimentation, monotony and standardisation; where the people's mental
> and spiritual inspiration comes from such arid sources as Hollywood,
> the rotary Press and the pulp magazines; and where men like Zanuk,
> Luce and Hearst can determine what and how people should think and
> dream.[27]

He also reviewed translations of Arabic works, and books dealing with
the effects of the "unparalleled slave system the Germans created during
the last war."[28]

Snapshots from this period testify to analogous variegated textures of
life lived in other countries: a packed hall full of attentive parents in

Aleppo in 1936; girls in wide silk trousers and vests posing before a dance performance at the Alliance in Damascus in 1939 or joining other students in the streets to demonstrate against "Imperialism" that same year; groups of scouts holding signs celebrating Israel's first independence day in Tripoli; exhibits at Hebrew book week in Tunis in 1956; lines of neatly dressed students under trees shedding their autumn leaves in a schoolyard in Rabat; camping trips and school plays in Teheran and Abadan; flower girls before the bride and groom at a fashionable wedding at the Magen Abraham Synagogue in Beirut in the 1960s.[29]

But beneath the surface of these contained images, a tremendous push and pull of often diametrically opposed forces was being exerted on and within the Jewish communities. The ideology of the Zionist movement, with its Eurocentrism and utter disregard for Arabs, did not simplify matters. By essentializing all of Jewish experience into the single objective of recreating the "homeland" and having all Jews settle in it, the prevailing forces within the movement often allied themselves with precisely those reactionary forces that would rather lend their support to a far-off Jewish state than open their own gates to the suffering and persecuted Jews of Europe.[30] Besides attempting to appropriate Jewish history in one fell swoop, the practical repercussions of Zionists' push to materialize projected historical claims through the establishment of new physical, economic, and cultural realities in Palestine produced a ripple effect throughout the Arab world. Naturally, this was felt most acutely within the Jewish communities. On one hand, they were generally ignored by the Zionist establishment. On the other hand, some either identified with it as a revival of Hebrew culture and the Hebrew nation or else were *put* in the position of somehow being allied to the movement. Thus many found themselves accused of harboring a double allegiance. As Menahem S. Daniel, later a senator in the Iraqi Parliament, explained to the secretary of the Zionist Organization in London in a letter dating from 1922:

> You are doubtless aware that, in all Arab countries, the Zionist
> Movement is regarded as a serious threat to Arab national life. If no
> active resistance has hitherto been opposed to it, it is nonetheless the
> feeling of every Arab that it is a violation of his legitimate rights, which
> it is his duty to denounce and fight to the best of his ability.
> Mesopotamia has ever been, and is now still more, an active center of
> Arab culture and activity, and the public mind here is thoroughly stirred
> up as regards Palestine by an active propaganda. At present the feeling
> of hostility toward the Palestinian policy is more strong, as it is in some
> sort associated in the mind of the Arab with his internal difficulties in
> the political field, where his position is more or less critical. To him any

sympathy with the Zionist Movement is nothing short of a betrayal of the Arab cause.

On the other hand the Jews in this country hold indeed a conspicuous position. They form one third of the population of the Capital, hold the larger part of the commerce of the country, and offer a higher standard of literacy than the Moslems. In Baghdad the situation of the Jew is nearly an outstanding feature of the town, and though he has not yet learned to take full advantage of his position, he is nevertheless being regarded by the waking up Moslem as a very lucky person, from whom the country should expect full return for its lavish favors. . . . This country is now trying to build up a future of its own, in which the Jew is expected to play a prominent part. . . . The Jews are already acting with culpable indifference about public and political affairs, and if they espouse so publicly and tactlessly as they have done lately, a cause which is regarded by the Arabs not only as foreign but actually hostile, I have no doubt that they will succeed in making themselves a totally alien element in this country and as such they will have great difficulty in defending a position, which, as explained above, is on other grounds already too enviable.[31]

As these conflicts developed, the use of historical right did not pass unnoticed or unopposed. Skepticism and outright antagonism (not to mention resistance) came from the people the Zionists proposed to displace, the Palestinians, as well as from Arab nationalists and Jews of the region who foresaw some of the potential dangers involved. Yusuf al-Kabir, for example, a prominent Jewish lawyer from Baghdad, had this to say regarding the Balfour declaration in a letter to the *Iraq Times* on November 5, 1938:

Reconstruction of historical geography, if accepted as practical theory, would for instance bring the case of Ulster to ground, and provide a recognized legal basis for German claims on Eastern Europe. In a certain influential section of the German press, the theory is now being held out that Eastern Europe, up to the Volga, was in some remote time wholly occupied by Germans. If the legal basis is accepted, there remains nothing but to work out history in detail for a suitable epoch, and everyone knows that modern science can do anything. Moreover, if one goes reconstituting history two thousand years back there is no reason why one should not go still further back, say four or five thousand years, and presently have the world ruled by militant archaeology.[32]

This archaeology would indeed become more and more militant as the impending shift from "strife" to war in Palestine, and the subsequent intensification of the stakes implied in that transition, exacerbated many of the already tenuous social and political relations in the surrounding countries. At the same time (while the ultimately meaningless, in these historical contexts, categories of "Jews" and "Arabs" have been bandied about), too little attention has been paid to the specifics of each situation. Class structure, for example, and the social struggles involved, also played a decisive role in determining the direction things went. Often, as in other periods throughout the history of the region, wealthier Jews could find themselves in a much better position than poor Muslims while the fate of poor Jews was often more closely linked to that of the Arab masses. Among Jews themselves, there were distinct divisions. The more culturally Arab working class lived in the traditional old Jewish quarters, the *hara* or the *mellah*, while the more Europeanized middle and upper classes lived in the newer quarters. Jacques Hassoun, an Egyptian Jew, described the division:

> From the late 1920s one could observe in some of these synagogues the ceremony of the "Initiation Religieuse des Jeunes Filles" in which young girls, all dressed in white, their heads veiled, candles in hand, would walk in procession in a manner all too reminiscent of a Catholic ceremony. What relation could have existed between those Jews and the Jews of the *hara*? Between the world of the Jewish *khawagat*, oriented to Paris and London and crowned by the glittering circle of Jewish beys, pashas, and barons—and the world of *galabia* and caftan, of *ful*, *malukhia*, and *qulqas*, of those for whom even the *siddur* (prayer book) had to be translated into Arabic?[33]

In addition, changing relations of authority and generational dynamics fueled new conflicts. Within the Jewish community, manifestations of this can be seen in the record of an extended and deep involvement on the part of younger people with various Arab nationalist, communist, and socialist movements, as well as with branches of the Zionist movement itself. This often came against the wishes of an older, more conservative and traditional generation. Those who won the struggle, however (a new Arab ruling class and a united Zionist movement), did so at a cost: the suppression and defeat of movements based on principles cutting across ethnic lines and religious differences, and the loss of any genuine tolerance that the older, more traditional generation might once have possessed. Here, the warring parties managed to find common ground. The increasingly reactionary Arab regimes also had their proverbial two birds and they, too, could be killed with one stone. By expelling the Jews, they could confiscate a substantial amount of wealth and property; at the same time, the Jewish question could be manipulated as a scapegoat to mask their own inert rhetoric, indifference, and lack of resolve regarding the question of Palestine. This, in turn, could help deflect attention from the more pressing, volatile, and brutal power struggles and social conflicts transpiring in their own countries; as Stillman notes:

> Much of the attention and the passion of the Arab masses was directed almost exclusively toward Palestine and temporarily, at least, away from the local Jewish communities and, it might be added, from the serious internal problems plaguing their individual countries. . . . In Egypt and Iraq, the governments took advantage of the state of emergency to round up communists, which in both countries included a considerable number of Jews. . . . The treatment meted out to the internees was generally far better in Egypt than in Iraq. Many more non-Jews were also arrested at this time since the two governments took advantage of the imposition of martial law to suppress internal opposition. In addition to communists, for example, many Muslim Brethren were rounded up in Egypt.[34]

Again, contrary to current mythology, resentment and violence were not necessarily directed exclusively at Jews. Jean Said Makdisi, whose life has been lived in all the cities on this itinerary—Jerusalem, Cairo, and Beirut—writes of her view as a child of these events:

> In Cairo, we lived well in the midst of vast poverty. . . . I remember arriving home to quiet, tree-lined Zamalek, with its embassies guarded by policemen in white uniforms; polite dogs lifting their legs against dry trees, held on leashes by well-dressed women or their servants; children spilling out of the large car and racing into the cool darkness of the building in which we lived. The majestic Nubian *bouab* in his white robes and turban, standing aside like some gigantic phantom, held open the door of the lift . . . Still, even in those heedless days—not, perhaps, so heedless after all—I wondered why he had to open the door for me . . . Always there was that crack in my contentment.

After describing a luxurious night at the opera, attended by the royal family in their red limousine, Makdisi remembers this:

> When we reached our own car, my mother held the door open for me to climb in—and then suddenly the magic ended as two children, barefoot and in rags, palms outstretched, came between me and my mother. It was from that moment, I think, that I came to see that mine was a dream world, a world of operas and fairy princesses, and that the real world—their world—was one of rags and shivers and the cruelty of a cold winter night.
> Indeed one January Saturday in 1952, the masses of Cairo rose up in fury and burned whole parts of the city to the ground. From the balcony in Zamalek where, on happier occasions, I dreamily used to follow the flight of falcons soaring high, high, up in the skies, and then

suddenly diving, and the crows that noisily flapped around the public
gardens near our house, we saw the red glow in the distance across the
Nile. That Saturday, charred paper floated in the air, and my nostrils
were black when I rubbed them. My father's business was among those
burned, but he felt no rancor. He received the news stoically, with
sadness.[35]

It was in the context of this history—the cataclysmic developments
that would shape the future of the region for generations to come—that
the Zionists, desperately in need of a large influx of "raw material" to
inhabit and rebuild what remained after the "miraculous cleansing of the
land," suddenly rediscovered the world of Arab Jewry, upon whom it
had previously placed strict immigration quotas.[36] In this often cynical
"rediscovery," gathered into the place of "origin" (the site professed as
primordial source by the ideology of return), Levantine and Arab Jews
found themselves completely cut off from the most enduring sources of
their own culture, not to mention that of the peoples among whom they
had lived for thousands of years.

There can be little doubt that the most shortsighted and devastating
effect of the socialization process undergone by the Arab Jews following
their mass exodus was "de-Arabization." This was most acutely felt in
the loss of Arabic as a native tongue and, as corollary to that, the loss of
grounding in any native tongue, forced as the new immigrants were to
conform to the non-Semitic structure, syntax, and pronunciation of
"new Hebrew."[37] The repulsion for things Arabic projected by the prevailing ideology was thus inscribed phonetically within the very deepest
recesses of the personal psyche, within language itself. Even today, the
pronunciation of two Hebrew letters—the gutturals *het* and *ayin*—serves
as a clear marker around which people determine social class, cultural
background, and educational expectations. Most uncharacteristically for
"the people of the Book," Israeli Jews—like the unvoweled consonants
of Semitic alphabets or a voice without a text—have become disembodied, monolingual, monocultural.

The age-old system of critical checks and balances, illustrated by the
paradigm of following the reading of the portion of the week from the
Hebrew Bible in synagogue with an interpretive translation in Aramaic
or Arabic, has largely been replaced by the import of cultural commodities. The generative model of reading the outside world into the text and
then reprocessing it out again through active interpretation[38] has been superseded by a regressive instinct: the nostalgic desire to be relieved of the
strain of individual responsibility (represented by the burden of a "reading" whose high stakes and universal application are implicit) in order to

collapse within the collective. This "absorption" of the old world's ancient Jews within a national Israeli collective has managed "what no empire had been able, or wanted, to achieve":[39] the exchange of the legal, covenental, and communal basis of Jewish existence for the racial, the ethnic, and the national, a rupture whose further implications and deeper marks are only beginning to surface.

II. Gazing at Palestine: Yosef Haim Brenner and Albert Antebbi

One of the sources usually not considered in tracing the archaeology of this exchange can be found in the initial collapse of terminology used by European settlers to describe both Arabs and Arab Jews. This process can be seen, for example, by juxtaposing the writings of Albert Antebbi (a leader of the Palestinian Jewish community from Damascus who—along with many other native Jews—had sharply criticized the prevailing Zionist policies at the turn of the century) and the record of the initial encounter of the Hebrew novelist and critic Yosef Haim Brenner with the promised land. Brenner, born in the Ukraine in 1881, came to settle in Palestine in 1909. His first evening in Haifa, "seeing a band of Arab urchins insult him and his comrades," he noted, "There is yet another species of gentile in the world we must suffer. . . . We also have to suffer this filth."[40] In *Breakdown and Bereavement*, Brenner's most acclaimed novel, Yehezkel Hefetz, the protagonist, goes mad after a nightmare in which he awakens in the presence of an Arab woman who has come to his settlement to look for her brother just before Passover. Hefetz, in a state of frenzy, connects this woman to a blood libel in Russia. In his novella *Nerves*, the new immigrants on their way to the promised land feel assaulted by the sights and sounds encountered in Alexandria: "Arabs in long gowns that looked like dresses assailed us on shore and begged, practically threatened us, to let them carry our bags. . . . To make a long story short, then, we were standing there confusedly, uncertain how to proceed in this strange, primitive, deafening place." After a Jew comes to assist them,

> we ourselves proceeded on foot through the streets of Alexandria, which were as filthy as only the streets of an Arab city can be, staring at the nargilleh smokers in the cafes, at the veiled women with their shawls, nose rings, and breathing tubes, and at all the rest of that Oriental clutter.[41]

This Jew, however, ends up swindling the newcomers and, as they finally land in Jaffa, the narrator recounts his experience to a friend:

Have you ever paid attention to the faces of some of our predatory Jews
who haunt the cities of the Orient. . . . I mean those cocky, energetic,
wolfish ones with their oily black hair and their sharp little mustaches
that curl up at the edges? Have you noticed how they prowl when they
walk, as though stalking prey? I tell you, I can spot at a glance which of
them are merely pickpockets and sharks, and which also deal in human
flesh . . . [42]

Haifa, Jaffa, the Arabs, and even the Arab Jews simply become a backdrop
for superimposed images from another world: the Cossacks, Poles, and
Russians of the Ukraine. The space is transparent: for all their professed
but idealized "love of the land," many of the early European settlers had
x-ray vision, seeing *through* things without recognizing them.

The same year Brenner arrived, Albert Antebbi (who, after noting
that "the ill will of the local population coincides with the creation of Zionism," was characterized as an "arrogant, haughty, capricious, per-
verse, irascible, violent, despotic, ruthless Asiatic")[43] wrote a scathing
letter to Meir Dizengoff and Daniel Brill, two Zionist functionaries sta-
tioned in Jaffa:

As far as ties to our other compatriots in the Land is concerned—see
here, they can only be well-disposed towards us insofar as we identify
with them. From the first day I prophesied those disturbances to you,
and I now predict there will be even more severe disturbances. . . .
How exactly do you expect to prevent doubt and even hatred given
such provocation? Last Sabbath I came upon two Muslims and was
surprised to find several issues of *HaZvi* with articles in them blue-
pencilled, their intention being to seek a court order from the Governor
against Ben-Yehuda for incitement to murder. I can assure you that the
most lenient courtroom in the freest country in the world would find
incriminating evidence in reading the advice given Jews to arm
themselves and not rely on the government for protection. [44]

Antebbi's nonessentializing discourse moves from an assumption based
on common sense and common experience to a specific incident clearly
bringing his argument—based on an interpretation made in the form of a
prediction—sharply into focus. From the particular, he then moves again
to a plausible and more general conjecture that puts the scope of his opposition into a broader context. This mode of perception and analysis—
drawing upon personal experience, extensive knowledge (only beginning with language), and intimate familiarity with the people and
cultures of the region, is precisely what characterized the different approach of native Jews to the conditions of the time. Eliachar, like many

other prominent native Jews, wrote of the general state of ignorance of actual local peoples and conditions:

> There are many who write, lecture and and remain in a state of constant alertness regarding everything that touches on relations between us, the Arabs in our country and the surrounding states. Many of them are "experts" who determine Israel's course and reach in our region. But there are very few, very few indeed, who have studied outside the walls of colleges for Oriental studies, university institutes, or who have absorbed their knowledge through anything but books or newspapers. How many of the Orientalists in our country, how many of the journalists gushing forth innumerable pages on regional problems and Israel's position regarding them, how many members of parliament who determine policy in everything regarding our future in the region—how many of these have, for example, ever visited the house of an Arab? How many of them can be found within their domain, living with Arabs, learning their ways and understanding the depths of their nature through daily contact, in their houses, on the street, in society, in commercial relations and recreational activities? Only a child could count them.[45]

In other letters, Antebbi applies his experience and knowledge to shake his correspondents out of the stupor of unexamined assumptions and generalizations, castigating them for incompetence and pointing out the real dangers that can result from the ignorance or "misreading" of local conditions and signs:

> How is it possible that you were unable to find someone of influence, a Jew or a non-Jew, in Damascus or Beirut, who could have opened the gates of those high-ranking officials before you? Why didn't you prepare yourselves with letters of introduction from your coreligionists in Constantinople? The matter could have been handled easily, and I know many people in Constantinople, Beirut and Damascus.[46]

Antebbi remained unequivocal in presenting plans that he thought would meet the requirements of a local population of which he considered himself an integral part, always stressing the need "to defend general political equality as well as safeguard regional economic interests."[47]

In his last piece of writing, "From the Notebook," Brenner referred to Arabs as "those Poles of the Orient." A contemporary Israeli critic pointed out that this, like Brenner's other works, "did not conceal the depths of hatred dividing him from them—seeing them as a collective with a nightmarelike essence, alien, seething with hatred. . . . He saw something foreign on the lowest erotic, aggressive level, the level of the threat of distorted eros, perverted and brutal sex, homosexuality, besti-

ality. In Brenner's opinion the latter danger was no less than the sword
and perhaps seductive to the same degree. He also feared the Jews would
be swallowed up by the Arabs."[48] Several days after finishing this piece,
Brenner himself fell victim (killed in the riots of 1921) to the fatal consequences of irresponsibility and incitement prophesied by Antebbi. For
Antebbi, it was simply the refusal to recognize the political and economic
rights of "others," the "natives," and the rage and frustration arising
from this injustice, and not the hatred of some abstract "species of gentile," which led to such tragic results. As entrenched ideologies continued
to invent ever more ingenious ways to mask political and economic im-
balances (those two fundamental realities most often subsumed in essentialist discourse, that "fantasy of understanding at no cost"), the price exacted kept getting higher and higher.

In the prevailing climate of self-fulfilling prophecies, where things
seem to be based more on "proving" projected and unchallenged
"truths" in order to maintain power than on testing possibilities based on
the interpretation of knowledge and experience, Brenner has come to be
seen as a "realist" who "harbored no illusions," while someone like Antebbi is labeled a hopeless romantic, catalogued with those "charmed by
the exoticism of the Orient."[49] Nor are either of these cases isolated examples: the kind of assumptions from which Brenner's texts emerge (in
which the "Arab" serves as a collective projection of imported fears and
the Arab Jew is little more than a mirror image of vulgar stereotypes)[50]
constitute fundamental codes and points of reference in almost all "official" contemporary Hebrew literature. On the other hand, intellectuals—
writers, historians, political or spiritual leaders—emerging from a
Levantine/Arabic milieu are either ignored, treated condescendingly as
part of a "rich folklore," or made into "race representatives" of the latest
cultural ghetto. At the same time, Antebbi was by no means a lone figure. Even a cursory examination of accounts by Levantine and Arab Jews
of this (and the following) period reveals that his concerns about political
and economic parity between Jews and Arabs were not extraordinary but
reflected the consensus among native Jews in the region. The most representative and accessible of these figures is, of course, Eliyahu Eliachar.[51]

While no comprehensive history of these attitudes has been written,
there are many hints indicating just how widespread they were. In speaking about Haim Arlosoroff, a Zionist leader whose way of thinking
strayed from the consensus and whose assassination remains unsolved to
this day, an Israeli historian of the conflict, Aharon Cohen, brings up
other dissenters:

Arlosoroff was to some extent "exceptional" in official Zionist thinking. The Zionist leaders who came from Europe were far removed in spirit and mentality from even the Jewish intelligentsia of Eastern countries, some of whom were solidly established in the Arab cultural world and could have constituted an excellent bridge between the Jewish and the Arab national movements. Men like Professor A. S. Yahuda, David Yellin, Rabbi Nahum of Egypt, and several leading Sephardi Jews in Palestine, could have contributed a great deal to the creation of a relationship of understanding and cooperation between the two peoples, but were not given the opportunity to do so. The upshot was that they resigned in an atmosphere of bitterness, and some of them even became confirmed opponents of anything connected with Zionist leadership and policy.[52]

Nor did such attitudes wane in the years following the initial encounter between European Zionist and prominent Middle Eastern Jews. The chief rabbi of Alexandria, the great scholar Moise Ventura, for example, in a New Year's synagogue sermon delivered as late as 1942, had this to say:

After the lamentable failure of Western civilization, the Orient is again called upon to play an important part in the cultural life of Nations. The Orient means Egypt, Palestine, Syria, Iraq; more specifically, the Semites—Jews and Arabs—are again called upon together to play a vital role within the scene of history. . . . Everyone whose mental capacities are in free working order must recognize that today the enemies of the Jews are as well the enemies of the Arabs—that is, the enemies of civilization.[53]

Needless to say, Ventura's sentiments were a far cry from the prevailing ones of Zionist leaders. Even within the crucible of the Palestinian uprising, where feelings and opinions have been steadily galvanized, Rabbi Ovadiah Yosef (Israel's former chief rabbi and still the most respected Sephardi rabbinic authority now practicing) has formulated *halakhic* (legal) opinions stating that giving up portions of the Land of Israel is desirable and even necessary for the sake of peace. Needless to say, again, like the thought of the figures mentioned above, such opinions are not only not studied or granted legitimacy but are even suppressed within the Israeli context.[54]

The legacy of Brenner's initial gaze is still operative through more or less subtle means in many aspects of Israeli life and culture. The bottom line of even the liberal "peace camp" represented by a figure such as Amos Oz does not seem to have moved much beyond S. Y. Agnon's harsh judgment regarding the Arabs after the disturbances of 1929: "My attitude is now this: I don't hate them and I don't love them, all I want is not to see their faces. In my opinion we must now make a great ghetto of half a million Jews in *Eretz Yisrael*, for if not we shall (God forbid) be lost."[55] The size of the ghetto has grown, but the nature of the problems seem frozen in time. From 1931 to 1986, for example, only a thousand items—mostly single poems—were translated from Arabic into Hebrew. Although the situation has improved somewhat in the past several years (through the continued efforts of Jewish scholars such as Sasson Somekh, David Semah, and Shime'on Ballas, as well as those of Palestinian Israeli translators like Anton Shammas, Salman Masalha, and Naim Arayde), presently there is not a single full-time Arabic/Hebrew literary translator in the country.

This lack of translated texts is indicative of the lack of many different kinds of translation and exchange on the official level. The "vaguenesses of vocabulary" and collapse of terminology have assumed endemic proportions, while "militant archaeology" has reapportioned physical and cultural space on a massive scale. The original terms of the conflict (drained of any real exchange value by their constant deployment as covers masking a more pragmatic and covert distribution of power) have been turned into what Meron Benveniste calls "a new Latin for the Middle East." This arcane and exclusive language is used by "the subculture of the mighty" to give the impression that something is actually being done to alleviate the constant tension that by now everyone simply assumes to be an unavoidable function of the essentialized, eternal qualities of strife implicit in and between the terms "Jew" and "Arab." Despite its enormous potential for effecting real change, the Palestinian uprising's bold initiative—met only with more settlements and more Jewish immigration, the creation of "facts on the ground"—seems to have, at least for the present, simply further entrenched these qualities.

It is not only in Jerusalem that the number of people born into this new reality has multiplied: all over the Arab world (except in Morocco), there are fewer and fewer people who can still recall either the diverse Jewish cultural presence or the full range of human encounters with people who just happened to have been Jews. At the same time, there are more and more people for whom Jews can only be seen through the dull and often bloody film of "Zionism," "Israel," war, and the constant brutality of military occupation. Ironically, it is only the protracted occupation following the 1967 war that has

> broken the geo-cultural isolation of Israel in the Arab world. . . . This transformation, which marked the movement from self-contained settlement colonization to expansionism, also affected the Arab Jews.

They who had attempted to forget the language of their parents could now, thanks to their knowledge of Arabic, do good lucrative business with the Arabs in the occupied territories, speculate and trade, and even move up a military and police hierarchy in which knowledge of Arabic became a professional advantage of extreme importance. Culturally, the occupation after 1967 marginalized the Europeans in terms of linguistic, musical, culinary or family traits, and made their monopoly of power appear more flagrant and more shocking.[56]

This ironic return has engendered another situation entirely, that of a seemingly unending status quo characterized by its blatant imbalance of power. One vision of this new reality, now the primary site and filter through which the terms "Jew" and "Arab," floating signifiers bloated to the point of explosion, take on meaning, is described in a nightmare recounted by the Palestinian writer Raja Shehadeh:

> I feel empty: in the hollow center of a wheel with rusty spokes. At the end of every spoke is a head—a haunted, hunted, greedy, cruel death-mask. The wheel begins to spin and I get dizzy trying to find my face among the masks. I look out into the other side, the backs of the masks, and instead of hollows I see twin masks—the fragmented faces of our occupiers: riveted to the backs of ours in a way that ensures that we will never see each other, as the wheel spins faster and faster.[57]

This metaphoric account is only buttressed by the very real nightmares of Palestinian children whose fathers, brothers, and sometimes even mothers and sisters have been taken away in the middle of the night by "the Jews" during and before the uprising. David Grossman writes of these children's perceptions in The Yellow Wind:

> Naji is two and a half years old, short for his age, black eyes, curls.
> "A month ago they took his father, and he doesn't know where he is, or if he will ever return."
> "A little while ago," says the second teacher, somewhat heavy, blue-eyed, and delicately made up, always on the edge of a giggle or a blush, "a little while ago the military governor visited the kindergarten and asked if I teach the children bad things, against Israel and the Jews."
> "And what did you say to him?"
> "I said that I don't. But that his soldiers do."
> "What do you mean?"
> "What do I mean? I'll explain. When a child goes outside and sees a tree, he knows that the tree bears fruit and leaves, right? When he sees a soldier, he knows very well what the soldier does. Do you understand?"
> "What do soldiers do?" I ask a girl of about four, called Naima, green-eyed, little gold earrings in her ears.
> "Searches and beatings."

"Do you know who the Jews are?"
"The army."
"Are there other Jews?"
"No."[58]

These floating signifiers have taken on the role of soldiers—willing and unwilling, young and old, refugee and resident, armed and unarmed, Israeli "Jew" and Palestinian "Arab"—who keep on killing and getting killed in this continuing war of attrition. While Brenner's fate and nightmare is still rooted deeply in the psyche, experience, and discourse of many Jews, Shehadeh's vision has almost fully occupied the once qualitative but now quantitative space that remains the site of a riddle.

This riddle, God's most treasured pun, 'eber ve 'arab (the two displaced letters—the "b" and the "r" of Hebrew and Arab), and its two unvoweled peoples built around consonants, both each other's vowels, shape, and story, seems most difficult to resolve without succumbing to some provisional "answer" that relegates apparently contradictory phenomena to some identifiable and unthreatening limbo. In a world governed by "indeterminacy and the code," words and sites become whatever one invests in them. It is left up to the reader, the "seer," to declassify the material, renegotiate the signs and produce intelligible and defensible meaning. Ideologies of power, on the other hand, assure secure returns by suppressing, denying, or co-opting the ambiguities and particulars of experience that stand in contradiction to the ideology. The events of history, "what it was before it damn well was history, what urgency or laziness or misery it was to those who said and did what they did," demand that the remains be redressed, that the writings and objects not collapse into a "demonstration, a separating out, an act of classification," but serve "the present, which is the only place history has context."[59] The land will not rest until all the sources of her memory have been tapped, until the interrupted synapses pass from one neuron to another, until the signals are picked up, the discontinued routes reinstated, and new blood can freely flow through the severed veins. It is only then, in the words of Mahmoud Darwish, that the witness, as writer, will have a chance to "guard the plot of the Book against the prophets."[60]

III. 1938: Beirut to Jerusalem via Damascus/An Itinerary for Edmond Jabès

The Hachette *Illustrated Blue Guide to the Eastern Mediterranean and Egypt* for 1938 (the same year Yusuf al-Kabir voiced his skepticism about accepting the "reconstruction of historical geography" as "practical theory") suggests the following four-day trip:

Beirut to Jerusalem via Damascus

Setting out from Beirut in the morning by car, you can reach Damascus in three hours; once there, the afternoon can be used for sightseeing. The second day should be devoted to the trip from Damascus to Jerusalem, and the third for touring Jerusalem. This itinerary also gives you the chance to be in Cairo—or Alexandria—the fourth day after leaving Beirut. By skipping Damascus and traveling along the coast, an extra day can be gained.[61]

The trip to Jerusalem and the sites within it are removed from time: "What one seeks in Jerusalem is the material testimony of historical events whose consequence has traversed the globe to our very own era."[62] Two-and-a-half pages devoted to the three varied types (places and artifacts unaltered by time; those changed or reconstructed; and those only authenticated by more recent traditions) of "material testimony of the Savior's life and the great drama of the Passion" follow. In between this enumeration and three-quarters of a page devoted to the Jews, "who have returned to the Promised Land . . . despite Arab hostility,"[63] the following lines are devoted to Muslims:

The Muslims are numerous in Palestine but, even though they are the majority in every city except Jerusalem and Tiberias, there is nothing particularly notable about them for the traveler. Thus, we shall wait until our arrival in Egypt before describing some Islamic customs.[64]

This majority (the "natives," in guidebook parlance) were in the process of having their fate decreed for them by a complex and increasingly distant network of force and circumstance. The first drafts for the partition of Palestine were drawn in 1938, containing a plan in which the proposed Jewish state would receive 33 percent of the total area of the country at a time when Jewish ownership did not exceed 6 percent of the land. The battle for land—not in any projected ideological, religious, or mythic sense, but on the purely economic level—remained central, and it is only in the most recent research that scholars have plumbed the impressively accrued layers of the conflict to reach the certain knowledge possessed by someone like Albert Antebbi.[65] In the fierce trilateral struggle between Palestinians, Zionists, and British colonizers, the primary issue at stake for the "natives" remained the demand for at least some form of representative government.

Protests were centered on the transfer of land, mass immigration, and the segregated labor policies of the new settlers. In other words, what was sought was political and economic equality and participation, precisely those issues foreseen by Antebbi as crucial and whose protracted irresolution would create Shehadeh's nightmare vision. The subsequent events—the actual partition of Palestine, the establishment of the state of Israel in 1948, and the mass population movements of "exile" and "return"—made following the itinerary of the *Blue Guide* difficult for many, impossible for some. Old and familiar routes with their enduring lines of communication had unnaturally and abruptly been cut off. As the parties to the extended conflict (determined by an asymmetry of power embedded within an already rigidly established set of possible claims, counterclaims, and tactics on the part of all the sides involved) moved into the open to take on the guise and jargon of nation-states, the more tangible and concrete reasons for the intransigent nature of the fight, and its broader consequences, seemed to recede further and further into obscurity.

While an old Levantine world whose Jewish and Arab presence is accounted for and considered in relation to Europe still remains largely unexplored, a new Levant—more discrete and fragmented but still aware of the possibilities of its space—is in the making. It is within the gap of these two worlds, along the margins of the many struggles fought to reorder its constellations, that the texts of Jabès and Derrida—for whom the qualitative space of the *Blue Guide's* itinerary was still real—emerge. In *Glas*, Derrida writes:

> In Algeria, in the middle of a mosque that the colonists had changed
> into a synagogue, the Torah once out from *derriere les rideaux*, is carried
> about in the arms of a man or a child. . . . Children who have watched
> the pomp of this celebration, especially those who were able to give a
> hand, perhaps dream of it long after, of arranging there all the bits of
> their life.
>   What am I doing here? Let us say that I work at the origin of
> literature by miming it. Between the two.[66]

Writing in a mode that attempts to situate Derrida's approach to textuality within and on the outskirts of a rabbinic tradition, Susan Handleman points out that

> *Glas* was written shortly after the death of Derrida's father, just as *The
> Interpretation of Dreams* was written after the death of Freud's father, facts
> which have much to do with the nature of both works. Indeed, what *is*
> Derrida doing here: unveiling the veiled scroll, the veiled writing, and
> here arranging all the bits of his life? Gayatri Spivak interprets this
> passage as the Jewish child's inspiration at the absence of the Father, or

truth behind the veil, an inspiration that allows him to place his autobiography in that place, producing the "origin" of literature. We would also again find here the displacement of the Father, the reappropriation-repetition (miming the origin) of his Scripture. Like Freud, like Paul, like Jesus, Derrida, in spite of all, is another in the line of Jewish prodigal sons, who try to perpetuate the law in its own transgressions, indeed who make the very concept of "perpetuating the law through its transgressions" the center of their theory.[67]

This reading, however tempting it might be, places Derrida squarely within the terms he himself chose to participate in; that is, within a discourse that leaves the current scene of the dream far behind. Here, a curious but telling reversal has been effected, particularly in certain areas of academic discourse. Jews from the former colonies—whose immediate concerns with the actualities of that Levantine/Arab world have receded to the point of internalized loss or the textual material of memory—have been reinscribed within a resurrected "humanist" tradition of "Jewish" textuality that usually ignores the context within which such works were produced. This reversal, in turn, operates within two clearly reciprocal but presently discrete spheres which are, themselves, the result of the reapportioning of "historical geography" and cultural space. The first sphere—that of retrieving rabbinic concepts of textuality in literary theory—finds itself progressive in one context and reactionary in another. As the discipline of Jewish studies opens its discourse to the vocabulary of écriture, it seems only to buttress its distance from a gesture of reconciliation that would at least signal the acknowledgement of a "reoriented" nexus of elements going into the making of a very new textual tradition. This new textual tradition, forged by both native and exiled Levantines, Jews and Arabs, encompasses a very wide referential space. Yet the aesthetic, social, and political concerns of these writers remain inextricably linked to the topography, archaeology, and possibility of their origins.[68] In discussing the development of the Arabic novel, to give just one example, Evelyn Accad gives a very precise sense of the kinds of issues confronted:

> Most of these [Arabic] works have been written in the context of
> societies in transition, in a state of stress born of numerous economic
> and political conflicts. It is a young, often experimental literature. . . .
> As such, it displays a very significant tension between anthropological
> "realities" and literary solutions. Conflicts created by colonialism,
> neocolonialism, imperialism, and other forms of oppression and
> solutions to these conflicts come out both in form and content. Using a
> genre usually considered European while wanting the destruction of
> Western models, the novelists work in a contradictory mode. The

schizophrenia resulting is often expressed by the authors with originality, in a unique voice that creates its own identity.[69]

Above all, their work is intrinsically committed to activating the past, to charging material that has too often been relegated to static forms of transmission with new artistic and formal intent. By recognizing this fertile ground, in which linguistic and cultural multiplicity takes place not on an interdisciplinary level but within language itself inscribed upon a political scene, vital and innovative areas of inquiry can be developed.

To ignore the possibilities of such a configuration also reduces the yield this kind of contextual relocation can produce in a text like Derrida's, with its sense of leaving something behind as it moves into another discourse that opens the possibility of inscribing other routes not taken. Such a reading could take its "here" to mean both "here" as the place of the writing and "there" as the dream of memory, a "there" that maps a succinct directory of crucial presences and absences. The mosque that "the colonists had changed into a synagogue" limns both the preferential and precarious position of the Jews since the time of Crémieux's Decrees proclaimed in 1870, in which "the local Jews became Frenchmen in the eyes of the law, enjoying civil rights not enjoyed by 90 per cent of the Algerians."[70] The arms of the man or the child embracing the Law emerging from behind the curtains—and the subsequent patrilineal line of power and interpretation—seek the specific and only more recently addressed location of the women. Yvette Chamache, an Egyptian, writes of this territory:

> He carries the mark of his pact with God and with his fathers upon his body: he is a Jew, he knows it, and will occupy the place inscribed for him naturally. But in tranquility?
>
> And the woman? She is there, up in the gallery, watching. Is it possible to say she feels excluded? She doesn't even know herself, she's gotten so used to it all . . .
>
> The woman, in the gallery of the synagogue, watches. She watches and she follows them. She will testify. Out of the silence. To anticipate oblivion.[71]

And Hélène Cixous, another Algerian Jew, has written of a time before the curtains veiling the Law obstructed her gaze, when she too could have been a child let down from the gallery:

> Yesterday I was small. Today I'm different and something of another. Yesterday time, the world, History, life, every science was in my father's head, and I was in his hands, and I didn't need anything. All I had to do was grow.[72]

Mining and miming these origins can trace the *gaps* between markers given as clues to what is present and the absences they adumbrate, the space *of* and *between* two worlds, the growing into and out of a rite; the "here" of writing and a "there" forever past but still insisting to know: What am I doing *here*? This question also implies asking: How did I get here? Derrida's reading of Jabès poses this poignantly in what amounts to a cautious burrowing into the more openly grounded and obsessive pre-occupation with loss that clearly marks a point of departure in *The Book of Questions*. This point is the core of a theme and problematic that has been seized on by commentators only too willing to appropriate the work of Jabès into an ethnocentric and simplistic ideology of equivalence (that of Jew = Writing = Book), without being attentive enough to the actual linguistic and cultural "collective duration" from which the work emerges.

This collective duration can be seen as a set of concentric circles of varying circumference, each circumscribing a range of sequences, events, activities, and attentions. The first, in the case of Jabès, would include a dense and palimpsestial biblical text intimately shaped by Egypt's contours and transcribed by Moses, the perfect writer who never reaches his destination. A second circle would encompass the "semiotic" parameters of classical Sephardic culture: social, psychological, and aesthetic expectations and markers; the legal, liturgical, poetic, and mystical texts engendered by Sepharad/al-Andalus and disseminated all over the Levantine and Arab world. A third circle could be that of the last generation of Jews in Egypt, a delineation of the pressures of their time impinging upon that space, and the position of Jabès himself within that configuration. Each of these circles would have to confront the question of linguistic and cultural choices and intersections, not as they affect some ideal and essentialized Jew but in terms of concrete political, economic, geographic, and generic exigencies. If the problematic is a "Jewish" one, then it must be grounded in a context that is both broader and more specific than the standard binary approach, which would see "rabbis" on one side and thought that "dislikes residence and offers itself as a philosophy for nomads" on the other.[73]

These distinctions have not been introduced in order to turn Jabès into something other than the very French writer he is, but simply to emphasize that he was part and parcel of a culture deeply rooted in and clearly informed by both Hebrew and Arabic antecedents and surroundings. When asked in an interview whether Arab culture had entered his education, Jabès had this to say:

> Not right away. Because at first of course, there were the French

schools: French philosophers, French writers, the history of France. But fairly quickly I became very interested in the great writings that are the masterpieces of these countries. Unfortunately in translation. I read Arabic, but still it was an effort. So, I had a certain rapport with Arab literature and philosophy, and then I realized in the Moslem tradition, with the Sufis for example, there were completely amazing things, as in the questioning of language. And at the same time I was also beginning to read the great Jewish mystics, who wrote in Hebrew and Arabic at the same time. All that is a part of the East, which is a world quite apart. The West, which penetrated quite considerably, didn't deeply mark the East, didn't shake things up. For example, in the time of Romanticism, they created an East of fantasies, the men with their harems, the sad women and so on, it's not that at all. The West has lived on this image of the East which is completely false.[74]

In this imaginary combination of flight and mastery, the specter of Egypt loomed large in the European imagination as an ideal site for unmasking the secrets of the "East," containing and transforming the material and symbolic order of its history into another logic, "rendering it completely open, making it totally accessible to European scrutiny." The objective of a work such as Lane's *An Account of the Manners and Customs of the Modern Egyptians* "is to make Egypt and the Egyptians totally visible, to keep nothing hidden from his reader, to deliver the Egyptians without depth, in swollen detail." It also typifies the conceptual underpinnings and renegotiations of power that make possible such imagery and, ultimately, the snapshot—an aftereffect of the hundred or so years of "the Orient as spectacle, as *tableau vivant*."[75] Timothy Mitchell notes this link between technologies and ideology in *Colonising Egypt*:

> Among European writers who travelled to the Middle East in the middle and latter part of the nineteenth century, one very frequently finds the experience of its strangeness expressed in terms of the problem of forming a picture. It was as though to make sense of it meant to stand back and make a drawing or take a photograph of it; which for many of them actually it did. "Every year that passes," an Egyptian wrote, "you see thousands of Europeans travelling all over the world, and everything they come across they make a picture of." Writers from Europe wanted to make pictures in the same way. They wanted to portray what they saw in words with the same chemically-etched accuracy, and the same optical detachment, as the daguerrotype or the photographic apparatus, that "instrument of patience" as Gerard de Nerval described it, " . . . which, destroying illusions, opposes to each figure the mirror of truth." Flaubert travelled in Egypt on a photographic mission with Maxime du Camp, the results of which were expected to be "quite special in character," it was remarked at the

Institut de France, "thanks to the aid of this modern travelling companion, efficient, rapid, and always scrupulously exact." The exact correspondence of the image to reality would provide a new, almost mechanical kind of certainty. The publication in 1858 of the first general collection of photographs of the Middle East, Francis Frith's *Egypt and Palestine, Photographed and Described*, would be "an experiment in Photography . . . of surpassing value," it was announced in the *Art Journal*, "for we will *know* that we see things exactly as they are."[76]

In this respect, the difference between the narratives of sojourners and natives is striking. For the visitor, the surplus value of tourism (even in its earlier forms of voyage and pilgrimage), is reinforced by investing the scene at hand with psychological baggage. Events, people, and places serve as a backdrop, insignificant in themselves unless their value has been "culturally" sanctioned or shaded. Instead, the view, and even the experiences themselves, seem like a Rorschach test. Thus the discrepancies between text and place, the imagined, dreamt, and yearned-for vision and the concrete particulars mirrored back to the viewer can be a cause of bitter disappointment and even personal loss, as in this *locus classicus* of Nerval's:

> I have already lost, kingdom after kingdom, province after province, the most beautiful half of the universe, and soon I will know of no place in which I can find a refuge for my dreams; but it is Egypt that I most regret having driven out of my imagination, now that I have sadly placed it in my memory.[77]

And how could the outcome be any different, once such loss assumes prior possession, or at least the right of inheritance? As Edward Said points out, one of Napoleon's great projects—the *Description de l'Egypte*, "published in twenty-three enormous volumes between 1809 and 1828"—presented an Orient that "existed as a set of values attached, not to its modern realities, but to a series of valorized contacts it had had with a distant European past." Egypt's significance had less to do with itself than with the fact that "Homer, Lycurgus, Solon, Pythagoras, and Plato all went there to study the sciences, religion and the laws," or that "Alexander founded an opulent city there."[78] Moreover, as Timothy Mitchell documents, the stunning reproductions of the Orient to be found at European extravaganzas such as the 1867 Exposition Universelle or the 1889 World Exhibition, held in Paris, were no match for what these new pilgrims of sensation would encounter:

> Since the Middle East had not yet been organised representationally, Europeans found the task of representing it almost impossible and the

results disappointing. "Think of it no more!" wrote Nerval to Théophile Gautier, of the Cairo they dreamed of describing. "That Cairo lies beneath the ashes and dirt, . . . dust-laden and dumb." Nothing encountered in those Oriental streets quite matched up to the reality they had seen represented in Paris. Not even the cafes looked genuine. "I really wanted to set the scene for you here," Nerval explained, in an attempt to describe the typical Cairene street, "but . . . it is only in Paris that one finds cafes so Oriental." His disappointment resulted from the failure to construct representations of the city that were to serve, as so often, very practical purposes. As I mentioned, he was supplying Gautier with descriptions that could be reproduced as stage sets and pantomime acts for the Paris Opera. Nerval finally despaired completely of finding "real Egypt," the Cairo that could be represented. "I will find at the Opera the real Cairo, . . . the Orient that escapes me." In the end only the Orient one finds in Paris, the simulation of what is itself a series of representations to begin with, can offer a satisfying spectacle. As he moved on towards the towns of Palestine, Nerval remembered Cairo as something no more solid or real than the painted scenery of a theatre set. "Just as well that the six months I spent there are over; it is already nothing, I have seen so many places collapse behind my steps, like stage sets; what do I have left from them? An image as confused as that of a dream: the best of what one finds there, I already knew by heart."[79]

In writing, the symbolic tension gleaned from an education based on accumulation, detail, and description finds itself embedded and subli- mated within a contradictory "cultural" urge: the wish to "civilize" the native and at the same time be inspired by their "barbaric" energy. Yet, much more than an individual psychological situation, this process masks an almost total disregard for the particulars of the human condi- tion in specific places while cordoning off areas in which power can fulfill its function within an ideology of supremacy. If the "natives" amount to nothing more than romantic landscape (or, as in Brenner's narrative, nightmarish obstruction), refracting material that only reflects distorted or idealized images of the visitors back at themselves, then it stands to reason that the *land* of the natives is of no particular value unless that value is invested by someone else: namely, the colonizer, imperial power, corporate shareholder, or tourist.

An insufficiently examined irony coursing throughout *The Book of Ques- tions* is that of the exiled writer/narrator producing and inhabiting a *native* space contained by the text but clearly arising from and alluding to the very personal circumstance and situation of Jabès himself. Born in Cairo in 1912, he only left when forced to—in 1957, at the age of 45. There is nothing "exotic" in the Egypt of Jabès. The reliefs, the desert, the Nile, and the pyramids are not filtered through any hierarchy of significance that doesn't grow out of the logic of memory, narrative, and language. References to Egypt (written in Paris) have the certainty of intimate gesture, as in these two passages from volumes 3 and 4:

> I shall always remember a bas-relief in the temple of Abydos where the god Horus and the sun-god Ra united in one body under the name Rharakhti, Horus of the Horizon, let Ramses II smell the "ankh," the symbol of life. I dreamed of my pen infusing this sign, which in ancient Egypt represented eternal life, into words so that every letter would be charged and enriched with it.

> I also remember well how I first became aware of the gravity of silence: watching the Nile flow with its cargoes reminded me of an unbroken line of red ants carrying their food. Hope made breath bolder. The world, all brightness, was dead to itself, was revealed to death in the most surprising lesson of life it had ever had. And I thought that a book ought to oscillate between these two silences, just as the tip of the pen should temper and bend it toward the words which people would read after God.[80]

While the work does not delineate what might be termed a "social space" in the sense depicted through the works of Egyptian writers like the late Yusuf Idris, Naguib Mahfouz, or Nawal el-Saadawi (to mention only a few of the more well-known and available examples), it also, on the other hand, refrains from valorizing the "scene" of its events. Sequences of perception and event, rather, manage to mime the process of coming to know, as "the unbroken line of red ants" that parallel the flow of the river mimes a first coming to awareness of the nourishing quality of silence. Characterized as a whole by its almost complete lack of any kind of description and a language that often appears amorphous, the work still manages—as well—to refrain from projecting and consuming the specific. To reach the temple of Abydos meant traveling through the desert, a place which—no matter how many different ways it appears and is used in the book—remains absolutely grounded in the experience of Jabès as a "great fascination." Like any fascination, it is returned to again and again, each time initiating another process, another encounter. As Jabès notes, the desert was

> a place I went to depersonalize myself, to no longer be who I was in appearance to others in Cairo. . . . In Cairo, I felt a prisoner of the social game. . . . In those days, the mainly European quarter where I lived and worked—the commercial and business quarter—was barely the

size of the Opera quarter in Paris. In such a confined atmosphere, the texts I published were considered at best a kind of intellectual entertainment. . . . Hence, the desert, which started at the very city limits, was a life-saving break for me. It fulfilled an urgent need of both body and mind, and I would venture into it with completely contradictory desires: to lose myself, so that, some day, I may find myself. So the place of the desert in my books is not a simple metaphor.[81]

The text constantly seems to reproduce this process of contingency, appearance, and perception, to describe and redescribe a desert of words, a gallery of rabbis, a bundle of narrative fiber in the form of journals, letters, and a love story. The desert of the words, like the vacuum-packed realm of the rabbis, the journal, and the story of the lovers, is itself the space of interpretation, the place the reader goes to find him- or herself. The self in Cairo is only constituted through its appearance to others. In this sense, paradoxically, the city is so fully a part of the self, so clearly there within, that it need not be described. Yet Jabès himself was clearly consumed by the sights and sounds, the texture of that world:

Just as the countryside hits you with its bareness—it is only sand torn from the desert and fertilized by the river—so the city hits you with its many colors and its all-pervading sensuality, with its crowded streets where the smell of sweat contends with the odor of the spices, jasmine, incense; with its overcrowded, stuffy cafes beloved by flies, where customers and backgammon players share rickety tables; where water pipes awake insatiable erotic dreams in the lonely, dazed smoker.

The old quarters of Cairo with their low shanties, their badly lit filthy alleyways—the quarter of the bazaar and the mosques, kept at arm's length by the residential quarters of the island of Gherzireh or Zamalec and by that portion of the capital dotted with imposing buildings, movie theaters, large stores, banks, luxury hotels; with its prestigious squares, its spacious roads where the common man, too poor to feel at ease in such surroundings, rarely ventures, though here and there a few beggars—the one-eyed or blind, the armless or legless— bring back the reality of the surrounding poverty and squalor.

All of that is part of my intimate landscape. Like those unforgettable spectacles, the feast days or days of mourning, that one takes part in regularly.

I'm thinking especially of the Feast of Spring, the Mouled El Nabi, when for twelve hours, men, women, children, all gaudily dressed, crisscross the city in donkey carriages while clapping their hands, singing, dancing and brandishing sugar dolls made for the occasion, before flooding the public gardens—and its opposite: the sad nearly daily, spectacle of the black funeral processions—no two alike—with their professional mourners, screaming, tearing their faces smudged with earth, miming pain in the face of death, miming death and the dead man or woman in their last struggle, in their ultimate embrace, like a couple locked together since the beginnings of time.[82]

The further paradox of the undescribed and indescribable city is that, having once lost it and the world of others within it who literally made up the self, recollection may simply turn into an ordeal too painful to bear. The following catalogue from volume 3, rare in the desert/"no-place" bookscape of Jabès, touches the core of this pain:

> In the cemetery of Bagneux, *département de la Seine*, rests my mother. In Old Cairo, in the cemetery of sand, my father. In Milano, in the dead marble city, my sister is buried. In Rome where the dark dug out the ground to receive him, my brother lies. Four graves. Three countries. Does death know borders? One family. Two continents. Four cities. Three flags. One language: of nothingness. One pain. Four glances in one. Four lives. One scream.[83]

A map of the shattered self in which each city is a private monument, an identical signature of death, significant only insofar as it points to the life once within. By domesticating and then inhabiting the book, Jabès leaves the space of one world behind and situates his text on the threshold of another:

> Strangely enough, in Cairo I felt closer to—I could say more dependent on—French culture than in Paris. I should add that my uprooting was total and happened practically from one day to the next . . . You have to understand the following: to claim French culture as my own in Cairo nearly took the place of real filiation. In Paris, the earth opened under my feet. To recognize a filiation meant to amputate myself. Paris aggravated the problem in that, by settling there, I gave the impression of having sought out that integration. Roughly speaking, to claim Baudelaire, Mallarmé or the Surrealists in Cairo functioned as a reference rather than anything else. In Paris, Egypt, its desert, the rhythm of life these had imposed on me, suddenly stood between those authors, their writings, and me. Another obsession with the book emerged though I was as yet not yet completely prepared for it: a book outside of time—which is how Egypt suddenly appeared to me—that would integrate the break on all levels; a book in which the very words would be confronted by the infinite that undermines them.[84]

Shaped by the shock of his own exile, the writing of disaster and the disaster itself, Jabès sums up a lost and finally internalized world of activity by translating it into another consciousness and set of conditions, just as the consciousness and conditions of the world he left behind have themselves changed radically since his departure.

This departure, and the subsequent development of the writing out of that rupture, can be seen to mark a watershed point in one particular area of a "history of things" that would "aim beyond narration to find cleavages in history where a cut will separate different types of happening." This approach sees "any work of art as a portion of arrested happening, or an emanation of past time" in which the work is also "a graph of an activity now stilled, but a graph made visible like an astronomical body, by a light that originated with the activity."[85] In concluding *The Shape of Time*, George Kubler goes on to make these remarks on the "plural present":

> Everything varies both with time and by place, and we cannot fix anywhere upon an invariant quality such as the idea of style supposes, even when we separate things from their settings. But when duration and setting are retained in view, we have shifting relations, passing moments, and changing places in historic life. Which is now valid: the isolated work in its total physical presence, or the chain of works marking the known range of its position?[86]

The graph that the work of Jabès charts includes many of the sequences and concerns falling within the concentric circles making up the very particular "collective duration" of which he forms a terminal part. The Talmudic and kabbalistic aphorisms serving a certain function in one age are translated into terms comprehensible to another. The search for the truth once taken into the desert by the saintly mystic leads into the labyrinths of a book challenged by despair, suicide, and mass murder. The exile from Egypt is met by graffiti on the walls of Europe. The source of light making this graph visible goes back to the distinctions among sun, moon, and fire made by Maimonides. This Maimonides, however, lived and worked in Cairo, and wrote as a Levantine between and within an intersection of cultures and languages in the sense conveyed by Jacqueline Kahanoff, another Cairene who found herself at the threshold of a cleavage:

> The Levant is a land of ancient civilizations which cannot be sharply differentiated from the Mediterranean world, and is not synonymous with Islam, even if a majority of its inhabitants are Moslems. The Levant has a character and history of its own. It is called "Near" or "Middle" East in relationship to Europe, not to itself. Seen from Asia, it could just as well be called the "Middle West." Here, indeed, Europe and Asia have encroached on one another, time and time again, leaving

their marks in crumbling monuments and in the shadowy memories of
the Levant's peoples. Ancient Egypt, ancient Israel and ancient Greece,
Chaldea and Assyria, Ur and Babylon, Tyre, Sidon and Carthage,
Constantinople, Alexandria and Jerusalem are all dimensions of the
Levant. So are Judaism, Christianity and Islam, which clashed in
dramatic confrontation, giving rise to world civilizations, fracturing into
stubborn local subcultures and the multi-layered identities of the
Levant's people. It is not exclusively western or eastern, Christian,
Jewish or Moslem. Because of its diversity, the Levant has been
compared to a mosaic—bits of stone of different colors assembled into a
flat picture. To me it is more like a prism whose various facets are
joined by the sharp edge of differences, but each of which, according to
its position in a time-space continuum, reflects or refracts light. Indeed,
the concept of light is contained in the word Levant as in the word
Mizrah, and perhaps the time has come for the Levant to reevaluate
itself by its own lights, rather than see itself through Europe's sights, as
something quaintly exotic, tired, sick and almost lifeless.[87]

IV. Cairo: From Umm Kulthum to Nawal Saadawi

In "The South," the last chapter of *The Book of Yukel*, the writer, after
learning of the death of Yukel's lover Sarah, goes out into the rainy
streets of Paris. While walking,

> he remembered a phrase (but why did this one rather than any other
> pop up in his memory?), a single phrase from a forgotten story whose
> tone he recalled in quoting:
> "Father, which was this city
> of which we were guardians?"
> This city is not Paris. And yet Paris is the Capital of his senses.[88]

Outside, in the rain again, it is Yukel this time who is on his way to a
tailor whose card he finds in a suit he wants redone. The tailor, a Central
European Jew, recognizes Yukel as the writer of the story of Sarah and
Yukel and calls in his wife to meet him:

> "Ach," said the woman. "You're Jewish, like us . . . You know," she
> went on, "we were deported too. My husband and me, we came back,
> but our children, our son and daughter died over there. Were you in
> France during the war?"
> "No. I was in Egypt."
> "Then you're a lucky Jew. No matter what you've suffered, you're a
> lucky Jew."
> "That'll do, mama," said the old man. "You're not going to bother
> the gentleman with . . . "
> But the old woman interrupted.

"He's a Jew, no? He's a writer, no?"
And she talked of the days of coming back, the interminable nights
of coming back with death inside them . . .

Yukel is reduced to silence as the scene in the small, crowded shop becomes more and more claustrophobic; the chapter, and the book, end
with this:

> What pressing urge pushed Yukel to take a train south a few hours later?
> To see the Mediterranean again, listen to the lesson of the sea which
> keeps forever its salt and its color.[89]

The next volume, *Return to the Book*, opens with the catalogue of graves
quoted earlier and suggests Cairo as this city, not Paris, in a forgotten
story, "of which we were guardians." Even though the Mediterranean is
an eternal opening, the sequence emphasizes those markers of death that
circumscribe the borders of both forgotten cities and forgotten stories.
Jabès himself left that world behind, never returning to Egypt: "Perhaps,
to put it simply, I invented a mythical Egypt. Maybe I was scared of confronting Egypt—or that one that is in my books—with a reality which,
at any rate, no longer corresponds to the one I knew. And that would
mean losing it a second time."[90] Even given this admission, by maintaining the integrity of an interior space inextricably linked to the fate of the
writer himself, Jabès manages a mythology that differs unconditionally
from the projections of flight and mastery so characteristic of either Romantic or colonial narrative sequences. At the same time, this nativity is
contained and frozen in exile, far from the scene of its inspiration, caught
in the gap and cleavage that marks the drawing to a close of one world
and the possible initiation of another, reinvested with the sources of "its
own lights."
    Despite the facility of the equation, Jews had no monopoly on es-
trangement or exile. For many of a certain class and education, arriving at
the sources of self-definition could be a daunting experience within the
divisive terms set by colonialism; as Jean Said Makdisi writes:

> We were not taught Arabic literature, the names of our great poets
> remaining for us at the time just names, but the study of English
> literature, taught as well and as thoroughly as it was, was not the less
> valuable. It made us, it is true, familiar with the skylarks and the
> nightingales, the daffodils and roses of England, leaving us strangers to
> the flora and fauna of Egypt. It made us think in terms of English rather
> than Egyptian seasons, putting us out of pace with our own climate.
> There was, for instance, a poem we had to memorize. It had to do with
> November and presented that month as a gloomy, wet, most English

experience. As it is, November is one of the loveliest months of the year in Cairo, and the fact that this very negative approach to it was totally contrary to the actual experience didn't seem, somehow, to matter very much. I don't know that I ever at the time noticed the conflict. It was as though we lived in two worlds simultaneously, neither encroaching on the reality of the other; or, to put it another way, each cancelling out the other's reality, so that we were suspended in unreality altogether.[91]

This "unreality" is named by Etel Adnan who, like Jabès, had been closely associated with Gabriel Bounoure; in her case, as a student of Bounoure's in Beirut:

Lebanon was newly created as a state by the French. The French turned Syria and Lebanon into mandates under their rule. They expanded the already existing French schools in the country and favoured the stablishment of new ones. They created in Lebanon, and imposed on it, a system of education totally conforming to their schools in France, an education which had nothing to do with the history and geography of the children involved.

So at age five I started speaking French and then, only French, as Arabic was a forbidden language in these French schools. They were in their entirety run by members of the French Catholic Church. And Arabic was forbidden. The Lebanese children spoke it at home. My mother not knowing Arabic, French took over as the language at home: we spoke less and less Turkish or Greek and more and more French.

These schools were for boys or girls only. The coeducational system was instituted in Lebanon in the fifties.

The French nuns were stern. They behaved like colonialists and like missionaries: they had the dual purpose of extolling French civilization, and the infallibility of the Church in matters of religion. They created for children an authoritarian and dogmatic environment. They were so thorough in their system that very few students of their schools ever questioned the education they received. Dogmatism has the effect of occupying the totality of one's mental space to such a degree that the things it purports to be true become as "natural" as the sky or earth: they become the only things the mind can distinguish, they become the very tools of one's thinking. They become taken for granted.

So I grew up thinking that the world was French. And that everything that mattered, that was "in books," or had authority (the nuns), did not concern our environment. This is what is called alienation.[92]

In a topological approach to writing attentive to setting and duration, fundamental distinctions could be made between writers who have stayed in a given area; those who left entirely; the newly arrived; and others relocated within the wider sphere of the same area but whose work has been realigned by altered conditions. Of the writers touched on so far, Antebbi can be seen as an example of the first category; Jabès, Derrida, Cixous, and Chamache examples of the second; Brenner an example of the third, and Kahanoff—an Egyptian who emigrated to Israel—an example of the fourth. A very different Egypt, gleaned from an account that would find its place in the first category, can contribute to tracing an understanding of the present context. In this account, an autobiography, the legendary Egyptian singer Umm Kulthum writes about the beginnings of her career, singing "on hundreds of station platforms in many, many stations along the Delta railroad line . . . ":

> As the months passed, I began to realize that there was a world beyond the Delta railroad line, that there were other cities, even bigger than Zaqaziq. One day we were invited to a big city called Cairo, which I had never heard of before. This is how it happened. A well-known pasha, 'Izz al-Dinn Yakun, was speaking with the estate manager in our village, telling him about the special festivities planned in his palace at Hilwan, to celebrate the night of the Mi'raj (the night when the Angel Gabriel first spoke to Muhammad).
> The estate manager said, "By God, we have a girl right here in Tammay who has a beautiful voice."
> "Well," said the landowner, "bring her to sing for us, why not?"
> We traveled with the estate manager to Cairo. I don't remember anything about the city, and I have no impression of it at all in my mind, except the Bab el Luq station, where my father bought me a piece of candy better than any I had ever had before.[93]

The understated tone almost camouflages the compression of the narrative in this account, the extent of the distance traveled in such a short space. Events are allowed the significance of their own order and names left to the domain of their singularity. There is no imposition or restructuring of events. The gaps between things provide a transparency in which the reader's imagination can wander and work at the range of emotions each incident might imply. In referring to the night of the Mi'raj, the narrative thread almost unnoticeably weaves itself into an event whose significance reaches far beyond the parameters of the particular story being told, but with no need for commentary since the teller of the tale remains part of a sequence that still maintains the integrity of its own structure. The internalization of this structure, and the irony of the narrative position in Jabès, slightly alter the qualities of even the most intimate gestures in *The Book of Questions*, reverting and referring them to the circularity of the whole. Going through the desert to reach the temple of Abydos is not connected to a rite but to the larger—although still absolutely integral—scheme of writing, the book and exile. In Umm Kulthum's movement within a space *still* inhabited, there is no projection and the city—although nothing about it is remembered—is also not forgotten. The walker in it, the traveler to it participates in its life, interacting as the city drops its own hints, projects its own codes and signals.

After having spent some time in Cairo, Umm Kulthum tells of an incident in which a magazine article puts her honor and reputation in question. As her father packs the family bags in preparation for the trip back to their village, people begin coming to their apartment to try and convince him of the error of his ways. Among them is Amin al-Mahdi, a famous 'oud player, who finally says,

> "Let me tell you something, Shaykh Ibrahim. You realize, of course, don't you, that leaving Cairo right after this article appears means only one thing to those of us in the city."
>
> "Yes," said my father. "It means that I will not listen to such stories about my daughter's honor."
>
> "No," said Amin al-Mahdi. "To the people of Cairo, it will mean that the story is true. Here honest people do not run away from false accusations."[94]

The message, naturally, is grasped immediately and the family stays. The experience is translated into knowledge and Umm Kulthum breaks her narrative, precisely after this incident, to outline the extent and implications of this newly gained recognition:

> Before I go on, my readers might like to know something about Cairo at that time, the kind of city I came into in the early twenties, a young village girl wearing a long blue coat and a black head scarf and singing the religious songs of the Prophet. For the boy's clothes had now been given up. My father had stopped deceiving himself. I was a girl, I was a singer, and I was making slow progress in the city. But it was not easy for my father, and it was not easy for me.

Cairo, 1926

An egg cost one millieme.

A kilo of meat cost 2 piasters; barbecued, 3 piasters.

A pack of al-Anbarul cigarettes: 2 piasters.

A luxurious sedan car: 360 pounds.

The school text for the government exam was *Zahrab wa-Rustum*.

On the stage 'Ali Effendi al-Kassar was playing the comic role of the Nubian in the Army.

Yusuf Wahbi was the star of the world of the theater.

The chief of the mixed courts was Mr. Sansom.

The population of Egypt was twelve million. Twenty-six percent of the population died at birth because of poverty and malnutrition. Those who could read and write, over the entire country, totaled 197 per thousand. Traveling from Cairo to Alexandria took seven hours on the new express trains.

The revolution of 1919 was over, and Egypt fought within itself and with the British army of occupation. Sayyid Darwish summarized the political situation in his satirical operetta, *A Good Relationship*, where the song that brought down the house was "To Rise and Rise and Rise We Have to Bow and Bow and Bow!"[95]

Here the city—its possibilities and magnitude—is both listened to and heard. To fully rise, though, would take another thirty years, a period marked by Nasser's triumph in the 1956 Suez crisis, an event that no less a historian than Marshall Hodgson called "a corollary of the end of European world hegemony."[96] A year after this, Jabès, along with most of Egypt's Jewish community—and other foreign nationals—left, some for Europe, some for America, some for Israel. Colonialism, officially at least, came to a close during the 1950s and 1960s, but the newly independent states were left with a staggeringly compounded set of problems. Like the young village girl and her father coming into the city, progress was slow and not easy. The boy's clothes had been given up and, like the other girl who "didn't need anything," since "time, the world, History, life," and "every science" was in her father's head, all that was left "to do was grow." Processes that proceeded internally in the "developed" countries, from the industrial age onwards, were squeezed into the suffocating framework of a short time span and the limited means of severely dependent and depleted economies. Advances that were of the utmost importance—lower infant mortality rates and longer life spans, for instance—put enormous pressure on housing, the labor force, transportation, and, ultimately, the environment. Nothing took place in isolation: each element in the process, each revision or innovation affected a chain reaction coursing throughout the system. Cities, naturally, became the nerve centers and shock absorbers into and out of which all these impulses charged.

In these often bewildering, chaotic, and sometimes desperate conditions, the rhetoric of nationalism over the airwaves was only topped by the constant sound of music, "wounded kinship's last resort."[97] In the following passage, the exiled Lebanese writer Etel Adnan precisely locates the social meaning of Umm Kulthum's presence, but without sacrificing any of the possible ironies that her position entailed:

One being escaped the total fate of Arab women: Umm Kulthum.
When the Arabs were thinking that they had nothing, they were saying
that after all they had Umm Kulthum and that, all by herself, she
represented their will to be, the religious essence of their culture; she
pulled to herself, by the quality of her voice and the tone of each one of
her words, the human tide that was coming towards her. This human
tide became the tide of history, the tide of all the frustrations
transfigured in a kind of bliss.

She sings "on target," like a whip to whatever in each one of us is
dormant. And also, we can't forget it, a whip against anything foreign,
because, then, the foreigner was the colonizer. She took it on herself to
tell the world that the Arab world existed.

To all those castrated by under-development and occupation, she was
saying that she loved them. She sings as for you alone, and in this love
as deep as valleys and the ocean floor, the fellah and the prime minister
found, each, what forgives all sins and recycles the son in the grace of
the mother.

Erotic being, like the soufis, she reconciled the flesh and the spirit.
She has been this century's thread. I heard her when I was twelve in the
Grand Theatre of Beirut. It was a beneficial trauma.

Then, I followed her: in Cairo, where on the first Thursday of each
month she made people leave home with a transistor radio, or they
gathered at night in shops to listen to her in their long and white robes.
Listening to her songs, which lasted for four or five hours, I heard the
Nile moan and the human species give birth. In the divisions which
break a world and make it explode, she was the unity we had.

I follow her in Cairo, for her death. On February 5 I go to her
funeral. On the tent near the Omar Makram mosque, where the human
river is going to flow behind her coffin, a huge picture of her has a
green ribbon on which it is written that she is the martyr of divine love.
Yes, the sky is light, cloudy. The people are coming from everywhere,
and the noise is like of trees in the wind. La Illah illa Allah, says the
crowd. The army was here, but it is gone. The people become the sea
and engulf the body.

And it floats, small coffin covered with an iridescent blue and green
veil. The people possess her and in their collective memory they take
her away like a pharaonic boat.[98]

The fate of woman as symbol; the transference of the collective sense of
violation following the colonial period; historical revision in the service
of power; the replacement of foreign colonizers by native colonizers; the
shock of recognition; the reversion to transcendent meaning—all of this
is still grounded in very human needs that the narrative constantly refuses

to diminish, circumscribe, or judge. Instead, experience is at once collective and cumulative, centered around "a beneficial trauma" leading to those fissure points where "master narratives" can be interrogated from within.

In "A Tale Told by a Dog," the Egyptian writer Yahya Taher Abdullah also describes an arrival from the village to the city:

> The night of the city has two days, each day has two suns, and the people in the city run about on the streets like flood water; their clothes are odd—it's as though they're at a festival or a saint's day.
>
> I saw the most extraordinary things as I loitered around the city's souks:
>
> Colored birds imprisoned, singing inside their cages. Lights in all colors, colors winking and changing places. Human beings, shoes, clothes and children's balls imprisoned within glass cages. A woman hanging on the wall crying out soundlessly as she drowned in the water of the sea, and no one going to her rescue.
>
> The shops closed their doors, the light grew less and the people vanished. Were it not for the cars and the car owners, I would have barked into the face of the city: "O city, your inhabitants have forsaken you."
>
> People are in heaps and the garbage is in heaps, and the houses are empty of men, populated by women sitting in front of their doors, cooking and washing and eating and throwing the scraps to us dogs. But the small homeless boys assault dogs with stones and seize the bones from their mouths: the day here is a sun without eyes, and life here is an unremitting hell.[99]

The Cairo of this story is a city of at least 12 million, the population of the whole of the Egypt described in Umm Kulthum's memoirs. The tale goes on to become a cruel allegory of upward mobility: Mahzouz the dog changes his name to the more "refined" Mizu and leaves behind the kind and patient ants who helped him when he first came into the city. Now he spends his time "divided between the circus, the cinema, television, broadcasting, evening parties, interviews, and agreements with producers, distributors, and directors, with the hairdresser, the masseur, the manicurist."[100] But the past pursues him—when the wise ant's mother comes in search of her daughter, Mizu scratches her away and tells her to go find Mahzouz. The story ends with the following awesome scene:

> Looking in the mirror, I addressed my reflection: "Tell me, O reflection—whose reflection are you? The reflection of Mizu or the

reflection of Mahzouz?" Before it replied the doctor came in and gave
me a fix; the yellow liquid coursed through my veins and the past came
back, and when sleep came and put spectacles on me I saw through
them that everything was burning, everything, and that the fire was
drawing close to me, while I did not move, did nothing.[101]

Confronted with his own reflection in the mirror ("an out-of-focus
confusion of an antique present, a precious past and a disjointed future"),[102] aware that "everything was burning," and "the fire was drawing close," Mahzouz/Mizu becomes paralyzed. This paralysis is more
than just the inability to act; it locates its antithetical thrust specifically
within the given ideological assumptions of "backwardness" and
"progress." In Baudrillard's terms, "the circular response of the polled,
the analyzed, the natives is all the same a challenge and a triumphant revenge . . . they place the spotlight back on the question itself, isolate it in
offering it the mirror of the answer it was awaiting, and show it helpless
to ever quit the vicious circle which in fact is that of power."[103] By simply staring back at his own undefined image, Mahzouz/Mizu mocks any
and all notions of "self-help," or "improvement." The irony of his own
"progress" gains the precise quality of allegory defined as "the epitome
of counter-narrative." In this, "allegory is also the epitome of the anti-
modern, for it views history as an irreversible process of dissolution and
decay. The melancholic, contemplative gaze of the allegorist need not,
however, be a sign of defeat; it may represent the superior wisdom of one
who has relinquished all claims to mastery."[104] The stakes are drawn between a vicious circle of power and the gaze that relinquishes mastery.
But for writers still inhabiting this realm, mirrors erected between practice and theory must be, if not shattered, at least turned to reflect more
than an image. The gaze over dissolution and decay is revelatory and urgent: it is only here the materials can be reclaimed and action, based on a
consciousness of the dilemma, be initiated.

Between the narrative of Umm Kulthum and Yahya Taher Abdullah's relentless fable, from the First World War to the 1970s, Egypt maintained a
central position in the Arab world. Edward Said describes this importance:

> Because of its size and power, Egypt has always been a locus for Arab
> ideas and movements; in addition Cairo has functioned as a diffusionary
> center for print publishing, films, radio, and television. Arabs in
> Morocco, on the one hand, Iraq, on the other, who may have very little
> in common are likely to have had a lifetime of watching Egyptian films

(or television serials) to connect them. Similarly modern Arabic
literature has spread out from Cairo for the whole of our century.[105]

A belated token of recognition for this literature in the West (in the form
of the 1988 Nobel Prize awarded to Naguib Mahfouz) ironically came at
a time when Cairo itself was already well past its once pivotal role. Although many critics unfamiliar with the context of the contemporary Arabic novel have attempted to assimilate Mahfouz into European models,
usually by calling him the "Arab Dickens" or the "Arab Balzac," narratives from this period in Egypt continually resist such facile exchange.
Besides the magisterial and compassionate work of Mahfouz himself,
particularly his *Cairo Trilogy* (depicting three generations of a Cairo family between the two world wars) and his allegorical masterpiece *The
Children of Gebelawi* (which was banned for many years), these narratives
include the works of Taha Hussein, Tewfik al-Hakim, the late Yusuf Idris, Sonallah Ibrahim, Gamal al-Gitany, Edwar al-Kharrat, Alifa Rifaat,
Nawal el-Saadawi, and a host of other writers such as Salwa Bakr and
Neamat el-Biheiry, only recently gaining recognition abroad.[106] No matter how reliant on the European novel or short story form they might
seem to be, closer examination reveals the highly particular narrative tra-
jectories, artistic intentions, and political implications that emerge from a
specific time and place.

Cairo, throughout, remains a presence. In the work of the late Yusuf
Idris, it is a city divided, rather brutally, along class lines. In his classic
story "The Dregs of the City," Idris describes the journey of Judge Abdallah in pursuit of a maid he has raped, turned into his mistress, and
whom he suspects stole his watch. The trip begins in serenity, driving by
"the open spaces and the tall stylish buildings" lining the Nile:

> At the bridgehead they are joined by streams of cars pouring from
> Zamalek and Gezira and Dokki and Quizeh. Bright, colourful, shining,
> like flocks of birds. In the whirlpool of Kasr el Nil Square their ranks
> are swelled by shabby cars and taxi-cabs before they diverge to other
> streets where movement never stops; narrower, with closer buildings,
> noisier, with more pedestrians. At Ataba it becomes one great merry-
> go-round. Automobiles and buses and tram-cars and pedestrians and
> horse-drawn carts mill around in utter chaos. It reaches a peak when
> they turn into Al Azhar Street. Here, it is a madhouse of pedestrians and
> automobiles, screeching wheels, howling claxons, the whistles of bus
> conductors and roaring motors. Policemen blow their whistles, and
> hawkers yell in the blistering heat. The roads and pavements are a
> moving mass of flesh. Everything is wholesale. Riding a vehicle,
> trading, and even accidents come wholesale. From time to time a

warning to be careful rises above the din like the last cry of a drowning corpse.[107]

As they park the car and continue on foot, everything the judge has known and thought about himself begins to crumble:

> He is Egyptian through and through. His father came from El Mounira and his mother from Abbassieh. He has poor relations in Upper Egypt. He has travelled a good deal, gone to many places, and seen the extremes of poverty. Yet, here he was in Cairo, and this place where he finds himself is part of it. The incredible scenes unfolding before his eyes amaze him beyond belief as he delves further in as though he were sinking in a bottomless pit.[108]

This bottomless pit is divided into further stages coursing from the living to the dead and the almost dead. Each stage is characterized by language: at first, "language is polite." Then, "language degenerates into abuse," before breaking "down to a jargon of grunts." They finally get within range of Shohrat's dwelling:

> As they keep on towards their destination the winding lanes and alleys lead to a place without substance where everything melts into everything else. The raised ground, compounded of years of accumulated dirt, welds with the dilapidated buildings groaning with age. The slimy ground is the same color as the dusty walls. The smell of the earth mingles with the smell of humanity, and the low broken murmurs mix with the barking of dogs and the creaking of old gates, and the dead slow movement of inanimate creatures. The low grimy dwellings are a continuation of the graveyard, stretching forward as far as the eye can see.[109]

From the flowing Nile, the image of birds and the drowning corpse, we are led further and further into the earth, to the point where everything returns and dust goes to dust. The figurative pilgrimage of this narrative (like the path along Umm Kulthum's ascendence depicted in the passage by Etel Adnan), takes place in an entirely different environment than the catalogue of graves and the suggestion of Cairo in Jabès. In the work of Idris, social and political meaning is not only implied through the subject matter but woven directly into the collective material of his art. What is particularly significant about Idris is the fact that he reproduces the sense of breakdown and recognition that his characters experience within the language of the text itself. The first writer to fully develop colloquial usage within the norms of standard literary Arabic, Idris's method becomes an urgent indictment of literate Arabic readers, calling on them to acknowledge both the *speech* and the *presence* of the "illiterate," no matter how deeply the city has buried them, blocked out at the end of so many blind alleys by the tunnel vision of social constructs.

The narrative space of Cairo is also the city where members of an even larger class, which includes characters like Shohrat the maid, are given history and inner life. Despite the fact that women, and their "plight," remained a constant presence in the contemporary Arabic narrative, "women in men's literature were carefully distanced from the writer's social context. Women's forms were seen. Their voices remained silent. Like the literature of a colonized people, women's writings have occupied a separate space that was not deemed worthy of consideration, except when it used the colonizer's language, and thus evaded its own particularism."[110] In the writing of the Egyptian feminist, psychiatrist, and novelist Nawal el-Saadawi, the stylish boulevards lining the Nile also become a place where girls once abused by uncles or brothers or bosses have turned into women possessing a deceptive but nevertheless highly resolute sense of independence:

> I walked down the street, my head held high to the heavens, with the pride of having destroyed all masks to reveal what is hidden behind. My footsteps broke the silence with their steady rhythmic beat on the pavement. They were neither fast as though I were hurrying away from something in fear, nor were they slow. They were the footsteps of a woman who believed in herself, knew where she was going, and could see her goal . . . No one would have easily recognized me. I looked no different from respectable, upper-class women. My hair had been done by a stylist who catered only for the rich. My lips were painted in the natural tone preferred by respectable women because it neither completely hides, nor completely exposes their lust. My eyes were pencilled in perfect lines drawn to suggest a seductive appeal, or a provacative withdrawal . . . But my firm, confident steps resounding on the pavement proved that I was nobody's wife.[111]

Yet, despite the power and importance of Saadawi's work—in all of her varied roles—its reception in America often seems contingent *only* upon assumptions about the victimization of women in the Arab world. The complex history of women's creativity—which in the modern period alone includes the innovations of Nazik al-Malaika (one of the pioneers of the Arabic free verse movement)[112] the Palestinian poet Fadwa Tuqan, or the remarkable group of women writers who "shared Beirut as their home and war as their experience"[113]— too rarely escapes the patronizing dichotomies of "underdevelopment" and "progress." Again, as in so many other instances, the question of context is crucial. One can see, for example, in younger Egyptian writers like Neamat el-Biheiri, an absorption of such issues into the text itself. In "Your Face, My Children and the Olive Branches," the narrator contends with the expectations of "a severe and miserly father" who claims that "it would be more useful to both of us . . . [for you] to learn a European language," by passing through the city toward a more ancient source, the river:

> I raised my head to look at the old buildings lining the streets of
> downtown Cairo. This was the first time, I recalled, that I had noticed
> the facades on both sides of the street reflecting the styles characteristic
> of old European architecture: the defeated face of Naopoleon and the
> slain countenance of Kleber gazed down upon me. Despite the heaviness
> of my gait I felt that the defeated and slain faces were driving me
> towards the river—the same river into which, my mother once told me,
> she had thrown my afterbirth on the day I was born. I loved the river
> with the same passion that marked my tireless search for deliverance.[114]

This "tireless search for deliverance" is also the search for a language earned through the progressive chipping away at externally imposed standards, images, and relations; it is the power of self-possession in the act of a restitution that is not nostalgic but exploratory, seeking not just re-creation but the creation of something new.

V. Discourses of the City

Less than fifty years after the *Blue Guide's* description of an itinerary through an intertwined network of cities in a still accessible space, some of those cities—Cairo, Beirut, and Jerusalem—have become limit points, endgames, each in their own way. Cairo, the city of the fourth day of that itinerary, now exists on "a scale and complexity that threatens incoherence at our level of discourse about the city. A sense that we really are not sure how to write 'Cairo' is evident in the urgency with which categories of the 'urban' are being questioned."[115] The description given by the Qadi of Fez, quoted by Ibn Khaldun in the fourteenth century, seems even more apt now than it might have been then: "What one can imagine always surpasses what one sees, because of the scope of the imagination, except Cairo, because it surpasses anything one can imagine." A Jewish traveler, Meshullam of Volterra, wrote: "We arrived in Cairo on Sunday, June 17, 1481. I had come to see the Cairenes and their deeds. However, if I were to write about its wealth and its people, all of this book would not be sufficient. I swear that if it were possible to put Rome, Venice, Milan, Padua, Florence and four more cities together, they would not equal in wealth and population half that of Cairo."[116] The city that seems so surreal and unmanageable to a "Westerner" (pyramids dotting a skyline of high rises, medieval mosques, and quasi-grandiose nineteenth-century buildings; people living in Mameluke tombs and under Roman aqueducts; five-star hotels, converted palaces and casinos catering to international businessmen and sheikhs from the Gulf; streets jammed with every possible means of transportation—horses, donkeys, cars, taxis, and buses with arms and heads sticking out of the windows and doors)—is certainly no less alarming or alienating to its own residents: the crucial difference still remaining seems to be who is doing the negotiating and how one reacts to or uses those negotiations.

This process of "scaling" occurs in many discourses about many cities. How does one react when confronted with the wild discrepancies, the misery, impossibility, privileged abundance, and size of cities like Cairo or Bombay; cityscapes divided into nameless "inhabitants" crowded into densely populated, outdated, and underserviced neighborhoods, the more and less well-off who would rather not think about what is usually artfully hidden, and those who might stop and catch a glimpse, though often through the window of a moving car?

> Bombay life has no order. It is so disordered it is magnificently disciplined. The city is an out of focus confusion of an antique present, a precious past and a disjointed future. It's a city that never stops. I could grow to love it. All the beauty and all the ugliness the world could ever muster has collapsed into an agonising and challenging heap called Bombay.
>
> In vivid afternoon daylight, looking with a panicky glance through a taxi window, Bombay is like any major city, except it's been left to rot and crumble. When it falls down no one will rebuild it.
>
> Roadside hoardings advertising fluoride toothpaste, the best brand of cigars, mentholyptus sweets and Cadbury's chocolate, mock the charismatic crisis of Bombay with explicit cruelty.[117]

As a "representative" of this explicit cruelty, how does one traverse the crisis? Not ease a guilty conscience galled by "the white man's burden" but gauge points of access, methods of translating these extremities into other ways of thinking, acting, and forming different ideas of culture and value? Guides to the outsider, even the best of them, bluntly dictate the limits:

> This entire district is known as Darb el-Ahmar, a name which nowadays epitomizes a poorer, broken-down section of the city. At the Citadel end which is entirely residential the street is fairly quiet and fairly filthy; it becomes livelier, and you do not notice the filth so much, as you enter the bazaar area further north. Apart from the ruins of many old houses and some fine intact monuments, you may also encounter

the gaiety of a marriage procession, a great noise of motor scooters, car horns, tambourines, ululations, whistling, chanting and cries.[118]

The names, even the places are irrelevant. What remains essential is that the tourist avoid "filth," that the monuments remain "intact" and accessible, that whatever else might seem to be going on—birth, death, poverty, joy, rage—not impose too much on reaching the goal, the destination, the historical site itself from which the sojourner can emerge victorious, having "taken" its picture.[119] Vision is mechanized as the photographer's gaze gratuitously "reproduces" the "experience." Here, tourism becomes the surplus value of social relations totally divorced from "the economic, political and ideological contexts in which they are embedded and which they activate."[120]

Maybe such circumstances call for another possibility, one that can serve as prologue—what David Antin, in a talk recounting various experiences of misapprehension, calls "tuning" and the process of "learning not to understand." The phrase comes after one of the central events spoken of in his talk: a friend invites Antin to see an Egyptian movie at a neighborhood theater in Brooklyn and, although he had been studying Arabic at the time, Antin finds the movie progressively incomprehensible until "the movie is over and i haven't the vaguest idea of what it is that i've seen." On his way home waiting for the subway, Antin begins a conversation in French with an Egyptian who has also just gotten out of the movie. Someone else appears in the station and somehow enters the discussion which soon turns to politics and the involvement of the "powers" in the Suez crisis. Since the newcomer speaks neither French nor Arabic, Antin finds himself unwillingly elected to translate. The discussion ends as the train pulls in, but exactly what was said still remains uncertain:

> now i
> understood everything that had been said to me   i knew what
> the words were   what they appeared to signify   and I kind
>   of had a feeling i understood roughly   what kind of
> conceptions were being pointed to   but i wasn't sure   my
>   impression was that there was something here that was too
> subtle for my understanding altogether   i gave up on it
>   because i think i had reached the point where the cell divides
> and there was no way i could get through that wall
>   i thought
>   about it all the time i was on the train and when i reached my
>   station i got off the train and went home   and i felt that
>   i understood as well as i would ever understand   what he
>   had said to me and what i had said to him   without a great

deal of further effort   at tuning   as i also knew i was not
    even close to an understanding   of what he meant by
    "england" or "france"   as he was not even close to what
        the american had understood as the "united states" and "russia"
                            and still   i could imagine   i suppose
            with the help of all sorts of historical discourse
                                            i could
        imagine such a frame of mind   but i would
            have to imagine it without experiencing it

                            but that i can only imagine it is
    what makes this a trivial illusion of understanding because
        there would still be no common knowing
                there would have been no tuning only my own
            arrogant fantasy of standing in that egyptian's place
    because   after all   his place was still egypt and much closer
        to cairo   and the suez canal   than mine

                                            i was
        beginning to arrive at a notion of how far we might be from
        each other and what sort of distance we might have to travel
                                            i would
    like to contribute to human not understanding   i would like
    to slow down the fantasy and illusion of understanding   so
        that we could inspect the way and the pace at which we are
        approaching or leaving other people   and see how far away
    they are   and whether there is any reason or prospect for
        reaching them   because one thing that's been promoted
        endlessly in this world is the fantasy of understanding the
        notion that it is always possible   desirable   and costs
        nothing[121]

VI. Beirut: Setting the Standards

Beirut, the starting point on the 1938 itinerary, fully tests the limits of
this "fantasy of understanding." After prolonged civil war and periodic
invasion, Beirut has become "almost unimaginable—an icon of chaos,
anarchy, meaninglessness—an image saturated in signs and lacking all
sense; a kind of grotesque unreality surpassing the imagination and language."[122] Yet it is precisely in Beirut where some of the deepest struggles for meaning have taken place, primarily by those who simply
stayed. Jean Said Makdisi writes of the experience of staying:

As the violence reached paroxysm after paroxysm—and the world
watched with indifference, or, at best, revulsion, even while feeding it
with more weapons—I have felt as much impatience with that world as

anger at invading armies, local warlords and anonymous car bombers. Outsiders look at Beirut from a wary distance, as though it had nothing to do with them; as though, through a protective glass partition, they were watching with immunity a patient thrash about in mortal agony, suffering a ghastly virus contracted in forbidden and faraway places. They speak of Beirut as if it were an aberration of the human experience: It is not. Beirut was a city like any other and its people were a people like any other. What happened here could, I think, happen anywhere . . .

What does it mean, then, to have stayed? What have we hoped to accomplish? First of all, I think, we have reclaimed and redefined our humanity. We did not do merely what we were told; we did not obey the obvious command to leave, or to be divided. We were more stubborn than those who bombed and killed and burned. In the end we proved stronger, tougher than they. Where they sought division, we insisted on community. Where they wanted a monochrome existence, we carried a palette of colors that we defiantly splashed around everywhere we went. Where they sowed death, we reaped life. We refused their arguments, and we proved that life can spit at death . . .

Those who are outside looking in see only the war. For us, there are people, friends, life, activity, production, commitments, a profound intensity of meaning. It is these things that have given us the strength to continue, even when we are filled with doubt, for they reassert themselves during and after every battle . . .

We have paid a heavy price for this community. Let those who would comment lightly on us beware: We are unforgiving judges of those who have not shared our experiences. We are like a secret society. We have our own language; we recognize signs that no one else does . . . [123]

Some of these languages and signs were developed through various so-cial, political, and artistic movements of the 1950s and 1960s and, most recently, through the remarkable writing of women in the group Miriam Cooke has called the "Beirut Decentrists." Collectively and individually, these women interrogated the hierarchic power structures of Arab society—the lingering national, political, communal, sexual, and aes-thetic issues that only emerged more clearly during the war—in a more radical way than had previously been attempted. Etel Adnan's novel *Sitt Marie Rose* describes the depth of such interrogation:

I hover above this city, this country, and the continent to which they belong. I never lose sight of them. I have devoted myself to observing them up close . . . I remain among them because I want to know. . . . There are milleniums inside their bodies that should be exposed to daylight or examined under a microscope. There are superimposed layers of memory crammed in their brains as their dead cities are crammed under the hills. This civil war is a laser which has hit the center of their identities. It's a nuclear explosion, not from a bomb, not from the exterior, but from the very heart of the race's memory.[124]

This will to examine and know is a far cry from the urge to master the natives and "render them totally visible, totally accessible to European scrutiny," which characterized colonial knowledge. The struggle for knowledge as a basis for responsibility is described by Miriam Cooke:

> War is a "fragmentation of the individual" at the same time that it is a "collective production." How is this paradox to be resolved? Through the ideal of responsibility in the Lebanese war: a collective responsibility that recognized responsibility to the self to be part of responsibility to others. This is the utopian project of the Beirut Decentrists. It goes beyond awareness to action: reconstruction. Even though society was fragmented, its members would not acknowledge either collective or individual fragmentation and particularly not their own. It was the writer who had to clarify the discrepancy between fact and its perception, to adjust individual consciousness, to reflect the whole in the fragmented self as part of a revolutionary process. Individual reconstruction consisted in the pulling together of the collective fragmentation. The individual deconstructed in the image of society might eventually allow the society to be reconstructed—or collectively produced—in the image of the new individual. Social reconstruction depended on each conscious survival. . . . The goal of the Beirut Decentrists is double-edged: to survive but even more, to give survival meaning.[125]

Although Beirut, the site of this struggle for survival and meaning, is also an ancient city (like Old Cairo, Jerusalem, and Damascus), its true significance is belated and only comes into full play in the late nineteenth and twentieth centuries:

> Until 1853, Beirut was a completely fortified seaport of about one-quarter of a square mile, surrounded by gardens. From 1840 to 1876, expansion to the east and to the west resulted in the demolition of the remaining city walls, and since that time Beirut has developed and expanded in all directions, despite the surrounding steep slopes.[126]

Beirut played a key role in the growth of modernity in the Arab world, serving as one of the focal points for cultural and political developments. Albert Hourani tells us that

> printing in Arabic had scarcely existed before the nineteenth century, but

it spread during the century, particularly in Cairo and Beirut, which
were to remain the principal centers of publishing: government schools
in Cairo and mission schools in Beirut had produced a comparatively
large reading public. Apart from school texts, books were less important
in this period than newspapers and periodicals, which began to play a
large part in the 1860s and 1870s.[127]

In addition to newspapers and periodicals published by Lebanese Christians such as Ya'qub Saaruf (1852-1927) and Faris Nimr (1855-1951), and
Jurji Zaydan (1861-1914) in Cairo, there was an encyclopedia published
in installments by Butrus Bustani (1819-83). This encyclopedia served as
"a compendium of modern knowledge which shows what was known
and understood in Beirut and Cairo in the last quarter of the nineteenth
century. Its articles on modern science and technology are accurate and
clearly expressed; articles on Greek history, mythology, and literature extend far beyond what had been known of classical antiquity in the Islamic
culture of an earlier age; a work edited and written mainly by Arab
Christians, it speaks of Islamic subjects in tones not clouded by reserve or
fear."[128] But these intellectual developments did not take place in a vacuum; in fact, as Charles Issawi has thoroughly documented, they came
about as a result of and in tandem with the revolutionary antifeudal
movements and uprisings of the mid-nineteenth century:

> The 1840s and 1850s also saw greater activity in the social and
> cultural life of Lebanon; this was particularly marked in Beirut,
> which had become the economic, social and cultural center of the
> country. The rise in Beirut's population was accompanied by the
> development of bourgeois layers (owners of commercial companies,
> merchants, brokers) and those of the intelligentsia (teachers, clerks,
> journalists, men of letters). . . . All of this bears witness to the birth in
> Lebanon of new forms of social life, which could not but reflect
> themselves in the internal political situation of the country. Among the
> different layers of the people, antifeudal and anti-Turkish mood gathered
> strength. . . .
>   The uprising of May-July 1840 was a turning point in the history of
> the popular movement. It did not contain any new principles in the
> matter of demands but was incomparably larger in its scope and social
> composition than previous insurgencies, bourgeois as well as feudal
> elements participated in its leadership, and, finally, the demands of the
> insurgents had a new basis—the struggle for liberty and justice against
> tyranny. Although the leaders of the uprising did not advance a program
> of political reforms, their call for the elimination of tyranny contained a
> condemnation of all systems of government; this had an ideological
> influence on subsequent events. . . .

Notwithstanding its defeat, however, the peasant movement of the 1840s and 1850s had important consequences for the economic and social life of Lebanon. At first (i.e. in the 1860s-1870s), there was a spread of small peasant ownership, a rapid growth in silk-reeling factories, an increase in differentation among peasants, and a rise in emigration. All of these changes indicated an activation of the process of the birth and development of capitalist relations. In the field of political organization, the events led to the recognition of Lebanese autonomy. Finally, the antifeudal movement in Lebanon promoted the development of sociopolitical ideas, the rise of the movement for enlightenment, and a renaissance in the field of literature.[129]

By 1970, Beirut had grown to become the cultural and economic center of the Middle East. This growth and centrality was formed "during the fifties and sixties, decades when all around Lebanon revolutions and coups brought into the country a sizeable number of dissident or dispossessed classes, intellectual, political and commercial," turning it into a microcosmic reserve for both greater and more fragmented conflicts that either broke free or were banished from their own place of origin.[130] The city also served as a refuge, meeting place, and reference point for writers insisting on the unity and universality of the Arabic language. But unlike certain tenets of Arab nationalism that, like Zionism, attempted to reduce and homogenize a plethora of social, historical, political, economic, cultural, ethnic, and religious differences under the all-embracing rubric of either "Arab" or "Jew," these writers expressed their vision of a borderless and uncensored Arabic as a way of speaking for people without a voice. By extending the threads connecting all Arabs through their cultural heritage, they hoped to open a new space for creation between the manipulative rhetoric practiced by "regimes that exploited the Arab public's fascination regarding Western modernity in order to establish almost absolute power," and the corresponding sterility reigning within "acceptable" native or imported cultural productions.[131]

The natural contradiction between this poetic intent and the ideological monopolies or interests of states often resulted in poets finding themselves in exile. In fact, modern Arabic poetry *begins* in exile, through the work of Lebanese and Syrian writers who settled in New York and Sao Paulo in the 1920s. In many ways, the sway of the modern period also ends with the beginning of another exile, marked by the suicide of the great modernist Khalil Hawi at the onset of the Israeli invasion of Beirut in 1982. "Lebanon," probably Hawi's last poem, sums up the general despair as well as suggesting the limits of a way of expression.

We were walls facing walls
It was painful to talk
It was painful to feel the distance
Choked by the tragedy
It was painful to talk[132]

The pain is tangible but impenetrable, like the walls everyone has become. The pain of talking, the silence, suggests that only an act (suicide, violence?) or a knowing look emerging from the depths of a common fate could even hope to hint at the extent of the outrage. The invasion had come to drive the nails into the coffin: a new order was being ushered in, and not only in Beirut; all the poet could do now was numbly register the multiplying wounds of distance. Those distant wounds — colonization, Palestine, the shattered hopes for progressive independence — had been fully transformed by a massive diffusion of the locus of control. Imperial interests had found eager partners among the native ruling class, and in such a lucrative equation Arabic culture was certainly an outmoded and disposable commodity. Etel Adnan wrote this in a section of her astonishing and prophetic book-length poem (written in 1975-76), *The Arab Apocalypse*:[133]

the young king of Arabia is bathing in oil
his mouth is shiny and black his teeth sink in petroleum
his eyes are becoming blind inch by inch like distorted suns
the sea is a belly dilated to receive the still-born
Indians and Arabs give battle backwards backwards
Gold powder covers the fighters betrayed by their own
There is in every tribe a gold-thirsty traitor
There is in every Arab a traitor thirsting for the West
Pontiac and Faysal hand in hand sleep in the sunset
the last king of the humiliated races remains lain on the horizon

What the Moroccan writer Tahar Ben Jelloun called "the malaise" had set in: "No one is celebrating; the creators, like the consumers, are conscious that Arab culture is in a bad way. There is talk of crisis, of emptiness, and even of decadence . . . whether through the ideological control of one-party regimes, through the commonplace system of censorship, or through the disappearance of the contemporary centers of culture like Cairo (since Camp David) and Beirut."[134] The voice of the voiceless — the energy that carried Nizar Qabbani's banned 1967 "Footnotes to the Book of the Setback" by word of mouth throughout the Arab world, and maintained Beirut's conspicuous role as the nerve center of the Arabic printed word — had finally been drowned out, "choked by the tragedy." The tension between that earlier, vital Beirut and the one of disaster encompasses the experience of Arab modernity, and pushes its writing beyond collision and dichotomy into collusion with a world that can only be defined by shelving what came before it with an arbitrary, occult gesture: "postindustrial," "postcolonial," "postmodern."

An unequivocal critical thrust against constraints both formal and political has governed Arabic poetry in the twentieth century. There are a number of markers along a line leading from a modern confrontational poetics to what could be called—with a number of significant qualifications and for want of less-abused terminology—a postmodern "poetics of indeterminacy" engaged in creating the space of antithetical knowledge.[135] The fact of exile was instrumental in this history; Salma Khadra Jayyusi points this out in discussing the role of Kahlil Gibran:

> One of the reasons why he was able to experiment with so much freedom, why his creativity could remain pure and unhampered, was the fact that he was writing in America, away from the sages of Arabic literature at home—those entrenched classicists who watched, hawk-like, over the sanctimoniousness of inherited literary methods, and strove to stifle any radical attempt to tamper with tradition. After Gibran's experiment everything became possible in Arabic poetry, and all the adventures with poetic diction, which came in such a flood in the 1960s and after, happened only because Gibran had, early in the century, laid the foundation for a new departure from inherited modes, in favor of an audacious spirit of experimentation.[136]

The two emigrant movements, Pen Bond and The Andalusian Group, found models in the extended line of Walt Whitman and in Abbasid poets like Abu Nuwas, Ibn al-Mu'tazz, and Abu al-Ma'arri. From these movements, "the New York poets Ameen Rihani and Gibran Kahlil Gibran stand out as the most inventive, having revived the Jahili (pre-Islamic) and Sufi concept of the poet as visionary, and introduced two new poetic forms which Rihani called *shi'r manthur* (free verse) and *qasidat al-nathr* (prose poem)." In addition, "Rihani introduced mythological and Christian themes, and metaphors which would become trade-marks of modern Arabic poetry. Gibran's contribution was his revolutionary attitude to the establishment and to language; he brutally attacked the hypocrisy and corruption of the political, religious and social order of his day."[137]

By the 1940s and 1950s, the hypocrisy and corruption of those social orders had multiplied as poets "witnessed their countries being ravaged by *coups d'etat*, wars and civil wars."[138] Bringing things into relief and filling in what falls through the cracks of rhetoric, detailing the abuses of power, are acts that have traditionally put Arabic poets in a precarious position. Two of the most important Abbasid poets, Bashar Ibn Burd (d. 783) and Salih Ibn Abd al-Quddus (d. 783), for example, were both condemned as heretics and executed by the Caliph al-Mahdi. The poets of this period and the following decade are no exception to this tradition, as clearly manifested in the work of writers such as Nazik al-Malaika, Badr Shakir al-Sayyab, Abdul Wahab al-Bayati, and Bulund al-Haydari. Traditional symbols were undermined, confronted, rejuvenated, and newly created. Public demands were voiced out of the private rage and bitterness arising from the discrepancies between officially projected images and what everyone could see before their very eyes, as in this poem by the Kurdish poet al-Haydari:

> My apologies, my honoured guests,
> The newsreader lied in his last bulletin:
> There is no sea in Baghdad
> Nor pearls
> Not even an island,
> And everything Sinbad said:
> About the queens of the jinn
> About the ruby and coral islands
> About the thousand thousands floating from the sultan's hand
> Is a myth born in the summer heat
>   Of my small town
> In the burnt up shadows of the midday sun
> In the silent nights of the exiled stars.[139]

Here, the quality of exile is not literal but an expression, rather, of a deep and unsettling *internal* estrangement from all forms of "official" culture: its language, values, and denials. Much of this disillusion came out into the open only after the stunning defeat of 1967 in which rhetoric again outweighed action and Israel conquered the rest of Jerusalem, the West Bank and the Gaza Strip. Increasing awareness of and frustration arising from the internal problems and contradictions leading to that defeat had honed this bitterness to a new edge, as in these lines by Nizar Qabbani:

> It's painful to listen to the news in the morning.
> It's painful to listen to the barking of dogs.
>
> Our enemies did not cross our borders
> They crept through our weaknesses like ants.[140]

The Lebanese novelist, translator, journalist, and critic Elias Khoury wrote: "Since the June defeat, the corrosion has spread into the body of the seat of power. The conflict with the enemy has revealed its true face. The destruction of society from within is leading to the transformation of the external enemy into an internal factor. The conflicts between enemies, and the inability to resolve them, are opening the horizons of an extended civil war in the Arab social body."[141]

In another poem of Qabbani's, "The Ruler and the Sparrow," the death notice of a megalomanic strain of pan-Arab unity is finally delivered:

> I travelled to the Arab homeland
> To read my poems.
> I was convinced
> Poetry was the public's bread.
> I was convinced
> The words were fish
> And the public their water.
>
> I travelled in the Arab homeland
> With only a notebook.
> Police stations tossed me about,
> Soldiers tossed me about,
> And all I had was a sparrow in my pocket . . .
> The word in my country needs a passport.
>
> I waited for the pass
> Staring at the sandbags,
> Reading the posters
> That spoke of one homeland,
> That spoke of one people.
> I was discarded at my country's gates
> like broken glass.[142]

Out of the splinters and shards of this rupture, a new distinction emerges: the Palestinian experience as a true source of energy and its equivocal use as an empty sign, vulgarly bandied about in yet another round of exploitation. Nurtured by "Hagar's tears—the first woman to lament a migration without end," the Palestinian became a "universal" particular.[143] Again, as Elias Khoury put it, "Palestine isn't a country for it to have a flag. Palestine is a condition. Every Arab is a Palestinian. . . . Palestine is the condition of us all."[144] Since it was more obvious, or at least it then seemed more obvious in their case just who their enemy was, Palestinian poets could attempt to embody things that had been suppressed, deflected, or symbolized. Those parts of the identity (personal, communal, religious, ethnic, urban, economic, and sexual) that had been traded in or subsumed under some amorphous notion of "nationality"

began to emerge more freely. The key to a new storehouse of energy—
long poised in readiness and pent up—had begun to be unearthed. The
materials of history could be endowed with ironic substance and the private could begin to become political, as long as it stayed within the discourse of the "cause." In "Leaving the Mediterranean Coast," Mahmoud
Darwish writes:

> I am the living and ancient cities.
> Try to uproot your names, you will find both my hands.
> Try to strip your clothes, you will find my blood.
> Or try to burn these maps, you will see my body.
>
> I am the living and the homeland they inscribed in your chronicles.
> My remains initiate the marauders, the prophets, the refugees—
> and in my body they close their accounts to begin again.[145]

Unlike the escape in Jabès, the flight into haunting memories of death,
forgotten cities and stories, this Mediterranean bitterly celebrates its
"new migration." The sense of exile is honed here even more sharply
than in the previous generation of Arab poets. Here, biography can begin
anew, beyond the strictly critical, to become autobiography. Written so
long for and by others, the Mediterranean can begin writing itself, as it
literally does in this poem by Darwish.

Present as well (as in Jabès) is an underlying deep conflict between getting lost or losing oneself in the desert, and remaining open to the sea.
This antithesis was at the root of two of the region's most alluring and
potentially radical poetic movements: that of the Hebrew Canaanites,[146]
and that fostered by the ideology of the Syrian Social Nationalist Party
under the leadership of Anton Sa'adah. In reaching the conclusion that
"we are Syrians, and we constitute a distinct national entity"—despite
the influence of European fascism—Sa'adah "argued that national unity
was not based on race or purity of blood, but that it was the by-product
of historical continuity of a group of people who occupy a defined piece
of land; and a by-product of the interaction between these people and
this geographical spot."[147] This ideology was influential not just with
Syrians (most notably Adonis and Yusuf al-Khal), but with Arab modernist thought in general. Thus the people of Palestine, for example,
could be seen as "an Arabian (i.e. Semitic) blend of Amorites, Canaanites, Hittites, Jebusites, Phoenicians, Hebrews and late Arabians with
Philistine, Roman, Greek and Frankish flavoring—who have lived out
their centuries and moved from one Semitic tongue to another in a series
of religious-political experiences as animists, as Jews, as Christians, and
finally as Muslims."[148] In this context, then, the referential range (includ-

ing Moses, the crucifixion, baptism, Mary of Magdalene, the Crusaders, and the Caliphate) in the poetry of Darwish (a Muslim by birth and a Marxist by choice) does not seem at all out of place. Space does contain memory and in Darwish this palimpsest has been accrued casually, through language, custom, and gesture, not as the result of a programmatic construct.

Yet, in many instances, privileging the Palestinian experience simply meant creating alternative versions of master narratives. The suppressed but cautiously emerging aspects of identity were often redirected, in more and less subtle ways, through structural models that simply shifted responsibility by "naming the enemy." A sure indication of this can be seen in canon formation, particularly regarding women writers:

> With the Palestinian cause as an arch-Arab cause, a new literary tradition was being wrought. It was a tradition that did not per se exclude women, but it did make their inclusion dependent on adherence to the rules, the message before all else.[149]

The origins of this dialectic of inclusion and exclusion can be found prior to the 1967 war, in the writing of women who worked within, alongside, and sometimes in collision with or seclusion from the movements of the 1950s and 1960s that were reshaping contemporary Arab culture. In an atmosphere where only the ostensibly "political" or the newly conjured reconfiguration of historical mythology was considered "real," attempts to interrupt public discourse with avowedly private experience could be seen as "violence committed against fundamental beliefs and assumptions."[150] The obscenity trial against the Lebanese writer Laila Baalbaki for her book *A Space Ship of Tenderness to the Moon*, held in Beirut in 1964, is just one early instance of this.[151]

The successive breakdowns following the defeat of 1967 are seldom spelled out as explicitly, radically, or broadly as in the writing of women. Despite the succinctness and accuracy of the analysis offered by many, it still seems framed by *external* manifestations of power. As acute and caustic as Nizar Qabbani's poetry is, for example, he writes of general "weaknesses" while upholding a noble persona defeated at the hands of greater and seemingly indomitable powers. In "Politics," a section of Etel Adnan's "In the Heart of the Heart of Another Country," very different and more specific senses of power are depicted:

> The State. A man and a woman, together, already form a state. There is

everything between them: a principle of authority, a government, laws of behaviour, embassy and representation, diplomacy, weapons, periods of peace and war.

They also constitute, to make things harder than for matters of state, two different species. When they meet, they sometimes ignore each other. Sometimes they climb on each other like a pair of monkeys. At other times, a current of cool air passes from one to the other: there is love. And then, there are times when, at their contact, a short-circuit happens, and they burn each other and leave nothing behind them but a spot on the sun.

Youssef el Khal said one day that I was a poet. Yes. I am the poet in the heart of the city. A dot. I am the poet of the here and now.

But, being a woman, I am invisible. I have to hide my obsession for ants. They pursue me. If a woman went to the marketplace and cried for help because ants were climbing up between her legs, some men would throw themselves between her thighs, and search wildly for the tiny beasts, in order to relieve her from her fear, and hurt her, too. But she would be arrested and thrown into an insane asylum until she hallucinated and the water which fell from the faucet became a thick stream of black ants. In that case, I would pull up my blanket of flies and sleep.[152]

The specifics here are not those of borders or dates, historical or mythological figures, but relationships and the consequences of unbalanced power occurring in a constant present that demands a state of both ingenuity and total alertness. Yet such a text cannot be read as either the complaint of a victim or the expressive flight of deliverance. Granted legitimacy, named "poet" by the Poet, the writer of these lines recedes to the space of a dot in "the here and now," invisible but central. For Etel Adnan and other Lebanese writers (Hoda al-Namani, Ghada al-Samman, Hanan al-Sheikh, and Claire Gebeyli among them), only the severe breakdown in the structures of society during the civil war created the possibility of such a paradoxically liberating place — within the very heart of "chaos, anarchy, and meaninglessness" — from which to speak, testify, and redefine the world. As Miriam Cooke put it:

> Most women's writing which restricted itself to the private domain registered an awareness that saying something is sometimes as important as what is said and who is saying it. . . . Their concern was not to gain acceptance into a predominantly male preserve but rather to register a voice. These voices were rarely heard in what has been termed the public domain. Their content was deemed irrelevant. How could the expression of private experience become acceptable outside its immediate confines? How could the apparently mutually exclusive

domains of private and public, of self and other, be reconciled? Boundaries had to be challenged and shown to be fluid, elusive. Such a radical reassessment and construction of social and literary order could not be achieved spontaneously. . . .

The Lebanese war provided the context. Violence in this case represented universal loss of power, but it also undermined the private/ public dichotomy, revealing the private to be public, and the personal to be universal. Private space became everyone's space and it was appropriated literarily in a collective endeavor to express and thereby understand the reign of unreason.[153]

VII. Beirut and the Poetics of Disaster

In a long and complex poem called "The Desert: Diary of Beirut Under Siege, 1982," Adonis writes:

> The cities break up
> The land is a train of dust
> Only poetry knows how to marry this space.[154]

What was cultivated reverts to wilderness: the desert finally overruns the city, paradoxically marking an end to growth and a return to the primal place of purification—but whose place? The poetry of Adonis from the 1950s exclusively associated the desert with "the sterility of a senile and collapsing sand-culture."[155] Sand and the desert are always obstructions, atavistic and stifling throwbacks to an alternative and forward-looking Mediterranean, yet the circumstances of the new poem almost seem to demand a retreat. Although Adonis himself continues to speak of the current condition in terms of "modern Arabic poetry," the return of and back to the desert seems to delineate an enticingly rich terrain for a poetics not based on modernist assumptions, one whose impetus may derive from the West, but whose sources are decidedly native.

As early as 1967, Adonis wrote: "We no longer believe in Europe. We no longer have faith in its political system or in its philosophies. Worms have eaten into its social structure as they have into . . . its very soul. Europe for us—us backward, ignorant, impoverished people—is a corpse."[156] The irony of this condition is that, in its critique of received ideas, "Arabic thought—in dialogue with itself prior to the problem of its dialogue with Western thought,"[157] often reaches back to the texts of tradition for its most unsettling innovations and most potent ammunition, but through a circuitous route:

> It was reading Baudelaire that brought me to discover Abu Nuwas. It was reading Mallarmé that restored Abu Tamam's poetic language to

me. Rimbaud, Nerval and the Surrealists made me grasp the experience
of the mystics. Reading contemporary French criticism prepared me for
the unfolding of al-Jurjani's originality. I think many Arabs, poets and
critics, went through a similar process.[158]

Given the "malaise" described by Tahar Ben Jelloun, the fact that
"homecoming is out of the question," and "the mechanics of loss" have
been transformed "into a constantly postponed metaphysics of return,"[159] the path into a qualitatively different state of resolve than that
presented by a modernist poetics of confrontation seems clear. This resolve and the use of old materials is not exactly a search for a referential
Ur-text lost in paradise; neither is it a return to the sublimated energies
stockpiled and labeled "differences," nor a wish to reinstate the particulars of lives or texts gone by as "presence," something that could only
lead to a somewhat pathetic ethnography or roster of classics. The intent,
rather, is to play along the margins of absences, to both visit and inhabit
"the space in which literature can exist," in the sense defined by Blanchot:

> Blanchot's writings investigate the absolute responsibility the writer has
> to language. Civilization has convinced us that to speak is to control
> that which is spoken of; Blanchot's entire occupation has been to call
> that glibness into question. He has shown us that the void writing
> creates between itself and the world can never be filled adequately; the
> writer's hope to tell a story is futile, yet this void is, infinitely and
> mysteriously, the only space in which literature can exist. In Blanchot's
> words: to discover the language of literature is to search for the moment
> which precedes literature.[160]

Adonis manages to assimilate the poetics of Jabès and *écriture*, but in a
language that is still Arabic, in a space still Levantine, "penetrated" but
not "deeply marked" or "shaken," at "the beginning of a new era," but
"not looking for a new beginning." It is precisely this point of
departure—beyond the illusion of control, situated at these intersections
and paradoxes—that is conveyed in the major poems written from the
precipice and in the void that Beirut had become. It is these texts, as well,
that constitute the last word for all the poets within earshot of the tragedy.

"The Desert" remains acutely aware of both the classical and modern
texts behind it while ruthlessly interrogating them: "Whatever comes
will be old / So take with you anything other than this madness—get
ready / To stay a stranger."[161] In the tangle of styles that constitute the
text—narrative, fragmentary dialogue and monologue, litany catalogues
and lyric interludes—this aphoristic irony (while itself commenting on

his own earlier poetry) unmistakably refers to the work of the Abbasid Abu al-Ala al-Ma'arri, a poet who witnessed and survived one of the Crusaders' bloodiest campaigns:

> The soul driven from the body
> Mourns the memory it leaves behind.
>
> A dove hit in flight sadly turns
> Its neck and sees its nest destroyed.[162]

The more abstract statement of the first stanza in al-Ma'ari's poem is jolted into focus by the clarity of the second, a very common sequence in Semitic poetry.[163] In the lines of Adonis, both clauses in the formula are stretched to the point of indeterminacy—"whatever comes; anything other than"—while the preparation for a state of constant home-lessness—the condition of the dove whose nest has been destroyed—is also left within the space of this unspecified abyss. Beginning the new exile marked by the invasion and Hawi's suicide also means embarking on a much longer and more uncertain journey, one that plumbs and per-forates the ideology of the book:

> This is the beginning of a new era.
>
> Whenever I say: my country is within reach
>   And bears fruit in a reachable language
>
> Another language kicks me
> To another language.
>
> The papers that love ink,
>   The alphabet, the poets say goodbye,
>
> And the poem says goodbye
>
> All the certainty I have lived slips away
> All the torches of my desire slip away
> All that was between the faces of my exile
>   and me slips away
>
> I have to start from the beginning
> To teach my limbs to reach the future,
> To talk, to climb, to descend from the beginning
> In the sky of beginning, in the abyss of the alphabet.[164]

This retreat into the interior, into "the sky of beginning, the abyss of the alphabet," is not the escape one might have once thought in such a highly politicized arena, but precisely the opposite. It is an attempt to repossess what Mahmoud Darwish has cynically referred to as "the surplus value of the slaughter";[165] a demand not to let that surplus value be manipulated once again within a vicious circle of corruption and power, but re-located and reinvested within the terms of an altered political and cultural economy.

At the same time, the Israeli invasion gave new impetus toward a rever-sion to the symbolic, to creating new "master narratives" expanded— often stylistically—to be just accommodating enough to more radical in-novations without losing a grip on the nets circumscribing the possible:

> Writers who had shied away from literary interpretations of the war, because events were too immediate, too intense, could now start to write fiction and create history. When wars are over opponents fight on to establish whose story will be embraced by posterity. It is at the crucial point of "making history" that "canon formation is particularly aggressive."[166]

Even in the extremely powerful work of Darwish, for instance, there is an insistence at times upon "naming the enemy," albeit in more subtle ways than during the period immediately following the defeat of 1967. The poet's pleas, even in the most ironic and self-critical instances ("We have a country of words. Speak Speak so we may know the end of this travel"),[167] are still directed at the collective bodies—with all their attendant frames of reference and relation—as conventionally constructed entities. Interestingly enough, this kind of pressure, arising from traditional modes of address or conven-tional writer/audience relations, which impinges upon the poetry, is largely absent from Darwish's Beirut prose diaries.

At this crucial juncture of "history making," when the civil war would come to be read through the subsequent invasion (allowing both events to appear within an overarching narrative sequence, however in-terpreted or represented), the work of the Lebanese women writers be-came more and more marginalized. Once the "cause" had assumed such catastrophic proportions, the concerns of these writers could be made to appear "frivolous."[168] Yet, in retrospect, the ambitious project of these writ-ers (with its insistence upon allowing reality to dictate its own forms, theo-ries, and critical intentions) often makes even some of the most important other work emerging from Beirut seem merely literary or conventional:

> By the late 1970s, the Beirut Decentrists were using language to create a new reality. Their writings were becoming transformative, even prescriptive. As self-censorship gave way to uninhibited expressions of self-assertion, the hold of the oppressive male critic was shaken. It was only with the breakdown of Lebanon's identity as an independent patriarchal polity that women began to assert their female identity publicly. . . . As the violence persisted and men fought senseless battles

or fled, women came to realize that the society of which they were also
members was collapsing; unravelling seams revealed the need for
collective responsibility, but also for responsibility for the self. The
individual had to become aware to survive. The time that was right for
assertion of female identity coincided with the disintegration of the
country's identity.[169]

At times, as in the passage above, Cooke's strident characterization of
gender relations seems to itself revert into categorical closures that bypass
the eloquent testimony of human solidarity ranging across all lines
(whether sexual, confessional, or even political) offered in a work like
Jean Said Makdisi's *Beirut Fragments*, among many others. Nevertheless,
the fact remains that responsibility to the self, to reconstructing the self,
was intimately tied to the general state of collapse engendered by the war.
Two major works, Etel Adnan's previously mentioned *Arab Apocalypse*
and Ghada al-Samman's *Beirut Nightmares*, both completed in 1976, pre-
figure not only the further chaos and destruction to come but also many
of the formal and aesthetic possibilities that only find their way into the
city and the region's general literary discourse later on. The tyranny of
language, its exclusion of the poet's traditional role, and the need to locate a beginning "in the abyss of the alphabet" as seen in the work of
Adonis, were already central concerns:

> I always tried to convince myself that the inkpot was greater than a
> hand grenade, that the pen was greater than a bullet. And I wrote and
> wrote . . . But one day I got out from under the rock and decided that
> the inkpot is not always greater than the hand grenade and that it was
> time for me to learn a new language.[170]

Yet, particularly in the work of al-Samman, these figures are never abstract enough to drift far from the very real and comprehensive project at
hand: the *reconstruction* of a self within the totality of war, not simply a
commentary or critique of the crisis. Even al-Samman's dedicatory poem
prefacing the book directly addresses one of the many incongruities that
threaten to undermine the very basis of her endeavor:

> I dedicate this book
> To the printers
> Who are at this moment arranging its letters
>
> Despite the thunder of the rockets and the bombs
> And they know
> That the book will not contain their names . . .
> To them,
> The hard-working, faceless, silent ones.[171]

The quality of solidarity expressed here is remarkable in that it potentially encompasses factions or sides while still retaining a very clear sense
of where the writer is located. Not only the substance but the figure of
language is constantly evoked: Claire Gebeyli writes of "A life / between
one syllable / and another," or "those 'commas of flesh' that punctuate
life in war." As Miriam Cooke notes, "War as a pervasive fact of life
must be acknowledged and accommodated in discourse. Language and
war must be seen to be intertwined so that nothing *said* may be perceived
as separate from the war."[172] For Etel Adnan, the search for a new language led her to create symbols, glyphlike marks on the page that "seem
to grow organically out of the words," allowing them "to disintegrate
and explode."[173]

Two of the strongest works to come out of the ruins of Beirut are Hoda
al-Namani's "I Remember I Was a Point, I Was a Circle," the title poem
from a collection of the same name, and Hannan al-Sheikh's novel *The
Story of Zahra*. Both further problematize and throw into stark relief destruction and revolution, by countering the predictably patriarchal order
of those scenes through the fact of women's experience within them.
Both also interrogate conventional definitions of madness. In al-Sheikh's
novel, the seemingly passive Zahra simply tries to negotiate the horrors
of a "normal" upbringing. These horrors include a violent father and an
adventurous mother who compelled her daughter into collusion with her
affairs; two rapes and two abortions; the persistent advances of an uncle
she visits in Africa; and an arranged marriage that ends in divorce. Her
retreat into silence elicits the diagnosis of madness, for which she is committed and given electroshock treatment. It is only in the second half of
the book, "The Torrents of War," that the general insanity reigning in the
streets outside begins to illuminate Zahra's inner past. As she goes to the
heart of the conflict through an obsessive and passionate affair with a
sniper on the roofs of the city, there is a newly found sense of freedom,
possibility, and clarity:

> Here is this god of death who has scorned the loss of my virginity once,
> twice, a hundred times, the sniper to whom I am grateful for accepting
> me despite my plainness, because he realizes that beauty is not
> everything. I hear, close by, scattered gunshots, yet feel as if they are at
> a great distance. This war has made beauty, money, terror and
> convention all equally irrelevant. It begins to occur to me that the war,
> with its miseries and destructiveness, has been necessary for me to start
> to return to being normal and human.
>   The war, which makes one expect the worst at any moment, has led
> me into accepting this new element in my life. Let it happen, let us

witness it, let us open ourselves to accept the unknown, no matter what
it may bring, disasters or surprises. The war has been essential. It has
swept away the hollowness concealed by routines. It has made me ever
more alive, ever more tranquil.[174]

Throughout the affair Zahra creates and recreates possible romantic sce-
narios that are never reciprocated: a blank mirror, even the sniper's allegiance to one of the many sides engaged in the battles raging in the streets
below is never clarified. Pregnant, and with the promise of marriage, Zahra suddenly asks whether her future husband is a sniper. Zahra's story
ends as she dimly realizes — fading away — that her own death has come at
the hand of her "lover":

> The evening has descended. The street is empty, except at the
> barricades. The rain falls. I stumble. I hold on to a telephone pole to
> stop some force from dragging me down. My thigh hurts. It's hurting
> even more. I reach down to touch the place and feel something wet run
> down my leg, and on to my foot. Can it be the rain? It's surely not
> raining so hard. Am I miscarrying? I can't even walk, but must not
> stop . . . Somebody shouts, "Look out. There's a sniper." And I begin
> to scream as the pain leaps up to my neck . . . I stretch my hand out,
> not knowing in my hallucination whether these screams are mine or
> another's.
>
> The pain leaps to my belly and I rake the ground with my fingers.
> It was the sniper who put this foetus in my belly. Is he the one who
> now puts in all this pain as well? . . . A complete silence descends,
> for to scream has become an unbearable agony. My vocal cords are
> chained to my heart's root. The sniper is killing me. His first two
> bullets missed piercing my head. His third missed piercing the foetus
> inside me. I don't scream. I don't try to touch the streaming blood. I lie
> silent in the rain . . . [175]

In al-Namani's poem, the sense of relational breakdown is even further refined, fully woven into the very texture of the language itself. Sufi
elements culled from the poet's own family traditions are drawn into a
chilling kaleidoscope of blending and crashing figures, but nothing is
conclusive. Any kind of closure is constantly negated and denied; the line
recedes while going forward as the poem deconstructs and comments
upon itself:

> In death I find none but you,
>
> in the breeze too, and the scythe and the drizzle, the
> barricades and
> handguns and men in hoods, in live broadcasts and telephones cut dead,
> in bulletins of news, the safe roads and the unsafe, interrogations,

delays, prayerbooks and beads, chess pieces, tranquilizers, pine and
saffron, weddings, births and spare time, and arguments, arguments,
arguments,
> I find none but you.
> Here I am bending down to drink and I lose my memory.

I have not let my face leap like a bat, I have not kicked my foot
against the place of my exile, I did not move like phantoms over the
rooftops, I did not try child hunting, I did not steal the sea's wings,
I did not break glass over a breast, I did not eat my flesh that burns,
I have not withdrawn into despair, I did not go mad in gathering honey,
> I did not go mad, I did not go mad, I did not go mad.[176]

Men are involved in barricades, live broadcasts, bulletins, interrogations,
and prayer books. For the women, there are pine and saffron, there are
weddings: the time not spent in labor—giving birth—is "spare" time.
But faced with death, that restrictive space of "spare" time and the activities of the men are forgotten: memory is lost and with it "everything
other than this madness," all the "ordered" relations, and even the rebellion against them, seem dwarfed in comparison. Throughout the poem,
the "you" serves as an undefined shifter whose locus of reference is never
fully disclosed. Instead of being confined to either a religious or an erotic
allusion, the "you" and the "I" join up to become a kind of relational
scanner that skims across the surface of the whole poem, continually attempting to realign the tensions of everything within it. The repetition at
the end of the stanza, "I did not go mad," becomes madness itself: the
literal "meaning" of the sentence is turned into its exact antithesis. Yet,
through its utterance, some hold on the madness is gained, some sense of
it is made. In this kind of work, it is "not the appearance of a word, but
the manner of its reappearance that counts."[177]

Like the stunning presentation of Adnan's *Arab Apocalypse*, much of
al-Namani's work presents a radical visual field in which the text itself
only forms one part of the design. The totality of these works confronts
the "image of the authority of 'right thinking' conveyed primarily
through 'right printing'—justified margins and conventional punctua-
tion,"[178] but always out of necessity, never simply for the sake of exper-
imentation. What is also striking about al-Namani's poem, Adnan's *Arab
Apocalypse*, "The Desert" by Adonis, and another major poem that came
out of Beirut, "Brief Reflections of an Ancient and Beautiful City on the
Coast of the Mediterranean Sea" by Mahmoud Darwish, is the fact that
all conclude with paradoxes:[179]

> I cannot die in a death
> That has no death now . . .

Nothing moves death in this place.
                    (Darwish)

I remember I was a point, I was a circle.
She is a voice . . . any voice.
    He is a land . . . not every land.
                    (al-Namani)

My obsession is here now, loss.
My concern is the end

            Is not over.
They are falling, I am not looking for a new beginning.
                    (Adonis)

When the sun will run its ultimate road
fire will devour beasts plants and stones
fire will devour the fire and its perfect circle
when the perfect circle will catch fire no angel will manifest itself STOP
the sun will extinguish the gods the angels and men
and it will extinguish itself in the midst of its daughters
Matter-Spirit will become the NIGHT
in the night in the night we shall find knowledge love and peace.
                    (Adnan)

Darwish and Adonis express despair as they embrace the openness of a
paradox: "Nothing moves death" because the people are stronger; there
is no need to look for "a new beginning" because all beginnings are
present. For al-Namani the woman's voice is enough, "any voice," as
long as it has come back from the inferno bearing witness, while the man
can potentially be a land, but "not every land." Most significantly, for
Adnan (like al-Sheikh's Zahra), "knowledge love and peace" can only
come after great destruction, *after* the apocalypse.

    In winding down like this, all these poems seem to relinquish a certain
form of power, in turn perforating and picking apart the preceding text.
Both the materials and the mode of their use in these poems correspond
to many of the definitions that have been formulated to set the "modern"
apart from the "postmodern":

> The deconstructive impulse is characteristic of postmodern art in general
> and must be distinguished from the self-critical tendency of modernism.
> Modernist theory presupposes that mimesis, the adequation of an image
> to a referent, can be bracketed or suspended, and that the art object
> itself can be substituted (metaphorically) for its referent. . . .

> Postmodernism neither brackets nor suspends the referent but works
> instead to problematize the activity of reference.[180]

Maybe even more accurately, the poems correspond to what Marjorie
Perloff has formulated — again, with some qualifications — as the "poetics
of indeterminacy" alluded to earlier. In such a poetics there is, in John
Cage's words, "a demilitarization of language" which preserves "a respect for the unintelligibility of what can't be understood."[181] But this,
of course, engenders another paradox since "nothing *said* may be perceived as separate from the war."[182] Reverting to perplexing riddles that
send shock waves back "to problematize the activity of reference," the
poems both skirt and court despair while retaining an equilibrium that
forces the reader past feeling to intellect and participation in the crisis of
choice that goes into the production of meaning, even if that meaning
amounts to a renunciation of understanding. These poems remain an initial place — the place of initiation — even if the poets themselves wearily
tread the worn and varied routes of exile in successive waves. The work
contains no grand blueprint, lost paradise, or unreachable destination; the
voyage is all. It is journey work that chronicles events with the accuracy
and compression of ancient Near Eastern verse; it is a poetry that maps
contradictions, "makes amends with the past, dates the wounds and the
estrangement."

At the same time, the work does not succumb to the cult of the "text"
or the "book," since the political climate and consciousness in which
these writers work assume language to be just "one strategic part of the
total social fact" that bears on reconstruction of a diseased and battered
social body. The often deadly meaning that the configurations and constellations of interpretation can take on within the "reconstruction of historical geography" that has characterized the very turbulent modernity
of the region lends a very different weight to writing and its possibility.
As Ron Silliman has pointed out, "new meanings exist only to the extent
that they have been previously repressed, not permitted to reach consciousness. But it is necessary to seek the social base of any meaning not
in the self-reflexivity of the text, as such, but in its relation to the social
positionality of its audience & author."[183] While many parts of the academy seem to have moved comfortably into a highly technocratic phase in
which "the curricula of most literature departments are constructed almost entirely out of monuments, canonized into rigid dynastic formation, serviced and reserviced monotonously by a shrinking guild of hum-
ble servitors,"[184] much outside of that realm remains "unread." It is
reading and rereading that now is producing new writing out of the
dense and crowded palimpsest that comprises the old Levantine and Arab

world, and it has been the prism of Beirut—both in its days of brilliance and in its eclipse—through which many of the most characteristic lights of that old world have been newly refracted.

VIII. Jerusalem and the Crusader Man

Jerusalem rests between two limit points, 250 miles from Cairo (the city "whose scale and complexity threatens incoherence and questions the discourse and categories of the urban")[185] and only 136 miles from Beirut, the city whose poets struggled to keep routes to the sea open, only to be enveloped by the desert. Cairo, although accessible to Israelis, remains a tourist site and not an urban point of reference. Neither the interior city of memory and exile (through the work of Jabès) nor the exterior, social city (through weather reports, newspapers, trade, new translations of contemporary Egyptian writers, or any other significant forms of exchange) have fully entered Jerusalem's vocabulary. The assumptions of commonality and easy exchange described by Ya'aquob Yehoshua in *Childhood in Old Jerusalem* seem light-years away:

> The sons and daughters of Sephardic families in Jerusalem were avid followers of Arabic music. With great vigilance, they kept track of the latest songs composed in Jerusalem or brought in from Egypt. Everyone enjoyed the works of the Arab poet Salama Hijazi Muhammad al-'Ashaq as well as [that of] others who visited Jerusalem and led poetry and music get-togethers in the Arab coffeehouses, back when the audience used to sit on low cane stools and smoke the *narghilleh*. Everyone went to hear George al-Abyad's Egyptian group when they came to Jerusalem before the First World War. The coffeehouses of the Old City and Damascus Gate served as cultural and entertainment centers for Arabs and Jews alike. There is no doubt, too, that various melodies from Arabic poetry and music found their way into the *piyyutim*, the religious lyrics and hymns that rabbis and cantors sang on Friday nights, at home and in the synagogue.[186]

Beirut, its culture dispersed and transplanted, has not been appended to this lexicon in terms of a possible poetics of disaster and politics of restitution, but as a closed chapter in a reckless and disturbing adventure. The extraordinarily rich cultural history and the dense textual history of this neighboring city have barely begun to penetrate: it was only in 1989 that a selection of early poems by Adonis, along with the Beirut diaries of Mahmoud Darwish, were translated into Hebrew. This is not to say that Palestinian Israeli writers, Jewish Israeli scholars, or others have no access to these texts in Arabic, English, or French, but simply to emphasize that, although produced in such proximity, they have yet to enter the larger discourse of contemporary Israeli writing and culture.

Ironically (akin to the irony in which Jews of European origin found themselves more and more marginalized vis-à-vis both Palestinians and Arab Jews after the 1967 occupation), in putting the nails in the coffin of Beirut, Israel has bound itself to the fate of the region more firmly and inextricably than ever before. Many realities and realizations (a growing awareness of Israel/Palestine as the country of the people living in it, rather than some ever-expanding "home" for all Jews; the progressive re-localization of the Arab/Israeli conflict and its dwindling significance on the international agenda; an altered Israeli economy relying more on an internally colonized local Arab market than on the undated blank check of American aid), have all contributed to the creation of a potential for one of those "significant cleavages in history where a cut will separate different types of happening."[187] This cut (a truer rapprochement between Israelis and Palestinians and the Levantine and Arab worlds that could turn the potential into the actual, reconnect old and familiar routes, and realign the cultural constellations of the region) has little to do with current "official" discourse. Despite the bleakness of the present climate—the radical shift in geopolitical balance resulting from the Gulf War (not to mention the already unmentionable suffering of the Iraqi people), the huge influx of Soviet Jews into Israel, the continuing confiscation of Palestinian lands in the occupied territories, and the increased entrenchment of Israeli policies—the very desperation involved serves as an indication of precisely how high the stakes are.

As the Arab character of the city is continually being eroded, shriveling its links to the Levant, Jerusalem encloses the space of another incoherence. A complete microcosm of Levantine and Arab Jewry (and containing the full range of diverse Palestinian affiliations), it remains effectively cut off from significant access to the texture, substance, and wider sphere of determinants that comprise the world of which it forms a part. Jacqueline Kahanoff wrote of this estrangement:

> To those of us who were born in the communities of the Orient, the names of places which were once familiar—Baghdad, Damascus, Cairo, Tunis, Algiers—are now the far-away places in that mythical geography of hearts and minds, where distances do not correspond to those on maps.[188]

The mirror image of this sense of being locked in as "the far-away places in that mythical geography" shrink and recede into the interior is conveyed by Raymonda Tawil, a Palestinian, in the form of memory from the limbo of a divided city:

In 1954, I changed schools once more, moving to Saint Joseph's in Jerusalem. Mother used to come to see me there, taking me for walks toward the demarcation line dividing the city. We would stand on the roof of Notre Dame, gazing across the border. . . . Invariably, her thoughts and mine turned to her sons—my brothers—only a few hundred yards away, so near, but so unreachable. . . . We walked the streets of Jerusalem, as though we were trudging through the desert, from mirage to mirage; wherever we went, our thirst remained.[189]

A further refraction from the spectrum of experiences of the city, reflected by a native to the promised land unable to go back, is present in Jean Said Makdisi's description of her father's last visit to his divided home:

We went up to the top of the YMCA building near the Mandelbaum Gate, and he showed me with a hesitating finger, pointing across the barriers and the years, the streets of his childhood. His memory was dimmed by the passage of time, by the alterations of inexorable modernity, and by the tears that came as he saw again after so long the city that had once been alive to him with parents, brothers, cousins . . . I think that reliving of his childhood there at the top of the YMCA building, on the border of the divided city, his recounting it to me, was cathartic for him; and perhaps he came to terms of sorts with the loss and the barricades. But in passing his memories on to me, he passed also the burden of memory, central to the Palestinian experience.[190]

With the "reunification" of the city in 1967, Jerusalem found itself almost completely isolated from the "old and habitual" world of which it had once formed an indivisible part, with some intervals during the Crusades, since the time of the Jebusites "and Melchizedek, King of Salem, a priest of God Most High."[191] Twenty-five years later, the processes set in motion then have become institutionalized, despite the fact that the gains of the Palestinian uprising mean there can be no return to the status quo prevailing before it. The rising percentage of people knowing only victory or only defeat—those born into either side of the occupation—has increasingly muffled even the possibility of hearing voices that could articulate the knowledge of a different experience. As the nerve center of a globalized conflict, whose roots have been even further mystified through the manipulation of religious signs transplanted from a long symbolic order and reappropriated as national symbols, the city also serves as a testing ground. The city itself becomes a test—coding and recoding itself like an endless movie or news report constantly interrogating and sounding out its viewers about the claims and counterclaims of its contenders, forcing them to determine why this frame was shot at that angle, who edited what out.

The land itself vividly reflects this struggle as the face of the city finds itself irreversibly deformed. Instead of terraced olive groves and fruit trees, massive residential and institutional structures (built on the tops of leveled-off hills) surround the city like ominous fortresses, overshadowing rural enclaves and the remaining "natives" holding on to the little land they have left. Analogies between these current proclamations of intrusive presence and the Crusaders' bastions of alien power have often been made by city planners, historians, and even poets. In "The Crusader Man," by the Israeli poet Shelley Elkayam, there is no need to revert to the "proof" of archaeology or document. Instead, the poem relies on an even surer source: knowledge localized in traces of the land's memory encoded and inscribed in her own accumulated experience as a seventh-generation resident of it:

> The Crusader man paid the Land a visit
> and that was
> around
> so and so many
> years back
>
> The Crusader man did the country
> in this
> or that many days.
>
> The Crusader man became the landlord.
> An enemy with holdings.
> Full of trust,
> sword-bearing, armor-wearing, with a coat of mail.
>
> Kind of a jumpy guy, the Crusader man.
>
> The Land is a witness,
> she sees it from
> the way he
> laid his
> place out,
> from the fact
> that he never did make himself a home.
> From the way he'd attack
> and cut himself off on the mountain tops. [192]

The dates and facts are not that important: "so and so many years back," "this or that many days." What does count are the Crusader man's *intentions*. Here, it's clear that his "trust" only amounts to holdings, whatever can be kept by sword and armor: booty seized or paid for, the pleasures of a whore and not a companion. The Crusader man's trip to the Land is just a visit. He "sees" everything he has to in a matter of days before becoming the landlord and lording it *over* the land—laying the land without grasping the lay of it. By cutting off the tops of mountains, the Crusader man cuts himself off from the source of wisdom she can provide, the knowledge needed to build a home. Far from being a passive object, the land as subject absorbs the architect's intent and reacts accordingly. Recalling the Crusader man's insult, she stores up the scars inflicted upon her.

The figure of the Crusader man pours salt on very old as well as newer wounds, recalling allusions in the text of Adonis to the great Abbasid poet al-Ma'ari and his experience of the unspeakable atrocities committed by barbarian hordes as they overran the ancient cities of Syria and Palestine. In concluding *The Crusades Through Arab Eyes*, Amin Maalouf writes of the consequences of these campaigns:

> Although the epoch of the Crusades ignited a genuine economic and cultural revolution in Western Europe, in the Orient these holy wars led to long centuries of decadence and obscurantism. Assaulted from all quarters, the Muslim world turned in on itself. It became over-sensitive, defensive, intolerant, sterile—attitudes that grew steadily worse as world-wide evolution, a process from which the Muslim world felt excluded, continued. . . . The Arab world—simultaneously fascinated and terrified by the Franj, whom they encountered as barbarians and defeated, but who subsequently managed to dominate the earth—cannot bring itself to consider the Crusades a mere episode in the bygone past. . . . There can be no doubt that the schism between these two worlds dates from the Crusades, deeply felt by the Arabs, even today, as an act of rape.[193]

IX. Jerusalem: The Islamic City

Fulfilling almost every imaginable cliché of the city as palimpsest, one embedded layer of Jerusalem has been further and further marginalized in a discourse within which gratuitous tourism—the search for or affirmation of an often vague, amorphous, or negatively defined ethnic identity—has replaced the ritual of pilgrimage. Despite the short shrift given Muslims by the *Blue Guide*, during the 1,310-year period dating from the Arab conquest in 638 until 1948, there were only 129 years in which Jerusalem was *not* under one form or another of Islamic sovereignty. While this is not to suggest that such sovereignty was in any way uniform, ideal, or free from the practice of various kinds of occupation or exploitation, it can sketch a context in which the city and its inhabitants acted and expressed themselves using a vernacular idiom of preindustrial knowledge, the lingua franca of the old Levantine, Mediterranean, and Arab world. Implicit connections spanning this vernacular idiom's terms of currency can be sensed in two descriptions of the city, written almost a thousand years apart. The first is by the historian and geographer al-Muqadassi, a tenth-century native Jerusalemite:

> The buildings of the Holy City are of stone, and you will find nowhere finer or more solid construction. . . . The grapes are enormous, and there are no quinces equal to those of the Holy City. In Jerusalem are all manner of learned men and doctors, and for this reason the heart of every man of intelligence yearns towards her. All the year round, never are her streets empty of strangers. As to the saying that Jerusalem is the most illustrious of cities—is she not the one that unites the advantages of This World and those of the Next? As for the Holy City being the most productive of all places in good things, why, Allah—may He be exalted!—has gathered together here all the fruits of the lowlands, and of the plains, and of the hill country, even all those of the most opposite kinds: such as the orange and the almond, the date and the nut, the fig and the banana, besides milk in plenty, and honey and sugar.[194]

The second account, by the Palestinian writer Jabra Ibrahim Jabra, speaks of the city in the late 1930s and early 1940s from the other side of catastrophe, through memory, in a voice already shaded by the tone of commemoration:

> Do you know Jerusalem? I don't know whether it really has seven hills, but I have walked up and down all its hills, among its houses built of stone—white stone, pink stone, red stone—castle-like houses, rising high and low along the roads as they go up and down. You'd think they were jewels holding the mantle of the Lord . . . those long walks on Jaffa Street or in the labyrinth of rocks and olive trees that surrounded the city. Have you ever sat down on the red earth, under an old, knotted olive tree, surrounded by thorn bushes and a few anemones that fought their way out through the struggling thorns? Or by those little yellow flowers that our farmers called *hannun*? How beautiful the olive groves were in Talbiyya, Katamon and Musallaba! How beautiful was the valley that stretched all the way to Maliha! It was there that we left part of our lives as a gift, as a pledge that we would return.[195]

Jabra's piece, even though located within the selective parameters of memory (written, as it is, from the backward glance of exile), still manages to fully express what is most striking about both passages: the fluid exchange between organic and human creation, between the urban and the rural.

The finely constructed stone houses, the handcrafted jewels celebrating divinity, the learned people (implying the existence of libraries and schools), the constant traffic of pilgrims and visitors—all blend in unnoticeably with the vegetation of the lowlands, the plains, and the hill country; with the uncrafted labyrinth of rocks, the red earth, knotted olive trees, thorn bushes, and anemones. The diverse terrain and the varied crops delivered by each part of the land also seem to indicate, without explicitly stating it, that a delicate balance of agricultural technique and urban economy can yield true riches. Tracing the threads that bind such a social structure together confirms this sense:

> The Muslim city can be defined less as a willed, conscious, so to speak
> "programmed" social and physical entity than as a series of tensions
> between contradictory and at times downright incompatible poles,
> always subject to the variables of time and area. The city is commercial
> and artisanal, but much of its wealth derives from agriculture, and the
> physical separation between urban living and the cultivation of land is
> never very clear.[196]

Both terrain and architecture, repositories of the most cohesive lexicon of the lingua franca mentioned earlier, provide a means for illustrating how the Islamic context enriched and informed the age-old intent of "traditional" culture to create objects imbued with the aura of events.

The labyrinth of rocks and terraced olive trees described by Jabra as surrounding Jerusalem mime the concentric nature of the architectural layering that attempted to redefine certain sites without fully usurping them, most obviously the Temple Mount area where the Dome of the Rock now stands. This monument, initiated in 685 and completed in 692, set not only the visual but also the structural tone of the city as "a mosaic of religious, ethnic and linguistic communities within the unifying field of a broadly defined Islamic civilization: a civilization that drew its characteristic qualities as a social order from the overwhelmingly Muslim character of the population without restricting participation in that civilization to Muslims."[197] Yet this "overwhelmingly Muslim character" was itself a palimpsest and prism of the people, languages, texts, material culture, and places within which the faith was revealed and sought its new adherents. The Dome of the Rock clearly expresses the nature and needs of such a social order and the choices offered by it. The stunning vigor of the Prophet Muhammad's revelation is announced through the brilliant engineering of a building that squares the circle and hovers along the divide between earth and heaven, between the proposal for a new set of relations and a tribute to those already existing. At a time when Islam had little material proof to entice the more ancient and well-endowed civilizations it encountered, its new monuments were determined to impress, astound, and directly engage "the people of the Book," both Jews and Christians.

By situating itself where it did, the Dome of the Rock completely redefined the "memory of the qualitative space upon which all religious rites and orientation are based." This sense of qualitative space is particularly apt for the Dome of the Rock since "in Islamic architecture space is never divorced from form: it is not the materialization of abstract Euclidean space which then provides a frame into which things are 'placed.' Space is qualified by the forms that exist in it. A sacred center polarizes the spaces about it."[198] By incorporating the complex network of existing event and myth regarding the sacred center of its own location (Mount Moriah as the earth's navel and place of Adam's creation and death; the rock where Abraham brought Isaac to be sacrificed; the area of the temple of Solomon and the Holy of Holies; the spot from which Muhammad ascended to heaven), the Dome shares the characteristics of a mode called "building the site." In this method,

> the specific culture of the region—that is to say, its history in both a geological and agricultural sense—becomes inscribed into the form and realization of the work. This inscription, which arises out of "in-laying" the building into the site, has many levels of significance, for it has a capacity to embody, in built form, the prehistory of the place, its archaeological past and its subsequent cultivation and transformation across time. Through this layering into the site the idiosyncracies of place find their expression without falling into sentimentality.[199]

Just how successful the Dome of the Rock has been in "polarizing space" and maintaining the "aura" of a complex occasion of events transformed across time can be seen through its present situation. Surrounded by sprawling modern suburban settlements crisscrossed by highways, the Dome is now witness to a radical transformation of a once familiar structure and economy of relations. Although threatened by the possibility of being "symbolized" out of actual time and place, hijacked into the sterile realm of ideological imagery and swamped by the scale of a new order (not to mention being blown up by new soldiers of faith bent on inducing a preview of the apocalypse), the Dome seems to have remained impervious to the kind of reductive reproduction that would deprive it of its "integrity and otherness." Edward Said comments on a telephoto shot in which the Dome is seen through a compressed foreground of minarets and TV antennas against a background of trees and white gravestones lined along the Mount of Olives:

All across the Arab world there is a mixture of cultural styles that characterizes rapid development: Modern Western modes of dress, activity, and architecture are superimposed on traditional settings and ways of being. The commonest symbol of this is to be found in the typical photographs of an old city across which is laid a grid of radio and television antennae. What we get is a site of intensity that makes reference to two traditions, one native, the other foreign or Western, held in a kind of awkward check by each other. You are left to compute the various gains and losses resulting from this kind of balance, and you are also led to think of two worlds in sustained tension. A more just representation of how the mixture of elements actually occurs and is experienced in modern Arab life is found, I think, in photographs of traditional sites whose undeniable centrality stands out, and draws in, by subordinating, the intruding symbols of metropolitan modernity. This is the slower way everyone absorbs and reorients the new according to the still redoubtable force of the old and habitual.[200]

More than "drawing in" and "subordinating," the ability to look back in return with the ironic gaze of allegory lends the Dome an "aura" in the precise way defined by Walter Benjamin:

Experience of the aura rests on the transposition of a response common in human relationships to the relationship between the inanimate or natural object and man. To perceive the aura of an object we look at means to invest it with the ability to look at us in return. . . . The uniqueness of a work of art is inseparable from its being embedded in the fabric of tradition. This tradition is itself thoroughly alive and extremely changeable. That which withers in the age of mechanical reproduction is the aura of a work of art . . . the technique of reproduction detaches the reproduced object from the domain of tradition.[201]

X. Turning the Page: Back to Damascus

The inscription of time within a site marks a spot that is not necessarily a "progression" but is certainly a fact: Islam comes after and evolves out of the earlier texts and prophecies of "the people of the Book" and in so doing redefines them. Its social order and the variety of writing produced within it occupy a large block of time, even though the interstices and nuances of that duration have largely collapsed into even larger, but more amorphous and safely uncontradictory categories. As Ilan Halevi writes: "There must be a way out of this sad history. A way of neither remaining prisoners of its sad parameters, nor remaining entranced by the turn of phrases, the echo of visions, the texture of the paper. The page must be turned."[202] The turning of the page, the further mark that another newer social order has superimposed over its predecessor, the definition and location of the "cleavage" that will initiate another "collective duration": this sort of change relies very much on the generosity of interpretations, and the help art and imagination can provide in piercing the "sad parameters" of unchecked assumptions. As John Cage has remarked, "the function of art at the present time is to preserve it from all the logical minimalizations that we are at each instant tempted to apply to the flux of events. To draw us nearer to the process which is the world we live in."

The old Mediterranean world, the prism of the Levant, is still in the process of finding the right angle through which the rays of its own light can be refracted. Although the cities may remain parenthetical (bracketed off in expectation of either perfect time and the final correspondence of words and things, or the aftermath of global disaster), they are inhabited, and the people within—conditioned by what they and their cities have gone through—exert unyielding pressure on the remaining and "unrelieved" traces. The once qualitative space that is the site of a riddle circumscribing two ancient peoples is now as densely crowded with claims and counterclaims as Cairo, the city that "escapes us." It is as filled with rough-edged shards (pieces of the puzzle) as Beirut is with rubble ("The most interesting things in Beirut are the absent ones. . . . The absence of an opera house, of a football field, of a bridge, of a subway, and, I was going to say, of the people and of the government. And, of course, the absence of absence of garbage").[203]

But a dream can lead away from mirages and out of the desert, to Damascus and the next part of the itinerary: Haim Vital, the renowned mystic who recorded the following, was born in Safed in 1542; in 1593 he was known to have been in Jerusalem, most likely staying there until his arrival in Damascus in 1598 where he remained until his death in 1620:

The   Muslim: A Dream

Friday   full moon in Adar 5355   a Sabbath evening   dreamt
that I was in Jerusalem. A Muslim with a brilliantly white cap came up
to me. He smiled. Salaamed. He placed a hand over my head & said in
a soft but audible voice "Rise up o God and scatter all thine enemies."
Then Rabbi Yakob Massod led me to the house of Rabbi Ashkenazi. He
rose for me bowed down & sat me at his right side. He took the Zohar
in his hand & told me "Let us study." There was a passage that he
couldn't understand but I explained it. It was a section of the *Zohar
Shemot* that tells about a man who danced for Rabbi Eleazar & so
showed him he would enter Paradise

In the dream I thought the Muslim was the prophet Elijah[204]

Chapter 2

A Garden Enclosed: The Geography of Time

> When I was a small child, it seemed natural that people
> understood each other although they spoke different languages,
> and were called by different names—Greek, Moslem, Syrian,
> Jewish, Christian, Arab, Italian, Tunisian, Armenian.
>
> Jacqueline Kahanoff

> To see the Mediterranean again, listen to the lesson of the sea
> which keeps forever its salt and its color.
>
> Edmond Jabès

I. Traveling through Glass Walls: Defining the Levant

Sometime around 1160, Benjamin of Tudela set out from his native city
on a journey that would take some thirteen years. His itinerary covered
most of the known world and included stops in several hundred cities in
Europe, Asia, and Africa. He described the Great Mosque of Damascus:

> Here is a wall of crystal glass of magic workmanship, with apertures
> according to the days of the year, and as the sun's rays enter each of
> them in daily succession the hours of the day can be told by a graduated
> dial. In the palace are chambers built of gold and glass, and if people
> walk around the wall they are able to see one another, although the wall
> is between them.[1]

Not everyone, of course, lived in palaces with chambers of gold and
glass. Yet what Benjamin saw—and the way he described it—is precisely
the figure that Jacqueline Kahanoff chose to convey her sense of the Levant as "a prism whose various facets are joined by the sharp edge of differences, but each of which, according to its position in a time-space continuum, reflects or refracts light."[2] The image of people walking around
walls through which they can still see one another remains a most fitting
metaphor for the way the many heterogeneous communities of the preindustrial Levant both knew about and related to each other. For Jews,
the poetics of this knowledge certainly lasted as long as the communities
did: that is, until the middle of the twentieth century. This is generally
true, even despite the deeper schisms and changing power relations lead-

ing to the dissolution and displacement of those communities that had begun with modernity proper, at the French Revolution. The poetics of this knowledge, though, takes into account not just the possibility of seeing through the walls and into the chambers but the facility of accurately calibrating the effects and nuances of the play of light through the apertures.

Marking the start, however, of the effective lifespan of the transparent walls/prism metaphor, as representing this Levantine heterogeneity, is more problematic than declaring its demise, given that more than the fact of physical presence is in question. After all, fully autonomous Jewish communities flourished throughout the Mediterranean and Near East since the Babylonian exile in 586 B.C. (under the aegis of Mesopotamian, Greek, Carthaginian, Roman, Persian, and Byzantine rule). This was long before the great "bourgeois revolution" that made such a journey as Benjamin of Tudela's not only possible but commonplace, before the enormous expansion and "internationalization of space" brought on through "the trading civilization established by Islam between the ninth and eleventh centuries."[3] Nor were the sharp-edged differences, the various facets refracted by Jews through the very "distinctive epicentre" of and from the Mediterranean Levant all the way back to southern Arabia, a negligible factor by any means in the earlier formation and subsequent unfolding of the new religion itself. Wasn't Mashallah, for example, an eighth-century Jewish engineer, astronomer, and heir to Hellenic traditions, one of the choice few picked to determine the optimal location to lay out *Madinat-as-Salaam*, the utopian project better known as Baghdad? This project, and the city that emerged from it, would decisively mark the Islamic ascendancy over and transformation of the rich and varied cultures and civilizations it encountered. Like the earlier construction of the Dome of the Rock inscribing the "older" peoples of the Book within a new religious/textual order, "the new city was intended to begin a *novus ordo saeculorum* or, as the 'Abbasids called it, a 'turning' (*dawlah*), in Islam," which would, from then on, "pursue its course as a universalist religion with Baghdad as its symbolic Constantinople."

Although symbolically linked to Constantinople,

> intellectually, commercially and circumstantially, Baghdad inherited within the *Dar al-Islam* the role played by Alexandria in the old Hellenic *oikoumene*. Turbulent, cosmopolitan, invincibly successful, given more to scholarship and trade than to piety, the unrivaled center of arts and letters and the seat of the secular and religious power in Islam, Baghdad had, like its Egyptian counterpart, no past. Its present was frequently unruly, since rich and poor, Arab, Iranian and Turk, Shi'ite and

traditionalist, Christian and Jew, scholar, merchant and soldier rubbed shoulders within its walls.[4]

The fact that the city had "no past" helped to emphasize and guarantee a sense of perpetual contemporaneity. This manifested itself most dramatically through the almost unprecedented extent of linguistic adoption and adaption of, within, and through Arabic. Many of the most innovative *users* of Arabic—those who indelibly marked the language from within—came from other cultural and linguistic backgrounds, particularly the Persian, such as the poet Abu Nuwas (d. 810) and the philosopher Ibn Sina (980-1037), to give only two of the most striking examples. The spread of Arabic as the prestige language of science, philosophy, and literature—without necessarily being linked to anything particularly Islamic—also extended to the far West. As early as 854, Alvarus, the bishop of Cordoba, "lamented the transforming effects of that cultural prestige":

> Our Christian young men, with their elegant airs and fluent speech, are showy in their dress and carriage, and are famed for the learning of the gentiles; intoxicated with Arab eloquence they greedily handle, eagerly devour and zealously discuss the books of the Chaldeans [i.e., Muhammadans] and make them known by praising them with every flourish of rhetoric, knowing nothing of the beauty of the Church's literature, and looking with contempt on the streams of the Church that flow forth from Paradise; alas! the Christians are so ignorant of their own law, the Latins pay so little attention to their own language, that in the whole of the Christian flock there is hardly one man in a thousand who can write a letter to inquire after a friend's health intelligibly, while you may find countless rabble of all kinds of them who can learnedly roll out the grandiloquent periods of the Chaldean tongue. They can even make poems, every line ending with the same letter, which display high flights of beauty and more skill in handling meter than the gentiles themselves possess.[5]

In Baghdad itself, the remarkably heterogenous crowds of the city were only matched by the crowds of imported texts. The open book of translation served as a screen through which the regenerative field of raw materials could be sifted to form the basis for an Arabic renaissance, whose accumulation of knowledge irrevocably shifted to Europe only after the fall of Baghdad. Both the Umayyad (656-750) and the Abbasid (750-1258) courts not only encouraged and patronized translation but established schools to carry out the systematic transference of texts from Greek, Persian, Syriac, and the Hindu languages into Arabic. The influx of so many new and conflicting ideas made Baghdad, particularly under the leadership of al-Mansur (founder of the city), Harun al-Rashid, and al-Mamun, a place of intense speculation, bewilderment, and innovation. During the reign of al-Mamun (813-833), for example, Christian and Jewish scholars were invited, housed, and supported, so that they could devote themselves to the translation of hundreds of Greek manuscripts acquired from the Byzantine Emperor Leon of Armenia. Not only did mathematics, mechanics, astronomy, geography, and logic enter the field of discourse, but so did Hippocratic and Neoplatonic texts and doctrines, Zoroastrianism, Manichaeanism, Indian philosophy, and every possible form of Christian dogma as well, from different brands of orthodoxy to the Spanish school of adoptianism. Various sects (influenced by Philo, the Manichaeans, and diverse forms of gnosticism) also emerged among the Jews, and the switch from Aramaic to Arabic as a primary language proved decisive in fully involving the Jews in the revolution of thought, the wave of modernity that affected every aspect of life in the Islamic world from the eighth to the thirteenth century.[6] Menocal points out the symbiosis of the two cultures during this long period:

> The flourishing of Jewish culture went hand in hand with the heyday of Arabic, particularly secular Arabic, culture. In great measure, both cultural zeniths were due to the same liberalism and tolerance, and ultimately they would both be destroyed by the same intolerance. Averroës and Maimonides both wrote in Arabic because it was so dominantly the language of prestige, and though in the non-Arabic parts of Europe that received their work they might be distinguished as Muslim and Jew respectively, they were more often seen as bound together as Andalusians—as harbingers of new philosophical and intellectual currents, masters of the language and cultures of a world of myriad riches—than they were seen as divided by any religious doctrine. Both of their religions, in any case, were not Christian, and any further or more enlightened distinction than that was not characteristic or necessary. Both would be avidly and appreciatively read, used, and translated by Frederick II for the benefit of others and for the enlightenment of the rest of Europe.[7]

Simplistic approaches often see "Islam" as an all-embracing, pervasive, and conquering force subsuming everything in its vaguely imagined and frightening trail. Such generalities completely ignore the very complex phenomenon of the old meeting the new, a process that was both characteristic and pervasive as Islam negotiated an identity with and through its new constituents. The ensuing synthesis and relations developing from that encounter are of utmost importance in any accurate assessment of life within Islamic society, particularly the lives of "minorities." To fully weigh and register the precise give and take, the social, economic, psychological, and aesthetic push and pull exerted by the particular peoples, communities, religions, and sects incorporated within the new structure is an enormous and complex undertaking. As the art historian Oleg Grabar has emphasized, "If a Muslim writer like Muqaddasi could still in the tenth century complain that Jews and Christians had the upper hand in Jerusalem, it is likely indeed that by that time many cities of the Islamic Near East, not to speak of the countryside, had a strong, if not always predominant, non-Muslim population whose degree of cultural Islamization is as difficult to assess as it is essential to know."[8]

A glimpse of the depth and intricacy of these relations can be caught in a section of Benjamin's account of Baghdad, where even the Caliph himself seems a newcomer in the presence of the Jewish Exilarch, the *resh galutha*, head of the Gaonic Academy and rightful heir to the crown of David:

> And every fifth day when he goes to pay a visit to the great Caliph, horsemen, Gentiles as well as Jews, escort him, and heralds proclaim in advance, "Make way before our Lord, the son of David, as is due unto him," the Arabic words being "Amilu tarik la Saidna ben Daud." He is mounted on a horse, and is attired in robes of silk and embroidery with a large turban on his head, and from the turban is suspended a long white cloth adorned with a chain upon which the cipher of Mohammed is engraved. Then he appears before the Caliph and kisses his hand, and the Caliph rises and places him on a throne which Mohammed had ordered to be made for him, and all the Mohammedan princes who attend the court of the Caliph rise up before him. And the Head of the Captivity is seated on his throne opposite to the Caliph, in compliance with the command of Mohammed to give effect to what is written in the law—"The sceptre shall not depart from Judah nor a law-giver from between his feet, until he come to Shiloh: and to him shall the gathering of the people be."[9]

The precisely planned city in which this scene took place was meant to fully incorporate the dense texture of a crowded palimpsest, the whole spectrum of light diffused by the Levantine prism. Instead, "as Alexandria turned its back to Egypt and looked out on the Mediterranean, Baghdad faced the East."[10] This eastward entrenchment was not a choice but a necessity, marking one limit point of an expansive new radius stretching through Persia and Central Asia all the way to China. The sea route negotiating this space, from the Persian Gulf to Canton, was, as George Hourani points out, "the longest in regular use by mankind before the European expansion in the sixteenth century."[11] The importance of this opening to the East has often been overlooked, but Janet Abu-Lughod has described its scope:

> One hundred years after the establishment of Baghdad as the capital of the Islamic empire, a remarkable document was written that detailed the extent to which Arab and Persian sailors, exiting the Gulf, had become "at home" in the Arabian Sea, the Indian Ocean, and even the South China Sea. The descriptions of the voyage and the ports of call leave no doubt that by 851, when Suleyman the merchant wrote his account (to which Abu-Zayd al-Sirafi put the finishing touches a century later), the trade path between the Persian Gulf and China—via the Malabar coast of India, Ceylon, the Nicobar Islands, Kalah on the Malay Peninsula, the Strait of Malacca, past Cambodia and Vietnam to Canton—was already well established and of great interest to Arabic readers.[12]

Baghdad's repositioning embodies another much more easily upset and potentially cataclysmic aspect of that delicate balance between the urban and the rural described earlier as characterizing the material and aesthetic economy of the Islamic city. This aspect consists of the relations between a regional center of administration, wealth, and bureaucracy—the seat of power—and the diverse but unwillingly socialized tribes and peoples producing the food in the lands surrounding and lying beyond the city. This social phenomenon encompasses and goes far beyond the Islamic city. In *The Republic of Cousins*, Germaine Tillion describes this relation:

> Until Pasteur, in fact, town-country relations can be represented in the shape of a two-way current. The numerically larger stream flows inexorably but silently from the countryside to the town. No organized, conspicuous human masses (or at least only rarely), but the continuous arrival of isolated individuals: adult individuals, in other words, people bearing a heavy burden of convictions. So in each generation these convictions are revitalized by new contributions, thanks to the immigrants. The other current flows in the opposite direction—from the town to the fields and grasslands—bearing conspicuous objects: books, fashions, ideas. It is registered in directories and catalogues, and thus leaves historical traces that will provide a feast for compilers, but it has neither strength nor depth, because very few men accompany it. Those who do, moreover, are transient officials: merchants, travellers, soldiers. Only the bearers of religious faith constitute an exception and settle. For thousands of years a rough balance ensured the survival of the two currents, the "city" prospering thanks to the surplus of men surreptitiously drained off to it from steppe and hamlet. From time to time, a bigger wave swept through at ground level (which is the level of

history) and ravaged the town: such a wave was called "the end of a civilization."[13]

Baghdad itself witnessed just such a bigger wave—in the form of the thirteenth-century Mongol invasions—which certainly signaled the end of a certain kind of civilization. Harking back to this period, for Muslims and Arabs, has never meant reveling in the power wielded over submissive infidels, as common Western imagery would have it. It meant, rather, the acknowledgment that an openness and fluidity spanning a large part of the globe had been achieved and sustained for a significant period, despite conflicts, wars, and natural disasters. What characterized the practice of later European expansion, from the colonization of the New World to the later colonization of parts of the Old World, seemed held in abeyance; as Abu-Lughod emphasizes:

> In the earlier system, although there were certainly rivalries and no small amount of interregional conflict, the overall pattern of trade involved a large number of players whose power was relatively equal. No single participant in the thirteenth- and early fourteenth-century world system dominated the whole, and most participants (with the possible exception of the Mongols), benefited from coexistence and mutual tolerance. Individual rulers did jealously seek to control the terms of trade and the "foreign traders" in their own ports and inland centers, but the ambition to dominate the entire system seemed beyond their needs and aspirations (and probably capacities). The change in the "rules of the game" introduced by the European newcomers in the sixteenth century, therefore, caught the older players off guard.[14]

Naturally, as trade flourished, so did cultural production and exchange. It is no accident that the move from a monastic culture to the urban university-centered culture that fostered the height of interaction between Muslims, Christians, and Jews in Europe (during the reign of Alfonso El Sabio X, when at Salamanca and Seville astrolabes, celestial globes, armillary spheres, clocks, and quadrants were universal signs that could be understood in Hebrew, Arabic, or Latin) exactly coincides with Baghdad's demise.

Yet the earlier crowds of Baghdad can, in some sense, be said to have contained the elements leading to its dissolution. The carnivallike diversity of those crowds—like the early entrenchment toward the eastern front—also originated in necessity, not choice:

> In the great metropolises of Africa and Asia, where climate and overcrowding continually incubate the most deadly diseases, the extermination of children was more radical than anywhere else. From the moment of their foundation, the huge mortality of the ancient cities

obliged them constantly to attract numerous adults within their walls: only thus could they avoid disappearing for lack of inhabitants, and by remaining populous, remain also strong and wealthy. In the old countries of Europe, Africa and Asia, the adults in question necessarily came from the neighboring country tribes.[15]

Without relying exclusively on this theory of movement as applicable to all cases at all times, it does present a dynamic within which the position of Jews in "the republic of cousins," the Mediterranean Levant, can be reassessed. Even the movement of scholars and translators (and their roles in the rise and fall of cultural centers) can be seen in terms of the many continuing waves of migrant workers, skilled and unskilled, making their way from one end of the Islamic world to the other. Despite some agricultural activity and settlement (most notably in Mesopotamia, Palestine, Islamic Spain, the Atlas Mountains, and Central Asia) following the "great bourgeois revolution" of the ninth century, the majority of Jews were undoubtedly what Isaac Abravanel termed "not the builders of great cities, but the dwellers of them."[16] As such, like a number of other non-Muslim minorities such as Greek and Armenian Christians, they assumed a tremendous role as conduits between town and country. This, coupled with the fact that Jews maintained an extraterritorial legal status, often put them in a precarious position at the service or under the protection of unstable power structures. At the same time, these powers were themselves constantly struggling to deflect and assimilate the tensions and conflicts arising from what Tillion has called "the absurd maintenance of rural ideas within city walls,"[17] brought about precisely through the population movement she describes.

But this "absurd maintenance" included, to be sure, the legitimate complaints of overtaxed peasants or the perceived injustice felt by their newly urbanized descendants unwilling to support the extravagant whims of an often decadent and unproductive urban elite. Nor did these claims find their victims only among the minorities, as much modern ethnocentric history would have us believe. Wealth, status, and class played roles as decisive—if not more so—as faith, race, and tribal or ethnic allegiance. This is eloquently attested to not only in the merchant's letters of the Cairo *geniza* (dating from the tenth century to the thirteenth, the classical period of Mediterranean Arab culture), but through many other accounts up until the modern period.

In their roles as inhabitants of cities and travelers between them— whether as artisanal workers, scholars, medical professionals, traders, or administrators—Jews maintained certain positions and roles remarkably intact within the Levantine and Arab world until the colonial and nationalist period. A very precise (and late) sense of this can be gotten from the following passage by Mordechai HaKohen (d. 1929), a Libyan Jew whose *Book of Mordekhai* covers every aspect of Jewish life in Libya and among the Berbers with an interpretive scope and methodological precision worthy of the best in modern anthropology:

> Merchandise is brought from Tripoli on the backs of camels: pepper, cumin, coriander seeds, ginger, sweet calamus, and all sorts of spices — honey, sugar, tea, coffee and tobacco; the flower of the rose, the flower of the myrtle, spikenard, saffron, cassia, and cinnamon; buds of perfume, powders, pure frankincense, and women's cosmetics — antimony powder to darken their eyes, the bark of nut trees to paint their lips like a scarlet thread, henna plants to redden their arms and legs; mirrors, hair combs, glass and coral beads, matches, threads, and needles; and other kinds of merchandise too numerous to mention.
> All the Jews are tradespeople who scatter throughout the region with sacks on their shoulders, or on their donkeys, to sell their merchandise to the Berbers and the Arabs in exchange for grain, olives, olive oil, figs, butter, sheep's wool, goat's hair, silver, eggs and so forth.[18]

This figure of the wandering merchant, although in some sense almost a caricature of a certain kind of Jew, shall be encountered again, in the next chapter, fictionalized (in a novella by Yehuda Burla) just at the point when the social fabric still lending credence and meaning to that role was disintegrating. In HaKohen's account, though, the merchant — like those traveling intellectuals, the doctors and teachers — still embraces the full range of a role introduced and institutionalized many, many centuries before. But entirely unlike the confinement of Jews to certain professions in Christian Europe, this role — and its persistence — was not a boundary or limit point. As only one possibility among many, it serves as testament to the very different set of circumstances out of which the cultural fabric of Levantine and Arab Jewry is woven. This set of circumstances can be summarized by the following four concepts, each of which can be derived to a greater or lesser extent from as late and apparently marginal a description as HaKohen's: autonomy, translatability, diversity, and mobility.

As indicated by HaKohen, travel by Jewish merchants from Tripoli to the outlying Berber and Arab settlements throughout the region was commonplace. The land itself, however, was characterized in the following less-than-inviting terms:

> The traveler on those paths can easily make a fateful stumble if he does not pay attention to these dangers; his legs will take him to his death. The outsider who climbs up the mountains will become weary of the

difficult traps that his feet encounter. He will feel that he is marching in a wild land, and his legs are taking him into hell. But the inhabitants of the region skip barefoot through the mountains and skip over the hills with heavy loads on their shoulders.[19]

Yet, this "wild land" was clearly familiar to the itinerant Jews and it would stand to reason that such travel assumed the legal/communal autonomy motivated and supported by the social structure. In addition, and perhaps even more significantly, such free travel would assume the confidence born of nativity within that sphere itself. As Goldberg points out, the distribution of goods as well as the role of the merchant entail much more than simple exchange: "In distributing goods throughout the region, the Jew was a cultural merchant as well. Former peddlers have told me that when they came to a village and stayed at the home of a *ma'aruf*, or village sheikh, they would be expected to provide entertainment by telling stories. Presumably they also spread news and ideas."[20] Such activity must assume some of the many senses of translatability, through the introduction of new products as well as the inevitable bearing of messages transformed to fit the needs and expectations of each audience encountered. In addition, the barter of imported goods for raw materials (silver, wool, goat's hair, and most probably leather), all certainly destined to serve the artisan in making jewelry, religious objects (*mezzuzoth*, *kiddush* cups, adornments for the Torah scrolls), carpets, footwear, and other handicrafts, marks another occurrence of translation on the nonlinguistic plane. Finally, the enormous diversity of merchandise limns an astonishingly extensive transactional and physical network that produced and relied on an intricate, well-established, but extremely fluid communications system. It is this geographical range that brings us full circle, back to the time and space of Benjamin's journey and the conditions within which these characteristic modes took root and grew. It is here—before going on to locate the effective beginning of the transparent walls / prism metaphor in a more precise and specific way (as a means of connecting, as Jacqueline Kahanoff wrote, "the sharp edges of difference")—that a brief survey of the classical Arab Mediterranean, the *geniza* world, is needed.

II. S. D. Goitein and the *Geniza* World

In Hebrew the word *geniza* simply means "storage" or "hiding place" and refers to that part of the synagogue where old writings are kept. The term, however, has almost become synonymous with the Cairo *geniza* where, at the turn of the century, several hundred thousand Hebrew and

Arabic texts first became known to Western scholars. Many apocryphal stories surround the remarkable "discovery" of this treasure house, located in a windowless room in the attic of the ancient synagogue of Fustat/Old Cairo. While most of the credit has gone to Solomon Schechter, the scholar who traveled to Cairo in 1896 after receiving some fragments purchased as mementos by two Cambridge residents, the *geniza* was certainly known as early as 1750 (mentioned—and possibly used—by Mediterranean rabbinical authorities),[21] and most probably remained in continuous living use since its establishment in the tenth century. Again, we seem to have a case in which only the European can legitimize and validate knowledge. The very idea that the "natives" might have used this material seems so patently absurd as to appear unthinkable, reducing the possible space of discourse to that inhabited by ideologically sanctioned authorities.

Notwithstanding, unlike Rabbi Wertheimer of Jerusalem, David Kaufmann of Budapest, and Elkan Adler of London, Schechter showed little interest in the *geniza* material until realizing that one of the pieces of parchment he received was an original fragment of the Hebrew text of Ecclesiasticus, *The Book of Wisdom* by Ben Sira, written around 200 B.C. Regardless of the sequence of revelation, and even given the favorable climatic conditions, the preservation of the hundreds of thousands of extant fragments still remains somewhat of a miracle. Yet, for anyone who has visited the synagogue, now utterly desolate, this miracle might not seem entirely unlikely. Like so many facets of Levantine and Arab Jewish life, the synagogue has fallen prey to the exorbitant and often grotesque discrepancies of the drastically altered cultural and political economy in which it now finds itself. The lone attendant—left with neither community nor quorum—mutters in an ambivalent amalgam of despair and rage, clutching twenty-five-year-old Israeli postcards and demanding that foreign visitors explicate them in a mix of Arabic, Hebrew, French, Ladino, Italian, and English. At the same time, distant Jewish communities invest to restore the interior and turn the synagogue into a tourist attraction. Outside, in one of the poorest, most neglected sections of the city, children, Coptic monks, and potters emerging from their subterranean workshops in the shadows of the Moqqatam hills crowd the unpaved streets filled with donkeys, horses, and roosters. Within this web of circumstance and relation, an almost awesome aura conducive to the miraculous, and commensurate to the history of the site, still seems to permeate the place. It is close to the Nile; legend has it that Moses knew the place, that the temple of the prophet Jeremiah stood on the same site, that Joseph and the holy family went into hiding and worshipped there, followed by the apostles Mark and Peter. In the twelfth century, the great poet and commentator Abraham Ibn Ezra came from Jerusalem to inaugurate the reopening, while Benjamin of Tudela noted that the scroll penned by Ezra the Scribe could be found within. But more than a museum, a place of pilgrimage for "great men" or a site of "great events," the true value of the Cairo *geniza* lies precisely in the full spectrum of light the fragments found there cast on the life of common people, on a time and spirit quite remote from ours.

The major work (monumental would be more accurate) of reconstructing this lost world (a reconstruction based mostly on the thousands of personal letters and business accounts of Jewish merchants that formed part of the *geniza* treasure) was undertaken by the great scholar S. D. Goitein, and found its full articulation in the five-volume work *A Mediterranean Society*, the writing of which occupied the greater part of his working life. Like Gershom Scholem, Goitein was a German Jew who decided, early on, to venture into Palestine. In *From Berlin to Jerusalem: Memories of My Youth*, Scholem wrote of his journey with Goitein:

> With a very knowledgeable, somewhat younger member of the Frankfurt circle I arranged a joint passage from Trieste for after I had put my affairs in Berlin in order. That was Fritz (Shlomo Dov) Goitein, the scion of a famous Moravian-Hungarian family of rabbis; I had stayed with him on my earlier visits to Frankfurt and got along with him very well. He had had an excellent Jewish education—his father had been a rural rabbi in a Lower Franconian district—and had just taken his doctorate under the direction of Josef Horovitz, a first-rate Arabist. Goitein was a rare blend, for he was a person with an artistic, even poetic, vein who was at the same time a scholar and a born schoolmaster. This was immediately recognized by Dr. Biram, the director of the Haifa secondary school, when he came to Germany in the summer of 1922 in order to recruit qualified teachers for his school. He gave Goitein a firm contract for the fall of 1923, by which time he would have received his doctorate.[22]

There is general agreement on the fact that Scholem's work repositioned and thoroughly revolutionized the whole dynamic of Jewish history and interpretation. It has also served as a fundamental source in the new Jewish "humanist" textual tradition alluded to earlier. Yet there can be little doubt that Goitein's work—perhaps less alluring and dramatic, but no less poetic or methodologically rigorous—is now of greater cultural and political pertinence. The great sensitivity Goitein's work shows to the range of human and cultural interaction between Jews and Arabs in the Levant makes it a fertile, resilient, and antithetical point of reference in face of the unchecked assumptions and "logical minimalizations" that everywhere circumscribe the present scene.

In reading Goitein one suspects that in addition to being a scholarly endeavor, his work paid secret and tender homage to the many Levantine and Arab Jews that he encountered, people forming the last intact generation of a disappearing world whose formation he traced so meticulously in fragments of parchment buried in libraries from Leningrad and Cambridge to New York. Historical parallels are often drawn as he recounts experiences or incidents that seem paradigmatic, valuable as evidence of attitudes or ways of doing things that become fully intelligible only through seeing them in a living context. Receipts, for example, indicating expenses for garbage removal in Fatimid Cairo, along with his own recollection of the system of street-cleaning in mandatory Palestine, serve as two pieces of a puzzle that, completed, describes a whole system of medieval municipal services. In another instance, when analyzing the function of the synagogue, he tells this story:

> I recall vividly a visit to the mosque in Bursa, Turkey, some time before the sunset prayer, when I observed ordinary people from the neighborhood listening to an exposition of a sacred text, occasionally addressing the reader with a remark or question. A few days before I had been present in a small synagogue in Jerusalem between the afternoon and evening prayer, where Yemenites, mostly craftsmen, recited the Mishna in unison, thus concluding, or interrupting their day's work. In both cases, I was struck by the impression that for these people the House of God was theirs, it was the meeting place of the community.[23]

Again, in trying to determine which classes of people received full training in calligraphy, he tells of an encounter with a craftsman, also Yemenite, who had put him "to shame more than once with his knowledge of Jewish ritual law and cabala,"[24] but did not know how to write. Even more significant, though, than the numerous single instances of such clues and fine distinctions is the sum of the three major experiences Goitein found most directly applicable to deciphering, reconstructing, and interpreting the *geniza* documents. These include the years he spent in America, far from the "authoritarian Germany" of his youth, and "Jewish society in Palestine and later Israel, with its socialist, welfare and protectionist tendencies," both "utterly different from Geniza society, which was loosely organized and competitive in every respect." It also includes his work in the Oriental Jewish educational system during the mandatory period in Palestine and, finally, the many years of ethnolinguistic research he carried out among the Yemenites, "those most Jewish and most Arab of all Jews."[25] Throughout his work, whether implicitly or explicitly, he draws from each of these realms.

The Mediterranean of the *geniza* world comprised just the inner, entirely familiar region of a realm that casually stretched to the Indian Ocean before reaching only a little more cautiously to the ends of the silk route in Central Asia and China. Although readily identifiable barriers and divisions (the Muslim east and west, the *mashraq* and the *maghreb*; *al-rum*, the land of the "Romans"), as well as labels (the *franj*) existed, they were not an indication of lack of contact or unbreachable national boundaries. Just as the Arabs constituted an integral part of Europe during this period, Europeans appear frequently and everywhere, before, during, and after the Crusades. While the Genoese conquered the coastal cities of Caesarea, Acre, Tripoli, and Beirut, their compatriots were busy moving goods through the markets of Old Cairo or shipping and receiving in Alexandria. As Janet Abu-Lughod points out:

> Neither the violence of the Crusades nor the repeated Papal injunction enjoining Europeans from trading with Muslims could interfere with the prosperous trade that in the twelfth and thirteenth centuries traversed the middle route. A deeply symbiotic relationship had developed over the years between the Christian merchants of the Crusader kingdoms and the Muslim merchants who brought them goods from the orient beyond.[26]

One of the most striking aspects of the *geniza* world is the extent to which people, goods, and ideas continued to travel freely over a vast and incredibly diverse geographical area, despite political conflicts, wars, civil wars, invasions, unstable or tyrannical rulers, natural disasters, epidemics, and any and all other possible obstacles, whether human or divine. This sense of passage is reflected in both elite and popular culture:

> Living in the Christian society of medieval Europe did not predicate that one would find silk or sherbet distasteful or Arabic songs not worth listening to. Frederick II's position as one of the leading campaigners in the crusades did not deter his unabashed adoption of Arabic culture, from clothes to harem to intellectual traditions and other cultural patterns. His example is flamboyant and spectacular, but in many essential features it is representative. One of the things that must have driven the church authorities mad was the well-documented fact that so many crusaders, both in Europe itself and in Palestine, were culturally converted.[27]

As far as daily life among Jews and Muslims is concerned, the following letter, from around 1070, is fairly typical. Written during a civil war, and sent from Sicily by a native of the Tunisian port of Sfax to his partner in Egypt, it simply describes business as usual—except that the main carriers of goods and cash were Muslims, since the wealthier Jewish merchants had already taken the precaution of fleeing the city. After meticulously listing and describing all the goods that were sent out, along with a few business requests, the writer asks his partner to find him "a flame-colored robe, which should be short and well fitting, of fine, not coarse, material; I would like to wear it first on the Day of Atonement. Likewise, a turban of fine linen, which should be short and of pleasant, not coarse, material. Send with this some odorous wood, flasks of camphor and perfume. . . ."[28]

Another letter from the same period, even though written in the midst of an invasion, still manages to put personal and business matters before anything else. Only *after* inquiring about his friend's eye disease, describing how other duties had forced him to suspend work on some rabbinical texts, delineating a fine legal point of Hay Gaon's, elaborating on an inheritance case involving a local Muslim judge, and lauding the revival of study in Egypt, does the writer mention the chaotic state of things: "You inquired, my lord, about Sicily. The situation deteriorates constantly, and everyone is truly disturbed about the progress of the enemy who has already conquered most of the island. The prices here [in Tunisia] go up, for this place must rely for its supply of grain entirely on Sicily. Twelve families of our co-religionists have been taken captive, and countless numbers of Muslims. . . . "[29]

Both of these letters reveal another striking aspect of *geniza* society: the assumed familiarity of Muslims and Jews, and lack of either animosity or barriers between them as such, something that usually extended to Christians as well and, for those in the India trade, to close Hindu and Abyssinian friends and business relations, usually referred to as "brothers." Sentiments such as the following (from the eleventh century) are not uncommon: "I have another wish, my lord. Should a caravan set out in which trustworthy Muslims, who have given you sureties, will travel, let the merchandise of my brothers be sent with them as if it was yours."[30] In fact, seclusion in the *geniza* world—when and where it existed—was often initiated by the minorities and not by the Muslim majority. Jewish as well as Christian women, for example, "disliked sharing houses with Muslims" since custom or restrictions regarding the veil might apply to them as well. Because of this, Jewish authorities occasionally initiated statutes prohibiting the sale or lease of parts of houses to Muslims.[31] On the commercial level, however, partnerships between Muslims, Jews, and Christians in any and all combinations were not only common but completely normal and unrestricted in any sense. This fluidity extended into other areas as well:

As we know from Geniza documents coming from Fustat, Cairo, Alexandria, al-Mahalla and other places in Egypt, from Kairouan, Jerusalem, Damascus and Aleppo, Jewish houses often bordered on those of Muslims or Christians or both. There was no ghetto, but, on the contrary, much opportunity for daily intercourse. Neither was there an occupational ghetto. I have counted so far about 360 occupations of Jews, of which 240 entailed some type of manual work. There was constant cooperation between the various religious groups to the point of partnerships in business and even in workshops. In order to assess correctly the admissibility of the Geniza records for general sociological research, we have to free ourselves entirely from familiar notions about European Jews.[32]

It is only in light of such relations, and their deep-seated foundation, that later attitudes, such as those of Albert Antebbi and others like him, make sense. For such Levantines, political and economic parity between Arabs and Jews was not only natural, but an entirely unquestionable prerequisite for any possible Jewish endeavor in the Holy Land. Numerous examples illustrating such assumptions of familiarity and recognition can be drawn from all over this same Levantine geographic and conceptual space throughout and up until the late nineteenth and early twentieth century. The contemporary Palestinian writer Ghassan Kanafani, for example, in a narrative whose voice can only be the recollection of a previous generation, manages to convey some sense of this:

In Safad, even though there were four thousand Jews who had never, for one day, been farmers, no one minded. They'd lived in their small shops for a long time, selling their wares to the people, exchanging greetings with them and long conversations. They'd be invited to lunch and dinner. Because they'd been there for a long time, they knew how to speak Arabic. They were called by Arabic names and they read Arabic books and newspapers. It seemed logical for the inhabitants of Safad to call them Arab Jews."[33]

Writing about Cairo in the 1950s, Jean Said Makdisi recalls a similar harmony:

We went to church every Sunday, yet the sound of the *athan* from the minarets was as much a part of my life as the sunset or the very air I breathed. I sometimes used to watch men praying on the street; sometimes I watched Ahmad, our *sufragi*, praying at home and was quiet, feeling his piety. During the holy month of Ramadan, I used to stand on the balcony and wait, as if I were a Muslim, for the sound of the gun booming in the distance to announce the end of the fast, over the silence of expectation that was almost palpably covering the city. So many of my friends were Muslims, so many of them were Jews, so many of them belonged to other Christian sects, that religious coexistence in those days was not a matter of theory, principle or ideology. It was, quite simply, a way of life, and one that came so naturally to us that I became aware of it only when it was threatened later on.[34]

Even more graphically, with explicit historical and contextual detail and in a situation where restrictions regarding the veil and preferred tenancy obviously *didn't* apply, Ya'aquob Yehoshua (in his six-volume work *Childhood in Old Jerusalem*), describes the extent and intimacy of prestate ties between Sephardic Jews and Muslims:

Jews and Muslims had common courtyards, just as if we were a single family. We grew up together. Our mothers revealed everything to the Muslim women and they, in turn, opened their hearts to our mothers. The Muslim women even learned how to speak Ladino and were adept in its sayings and proverbs. We didn't live in shelters for the needy like the Ashkenazim and there were no large estates separating our houses from those of the Muslims. The Muslim women used to come down to our places across the roof at dusk to spend the evening in conversation. All the kids played together and if anyone else from the neighborhood bothered us, our Muslim friends would come to our defense. We were allies.

Our mothers would nurse any Muslim children whose mothers had died or were unable to attend to them, just as they would care and watch over them if their mothers were busy or otherwise occupied. And the same was true the other way around. The parents of Muslim boys born after great expectation and long suffering often asked their Jewish friends to arrange for a Jew to perform their circumcision on the eighth day, following Jewish and not Islamic custom. . . . According to Islamic custom, though, a baby nursed by someone other than the mother, was considered a relative. Nissim Franco, son of the *Hacham* Ya'aqob Franco, told me the following story: "Once my brother and I accompanied our father to the train station on the way to Haifa from where he intended to go and visit the saints' tombs in Meron. As we sat in the car a very dignified Muslim sheikh entered and, upon seeing my father, cried out: "*Ya akhi*" (My brother!). They grabbed each other and stood a few moments in a tight embrace. My father asked us to kiss the sheikh's hand. We both got up and kissed his hand after which he blessed us. When my father saw how astonished we were at the whole thing, he turned to us and said: "When I was young we lived with the sheikh's parents in one courtyard. His mother died suddenly and my mother nursed him until he was weaned. So we're brothers."[35]

The space described by Yehoshua also corresponds to that of the *geniza* world. Since Jewish institutions in Palestine were maintained through funds donated by other communities, rabbinical emissaries set out from the four cities—Jerusalem, Hebron, Safed, and Tiberias—to both collect donations and serve for certain periods of time in various functions, most often as rabbis, cantors, teachers, or a combination of all three. Egypt, where Yehoshua's father served on such a mission, was considered the most pleasant post: besides its vicinity to home, many Palestinian, Syrian, and Lebanese Jews lived there. Others went to the "inland west" (Tripoli, Algeria, Tunisia), and the "outer west" (Morocco); still others went to Turkey, Iraq, Bukhara, or India. Those going to Europe adapted themselves by shedding the long cloaks, headwear, and other traditional garb they felt at home in in the Levant, and dressing "European," like the *franj*. Besides the official emissaries, businesspeople, families, and individuals also traveled freely and widely, sometimes emigrating for a variety of reasons. The story of Asher Mizrahi, for example, is told: a musician well-known in the Arab cities and villages of Palestine and the composer of many tunes that became standards in the Arab world, he decided to settle in Tunis following the events of 1929, when many Palestinian Jews were killed in the waves of violence that swept the country.[36]

Far from being an unobtrusive, silenced, or submissive minority, the Jewish presence and way of life were not simply tolerated but were always acknowledged and recognized as part of the texture of the Levant itself. While stories about the port of Salonica coming to a complete halt on the Sabbath and Ladino serving as a lingua franca there are well-known, a similar state of affairs—as pervasive, though not as legendary as that prevailing in Salonica—could be found in Baghdad through the 1940s:

> It was on Yom Kippur that our community made the full weight of its presence felt in the city. The entire city involuntarily observed our solemn day. With the exception of the theatre whose Muslim owner presented only Egyptian productions, all the movie houses were closed. Rashid Street, the city's main artery, was practically deserted. Muslim passers-by would affect an air of nonchalance which made Baghdad look like an orphaned city. Christian and Muslim businessmen, behind their counters, seemed only to half believe in their work. In the textile bazaar, Shiite shopkeepers gossiped with their neighbours as they sipped on their narghilahs, waiting for their rare customers.[37]

In addition to the more obvious and legal bond of religion, it was to cities that people formed their deepest allegiances. Goitein remarks of the *geniza* world:

The cities preceded the countryside. They were founded and filled with populace immediately after, or even in the course of, the conquest and formed the nuclei of Arabization. Consequently, it was natural that the capital of a country or district be identified in terms of the region it dominated. The region, as it were, was subsumed in its capital. Countries were political complexes, often changing their borders and characters, cities were units of life.[38]

Among Arabs "al-hanin ila 'l-watan" ("yearning after one's home") was such a pronounced psychological and social phenomenon that a distinct poetic genre categorized by that expression existed. Medieval geographers such as Yaqut and Ibn Jubayr, astonished at how people could live in certain climates or under certain conditions, finally attributed such irrational predilections to love of one's native city, something that obviously went beyond the dictates of reason and logic.[39] Evidence of one of the ways Jews expressed this throughout the ages can be seen in the names of synagogues founded by new emigrants all over the Levant. Among the many synagogues in Old Cairo were those established by the "Damascenes," "Palestinians," and "Babylonians." After the expulsion of the Jews from Spain in 1492, congregations bearing the names of almost every city in Castille flourished throughout the Ottoman Empire. To this day Sephardi synagogues in Israel carry on the traditions or are named after particular cities. In one neighborhood of Jerusalem alone, the following can be found: the synagogue of the refugees from Hebron; the Ades synagogue of Aram Zoba/Aleppo; the congregations of Manastir, Ionnina, Baghdad, Sa'ana, Aden, Dir Bakr, and Teheran.

A perhaps even more significant expression of this characteristic in the geniza world proper was in the precedence one's identification with a native city took over religious affiliation. On the road, Jews had a tendency to feel more comfortable with people from their own city, regardless of their religion. A medieval merchant, the only Jew on the caravan, making his way back to Palestine from Libya, writes: "On this very day a big caravan is setting out for Barqa under the command of Ibn Shibl. I have booked in it for my goods at the price of 3 dinars, and have already paid the fare. Most of the travelers are [fellow] Barqis. They have promised me to be considerate with regard to the watering places and the keeping of the Sabbath and other matters."[40] Due to the long distances traversed and the frequent and extended periods away from home, the merchants' letters are filled with longing, not just for friends and family but for the specific temper and style of their native or adopted cities. Marriage contracts also attached stipulations assuring the bride-to-be that any move from her native city would have to meet with her approval. In one case, a divorcée from Fustat/Old Cairo "engaged to a divorced man from Alexandria, stipulated that the couple would live in the capital and that she was prepared to accompany him on his visits to his family in Alexandria, but for not more than one month per year." As Goitein adds: "A month, she obviously felt, was the maximum she could stand."[41]

Just as relations between the faiths extended far beyond the "logical minimalizations" that present circumstance and ideology allow, so did the range of possibilities for women. Without trying to construct an apologetic chapter in a book of women's "accomplishments" in which those of men are taken as the sole standard of measurement, Goitein presents the beginnings of a foundation for a more thorough social history of medieval Jewish women, one that could confront and pose a wide range of practical and theoretical questions.

Something as innocuous as naming practices—in which women's names are almost completely "secular" and highly individualized (as opposed to the more standardized Biblical names of men)—opens the field to inquiries regarding what Goitein refers to as "the chasm between the popular local subculture of women and the worldwide Hebrew book culture of the men."[42] Nevertheless, the basis outlined, the exceptions to the rules (the mention of "the son of the female astrologer"; the world-famous women bankers and merchants along with the more commonplace brokers and agents; the teachers, doctors, and oculists) certainly provide food for thought. Being members of an affluent society, the women of the *geniza* world were freed from many of the more prevalent forms of female bondage. Besides being employed in a variety of vocations, women were engaged in business and were property owners. Marriage contracts not only stipulated the bride's choice of domicile but also provided firm safeguards for economic independence should the marriage break up. Often this provision for independence even preceded marriage and was simply a matter of course in a family's distribution of wealth. Goitein notes: "Women of all classes appear in the Geniza documents as being in possession of immovables. They receive as a gift or donate, inherit or bequeath, buy or sell, rent or lease houses (more often parts of houses), stores, workshops, flour mills, and other types of urban real estate, and also take care of their maintenance."[43]

While clear lines of demarcation between the worlds and activities of men and women certainly existed, women within Jewish society—like Jews within Levantine society—were far from a secluded and submissive minority. Single women traveling overseas—whether for business, pleasure, or religious pilgrimage—were common. It was also an ordinary occurrence for women to initiate judicial actions and then appear in their own defense: "I went to the *qadi* [Muslim judge]," writes a widow from

Alexandria quite casually in a letter addressed to the attention of the Jewish Vizier Mevorakh.[44] Despite the chasm between the male-dominated book culture and the generally vernacular literary parameters of women's culture, great attention was paid to both securing and providing for the education of children. This, in fact, was considered a woman's duty. A particularly moving letter written by a woman on her deathbed beseeches her sister to provide for her youngest daughter's *formal* education (*ta'alim*), which would include reading and writing. Whether or not this letter—and others like it—was actually ever sent, it provides indications as to the prevailing parameters of the possible. This is further buttressed by the fact that, in making the request, the woman refers to the example of their mother, herself an educated and pious person:

> This is to inform you, my lady, dear sister—may God accept me as a ransom for you—that I have become seriously ill with little hope for recovery, and I have dreams indicating that my end is near.
>
> My lady, my most urgent request of you, if God, the exalted, indeed decrees my death, is that you take care of my little daughter and make efforts to give her an education, although I know well that I am asking you for something unreasonable, as there is not enough money—by my father—for support, let alone for formal instruction. However, she has a model in our saintly mother.[45]

The affluence of the *geniza* world was reflected not only in the status of women but also in its incredibly rich and diverse material and culinary culture. While the medieval Cairene working class ate lunch out, the middle class usually brought a wide variety of hot, ready-made dishes home from the bazaar. Imported foods were not considered luxury items but basic staples. Highly perishable fruits such as apricots, peaches, and plums came into Egypt from the eastern Mediterranean in a half-dried or glazed state. Almonds, pistachios, walnuts, hazelnuts, and olive oil came in from the east and the west, cheese from Crete, Sicily, and Byzantium, the land of the "Rum." Sugarcane was exported by Iran and southern Iraq, honey by Tunisia, Palestine, and Syria. Spices, as one might well imagine, came from everywhere and formed the ingredients of both the druggist's and perfumer's trades. A relatively simple medicinal mixture could contain as many as twenty different items, each coming from a different corner of the known world.

As the large number and high specialization of occupations testify, the sophistication and variety of commodities readily available was truly astonishing. Local styles and specialties were the pride of many branches of endeavor, among them the metals, glass, pottery, leather, parchment, paper, and furniture industries. One of the major industries, the real "big

business" of the time, was the dyeing and textile field, an area embody-
ing, literally, the highly individualized and "exotic" tastes of *geniza*
people. Our merchant's "flame-colored robe," mentioned above, was
not particularly extraordinary. People ordered every possible nuance and
shade of every available color on the spectrum, using highly distinctive
epithets like silvery, sandal-colored, clean white, bluish-iridescent, olive
green, gazelle-blood, pure violet, musk brown, intensive yellow, sky-
blue, crimson, pomegranate red, pearl-colored, ash-grey ("color of bamboo crystals"), basil (brownish-violet), blue-onion, lead-grey, turquoise,
gold, indigo, and emerald. Taste was both exquisitely refined and extremely picky. In one letter a trader entreats his supplier: "Please, my
lord, the red should be as red as possible, likewise the white and the yellow should be exquisite, I was not satisfied with the yellow. . . . The si-
glaton robe is of the utmost beauty, but not exactly what I wanted, for it
is white and blue, while I wanted to have instead of the latter, onion
color, an 'open' color. The lead-colored [bluish-grey] robe is superb, better than all the rest." As if this were not enough, clothing was embellished with numerous kinds of "glitter" and "gloss," iridescence, stripes,
waves, and patterns; sleeves often featured calligraphy made to order.[46]

The textile industry, maybe more than any other, fully represented the
geographic range and the mobility of the *geniza* world, the intricate network of its cities. Brand names manufactured in Spain but originating in
the heart of Asia, the Jurjan dress for instance, indicate the migratory
movement of both manufacturers and craftspeople. Often it was difficult
to discern whether one was getting the real thing or if the market was
flooded with imitation items bearing only the name and the style of the
original, such as the clothes named after remote regions of Iran imported
to Egypt from Spain or North Africa but actually produced in Palestine.
Always up on style, *geniza* people also imported the latest from Europe.
One of the most popular items among the brides of Damascus and
Fustat/Old Cairo from the tenth to the twelfth century was a *mandil
Rumi*, a "European mantilla." This later was embellished by the Yemenites until it could be ordered as a "European mantilla in the Yemenite
fashion"; with this modification, it became very popular in Egypt.[47]

Besides serving as a center of wealth and commerce, the city assumed
a stature and character much greater than the sum of its parts. Trade and
urbanity—the urbanity of trade—formed a nexus of taste, quality, standards, and expectations. Oleg Grabar describes its importance: "Trade,
altogether, was much more than the main source of wealth in the city. It
was its cultural mix, its source of ideas and adventures, and in many ways
the means by which almost everything from a Chinese ceramic to an ab-

surd story could penetrate across social classes and from one end of the Muslim world to another."[48]

Business practice paralleled the range and movement of the *geniza* world. Capital was never allowed to sit idle. Rapid exchange and quick turnover was the general rule, as summed up in the often paraphrased ancient Near Eastern proverb: "Sell while the dust of the journey is still on your feet."[49] Because of this, merchants handled an "almost bizarre diversity of goods," as shown by the following list of items dealt in by Nahray ben Nissim, a well-known eleventh-century wholesaler:

1. Flax, exported from Egypt to Tunisia and Sicily.
2. Silk (from Spain and Sicily) and other fabrics, from Syrian or European (Rum) cotton to North African felt, and textiles of all descriptions, from robes to bedcovers.
3. Olive oil, soap, and wax from Tunisia, occasionally also from Palestine and Syria.
4. Oriental spices, such as pepper, cinnamon, and clove, sent from Egypt to the West.
5. Dyeing, tanning, and varnishing materials such as brazilwood, lacquer, and indigo (sent from East to West); sumac and gallnuts (from Syria to Egypt); saffron (from Tunisia to the East).
6. Metals (copper, iron, lead, mercury, tin, silver ingots), all West to East.
7. Books (Bible codexes, Talmuds, legal and edifying literature, grammars, and Arabic books).
8. Aromatics, perfumes and gums (aloe, ambergris, camphor, frankincense, gum arabic, mastic gum, musk, betel leaves).
9. Jewelry and semiprecious stones (gems, pearls, carnelians, turquoises, onyxes, and the like).
10. Materials (such as beads, "pomegranate" strings, coral, cowrie shells, lapis lazuli, and tortoise shell) used for ornaments and trinkets.
11. Chemicals (alkali, alum, antimony, arsenic, bamboo crystals, borax, naphtha, sulfur, starch, vitriol).
12. Foodstuffs, such as sugar, exported from Egypt, or dried fruits, imported from Syria.
13. Hides and leather. Also furs and shoes. All coming from, or through, Tunisia and Sicily.
14. Pitch, an important article.
15. Varia, such as palm fiber, and items not yet identified with certainty.[50]

A much less conspicuous merchant, Isaac Nisaburi, a Persian living in Alexandria around 1100, dealt in goods as varied as dyeing plants (saffron and brazilwood), medical and culinary herbs (scammony and cubeb), glass, silk (along with a variety of other textiles), corals, perfumes (ambergris and musk), wax, and millstones.

The range of things handled by such merchants, and made available by them in turn to a common market, parallels the continuous movement of people between cities that distinctly marks the *geniza* world. If, though, we could concentrate on less obvious aspects and look, not through the gold and glass chambers of a crystal palace as Benjamin of Tudela did, but through the walls of an ordinary house in the Old Cairo of that time, we would find the same sense and practice of mobility as that found in such lists, along the trade routes and in the bazaar itself:

> Mobility within the house conditioned the rhythm of life. Despite the rich architectural nomenclature of the Geniza and contemporary Muslim documents we would look in vain there for such terms as dining room or bedroom. In winter one slept in a small closet, which could easily be warmed by a brazier; in summer one sought relief from the heat in the spacious living room with its ventilation shaft, which brought the cool north wind from the roof into the interior of the various floors. The meals were taken where it was appropriate in accordance with the circumstances. There were no fixed tables surrounded by chairs; food was brought in from the kitchen on trays and put on movable low stools. Thus, whether resting or being with other people, one could enjoy either roominess or intimacy. But the emphasis was on space.[51]

And if we could draw up a list of a person's belongings, all the material objects they had left behind in this world at their departure for the world to come, we would, as well, find concrete traces of all the traders' routes and bits of the varied treasure they had brought back with them. In our case—although the remnants we have been given to examine are not those of a vizier but of a coppersmith who had emigrated from Spain to Egypt—we shall find a clue taking us right back to the palace, its transparent walls and refracting prism. The coppersmith was a craftsman as well as a dealer. The list of his belongings "contains about one hundred and forty brass, bronze and copper vessels of all descriptions, kept on the middle floor of the house where he lived, while, as usual, his workshop was on the ground floor. There, no doubt, he exhibited other products of his art for his customers. The middle floor harbored also his personal belongings, and the third floor was probably occupied by a tenant or by the proprietor of the house." After "three old carpets, a threadbare blue robe, a worn linen robe, a new Spanish robe, a lined chest containing ten Spanish 'raw' [unfulled] robes, an Iraqi *burd* gown, a Nuli turban, a piece of Sicilian cloth, two shrouds in which some china is packed, various pairs of pants and overalls, an 'Abbadani mat, a woolen curtain and some water jars made of stone," we find "a small chest containing the prayer book of Rabbenu Saadya of blessed memory, a section of the Book of Psalms, a Maghrebi prayer book, and a book of poetry in Arabic characters."[52]

III. Cities and Texts

The cities, trade routes, bazaars, and houses—the qualitative inner and outer spaces of the *geniza* world—constitute the overall site without yet marking the specific start or duration of the transparent walls/prism metaphor and the poetics of knowledge so accurately refracted by it. This metaphor extends from Benjamin of Tudela's description of the Great Mosque of Damascus, in which the walls both separate people and allow them to see each other, to Jacqueline Kahanoff's prism that reflects light through each of its facets differently. For that, as George Kubler put it, a "cleavage, an inscription in the history of things aiming beyond narration, a cut separating different types of happening to initiate a new collective duration" must be identified, ferreted out of the clues left in the coppersmith's "small chest" and the four books found there. Each of those books channels a possible history of Hebrew and Jewish writing. Together, they can serve as a focal point around which unconventional modes of grouping and a new working order of this history can be proposed. The chronological tags of this proposed new order, for want of better or more exact terms, consist of the biblical/rabbinic ("premodern"); the Levantine ("modern"); the Enlightenment ("neomodern"); and the New Levantine ("postmodern"). These categories cannot be conceived as inclusive or rigid, defining strict and essential characteristics. They must be considered, rather, as relational scanners, places on a map to refer to for orientation. Thus the Levantine ("modern") category, for instance, would include within it "classical" or "traditional" periods, phases, or writers. Such a proposal corresponds to the two other sets of qualities and distinctions already introduced: those of place, and of social and economic condition.

The first set specifically relates to the actual geographical circumstances of writers: those who have stayed in a given area, those who left entirely, the newly arrived, others relocated within the wider sphere of the same area but whose work has been realigned by altered conditions, can also be applied to other kinds of "movement." This kind of "movement" would include the ideological ends or uses to which works have been put within the same or another geographical area by different people, groups, political or educational structures and hierarchies. Although obviously pertinent to the Levant in particular, examining such ends or uses within as vast a sphere of influences as the Hebrew/Jewish context provides can open up a whole range of questions that probe the limits, formation, and perpetuation of "national" literatures in general. These hypothetical fields of inquiry would include the ideological uses of literature in the solidification of national/political characters and structures, and the effects these political structures and alliances have superimposed over other forms of connection. These other forms would naturally include the postmodern trivium of race, class, and gender. At the same time, this category would extend to investigate things such as pluralistic interurban culture and the effects its allegiances and connections might have on cultural formations *not* based on narrowly national, religious, or linguistic lines.

Other issues—such as the relationship between the standardization of dialects, the establishment of "centralized" curricula, and the canonization of reduced or decontextualized interpretations based on functional hierarchical ends—could also be examined. Such lines of analysis are by no means marginal in accounting for the range of assumptions and choices that went into, and still go into, the formation of European literatures emerging from the combination of Latinity (with *its* curriculum and agenda) with the Arabic renaissance. In fact, these concerns are central to gaining a richer understanding of the thematic, generic, and linguistic decisions made by the troubadours, Dante, Boccaccio, Chaucer, and many other canonized European Christian writers, not to mention the reasons for their canonization. Tracing the various interpretations of the origins of romance, courtly love, and the vernacular lyric in Europe, for example, provides a virtual cultural and political history of spheres of influence.

The first canonical European text to deal with this problem is, of course, Dante's *De vulgari eloquentia*, written in 1303-4. Interestingly enough, "Dante seems not in the least concerned with the bases, inspirations, or roots of the Provençal poets themselves. His silence concerning these subjects is noteworthy, and it is conspicuous, because the *De vulgari* is palpably driven by the desire to establish antecedents, authorities, and standards in an area where they are totally lacking or few in number."[53] At the same time that Dante promoted the troubadour lyric, he turned his back on the "reputed twenty thousand verses written by a hundred and seventy poets"[54] in Sicily, in Arabic, from the tenth to the thirteenth century. Certainly one possible reason for this omission has to do with Dante's own relationship to the formation of a vernacular Christian culture, at a time when "the primacy of the Christian system and the Christian ethos that Dante so deeply revered and cherished was under severe challenge. . . . It is not unreasonable to assume that some great challenge to the established Christian order must have existed to provoke Dante to write his *Commedia*, so magnificent an apologia for fundamental Christianity . . . and he would have certainly identified that challenge, which to him must have seemed an omnipresent danger to many of those he respected and loved most, as Arabic in origin."[55] In a truly informed and highly suggestive reading of Dante's career, Maria Rosa Menocal concludes that "the repression of the influence of the Arab world on the rest of Europe may well be dated to Dante."[56]

From the sixteenth to the early nineteenth century, the assumption that Andalusia and Arabic culture *did* play a significant role in the formation of European thought—with a few challenges here and there—held fairly firm ground. The first substantial revision proposing a fundamentally different pattern, one that would exclude Islamic Spain not only from any sphere of influence within Christian culture but from Europe itself, came in the early nineteenth century from Madame de Staël, Chateaubriand, and Schlegel. These beginnings burgeoned into a full-fledged institutional ideology that went hand in hand with European domination:

> It is evident that a number of critical perspectives on the poetry of the troubadours and on the Europe in which they lived had crystallized shortly after the midpoint of the nineteenth century. But this was also a period of crystallization and definition, both for the field of Romance studies and for the Europe within which that area of inquiry was formed. And it was a Europe that was at precisely that moment shaping its views of the Arabs as colonial subjects. . . .
>
> The vaguer, more romantic, and in some ways more positive views that had been common even fifty years before were replaced with far less tolerant ones. . . .
>
> By the time the great debate about the etymology of *trobar* formally commenced in 1878, two years after Victoria had become empress of India and four years before the British occupation of Egypt, it would no more have occurred to any of the participants to trace the world's etymon to Arabic than to propose an origin in classical Chinese.
>
> This academic conceptual banishment of the Arab from medieval Europe was to have extraordinary power. While versions of the Arabist theory were to be brought up again and again, it would not be reinstituted as part of the mainstream of philological thought. The sporadic suggestions of Arabic influence on this or that aspect of medieval European literature or on salient features of its lexicon, such as *trobar*, were largely ignored, were dismissed as unworthy of serious consideration, or at best were subjected to unusually heated and vitriolic criticism. The proponents of such ideas, predominantly Arabists, were dismissed as individuals who simply had an ax to grind rather than a

conceivably legitimate contribution to make and who, in any case, were not knowledgeable in the field of European literature.[57]

This single example, presented only in the most digested form, goes some of the way to show what kinds of areas can be opened up to new inquiry through the application of such a contextual framework. The peculiarities of the Hebrew/Jewish situation (in which a legal/communal/religious but completely extraterritorial focus has been replaced by a national entity, itself not just the icing on some teleological cake but a new country with a very particular and exacerbated political, social, and literary history) make the examples and paradigms offered by its present repositioning quite provoking, open to scrutiny, and potentially applicable to many other areas of inquiry.

The second set of descriptive characteristics (autonomy, translatability, diversity, and mobility) relate specifically to the connection between the social and economic conditions of Jews in the Levantine period and their "reproduction" in writing and cultural practice through the assimilation and transformation of an enormous range of materials. But these characteristics, too, have wider applications: first, for the general history of Hebrew/Jewish writing, which spans some 3,000 years with centers of activity and production in Canaan, Palestine, Babylonia, Egypt, North Africa, Yemen, Central Asia, Kurdistan, India, Spain, Byzantium, Turkey, Greece, the Balkans, Provence, Italy, northern France, Germany, Holland, England, central and eastern Europe, the New World, and Israel. Any history of this writing must take into account the peculiar circumstances and conditions of its production. In a book investigating the Egyptian context of the Bible, the great Semitic scholar Abraham Shalom Yahuda addresses this:

During the years of their history with which we are fairly familiar, the people of Israel voluntarily or involuntarily led a wandering life; and indeed not as an uncivilized nomadic tribe, but as a people, seeking, creating, and transmitting spiritual and material culture did they wander from nation to nation, from land to land. Through all the different periods of Jewish civilization, it was in the first place the language of the peoples among whom they dwelt that exerted the most extensive influence upon them. The Hebrews, with their staunch conservatism, preserved the Hebrew language throughout; this language, even at times when only in literary and scholarly use, did not by any means cease to live in their midst but was continually enriched by the adoption of new elements through close contact with many other peoples and the most varied cultural surroundings. In the development of the Hebrew language, one can even follow the very route of Israel's wanderings. In its expansion and enrichment, we can see reflected the fresh cultural values acquired in all periods. All the newly created conceptions, all the borrowed or imitated phrases and modes of speech, as well as the adopted, partly hebraized foreign words, are to be found embodied in the language and worked into its texture.[58]

The writing shaped by the circumstances of such a language can be called "inaugural," a sense described by Derrida as "the anguish of the Hebraic *ruah* [wind/spirit], experienced in solitude by human responsibility; experienced by Jeremiah subjected to God's dictation, or by Baruch transcribing Jeremiah's dictation. . . . It is the moment at which we must decide whether we will engrave what we hear. And whether engraving preserves or betrays speech."[59] It is also the moment at which one preserves or betrays real or imagined constructs of the self, shaped and inherited through language and geography. The sense of writing as "inaugural" opens both the doors and the floodgates. Extending the itinerary and increasing the number of way stations along the route, it also blurs, relocates, and redefines the markers distinguishing the "sojourner" and the "inhabitant." When Moses admonishes the people of Israel to remember Egypt, both the sojourning and the slavery, perhaps he meant—as Yahuda implied in his study—"inscribe your experience within the very fabric of the language, take the land and the cities and the people with you and make them live in your book, reinscribe Egypt in such a way that you remain responsible for the Egypt within, the interior exile." Freed by the desert and the breaking of the tablets and graciously exempted by God from the disappointment of seeing the promised land become a monarchy modeled on the one from which they were banished, only a child of Egypt like Moses could so thoroughly accept the exterior Egypt—since it posed no threat to him—as to permanently interiorize it by inscribing it within the palimpsest. As David Shasha has argued:

> The tradition of Judaism preserves a version of history, that is the best
> that language can do for us, but this version is not empirically
> verifiable. As Derrida has shown, empiricism is a specific philosophical
> mode which can itself be put into question. The traditionalist claims that
> the events did actually happen, but that the actual narrative construction
> of events is far more important, i.e. *how* we remember as opposed to
> *what* we remember, in regard to the epistemological traces which give
> history its significance.[60]

This way of acceptance, this manner in which the exterior is internalized without being disowned or renounced, is a stance of utmost respect and recognition toward the other, as well as being an acceptance of the otherness of one's self. A fertile path furrowed in the very humus of the "bookish earth" by the biblical and rabbinic tradition, the Jewish writers of the Levant kept well within its course. Traveling through Egypt from Spain in the twelfth century on the way to his intended destination of Jerusalem, Yehuda Halevi wrote:

> See the cities:
> Behold the unwalled
> villages held once
> by Israel and pay
> homage to Egypt.[61]

This constant referral back to something always anterior but newly inscribed in the text can be seen as the reverse of apocalypse—or of what apocalypse has been taken to be, the tone of defiance and urgency announcing the coming of the end. This seems to say, rather, that the *beginning* is always at hand, and may refer to what Derrida has characterized as a "non-question":

> The non-question of which we are speaking is not yet a dogma; and the act of faith in the book can precede, as we know, belief in the Bible. And can also survive it. The non-question of which we are speaking is the unpenetrated certainty that Being is a Grammar, and that the world is in all its parts a cryptogram to be constituted or reconstituted through poetic inscription or deciphering.[62]

If the world is seen as an act of God's speech, then the study of grammar includes all the disciplines that have become disparate and even conflicting in the Western tradition, since all categories of thought must ultimately struggle for and find their expression in language. Humans are both God's speakers and readers, and grammar is not the aftereffect of language but the genesis of meaning. To hear, in Hebrew, is to understand.

Much of the "certainty" of the Hebrew tradition owes itself to the acceptance of this grammatical non-question and its relation to the "question" of personal, communal, legal, and cultural autonomy. This, in turn, immediately raises the issue of "originality" and "tradition" as they impinge upon the given possibilities within any cultural space. In the case of the Jews, then, there is nothing surprising in seeing how part of the creative genius of their tradition manifested itself in grammar, codification, and literary/philological commentary, three of the great rabbinic projects. Almost all the important Levantine rabbinic writers, in addition to being physicians, diplomats, judges, astronomers, teachers, or merchants, were first and foremost grammarians, but grammarians whose standard form of currency was poetry. Instead of the sterile discipline usually associated with the study of grammar, the rabbinic grammarian/

poets practiced their art of inscribing and deciphering the word's poetic cryptogram as if the world depended on it, for in their terms it actually did. At the same time, these questions and concerns—of exile and the book, the sojourner and the inhabitant, inaugural writing and the responsibility of inscription and how they relate to the distinctions that have been described here—cannot simply and smugly be relegated to permanent "residence" within an ethnocentric domain. It is only in this sense that Anna Akhmatova's aphorism "all poets are Jews" can be fully understood, since the particular nomadic state of the Jews—and the specific development of Hebrew literature as a paradigm for other "Jewish" writing—only enact the possibilities of any writing in a more drastic and exacerbated way.

IV. The Common Currency of Verse

"Translation" in its most variegated sense—the means through which the experience of diversity can be mobilized, the process through which movement and difference of all kinds can be expressed—was not only a casual and inherited way of life for Jews throughout their odd nomadic history, but the key to their very sustenance, a paradigmatic model of generation and regeneration. Writing is only the most visible and resilient evidence tracing this transaction. In a tradition where reading and the transmission of writing are ritual acts, where hundreds of thousands of *geniza* fragments could survive partly due to the taboo against destroying the written word, there should be nothing surprising about finding our prism—the mode through which differences can be articulated—within the measure of a poetic line. Such a vessel might seem entirely unlikely, too weak to hold the ballast of a thousand years and circumscribe the space of more than a hundred cities, yet the act and the gesture of this particular innovation proved enduring. The act—which triggered an explosion of new writing—came in the form of introducing quantitative meters, verse forms, themes, and genres from Arabic into Hebrew poetry. The acrobat responsible for initiating this "collective duration" was Dunash Ben Labrat. A tenth-century native of Fez with a Berber name, he had gone east to study in Baghdad with the master, Sa'adiah Gaon. It was Sa'adiah who served as a bridge between the period preceding the Arabic renaissance and its height. He did this by both preserving and reviving the use of Hebrew while confirming and even "institutionalizing" use of the richer, semantically and philosophically more adept and versatile Arabic, the language of almost all the significant prose works written by Jews of that period.

Although Sa'adiah's work formed the foundation for this modernity, the poet's gesture more clearly marks the beginning of the "modern" Levantine period. This period inextricably inscribed Arabic within the palimpsest, opened a completely new space for Hebrew, and formed the basis of a poetics that permeated the whole Levant to continue with stops, starts, and diverse flirtations through to the present and its last significant practitioners. More obvious at the start, the Arabic inscription (with further Spanish, Greek, Turkish, and other layers added) was retained right through the "traditional" phase that closed the Levantine period. This closure coincides with the radical changes in the conditions of production for Hebrew/Jewish writing in the region caused by the proletarianization of Levantine and Arab Jews and the shift from a communal to a national identity.

Examples of the persistence of the Arabic element in Hebrew poetry abound. In Egypt, for instance, the *Laylat al-Tawhid* (the custom of studying the Torah on the eve of the ancient New Year), assumed a particular form. Hebrew liturgical poems were sung to Egyptian tunes before being translated, verse by verse, into Arabic. The climactic text—all in Arabic and recited at midnight—contained many Islamic formulas. Beginning with the Muslim invocation (*B'ism Allah al-Rahman al-Rahim*), it invoked the ninety-nine divine attributes in the Sufi manner and used Koranic epithets for biblical figures: Abraham as *al-Khalil*, Aaron as *al-Imam* and Moses as *Rasul Allah*. Kept intact as long as there was an active Jewish community in Egypt—until, in fact, the period during which Jabès emigrated—this solemn service that "renders the heart and fills the soul with terror" seems to have been originated by the Nagid Avraham, son of Maimonides. Remarkably enough, the ceremony has continued in the Egyptian Jewish community of Brooklyn, where even during the Gulf War Egyptian musicians (former members of Umm Kulthum's orchestra) shared the stage with rabbis and cantors as they celebrated the ancient expressions of common unity. Again, in what may very well be the last "old world" collection of Levantine Hebrew poetry edited and annotated by a genuine exponent of that tradition, the resonant Arabic core is retained most tangibly through writing's relationship to music, "wounded kinship's last resort."[63] This collection (*I Shall Arise at Dawn*, three volumes of North African works from the seventeenth century to the twentieth) was completed by the Moroccan liturgical poet Rabbi Haim Raphael Shoshannah (1912-87) just before his death in Beersheba. In his introduction, before an elaborate description and set of stage directions for the performance of liturgical poetry, Rabbi Shoshannah writes:

The ancient poets of Arabia came to the conclusion that every melody that had ever been or might possibly exist could not but correspond to one of the eleven melodic modes. . . . These ancient musicians, with sound, subtle and acute sense, also stressed that each melodic mode corresponded to a particular time of day. And naturally anyone of judgment and taste can effortlessly feel that the 'ashaq mode, for instance, is clearly meant for the morning, with the throat's protestations and the voice's resonance after sleep. The subjects of the poems—I refer here to Arabic poetry, of course—also revolve around sunrise, the glitter of the sun, the dew's caress, the smell of the field, wind at daybreak and the battle with nightfall, as it is driven off to give way to the light of day. Thus, you find that a melodic mode like the *maya* corresponds to evening and poems set in this mode concentrate on descriptions of twilight and the setting sun, subjects invoking melancholy among those who must put an end to their gaiety and dissolve the bonds of friendship with the coming of night, but joy to those whose designs can only be fulfilled under cover of darkness. There are melodic modes characterized by delight and pleasure, such as the *hijaz*, while others—such as the dramatically structured *ghariba*—evoke an undercurrent of grief and sorrow.[64]

Like the coppersmith's medieval prayer books, Rabbi Shoshannah's twentieth-century collection serves the double function of ritual guide and poetry anthology. The poems are divided by subject, in relation to the biblical portion of the week and, more significantly, by the ancient Arabic melodic modes described by Shoshannah. This poetry is also performed, sung by the congregation according to fairly strict standards, particularly during the High Holiday services and the month preceding them. This custom is still fairly intact among traditional Jews, particularly in the working-class neighborhoods of Israeli cities and development towns, and it marks an achievement in cultural transmission that should not be taken too lightly. The equivalent in England, for example, might be if a good part of the population spent several weeks reciting selections from Chaucer, Wyatt, Campion, Marlowe, Shakespeare, Jonson, and another few dozen poets. The continued popularity of this often extremely complex poetry, its constant production and performance, also seem to indicate the persistence of a quality noted by Goitein as common to the *geniza* world:

> The attainments of laymen must sometimes have been impressive. We are able to recognize their achievements in several business letters that have been preserved, on the reverse side of which the recipients— merchants whose handwriting is well known to us—discuss theoretical problems or actual cases to be decided according to the sacred law. Their discussions are on a high level and do not differ in character from legal

opinions written by a scholar. These instances should not be regarded as exceptional. Many letters contain quotations from the Bible, and sometimes also from postbiblical literature, which are by no means mundane, and the poetical proems frequently preceding letters are seldom confined to conventional phrases. Thus, the general standard of adult education, or rather of the regular study by middle-class adults, cannot have been low.[65]

Without yet entering into the complex relations between Arabic and Hebrew poetics, between Hebrew liturgical and nonliturgical poetry, all part of a longer tale, suffice it to say that thousands of such anthology/ prayerbooks kept poetry "in print." This made Hebrew poetry, with its intimate and pervasive allegiances to Arabic, common currency for a Jewish audience spread out from one end of the Levant to the other. This Levantine space was circumscribed by the *geniza* world on one end, and its corresponding "prestate" parameters, as described by Ya'aquob Yehoshua and others, on the other.

During the height of the Andalusian period, in his Arabic work on poetics, *The Book of Conversations and Memories*, Moses Ibn Ezra stressed that great poems were "recited and conveyed, heard, read and noticed by everyone. In fact, I find no need to cite the choicest pearls of the most outstanding poets nor have I noted their beautiful phrases here since they are already so well known and flow so freely through the mouths of the reciters: after all, if the morning light has no need for a lamp—how much less is the sun in need of a candle!" Speaking specifically of the poetry of Samuel Hanagid, Ibn Ezra notes: "His writings are known in the remotest regions of the East and the West. . . . They reached the Heads of the Babylonian Academies and the Sages of Syria, the learned of Egypt and the Viziers of Tunis, the western patrons and the Spanish aristocrats."[66] In a thirteenth-century *geniza* letter, information can be garnered on "a Hebrew liturgical poem available in France, so cherished by those who had heard it in Alexandria, that a cantor in Old Cairo who already knew of it was eager to obtain a copy, but the colleague in Alexandria reserved the exclusive privilege to its use for himself."[67]

A seventeenth-century poet such as Israel Najara, with firm roots in Andalusian poetics, tailored his verse to fit popular Turkish, Armenian, Spanish, and Greek melodies, a combination that made him popular not only throughout the Levant but as far as Aden, Calcutta, and Cochin. Like the "European mantilla in the Yemenite style" so popular in the Cairo of the *geniza* world, this kind of mobility, transfer of style, and ease of exchange remained very real to poets like Shoshannah or the master musician Rabbi David Buzaglio. Also Moroccan, Buzaglio in the 1940s set Yehuda Halevi's twelfth-century poetry to popular contemporary *sharqi* (Eastern) melodies from Egypt while modally and rhythmically modifying them to fit ears tuned and turned toward the "west," the Maghreb and its Andalusian memory.

Both the "literary" function and the actual publishing history of a collection like *I Shall Arise at Dawn* raises a number of crucial issues. Such a book, along with hundreds of others like it that appear in Israel, are unsubsidized, nonacademic and noncommercial. Money for printing is raised through contributions and subscriptions within the community. These circumstances pull into sharp relief the accumulated testament of Levantine Jewish writing, its very concrete allegiances, antecedents, and material conditions, with its present textual state and cultural status. The "modern" period, by upholding the difference of the Arabic facet of the Levantine prism, not only through poetic inscription but perhaps (with the preceding examples serving only some indication) just as significantly through musical practice, precisely counters the "neomodern" European Enlightenment and Zionist phase of Hebrew/Jewish culture, with its Orientalist under- and overtones. This drama, as pointed out in the introduction, is primarily played out in Israel through the discourse of an elite "Western" culture on one hand, and an "underdeveloped," albeit folklorically rich "Eastern" culture on the other. While the dominant side (just as in the controversy regarding Arabic influence on European thought) would like to see this perceived as an "internal" struggle, such a presentation clearly impairs the reception and appreciation of Jewish culture on a general level.

For all the invaluable and pioneering work done by Enlightenment Hebrew scholars, the deeper connection between an imagined Andalusia held up as an example of "successful" Jewish assimilation and the continued living tradition of Levantine rabbis and poets was never really made, despite contact and ample opportunities for such exchange. An intriguing study could be done on the relationships between European (both Eastern and Western) Jewish scholars and their Levantine and Arab counterparts, but from the point of view of the non-Europeans. This dynamic, of course, is multilayered and would have to include the contempt that, for example, German Jews often felt for the "Oriental" Eastern European *Ostjuden*, something that led them to romanticize the golden age of Spain while all but completely ignoring the living examples of that very culture.

A progressive curve tracing this rift can be drawn from an eighteenth-century figure such as Hayyim David Azulai, to nineteenth- and twentieth-century figures such as Hayyim Palaggi, Giusseppe Almanzi, Eliahu Ben-amozeg, Shaul Abdullah Yoseph, A. S. Yahuda, and Moise Ventura, to mention only some. All of these people had extensive contact with European Jewish intellectuals and institutions, yet a reading of almost any general history of modern Jewish thought would leave one with the impression that none of these persons ever existed, that the Levantine and Arab world remained plunged in darkness, totally unaware of what was taking place outside it. Needless to say, the work toward such an intellectual history has not even begun on an institutional level. In fact, the possibility of even thinking about it is only delayed by the legitimation of the "rich folklore" of Oriental Jewry in Israel. The more minute studies done on the type of henna used in Jewish wedding ceremonies in Iraq or Bukhara, no matter how valuable or interesting they might be, the less likely we are to get studies on the relationship of Abraham Shalom Yahuda and Freud, or the progressive marginalization of Levantine Jewish intellectuals within the Zionist movement, to mention only two enticing possibilities. As David Shasha notes:

> We must see that the modern historian too "believes" in something. The store of "prodigious arcana" corresponds to Yerushalmi's assertion that "no subject is potentially unworthy of his interest, no document, no artifact, beneath his attention." The vessel of modern historiography has become a repository for such arcana. Indeed, Yerushalmi himself describes how the failure of memory among modern Jews has indirectly led to the "explosion" of modern Jewish historiography. But, increasingly, the studies produced are far removed from the contours of memory, in addition to the fact that the texts themselves are increasingly estranged from *any* sort of context; outside, that is, of the academic context.[68]

Again, during the early state period of the Zionist phase, despite the effort to keep popular editions of classical Levantine Jewish writing available, absolutely no connection was made between that culture and the textual, musical, oral, and aesthetic traditions of the hundreds of thousands of immigrants pouring into the country. The academic institutionalization and elevation of those classical periods to a privileged but completely decontextualized status, along with the current social position of the practitioners of that culture, has created very discrepant sets of values and meanings. Thus, to take an example so stereotypical it verges on the comic, the "neomodern" Hebrew national poet, Haim Nahman Bialik, could spend a good part of his creative energy and a number of years collecting and editing Andalusian Hebrew poetry while saying that he couldn't "abide Sephardic Jews because they reminded him of Arabs."[69] At the same time, these very Jews whose living knowledge of musical and poetic performance constitutes an encyclopedia inscribed in rapidly fading ink have little or no access to the institutions that have privileged the basis and shifted the receptive space of those same counters.

The more recent reception of Ethiopian Jews in Israel only proves that these attitudes and practices remain deeply ingrained within the Israeli institutional system, despite valiant efforts on the part of many groups and individuals—as well as the Ethiopians themselves—to temper them. Practitioners of Jewish customs that are pre-Talmudic, these Jews were forced to convert on all levels, the personal, literal, spiritual, and intellectual. After being "given" Hebrew names (in precisely the way described earlier by the Iraqi who immigrated during the transit camp period), they were also given the "choice" of taking a ritual bath to mark their "conversion," and to adopt standard Eastern European Orthodox religious practices. To not accept such "choices" meant being considered gentiles, their marriages unrecognized and their children illegitimate. While such abominations existed on the public policy-making level and within the state's religious institutions, academia went into high gear in order to "preserve" the disappearing culture of this "rediscovered" tribe.

Ironically, the best source spanning the full range of Levantine Hebrew poetry currently available, T. Carmi's *Penguin Book of Hebrew Verse*, has to be imported into Israel. Many of the most important poets remain completely out of print while even classical Andalusian poets like Samuel Hanagid, Yehuda Halevi, Solomon Ibn Gabirol, and Moses Ibn Ezra can only be gotten whole in expensive scholarly editions. Dozens of poets and thousands of poems remain in manuscript, within the vocabulary of a few specialized scholars, remote from most readers of poetry and completely beyond the scope of even an imaginable curriculum. The revision of such a curriculum in Israel, even more radically than in the case of Europe, would entail an unequivocal recognition of the centrality of Arabic—in all its nuances—for the formulation of a great part of modern Jewish thought and culture. Given, however, the predominant policies of the Israeli government (whether in foreign affairs or in the educational system), and the way Israel's intellectual elite conceives of its cultural place in the world, such a project is entirely unimaginable. Nor do prevailing attitudes within the American context, on both academic and political levels, give much cause to hope for deeper systemic changes.

V. Dunash Ben Labrat and Classical Sephardic Poetry

The possible history that the coppersmith's books and the circumstances of their being together propose divides the two longest periods, the biblical/rabbinic "premodern" and the Levantine "modern." At the same time, they allude to the function of poetry as legitimate currency and immense popularity among people from all walks of life. The Book of Psalms, most obviously, surveys and contains the "premodern." This biblical/rabbinic period is an ancient semantic and narrative space that inscribes, revolts against, comments on, and commemorates the Egyptian, Sumerian, Akkadian, Ugaritic, and Babylonian poetic and mythic traditions. The fact that to this day most traditional Jews, even the illiterate, can recite the Psalms by heart as well as chant them to a variety of melodies, points to another significant act of cultural transmission, one reaching to an even earlier strata of the Levantine palimpsest.

The anthology/prayer books, along with the book of Arabic poetry, specifically place the coppersmith well into the period of Jewish history following the absorption of Baghdad's cacophonous plethora of contexts. It was only then that Jews steadily began navigating the waters of all the reigning discourses, with poetry kept as a favored reservoir. And it was also only after the bulk of that spadework had been done, following the "age of translation," that Sa'adiah Gaon, a native of Egypt elected to head the Babylonian Academy at Sura, found himself in the capital. Many of the projects that he saw as essential to firmly anchoring the criteria for a common vocabulary among the Jews, from the West to the East, were already behind him. These projects included the first translation of the Bible into Arabic (considered by many to be as significant as the Septuagint), the edition of the first "standardized" prayer book (the same one the coppersmith had), and the compilation of the first comprehensive Hebrew lexicon, complete with a rhyming dictionary for poets. Sa'adiah's centrality to the period that would follow him has been well documented; as Ross Brann writes, "Nearly all the revolutionary cultural changes wrought by the Jews of al-Andalus were prefigured in the work of R. Sa'adya Gaon al-Fayyumi (882-942), a brilliant Egyptian scholar and communal leader, and the first seminal figure in medieval Judaism."[70]

Before the Andalusian school, postbiblical poetry written by Jews could be roughly divided into two main spheres of activity. The first and longer tradition was that of the *paytanim* ("liturgical poets," the term being a derivation of the Greek *poietes* and appearing in Hebrew sources as early as the second century), lasting from about the sixth century to the eleventh, with important centers in Palestine and Babylonia. The second was the pre-Islamic Jewish poetry of Southern Arabia, of which only fragments survive, most notably those of Sarah and Samawal Ibn Adiya. The *piyut* (liturgical poem), went through many different phases. The most important, for our purposes, is the linguistic change from the relatively clean biblical usage in the early tradition, to a progressively more complicated and abstruse use of neologisms, obscure allusions, and highly specialized Talmudic and Midrashic vocabulary that characterizes the later *piyut*. Although the *piyut* often brilliantly managed to go beyond the very strict formal and functional constraints to which they were bound, Sa'adiah Gaon was the first to systematically practice the reforms needed to expand the possibilities of a Hebrew poetics that had exhausted itself. The main element of his approach consisted of the concept of *tsahut*. This term means "clarity," or "purity of style," and refers primarily to the adoption of the Bible—biblical vocabulary and usage—as the sole model of excellence for Hebrew poetry. Ross Brann has laid out some of the context for these innovations:

> The revolutionary, at least for Jews, literary approach to the Bible was spawned by life in an Islamic environment. Methodological innovations in comparative Arabic and Hebrew philology, lexicography, and grammar germinated in early tenth-century Baghdad and spread to regional centers such as Spain, where linguistic research and biblical commentaries proliferated and were studied with religious zeal. Several internal and external factors renewed Jewish interest in the Bible, and instigated the scientific study of its language and its literary qualities. On the one hand, Jewish intellectuals were impelled to reexamine the meaning of the Bible in order to counteract Karaite charges that Rabbinate Judaism neglected revealed scripture in favor of the rabbis' "counterfeit" oral Torah (torah she-be-'al peh [rabbinic tradition]). On the other, the sway of Arabism (al-'arabiyya) and the cult of the "inimitable wondrousness of the Qu'ran" (i'jaz al-qur'an; cf. Qur'an 90:18), the model of Quranic exegesis (tafsir), and interconfessional attacks on biblical anthropomorphism set the intellectual agenda and restored the Bible to the center of the Jewish curriculum.[71]

Without entering into elaborate technical, historical, or theological debates and descriptions, the following anecdote told by Moses Ibn Ezra in *The Book of Conversations and Memories* gives a very exact sense of the psychological and emotional weight carried by these Arabic linguistic concepts:

> Once, in the days of my youth, in the country of my birth, one of the great Muslim sages, a man extremely adept in all aspects of judgment, requested that I read before him the Ten Commandments in Arabic. I understood his intention: he wished to diminish the value of their "rhetorical purity." Therefore I asked him to read before me the Opening of the Koran in Latin, a language he knew perfectly. When he attempted translating the Opening into Latin, he found the original beauty was marred, and the whole thing laughable. Then he understood what I had meant and did not renew his request.[72]

Although the Arabic influence on Hebrew writing was absolutely pervasive, Arabic and Hebrew writers faced very dissimilar sets of past and
present references and relations, which made the context and the social
space in which their work was received quite different. No matter what
kind of agitation modernity and the innovations in science or philosophy
aroused, poetry—in both Hebrew and Arabic—maintained the logic of
its own linguistic and historical circumstances. Not that science or philosophy and the introduction of new texts on such a massive scale had no
effect on reorienting, circumscribing, diminishing, or expanding the
space of poetry. The effects of these things were certainly significant, yet
the functional role and position of the poet within each respective society
and culture remained very specific, and it usually dictated, in a subtler but
more unyielding way, the possible boundaries poets inherited.

By Sa'adiah's time, the history of "modern" Arabic poetry was already well over 150 years old and could be characterized by a very complex relationship to the Koran and monotheistic religious thought on one
hand, and to the rich pre-Islamic pagan oral poetic tradition (going some
300 years further back) on the other. As the encyclopedias of the tribe,
shamans believed to possess extraordinary powers, the ancient Arabic
poets of the *jahalliyah* (the time of ignorance) were powerful figures who,
in a very real way, witnessed and ritualized the being in time of their
people. As public poets of the desert, that space characterized by Jabès as
"at once everything and nothing," which is itself "listening pushed to the
extreme,"[73] the reciprocity between performance and reception, the song
and the memory of the song, crystallized into what can be termed "a critique of reality from the point of view of music."[74] It was against the
bedrock of this experience that the standards of all Arabic poetry were
measured, even following the radical transformation from orality to
writing and the ensuing changes in social structure that came with the
Prophet Muhammad's astonishing revelation received in the form of the
Koran:

> In the pre-Islamic period, the poet's role was to flout norms of caution
> and reasonable self-interest, and through such recklessness to fashion a
> model for the balanced life. Under Islam, the community lived the
> balanced life, which Koran, prophetic tradition, and religious law
> mapped out between the permissible and the forbidden. The poet
> moved out into the margin. He was still the reckless character of the old
> tradition, but his function had changed. He used to provide the
> structure; now he evaded it. He became an actor whose best role was
> some form of institutionalized disorder. For this role society had a ready
> slot, and there we very likely have a more important social cause for the

flourishing of love song and drinking song than either in the new elegance of Mecca or in the luxurious solicitations of the Iraqi cities.[75]

The dialectic between these two positions—between critical beauty (the oral/encyclopedic past) and received truth (the graphic/monotheistic present) embodied in the text of the Koran (a work unique and set apart, composed neither of prose nor verse)—opened a completely new space for poetry. This newly found space would again aspire to "providing the structure," but in very different terms. A poet like Abu-Nuwas, for example, could "transform drunkenness, which rids the body of the censures of logic and tradition, into a symbol of total liberation." In such an order, or disorder, "the symbol is an immense vestibule of metamorphoses. Wine is no longer wine. It is symbol and interpretant: transformative, annihilating, creative, negating and affirmative power."[76] For Hebrew poets using Arabic models, each term in these equations took on entirely different meanings and related to other sets of circumstances altogether. This phenomenon, of necessity, often led to those apparently anachronistic situations such as the one we have already witnessed, in which ancient pagan Arabic melodic modes—filtered through particular practices and conflicts—were retained for over a millenium as defining categories for Hebrew poetry written to be performed in synagogues.

Like almost all the Jewish writers born into the world of "new" Arabic poetry, Sa'adiah also tried his hand at verse, in an ambitious work that attempted a methodical union between "philosophic" and "poetic" discourse, based on his innovative rhetorical approach. Distinction as a poet, though, went to Sa'adiah's prize student, and it was there, in Baghdad, that Dunash Ben Labrat began the experiments that radically changed the course of Hebrew writing. The Eastern Caliphate had already come under foreign rule and was in a state of decay. Mutanabbi, one of the last giants of an Arabic tradition already 500 years old, "expressed the Zeitgeist—the anguish of the homeless individual personifying the lost empire—in textured language powered by a unity of intellect and emotion."[77] As an aside, it is not insignificant to note the presence of Mutanabbi in both Ghada al-Samman's Beirut Nightmares and "The Desert: Diary of Beirut Under Siege, 1982," by Adonis. In al-Samman's novel, which "chronicles 7 days and 206 nightmares spent in a villa next to the Holiday Inn and the Phoenicia Hotel during the Hotels Battle of 1975, the protagonist endures the helpless waiting, armed only with Mutanabbi's poetry and a fierce determination to survive."[78] In section 19 of "The Desert," Adonis writes, "What is it that touched Mutanabbi / Other than this soil that felt his tread? / He betrayed many things, / But not his vision."[79]

Dunash Ben Labrat, that younger Jewish poet of the early medieval period, transferred the accumulated knowledge of this Arabic tradition to initiate another age that, hundreds of years later, would also be looked back on, with nostalgia and pride, as source and model. Unlike the coppersmith, no record of any robes or rugs that Dunash might have possessed exists. We do know, however, that around 960 he went West, attracted by the efforts of the Jewish physician and minister Hasdai Ibn Shaprut to lure the leading intellects of the East into Abd al-Rahman III's court at Cordoba. It was from there that a poem by Dunash—sung to this day by all traditional Jews—must have entered the coppersmith's other volume, the Western or Mughrabi prayerbook. Partly because of the many tunes it has been set to, this hymn (*Deror Yiqera*, which could be translated as "Let Freedom Ring"), remained Dunash's most popular work, but not the work through which he gained such notoriety as a radical innovator. For this, one has to turn to his brash grammatical guerrilla raids on the older, more established Menahem Ibn Saruk (also aimed, by implication, at Dunash's master Sa'adiah, whom Ibn Saruk ostensibly rose to defend), and then to the poetry itself, specifically to the first Hebrew wine song:

And he said: "Don't sleep! Drink fine wine,
amidst myrrh and lilies, henna and aloes,
in groves of pomegranates, palms and vines
lined with lovely saplings, coursed by tamarisks,
the murmur of fountains, the strain of lutes
and the sound of minstrels with flutes and lyres.
Every tree is full, every branch graced by fruit
and birds, each in kind, lilt among the leaves.
The doves voice a plaintive melody and their
mates answer, cooing like deep-toned reeds.
We'll drink by the lily-bordered flowerbeds,
we'll eat sweets and wash them down by the bowlful,
we'll raise our goblets and act like giants.
In the morning I'll rise to slaughter
ample choice bulls, rams and calves.
We'll anoint ourselves with fine oil
and burn incense made of aloes.
Come on, before fate lowers its boom—
let's enjoy ourselves in peace!

    I lashed out at him: Be still, be still.
    How can this come first, when the Temple,
    God's footstool, has fallen to the uncircumcised?

    You spoke like a fool, you chose idle rest

Your talk is vain, like that of dolts and curs!
You left off studying the Law of God the Highest,
even now, as you rejoice, jackals run wild in Zion.

How can we drink wine
how even raise our eyes
when we are nothing,
loathed and despised?[80]

Although other similar works may very well have been written in Hebrew before or around the same time, this wine song has come to stand as
a marker clearly differentiating everything on either side of it. This cleavage dividing the two collective durations has, for the sake of convenience, here been labeled the "premodern" and the "modern." Interpretation of the poem has also, traditionally, been divided into two schools
of thought. One sees the first long stanza as a somewhat clumsy but nevertheless acceptable attempt at imitating an Arabic wine song with the
last three short stanzas apologetically tacked on as a reassuring nod to
"tradition." The second version sees things the other way around: the
first stanza as a preening, almost contemptuous display of prowess
mocking "oriental" indolence, with the last three stanzas carrying the
weight and the "real" message of the poem: the real message, again, being "tradition, tradition, tradition," but this time with the accent and intonation of Tevye from *Fiddler on the Roof*, heaping guilt upon a fellow
Jew wandering out of the fold.

Such approaches obfuscate both internal and external evidence. Both
parts of the poem display extraordinary skills that verge on bravado. Despite flaws, Dunash's act of transference—metrically, generically, the-
matically, and conceptually—would be tantamount to the hypothetical
case of a young American poet moving to London and deciding to write
pastoral poetry in "pure" Middle English using a combination of blank
and projective verse measured by variable feet! The differences between
the indirect speech of the first stanza (opening with a standard Arabic
convention, *wa-qal*, "And he said"), and the emphatically directed speech
in the following stanzas strengthen the rhetorical effect of a small drama
enacted within a particular setting. The irony of the setting, however,
must be sought outside that setting, using external evidence. The setting
is, of course, the site of the new Hebrew poetry: the garden of courtly
relations, where gatherings turned into literary contests. T. Carmi has
described this scene:

> Secular Hebrew poetry was born at the courts of Jewish grandees who
> served as courtiers to Muslim rulers, at first in the caliphate of Cordoba
> (927-1013) and later, after the dissolution of the caliphate, in the smaller

Muslim principalities. This aristocratic birth set its mark not only on the subjects of the poetry, but also on its style and character. Its main genres were panegyrics, laments on the death of the patron or his relatives, songs of self-praise, invectives aimed at the patron's rivals, the poet's rivals or, when the need arose, against the hard-fisted patron himself; aphoristic verse; stylized wine songs and love songs which, to the accompaniment of instrumental music, regaled the company gathered for a drinking session in the palace garden in springtime or the palace courtyard in winter.[81]

But this was not, by any means, the only setting for Hebrew poetry, as even Dunash's own production reveals. Nor did the setting of such a song have remotely the same meaning for Hebrew and Arabic poets. Beyond the world of the court depicted in panegyrics, love songs, wine songs, complaints, and meditations, Hebrew poets fulfilled a completely different function for a very different audience through the personal/communal religious lyric and liturgical poetry. Here, they were placed in a unique position: worldly people serving as intimate interlocutors between the community, the individual, and God. Most Hebrew poets wrote for the synagogue, in one form or another, and only a tiny minority of the hundreds of extant poets were exclusively courtiers or professionals. Yet even they, no matter how secular their verse appeared, still wrote according to the strict standards of an Andalusian poetics that insisted on the "biblical purity" of its language, with all the inevitable explicit and implicit religious allusions that entailed.

It is precisely this relationship of medieval literature to the "religious" that poses the most problems in many contemporary approaches to it. There is a marked tendency to lean toward either one of two extremes: the reductionist fallacy or the magnification fallacy. The reductionists gloat over any nondoctrinal chink in the wall of orthodoxy through which some secular spark might attest to the blinding light of reason. The magnifiers, on the other hand, disregard or distort whatever cannot be allegorized. Both, needless to say, miss the point, and display a kind of hysterical immaturity that only cliffhangers and those long accustomed to hovering over an abyss can appreciate. In a Jewish context this problem becomes even stickier, since Jewish "orthodoxy" is generally identified as a particular Eastern European brand. The seemingly casual approach to "religion" and the entirely different relationship to God that permeates the Levantine or Arab sensibility seems surprising and even anomalous in the context of such cultural assumptions.

In the case of this wine song, the external evidence, the possibility that Dunash—a favored student of one of the greatest legal and philosophical minds in all Jewish history and the foremost religious authority of the time—could even think in terms of the "religious" and the "secular," or of being "in" or "out" of the "fold," limns the irony of the situation. This irony is more precisely disclosed when one considers the discrepancy between the persona of the "rebuker" ("We are nothing / loathed and despised") and the actual status of Dunash the poet, an honored member of the Caliph's elite. But even this reading is further problematized by the poet's art. The very powerful dirgelike rhythm (*dóm, dóm . . . áykh tikdóm*) of the rebuker's entrance and the clipped, sharper beat of the rest of the poem force the reader/listener into an internalized sensual relationship with the lazier, extended measure of the drawn-out garden scene. This relationship is never really resolved but simply allowed to coexist within the space circumscribed.

This quality of being in-between, in between Fez and Baghdad, between the "world" and the "community," the space of the courtly garden and the place of kinship embodied in the covenantal relationship to a lost kingdom, does not relegate the poet to a state of limbo, being neither here nor there. The final *topos* of the poem ("Zion in ruin while we shamelessly indulge ourselves") emphatically asks that the context of the *geniza* world, where "Zion" was not some distant unreachable dream but simply another spot on a very familiar and accessible map, be seriously taken into account. In light of the poetics of "rhetorical purity" that Dunash and his followers practiced, the ingredients of this poem and the career of its author ironically chart what is most particular about the Levant, its people and their works: an almost anarchic lack of purity and exclusivity, the inexhaustible knack of being in many places in many times at once.

VI. Yehuda al-Harizi and Old Metaphors

In "Averroës' Search," Borges writes of the philosopher's perplexity at the presence of "two arcane words" that "pullulate throughout the text of the *Poetics* . . . tragedy and comedy."[82] Although the story dwells on the incongruousness of the philosopher's utter incapacity to decipher what the writer assumes as given for his readers, Borges goes on to dissect the tale's overly algebraic assumptions: "I felt that Averroës, wanting to imagine what a drama is without ever having suspected what a theater is, was no more absurd than I, wanting to imagine Averroës with no other sources than a few fragments from Renan, Lane and Asin Palacios." Interestingly enough, the Baghdad-born Israeli scholar Shmuel Moreh has done some pioneering work on the theater in medieval Islam, research that would further confound Borges's own labyrinthine sense of the available.[83]

The inability ever to be fully present in that other world, the absurdity of the narrator, is most evident in Averroës's longest discourse, a defense of the use of "old metaphors":

In Alexandria, it has been said that the only persons incapable of sin are those who have already committed it and repented; to be free of an error, let us add, it is well to have confessed it. Zuhair in his *mohalaca* says that in the course of eighty years of suffering and glory many times he has seen destiny suddenly trample men in the dust, like a blind camel; Abdelmalik finds that this figure can no longer marvel us. Many things could be offered in response to this objection. The first, that if the purpose of the poem is to surprise us, its lifespan would not be measured in centuries, but in days and hours and perhaps minutes. The second, that a famous poet is less of an inventor than he is a discoverer. In praise of Ibn-Sharaf of Berja it has been repeated that only he could imagine that the stars at dawn fall slowly, like leaves from a tree; if this were so, it would be evidence that the image is banal. The image one man can form is an image that touches no one. There are infinite things on earth; any one of them may be likened to any other. Likening stars to leaves is no less arbitrary than likening them to fish or birds. However, there is no one who has not felt at some time that destiny is clumsy and powerful, that it is innocent and also inhuman. For that conviction, which may be passing or continuous, but which no one may elude, Zuhair's verse was written. What was said there will not be said better. Besides (and this is perhaps the essential part of my reflections), time, which despoils castles, enriches verses. Zuhair's verse, when he composed it in Arabia, served to confront two images, the old camel and destiny; when we repeat it now, it serves to evoke the memory of Zuhair and to fuse our misfortune with that dead Arab's. The figure had two terms then and now it has four. Time broadens the scope of verses and I know of some which, like music, are everything for all men. Thus, when I was tormented years ago in Marrakesh by memories of Cordova, I took pleasure in repeating the apostrophe Abdurrahman addressed in the gardens of Ruzafa to an African palm:

> You too, oh palm!, are
> Foreign to this soil . . .

The singular benefit of poetry: words composed by a king who longed for the Orient served me, exiled in Africa, to express my nostalgia for Spain.[84]

Following Dunash, the Andalusian school—with antecedents in the "new" Arabic poetry and its ancient heritage—triggered an explosion of new writing. This explosion first rocked back and forth from the western to the eastern Levant, from city to city, according to fortune and the vicissitudes of power. Then, because of expulsion or immigration, it reached beyond the Old World and into the New. Of about 350 writers that could be chosen for a possible, very selective, anthology, only two were born, lived, and died in the same place: Sarah Coppia Sullam, a poet from Venice, and Haim Palaggi, a rabbi from Smyrna. Fully intent on the possibilities of each idiom they encountered, these writers turned their cities to books and lived in words, but never as a means of excluding themselves from the world they inhabited. Refusing to use tradition as a barricade, they avidly pursued and confronted the new: first in Hebrew, Arabic, and Aramaic, then in Spanish, Provençal, Italian, Latin, Catalan, Portuguese, Greek, Turkish, Persian, Berber, Serbian, French, English, Dutch, and more than a few other mother tongues. Every imaginable form appeared—in parchment and newsprint, divan and prayer book, question and commentary, document and fable—each with its own curious history and mode of transmission: philosophical, medical, legal, and mystical writings; mathematics, astronomy, alchemy, grammar, music theory, and dream interpretation; poetics, commentary, linguistics, and literary criticism; rhymed prose narrative, picaresque, pastoral, and realistic novels; geography, cartography, travel accounts, and history; drama, opera, and lyric.

But strict periodization emerging from only one or even several major lines of influence serves no real purpose in tracing the course of this writing. After all, the different peoples inhabiting the greater Levant literally lived in different historical times using different calendars. One has to imagine, rather than a chronological sequence, different traditions at different stages of development being influenced by different things in very different ways. Usually bi- or trilingual, like many medieval Europeans, these writers often used different languages for different audiences or purposes. The plethora of contexts delineating the range of choices possible in any writing—what one transforms, takes in, rejects, writes through or across—finds a remarkably concentrated form among these Levantine writers. Accumulatory and accretionary qualities operate on semantic, narrative, and generic levels. These occur through syntactic patterns, nuances, words, forms, and meters borrowed or adapted from other languages, as well as through the tiered texture of *fabulae* going into the common pool of image and event that could be drawn on and recast. Moreover, each generation would inherit what was current in its own surroundings plus all the baggage of the past. This both greatly intensified relations to the wider implications of each of the four concepts of autonomy, translatability, diversity, and mobility; and contributed to another marked characteristic that courses, never too far below the surface, throughout the writing. This characteristic is the persistence of "old met-

aphors" and the tricky process, to paraphrase "Averroës," of allowing
"time to broaden their scope."

The currency of familiar counters, however, and the almost obstinate
sense of conservation are accompanied by an apparently contradictory
urge: a great openness toward new idioms and forms. Hebrew poets, for
instance, could be arch-conservatives in their "own" tradition, and experiment freely using the material of others. Immanuel of Rome (c. 1261-
1332), the first poet to write sonnets in a language other than Italian (using the form in Hebrew over a hundred years before either the French or
the English imported it), is a perfect example of this. A poet like Immanuel lived and worked simultaneously in three sequences: his own ritual
and textual time, as commentator on the Song of Songs; the agitated
course of Dante and poets of the *dolce stil novo*, with whom he exchanged
Italian sonnets; and the opaque world of Arabic narrative, with its stock
of characters and situations, received through Hebrew versions and
translations. While extremely innovative in his adaption of Italian material, Immanuel still based his work on Arabic models, conventions, narrative structures, and metaphors already in circulation for over 300 years.

The very revival of Hebrew, the gesture initiated by Dunash on Sa'a-
diah's philological scaffolding and continuously rehearsed throughout
the "modern" period, itself enacts an omnidirectional movement. This
movement reveals other aspects of the contradictory relations between
the "old" and the "new," tradition and invention, the steady accumulation of time and the bright flash of novelty, tensions reproduced throughout the intersecting history of Jewish writing in the Levant. By adopting
Arabic "software" as the guiding system through which biblical antecedents could be programmed, the Andalusian poets achieved a radical rereading of their own Ur-text. By inscribing Arabic so deeply within the
palimpsest, they simultaneously preserved and obliterated it while creating both hybrid and completely original forms that went on to assume
the historical logic of their own particular circumstances. The double
movement embodied in the practice of this gesture opens a whole new
problematic and series of questions regarding different forms and expressions of social identity and allegiance within writing. These are particularly pronounced in terms of particularism and universalism, the possible
mobility between "high" and "low" culture, and the implications of formal and linguistic "choice" within the different spaces of expression
available to men and women, or to people of different social standing.

Part of this problematic remains open to scrutiny in the work of Yehuda al-Harizi (c. 1170-1235), the polymath after whose work Immanuel
fashioned his *Notebooks*. Although a native of Christian Toledo, it was
al-Harizi who summed up, crystallized, and, in a sense, managed to

transfer, transform, and recirculate the best of the Andalusian golden age into which he found himself belatedly born. By his time, the giants— Hanagid, Ibn Gabirol, Ibn Ezra, and Yehuda Halevi—were already dead. Although Spain itself had become the nexus of both rich exchange and violent confrontation between the Cross and the Crescent, the old cities newly conquered by the Christians remained Arabic in custom, taste, and style. In such a context, translation and the correct interpretation of signs could be a matter of cultural or actual life and death. In fact, the ability to solve riddles and read situations that called for decisions whose swiftness and morality could mean survival, whether physical or spiritual, re- mained a major theme in a genre that underwent a renaissance of sorts during this period. This form, the *maqama*, consisted of rhymed prose tales interspersed with poetry. Collections of these, forming books built around confounding circles of structural ploys, subtle and startling shifts between "fact" and "fiction," attained a remarkably dense and complex narrative texture.

As master of this genre, al-Harizi's own career was emblematically di- vided into three overlapping parts. Each role—whether translator, poet, or traveler—deftly played along the margins of the vigilant and ambiva- lent range of feelings internalized in his fiction. These feelings, ranging from intense pride to a vulnerable sense of precariousness, are certainly connected to Spain's position at the vanguard of a new world order, in- timating and ushering in the decisive westward shift whose eventual frontier would only end at the Pacific. Yet al-Harizi's decision to translate the most popular Arabic work of the age, move back to the East, and span the full generic range available to him in his own work, also indi- cates an acute and often very moving awareness of the need to document a past about to be lost. His position, then, for the Hebrew/Jewish culture of the Levant, is analogous to that of Aristotle's in the Hellenic world and Chaucer's in medieval Europe. All three gather paradigms in an attempt to fend off the sweeping effects of changing orders without realizing the overarching trajectory of their gestures, the fact that their work would go on to reanimate the life of forms by sustaining the specific knowledge contained within them. David Shasha has written a brilliant analysis of the historical meaning of al-Harizi's generic choices:

> Interestingly enough, it is the use of a relatively arcane Arabic genre
> which heralds the Arabs' departure from the territory as a ruling power.
> It is as if by writing in such a manner, the Jews and Muslims who
> remained (but particularly the Jews) would be able to summon the
> ghosts of the buried past back to Toledo. In the context of Jewish
> writing, al-Harizi served to rejuvenate a moribund intelligentsia. The
> narrative framework of *maqama*, as honed and perfected by al-Harizi,

well suited the nascent culture of Jews in Christian Spain. Gone were the expansive courtiers and their patrons who provided the material and intellectual context for the secular poems. Gone was the liberality of a Rabbinate which held liturgical and secular poetry to the same scientific standards as the philosophy so beloved of the scholars. In place of this cultural freedom was a narrowly confined religious system and a burgeoning feudal aristocracy which never really came to terms with the "moorish" culture that had become indigenous to the space of al-Andalus. Utilizing *maqama* as a variant framework, the writers of this period continued to feed off of their predecessors' hunger for language, but now fused it with what we might call the fictive impulse. For the first time in a long while, Jewish writers had the opportunity to tell stories, the tales being even more crucial to their way of life which was rapidly disintegrating.[85]

Again, a rather stark indication of the present status of the way of life and culture al-Harizi gathered is the fact that his work is presently out of print.

As translator, al-Harizi's "minor" works included versions of texts by Aristotle, Galen, and the Christian medical authority Hunayn Ibn Ishaq. His major translations included the *Guide to the Perplexed* by Maimonides and his masterful rendition of the enormously popular picaresque *Assemblies* of al-Hariri (d. 1122). This remarkable accomplishment became the first object of al-Harizi's often boundless pride. Seven Hebrew poets had attempted one or several of the fifty sections before him, but only al-Harizi took the *Assemblies* whole. By fully transferring it into a Hebrew context, with biblical equivalents and correspondences, it could serve as both primer and "proof" of precedence and, if not superiority, then certainly equality with the "poetry that Hagar, Sarai's Egyptian handmaiden, had borne."[86] Because of the sheer variety of scriptural fictions (and despite the obvious and blatant Arabic models), these claims led to an even more refined and firmly rooted appreciation of the Bible as linguistic, narrative, and metaphorical source than that achieved and practiced by the classical Andalusian Hebrew poets:

> And they said that our language is too narrow and its rhetoric is deficient. But they know not that the lack is in those who do not comprehend its speech and do not recognize its loveliness, like one who has disease in his eyes, and the sun, that shines before him, grows dark. He thinks that the accident or the plague is in the sun and he knows not that the plague is in his own eyes. Thus, most of our people despise the Holy Tongue because its themes are too wonderful for them. Eyes have they but they see not the light. The manna is before them but when they go forth to gather they find it not. The rivers of Eden are before

them yet they are athirst. And I took up my parable:

> Woe to the fools, like wild asses they bray;
> Beside fountains of Eden, yet thirst they all day.
> Manna is before their eyes—but their eyes are blind.
> They go forth to gather but none do they find.

Now many of those that slept in the soil of folly awoke and they made the chariots of their tongues race through the road of song. They planned to translate the book of this Arab Hariri, from the Arabic tongue into the Sacred Tongue, Hebrew, and they came in prosaic garments to serve in the sanctuary of the muse. And when they came forth equipped for the battle of poetry, they could only take as spoils one out of the fifty. For by the power of the metaphors of the book they were dismayed and terrified, and at the sound of its thunders and hailstones they perished and were exterminated, and the hail came down upon them and they died. . . .

Until I arose and wrought its armor. I translated the whole book with fitting prose and poems like pearls, pure and salty.[87]

The weakness of the "public," the callous vulgar audience, is an old theme, familiar in the work of Ibn Gabirol ("If your ears are uncircumcised, how / can my bell be heard? Your necks are not fit to wear my golden crescents"),[88] and prevalent with the later troubadours. For al-Harizi, once the test of translation was over, the transference accomplished, there had to be a further move:

Now when I had fulfilled their desire and had translated the book, I forsook my home and I wandered on roads, I sailed on ships. I crossed seas. I fled from the West and I shone in the East. And I saw that I had done foolishly and my iniquity was greater than I could bear in having neglected to compose a book of our own poetry, as though the word of the living God were not among us. I had hastened to keep the vineyard of strangers, but mine own vineyard I had not kept.[89]

Here al-Harizi's pride and arrogance seem tempered: first by his own experience as a wandering poet in search of patrons, and then through the clearly popular form of his new book. The *Tahkemoni*, addressed as an entertainment to a wide audience, has an obvious didactic thrust, even if the very assertion of that purpose is condescendingly put: "And how much this new book will help the people of all the provinces from Egypt unto Baghdad, many of whose tongues stumble and whose reading is deficient and bad when they speak the Holy Tongue. For through this book they will smooth their ways and will speak correctly—they will say well what they speak. Through it their thoughts will awake from the sleep of folly and their eyes will be opened and they will know that they are naked. And they will sew leaves of rhetoric and songs and will make themselves girdles."[90]

The leaves of this rhetoric were gathered from every possible branch of letters, as al-Harizi himself is careful to point out in the proem to his "fifty-gated" work:

> And I gathered in this book many parables and sweet themes. Among them various poems and striking riddles, words of instruction, songs of friendship, proverbs of right things; words of admonition, events of the time and tidings of the years. The remembrance of death and the place of the shadow of death; words of repentance, and pardoning of guilt. The delights of love and pangs of love. The betrothing of women, bridal canopy and marriage, and matters of divorce; the drunkenness of drunkards; the asceticism of ascetics; wars of heroes and events of kings; the adventures of the road; songs of praise, and supplications of prayers; ethics of the sages, and associations of the upright. The passion of lovers; gardens and hamlets; words of princes; the patter of children; the hunt of hunters; the treachery of deceivers, and the folly of fools; the slandering of scorners, the blaspheming of revilers. And wonderful songs and epistles written in a marvelous way: in order that this book may be as a garden in which are all manner of dainties and pleasant plantations. And in it each seeker will find their heart's desire.[91]

As in al-Hariri's *Assemblies* and, for that matter, almost all collections of rhymed prose narrative, the glue holding all these pieces together consists of the complex relationship spun among all these: the author as author; the author as narrator; the protagonists as narrators, authors, and witnesses; and every possible combination imaginable between and among all of these. As the late Dan Pagis noted: "In each episode (chapter, "gate," individual maqama) there are two recurrent characters. One is the protagonist (al-Hariri's Abu Zaid; al-Harizi's Heber the Kenite), a wandering poet, scholar and picaro–like rogue who often appears in disguise and does not shrink from deception and fraud, yet endears himself to the reader by his wit, inventiveness and zest for life. The other character, the witness-narrator (al-Hariri's Harith ben Hammam; al-Harizi's Heman the Ezrahite) relates his friend's, the protagonist's, escapades and presents his rhetorical achievements."[92] In addition to this narrative layering, it is important to note that the *maqama* presents a qualitatively different relationship between the poet's language and its biblical sources and referents:

> *Maqama* looks at the text as a map of broken-up (or broken-down) possibilities. The tableau is strewn with broken pieces of stray objects waiting to be picked up and pieced back together. The *maqama* creates

the illusion of order while in reality it remains variegated. In real terms, the prose and poetry of the *maqama* serves to harriedly juxtapose elements which are not so neatly wrapped up. The poem is an ornate edifice that builds and ends up as a splendid tower meant to be admired. The *maqama* is a quick lunge, an attack if you will, on the very conventionality of verse. It sends the verses of the Bible and earlier poets every which way and cares little where the pieces might fall. The stylistic and formal energy of *maqama* is overwhelming."[93]

Although the continued encounters and unlikely scenes might appear repetitive or tedious to the uninitiated, each episode plays subtle and more startling variations on an underlying theme. In al-Harizi's book, the protagonist Heber is a function of the literal meaning of his own name, derived from the Hebrew root *haber*: to join, connect, stitch together, unite, compose, or write. As he himself says:

> Indeed they call my name Heber because
> I write all scattered precious poetry.[94]

All Heber's efforts are put into gathering, retrieving the "scattered" pearls and putting them into some kind of order. Yet each episode—after Heman recognizes his "boon companion" or Heber gives up his own disguise—ends in parting. The intensity and meaning of each of these partings is very different but the fact remains: Heber and Heman are doomed to part at the end of every meeting. This division reiterates and adumbrates "the remembrance of death and the place of the shadow of death." One clue to uncovering al-Harizi's intent, his wish to fully compile the example of Spain in a book since its actuality had past, is that the most poignant parting between the companions comes at the end of Gate 18, a definitive chapter of *ars poetica* and literary history. Here, Heber doesn't even divulge his name, and only circumscribes his identity:

> I am the companion of all who seek me,
> Migratory Oaks is the city of my habitation.
> In the tourney of the intellect, my praises are my weapon,
> And I make my tongue—my lance.[95]

Embedded within an often hilarious narrative structure worthy of Flann O'Brien is a history that is also a tale of mutability. It is no coincidence that one of the Andalusian school's most effective weapons, a tool used both to stave off mortality and to regenerate meaning, was embedding, or the use of biblical citation within verse lines or rhymed prose. The Hebrew term, *shibbutz* (to embroider, inlay, ornament), derives from the Arabic *al-iktibas* ("The lighting of a candle from a lamp already lit, or the kindling of a flame from a fire already blazing, perceived as an analogue to the Koran as source of light").[96] Franz Rosenzweig, ever sensitive to the incredibly layered and intricate implications of citation for the translation of Hebrew poetry, stressed that it is "by no means an ornamental appendage," but a basic material. He called embedding the "coined form" of the poet's ideas, "the paper slip enveloping speech."[97]

Poets often begin from citations embedded within the body of a text so as to make them appear as if they were added on later, as fillers. This further confounds realization of the allusive nature of this practice. As al-Harizi himself, or rather a character speaking through the voice of Heman the Ezrahite, notes: "Know that there are ways to poetry, and paths and roads for rhymes. They have art forms, guarded and arranged. But the best of the arts is to take a verse from the prophetical books and build a choice and lovely theme on it."[98] The slip, then, is more often a veil, but one that can never be perceived as static. Rather, it remains perpetually mobile, hiding and revealing different things as it moves with the poet's relationship to the text within its new context, and with the "crisis of choice" faced by the reader in directing remembrance and intellect in the act of interpretation. This process gets to the root of what is unique and innovative about the Arabic poetics inherited by Hebrew writers.

As absurd as Borges felt trying to piece together "Averroës" from odd scholarly fragments, there is little question that Averroës, Ibn Rushd himself, did try to grapple with fragments of Aristotle and the poetic concepts that could be derived from them. Significantly, Averroës adopted the term "poetic discourse" (rather than "poetry") as a working category. Like al-Farabi (d. 950) and Avicenna/Ibn Sinna (d. 1036) before him, he remained intent not on determining, like Aristotle, "the *genus commune* in which all kinds of imitative arts converged," but "the *ultima differentia* of poetic art."[99] One thing that clearly does differentiate Semitic poetic discourse from all others is the extraordinarily high "degree of verbal consciousness" expected of the reader.[100] This kind of awareness assumes that figures of speech have the power to provoke psychological, intellectual, even mystical connections and correspondences. Again, terminology is of great significance. The Arabic term *takhyil* (a mental process by which the poet can cause mimetic representations to be imagined, effective and creative), was characterized by Ibn Sinna as "an acceptance."[101] The most powerful and evocative forms must allow the space needed for this "acceptance" to be shared, produced and reproduced by both reader and writer, a concept articulated in the astounding work of al-Jurjani, an eleventh-century rhetorician:

> If it is clear that an expression can be interpreted only in one way which
> is directly suggested by its apparent form without there being any

possibility of ambiguity in this expression, and if it can be realized that
the expression conveys what it conveys without any meditation,
reasoning and probing consideration, then there is no distinction in this
expression. For distinction and high esteem are qualities which are to be
reserved for what is (ambiguous, namely) that which in its apparent
form may be interpreted in a way other than its real interpretation, but
then one finds one's soul more intimate with the real (meaning) than
with the feasible one. . . . The noblest and most highly placed poetry
inevitably requires such participation, for the recipient needs to establish
structural relations between the various elements.[102]

For Hebrew poets, this participatory process was constantly reinforced through the practice of embedding, the effects of which are as varied as instances of its use. One of the essential keys to unlocking the secrets of the poetry of the "modern" Levantine period is the ability to
track words and phrases down. These must first be grasped in their original senses before one goes on to trace their histories and determine the
poet's possible or probable intent in using them within a new structure or
context. Time, naturally, broadens the scope of such verses. A biblical
phrase extracted from a narrative sequence may have legal connotations
in the Talmud, which can then be imbued with philosophic, cosmologi-
cal, or mystical implications, all of which—one can rest assured—poets
took into account.

Although al-Harizi is most known for his seamless use of citations to
achieve incongruous, ironic, and outrageously comic effects, he also initiated a new, very different form of embedding. By paraphrasing or even
directly citing lines from the classical Andalusian poets of the generations
preceding him, al-Harizi also displaces their citations in order to recon-
textualize them. Here, he renders a double homage that firmly fixes the
classical status of the Andalusian school, but within the criteria and terms
of his own text. This status, due to the narrative structure of al-Harizi's
work, is also injected with a note of "realism." This realism stands in
sharp contrast to prevalent "neomodern"/Enlightenment interpretations
and myths about Andalusian poetry and the world of which it formed a
part.

Like many before him, al-Harizi also made the pilgrimage to Jerusalem. This trip, as pointed out earlier, was entirely ordinary within the
parameters of the *geniza* world. It is, however, the journey of Yehuda
Halevi, al-Harizi's most famous pilgrim/poet predecessor, that has assumed the status of nationalist myth and model in the Zionist phase of
the "neomodern" period. The following poem, written by Halevi while
still in Spain before setting out for the Holy Land in 1140, can be seen as

a further, almost alchemical refinement on the rebuker's refrain in Dunash Ben Labrat's earlier wine song:

> My heart is in the East and
> I at the end of the West—
>
> How can I taste what I eat
> how make it sweet?
>
> How shall I fulfill my vows
> and binding ties while Zion
>
> is held by the cord of Edom
> and I by Arabia's bonds?
>
> I would find as much ease
> leaving all Spain's good
>
> as my eyes grace in seeing the
> dust of the ruined Shrine.[103]

Because of their grand but concise diction, purely crystallized emotion, evocative rhythms, and allusive language, all the poems left from
that journey (those from the outset and others, like the *Sea Songs* and the
"Egyptian sequence" composed in Alexandria along the way) rightfully
vie with the Psalms and the Song of Songs in the Hebrew canon. Yet, like
so many other works of the Levantine period, these poems have been less
read than used—like the perennial elephant of the Jewish joke—to hand-
ily answer one of the many forms of the "Jewish question," as another
piece of evidence to fit into the mold of a predetermined set of assumptions. At its most vulgar, this use makes Halevi into some kind of proto-
Zionist. This metamorphosis, naturally, precludes emphasizing the fact
that he was also known as Abu al-Hassan; that his Socratic dialogue, the
Kuzari, one of the most popular books among all Jews, was written in
Arabic; that most of his poetry, like that of his Andalusian counterparts,
was steeped in the material and spiritual culture of Islam; that the financial insurance behind his pilgrimage resulted from the holding in escrow,
through a business partner, of an expensive silk turban, probably as extravagant an item as any of those found in our traders' inventories.
Whether or not Halevi ever reached Jerusalem remains a mystery. His vision of the city, though, at a time when the Crusaders had barricaded
themselves in, remains ideal, exalted, removed from time, despite the
very personal, almost sensual tone of his magnificent poems:

> Lovely height, world's joy,
> city of the great King:
> my soul yearns for you

from the edges of the West,

the breadth of my pity
stirs remembering the East,
the exile of your Divinity,
and your Shrine's ruin.

Borne to you on eagle's
wings I'd drench your
dust in my tears until
they turn to mortar:
Though your King be not
within you, and in place of
your balm of Gilead venomous
snakes and scorpions are
found, I seek you. Shall
I not cherish and kiss
your stones, will not
the taste of that caked

mass be sweeter to
my mouth than honey?[104]

Some seventy-five years later, after the victory of Saladin, his cleansing of the mosques on the Temple Mount, and his decree allowing Jews back into the city, Jerusalem is portrayed as a much more worldly place. For a teller of moral tales such as al-Harizi, "Holy Land" was only part of an itinerary marked for the spirit within a whole ethical and qualitative space, unreachable and uninhabitable without an effective community. What concerned him, again, were questions of division, of gathering while being torn apart, from without or within:

The fire of strife flames day and night
Sundering the hearts of friends as blight
If pure and upright men don't put it out
God's wrath will burn against us without doubt.
For every ill men find a cure to make them well
But jealousy breaks and shatters one to hell.
All transgressions God can bear, even rage forbear,
But divisiveness He cannot, cannot bear![105]

VII. The Scarlet Thread of Song: From Samuel Hanagid to Yehezkel Hai Albeg

The scarlet thread of "old metaphors" binding the cities of the Levant together through its poetry never precluded either the personal or the original. Although steeped in conventions, poets set their very unique seal on what they were given. In the wide range of *carpe diem* motifs, for example, whether set in graveyards or in nature's open book, set pieces take unique and very real twists, as in this short poem by Moses Ibn Ezra:

> My thoughts roused me to stop by
> the resting place of my parents and
> my friends. I asked them, though none
> could listen or reply: have you all
> betrayed me, even my father and my
> mother? Mouthlessly they summoned
> me to them, and showed me my
> place at their side.[106]

Samuel Hanagid, the first major figure of the Andalusian school, for all the bravado he displayed as vizier and commander of the Muslim armies of Granada, was as intimately aware as Virgil of the inherent confusion and loss of self the individual faced through service to the state. Unlike Virgil's, Hanagid's world is not one of chiaroscuro. Even in the sublime space of creation, the blood of the battlefield seeps through:

> Look at the jasmine, whose branches, leaves,
> and stems are green as chrysolite, whose flowers
> are white as rock crystal, whose tendrils are
> red as carnelian—like a white-faced youth
> whose hands are shedding the blood of innocent men.[107]

Usually the setting of precious jewels in such a landscape presents a cameo within which a lover's face can be praised and beauty's transience lamented. In this poem, the progression from more common minerals such as chrysolite and rock crystal to the only precious stone mentioned, carnelian, immediately sets up a different response to that convention. A lover would not be compared to such relatively common materials, but the reddish hue of carnelian can begin to prepare us for the shocking end, the sudden switch from the expected erotic description to the blank youth—without eyes, ears, or mouth—fulfilling orders as changeless as the order of the correspondences in the world itself.

The ability to gather meaning from the conventional presumes familiarity with those conventions. The common Semitic and Arabic method (examined earlier in the work of Adonis and al-Ma'ari), of presenting an abstract statement, fixed later in the poem by a sharp image, becomes, in the hands of Hanagid, entirely his own:

> I survey the heavens and the stars; I
> look at the earth with its creeping
> creatures; and I understand in my

heart that they were all intricately
fashioned. Look up at the sky—like
a tent, whose clasps are joined to it
by loops; the moon and its stars—like
a shepherdess grazing her flock in a
pasture; the moon among the sweeping
clouds—like a ship sailing with raised
pennants; a cloud—like a girl walking
through a garden, watering the myrtles;
a cloud of dew—like a maiden shaking
the drops from her hair onto the ground.
But the earth's inhabitants are like
an army pitching its tents for a
night, looting the local granaries. And
all flee before the terror of death—
like a dove chased by a hawk. All are doomed
to be like an earthenware plate
which has been smashed to bits.[108]

In a sweep of the eye the poet sees a group of celestial objects and com-
pares them to a group of terrestrial objects, all held in absentia, in the
mind's eye. The imagination and the inner space of memory seem a safe
and fertile place—water leads to woman, a garden, home—but the spiral
down from the sky to the womb is intruded upon, crowded out by an
army, chased by a hawk, smashed like a plate. People plunder, loot, and
even rape the fruit of the earth's fertility without paying heed to the consequences. The impression of these parallels can be that of either an arbitrary, stock list or a perfectly ordered, intimately connected sequence.
Unused to trade in such currency, accustomed to not getting beyond
stock figures in treating the distant, and considering the poet whose tools
are honed by the rhetorical art to be some well-intentioned carpenter
whose material is not wood but words, we might choose the arbitrary.
But closer scrutiny (and familiarity with Hanagid's other work) shows
the imagery to have an inevitability and sense of tragic irony in its futility
that works backwards, each clause illuminating the one before it until the
last lines snap the whole picture into focus. The mind is free from the
ways of the world only insofar as it has the power to create its own order.
In one of the few profound readings of a medieval Hebrew poem available in English (in a book titled, significantly, *On the Art of Medieval Arabic Literature*), Andras Hamori concludes a long explication of this same
poem by Hanagid with the following:

Perhaps this impingement (that of comparison) is more than a poetic
mannerism; perhaps it goes some of the way toward redeeming the

experience of memory. Their end is to be compared; we do the comparing. We are imprisoned in time, every bit as much as the things that surround us; to compare, to sort out the relations about us, to actively experience our being in time is making the best of it.[109]

"Old metaphors" continued to channel the experience of memory and chart the geography of time within the enclosed garden of the Levant, long past the apparent dissolution of its early unity in the *geniza* world. Hebrew poets found the source of metaphor out of which they fashioned their art in the courtly and figurative scene of lovers' unions, the arena of song and the space of exile, as well as in the themes of fate and time's passing. Again, each of these "old metaphors" were marked by highly original twists and turns, as in this "Poem from Prison" by Todros Abulafia (c. 1247-1295), a native of Toledo:

> Debris and mire are spit up by the sea
> but corals sink to the very depths. This
> is Time's way: to raise the worthless and,
> in that elevation, humiliate the noble.
> Time turns good and bad upside down—
> it mocks those who think they've reached
> their station, but anyone of intelligence
> must come to taunt it, amuse themselves
> with a "perhaps" or an "if." After all,
> there is a balance in dust and heaven
> that pulls down the innocent
> and uplifts the wanting.[110]

This poem, like so many others, relies on embedding and the pun in the last line, a citation from Isaiah 40:15 ("the nations . . . are accounted as dust on the scales"), in which the word *shahak* means both "heaven" and "dust." Rather than being an ornament, the scriptural word here serves as the structure that can at least attempt to make the world's incongruities intelligible, though without justifying them.

By the thirteenth century, the Romance languages, though clearly part of the Andalusian vocabulary from the beginning (through the *khardjas*, those curious stanzas appended to Hebrew and Arabic girdle songs, and considered the oldest of any surviving Romance fragments),[111] began inscribing newer and deeper layers into the texture of the Levantine palimpsest. In addition to the classical Andalusian fare, it was al-Harizi's encyclopedic compendium that served as a directory indicating the repertoire available to poets born at these new intersections. The "picaro-like rogue," the wandering poet in search of patrons, now took on the guise of a real troubador, such as Isaac Hagorni, the thirteenth-century minstrel from Aire who drifted through the Jewish communities of southern France in search of a fitting audience. The apotheosis of song and the hermetic style of the troubadors (both typical of Hagorni), was then combined with the ritual discipline and cosmic implications of the kabbalah. This withdrawal of things into themselves can be seen in the work of Meshullam da Piera, one of the most innovative post-Andalusian poets:

> When they sang together, when my
> morning stars sang as the night was
> ending and light came from all sides;
> when the night was ending, the dark-
> ness expelled, and my sun rose in the
> East; when my thoughts shook off
> slumber and my limbs woke from their
> sleep of night—then I sought to greet
> the dawn with music and to worship
> the morning with song . . .
>   I began
> to sing and improvise, to see if my
> instruments would answer my words,
> to see if they would comfort me in my
> wandering, in this land of exile which
> is my home . . .
> O master of mysteries, have you ever
> known a musical instrument that would
> not strike up when I sing—and the
> birds voiceless among the branches, the
> swallow songless in my house? Yet I
> wish them well, for with their silence
> they counsel me to hide my works, to
> hide my words . . . [112]

As the confrontation between the Cross and the Crescent intensified in Spain, Hebrew poetry began to go underground more and more. No matter how precarious things sometimes got for the Jews within Islamic society, they remained a protected people, "the people of the Book." But Christian culture, particularly in Spain, asked things of the Jews that the Islamic structure never had. The kind of autonomy and recognition that had so long been assumed in the Levant underwent a process of erosion beginning in the thirteenth century and culminating in the first truly "modern" totalitarian project, the Inquisition, a structure whose logic would bring about the emergence of another truly modern phenomenon, the crypto-Jew; as Shmuel Trigano has written: "The Marrano Sephardic

Jews served, paradoxically, as the prototypes and the anguished laboratory of modernity, the 'political animal' divided into the fantasizing private person, and the universal citizen, abstract and theoretical. The citizen is 'free' but subject to law and the coercion of power. The private
individual is 'free,' but that liberty can only be exercised between the four
walls of 'cellular' rooms."[113]

Some writers, such as the remarkable fourteenth-century poet Shem
Tob Ardutiel, worked in both Hebrew and Spanish.[114] Others, such as
Solomon Bonafed, a member of the Saragossan "Band of Minstrels" and
the last prominent Hebrew poet in Christian Spain before the expulsion,
used the conceit of the love lyric to express an increasing sense of desperation:

> See how horses streak through the sea
> like lightning bolts, and ships sail
> through the market-place. A thread of
> linen splinters a bar of iron, and water
> blazes like wood. Leopards flee before
> kids and foxes give chase to lions. Nor
> should you marvel that the world is
> turned topsy-turvy and the times have
> strayed from their natural course. . . .
> Oppression grows from day to day . . .
>
> Oh, let us go, my fair companion, let us
> walk far afield, and amuse ourselves
> among the thickets . . . there we shall not see
> the vagaries of time nor pay heed to
> wicked betrayers. . . . Slowly, eagerly,
> we shall drink the wine of wisdom and
> feed on wafers of choice melodies—
> until time mend again what it had
> twisted and restore all it has ruined;
> until time set apart the lead from the
> gold . . . [115]

With the expulsion of the Jews from Spain in 1492, Hebrew poetry,
stuffing over 500 years into its itinerant baggage, set out for other shores.
Welcomed with open arms by the Ottomans, Jews settled throughout the
empire. They went to Safed, Constantinople, Smyrna, Salonika, and
back to the East to renew, rejoin, and reinscribe a new layer into the worn
texture of the Hebrew/Arabic share of the Levantine palimpsest. The Zohar, that most unclassifiable of books, itself an amalgam of the narrative,
poetic, and mystical conglomerate cutting through Christian Spain, in-
filtrated almost every aspect of the spiritual, communal, and intellectual

life of the Jewish Levant. The work of the extraordinary "Masters of Poetry" circle in Salonika, for example, could not be read innocently. As the children and grandchildren of the Spanish refugees who had survived the catastrophe, almost every standard figure and conceit could implicitly refer to the great questions about creation, good and evil, the suffering of the innocent and the coming of the redemption that the inward turning of the kabbalah had posed. The "old metaphors" took on new urgency, as in this almost ecstatic poem by Israel Najara, the most popular of all the "new" Levantine Hebrew poets:

> Sleep deserts my eyes and I toss like a
> ship in the sea of my yearning for You
> as I imagine these things: If I were an
> infant and you were my nurse, I would
> suckle your beautiful breasts, and
> quench my thirst. If I were a stream
> and you and I sat in the shade of my
> garden, I would look after your fruit.
> If I were a spear and you thrust me
> into your enemies' hearts, I would be
> drunk with their blood. If I were a tent
> and you dwelt in me, we would delight
> ourselves with love and clothe ourselves
> with joy. If I were a tongue and you
> were my words, I would soothe desire's
> flame with a song. If I were a slave and
> you were my lord, I would never choose
> freedom.[116]

Najara, al-Harizi, and the dozens of other compilers of narrative collections, the wandering bards from Provence, the "Band of Minstrels" in Christian Spain, the "Masters of Poetry" in Salonika, versifying Roman doctors, Venetian prodigies, the baroque Frances brothers of Livorno and Mantua, all felt the light cast from behind by Sepharad and al-Andalus through the Levantine prism. Their world is certainly akin to that of the English courtiers and metaphysicals; to Chaucer, Spenser, Wyatt, Raleigh, Sidney, Herbert, and Crashaw; to the picaro and *Book of Good Love*, the Spanish and Italian flourishes of Calderon, Gongora, Ariosto, and Marino; the German minnesingers and Provencal troubadors—to so much, in fact, that is familiar, it remains a mystery why the Hebrew poetry of the Levant has not entered the common vocabulary of the "European" tradition.

Besides the major poets of Andalusia and the many minor figures and schools only briefly mentioned here, literally hundreds of poets continued to people this Levantine world. Hebrew poetry wound its way through Renaissance and Baroque Italy, flourishing until the end of the nineteenth century, when the delicate work of poets like Abraham Ishaq Castello and Giusseppe Almanzi molded a unique place within the Romantic space that had been shaped throughout Europe. After the expulsion from Spain, Amsterdam became the site of a revival where poets took to the stage to create Hebrew drama, a genre that, along with opera, was also produced in Italy. The North African tradition, which began almost as that of a colony of Spain and whose output fluctuated in relation to the political situation on both sides of the sea, was most productive from the seventeenth century to the twentieth, with the already mentioned Rabbi Haim Raphael Shoshannah, the last classically educated traditional poet from Morocco, still writing until his death in 1987 in Beersheba.

Minor liturgical traditions, such as that of Aleppo, flourished in Brooklyn until the 1960s as a result of the same waves of immigration after the turn of the century that brought Kahlil Gibran, Mikhael Naimy, and Amin Rihani from Syria and Lebanon to the New World. Such newly established centers often adopted well-known poets, as this Syrian community took on Yehezkel Hai Albeg, a Baghdadi who had studied in Jerusalem before immigrating to America. Certainly the most interesting "old world" Hebrew poet still living, Albeg recently published his complete *Diwan* after retiring as cantor and house poet for the Brooklyn community. Albeg's work is living testimony to many of the intersections examined here; in the first chapter of a book-length poem, Albeg describes a Sabbath Eve in Iraq:

> This matter took place in the afternoon before Sabbath while each and every man and woman called an end to their workday, and each servant was freed from his employer. According to the custom of the Baghdadi Iraqis I changed my garment to a multi-colored tunic, in order to greet the visage of the Queen with a joyous heart and in song. . . . There we greeted the visage of the Sabbath Queen in a manner befitting Her radiance, splendor, glory and esteem. We sang the hymn *Lekha Dodi*, supple and pleasant, with an additional soul in holiness and spirit.
>
> After I had traveled nearly an hour, as in the days of my youth, my legs carried and placed me in the midst of the valley. There I met up with my friends who were enveloped in myrrh and cassia. When the balance of the congregants finished arriving, we all turned and climbed up the hill. Even as the time for prayer had yet to come, a quiet blanketed the crowd and some members began to narrate tales of the righteous, laying out their praises. . . . I arose to circle the hill and to wander about for I enjoyed to examine nature. . . .

And there could be found an Arab coffeehouse. The *narghileh* smokers and the coffee sippers were found there in abundance, and a western wind brought with it Arab voices. One could hear a passionate singer intoning profane songs. To this place each evening came an elderly blind man along with his cane and his knapsack. The patrons of the *qahwah* surrounded him on the right and left to hear him as he would speak edifying discourse. He would open with a legend and adumbrate the core with his own embellishments and exaggerations of turquoise. He was a true artisan who knew how to move the hearts of those who had assembled.[117]

Here we see some of the fluid transitions involved in nativity, from changing working clothes to donning a "multi-colored tunic"; from walking out of the synagogue with its sacred hymn to wandering through nature and into the Arab coffeehouse, with its own profane repositories of history and memory.

Another community, the Yemenites, those "most Jewish and most Arab of all Jews," did not, as is generally accepted, live in complete isolation, as the different strains coursing through their poetry clearly indicates. Like other Jews in various places and at various times, the Yemenites wrote quite a bit of poetry in Arabic, but based more on local traditions than on the classical Arabic verse that had served as the foundation for Andalusian poetics. Nevertheless, the light of that prism still reached them, mainly through the kabbalistic poetry written in Palestine and the Near East during the sixteenth and seventeenth centuries. This, then, remained the basis of a Yemenite practice that continued until 1951, when it was abruptly cut short and superseded by *The Yemenite Laments*. This group of poems, written in the transit camps of Israel to mourn the death of Rabbi Ya'qob Salim G'rafy (shot to death by police during riots protesting the authorities' unwillingness to allow freedom of worship), ironically came to mark what the poet/rabbis must have felt to be the "post-deliverance" death of the community itself.

VIII. The Spanish Inquisition and Jewish Humanism

In the beginning of *Don Quixote*, Cervantes has his narrator describe the discovery of a manuscript in the marketplace. This text, *The History of Don Quixote de la Mancha* by Cide Hamete Benengeli, Arabic historian, when translated from Arabic into Castilian, becomes the novel itself:

One day I was in the Alcana at Toledo, when a lad came to sell some parchments and old papers to a silk merchant. Now as I have a taste for reading even torn papers lying in the streets, I was impelled by my natural inclination to take up one of the parchment books the lad was selling, and saw in it characters which I recognized as Arabic. But though I could recognize them I could not read them, and looked around to see if there was not some Spanish-speaking Moor about to read them to me; and it was not difficult to find such an interpreter there. For, even if I had wanted one for a better and older language, I should have found one.[118]

The "better and older language" alluded to by the narrator, with more than some of al-Harizi's pride and prejudice, is obviously Hebrew. Although this was written well over one hundred years after the expulsion, as *conversos* the Jews still played a major role in all aspects of Spanish society and culture. But the inflationary nature of the hidalgo / Old Christian ethic, based on an almost unimaginable discrepancy in the distribution of wealth and power, infected the very nature of all relations in Spain, spreading the disease wherever Spanish influence reached (estimates reckon that the nobility in the Castile and Aragon of 1482, 1.65 percent of the population, controlled 97 percent of the land; a marquis could command 100,000 ducats a year, while one ducat was equivalent to eight days' wages of a skilled worker).[119] The ostensible reasons for establishing the Inquisition in Spain (quite late in the game for Europe, where anti-Jewish legislation had already been enacted at the Fourth Lateran Council of Rome in 1215) can be seen as economic. Again, because of their extraterritorial urban network and culture, the Jews often found themselves in a very precarious position. In his introduction to Moses Almosnino's *Extremos y grandezas de Constantinople*, for instance, published in Madrid as late as 1638, Iacob Cansino — a Jew — speaks of himself as a third-generation employee of the Spanish court in the capacity of Arabic translator. Besides his own diplomatic connections with the Barbary Coast, Cansino relates the experiences of his father (killed in service) and grandfather in their station as liaisons between the court and the "frontier" Moors, still holding out against the central powers. This office appears to be another instance of the city/country go-between and the inherent instability of that position, retained, in this case, from at least the fourteenth century, when Jews began serving in numbers as tax-collectors to rural areas.

Beyond economics, however, the *limpieza de sangre*, the purity-of-blood codes ensuring "noble" descent, soon stretched to cover "purity" of thought before finally suffocating thought altogether. The censor's coercion imposed a rule of silence and a set of linguistic and conceptual double standards from which Spain has only recently begun to recover. At the same time, the brutal machinery of the Spanish Inquisition and the kingdom's power struggle never stopped at repression of the Jews. Recent historiography suggests its primary target to have been the last vestiges of Islamic power in Europe and the larger struggle between "East" and "West,"[120] a conflict in which the Jews also found themselves in the middle. While the torments inflicted upon Jews by those such as Torquemada have assumed an almost iconic indelibility in the European imagination, little attention has been paid to the persistent oppression of the Moors, whose final decree of expulsion—affecting anywhere between 275 and 400,000 people—came in 1609.

Nowhere has Europe's Semitic heritage and debt been more apparent and more suppressed than in Spain. Spanish culture, whose palimpsest is so perfectly condensed in this passage by Cervantes, can almost be seen as the *result* of the struggle between, and against, the memory and reality of its Hebrew and Arabic past. It should come as no surprise that two of Spain's most feared modern writers, Garcia Lorca and Juan Goytisolo, directed so much of their work at both recovering the texture of Spain's "impure" Moorish past and destroying the myths of a "pure" Spanish history whose only logical outcome could be Franco, fascism, and sterility.

While Hebrew poetry with its Arabic antecedents continued to be written in Italy, North Africa, Yemen, and other old centers throughout the Levant, the exile from Spain was accompanied by another, and from many perspectives acutely ironic, phenomenon: the new Spanish and Portuguese literature of the Sephardic diaspora. In the eastern Levant, the Ottoman Empire added another language and culture to its already diverse makeup. Rabbinical works (such as the enormous *Me'am Lo'ez* project, lasting over several generations), popular narrative, historical works, travel accounts, drama, romances, and songs were all written in Spanish and readable in Palestine, Constantinople, Rhodes, Aleppo, Cairo, and Fez.

In the West, Amsterdam became a vital center for Spanish drama and poetry. Developments on the Spanish and European stage were closely watched as dozens of poets and playwrights formed groups, literary circles, and societies to disseminate their work. Italy remained the center of emigré printing, with lines of communication open to the Maghreb and the Mashreq, to Tunis and North Africa on one hand, Syria, Palestine, and Egypt on the other. The Levant itself may have been under siege and gone underground, usurped by the European renaissance, but the legacy of Andalusian enlightenment found its way into Europe through the auspices of Jewish humanists. These included Italian printers such as the Soncinos, scientists such as Joseph del Medigo (a student of Galileo's), philosophers such as Judah Abravanel, rhetoricians such as Judah Messer Leon, and doctors such as Rodrigo de Castro, David de Pomis, or Amatus Lusitanus.

Called in as a medical expert by the court of Ragusa (a city now known as Dubrovnik) in a case in which a woman was imprisoned and tried on the charge of causing a young man to become deaf, Lusitanus provided sufficient medical proof to convince the court that the young man's deafness had been caused by syphilis and not witchcraft. His "Physician's Oath," given at Thessaloniki in the year 5319 (1559), expresses the persistence of a very Levantine code:

> I have given my services in equal manner to all, to Hebrews, Christians, and Moslems. Loftiness of station has never influenced me, and I have accorded the same care to the poor as those of exalted rank. I have never produced disease. In stating my opinion, I have always told what I believed to be true. . . . In short, I have done nothing that might be considered unbecoming an honorable and distinguished physician, having always held Hippocrates and Galen before me as examples worthy of imitation. . . . I have been diligent and have allowed nothing to divert me from the study of good authors. I have endured the loss of private fortune, and have suffered frequent and dangerous journeys and even exile with calmness and unflagging courage, as befits a philosopher. The many students who have come to me have all been regarded as though they were my sons. . . . I have published my medical works not to satisfy ambition, but that I might, in some measure, contribute to the furtherance of the health of humanity; I leave to others the judgment whether I have succeeded; such at least has always been my aim and ever had the foremost place in my prayers.[121]

The schizophrenia imposed by the expulsion, the culture of the newly converted, and the Inquisition with its distorted ethic of brute power and superstition aimed against reason, seeped into many aspects of European life. Analogies can even be made within the new order of economics brought about by the establishment of the stock market. Here, the post-medieval European scene did not differ from the *geniza* world as much in geographic range or type of goods handled as in its methods of speculation. The fictitious nature of deals involving shares and options, in which "speculators thought in terms of the 'difference' between what one anticipated and what actually occurred," was a radical departure from the more concrete relations extant in the *geniza* world.[122] In this, the Marranos—already used to gambling away their very identities for life-and-death stakes—present a haunting specter. Joseph Penso de la Vega, the son of converts who had returned to the fold and a prolific writer in both Hebrew and Spanish, describes the state of affairs transpiring at the Amsterdam stock market in his *Confusion de Confusiones*, written in the form of a Socratic dialogue held between a philosopher, a shareholder, and a merchant:

SHAREHOLDER: To be sure, there is widespread honesty and expedition on the Exchange. . . . Such honesty, co-operation, and accuracy are admirable and surprising. But to make payments for obligations which according to the Exchange usances do not exist, when your credit is not endangered and your reputation not likely to suffer—that is not liberality, but insanity; it is not punctuality, but prodigality; not courage, but the foolishness of Don Quixote. . . . A witty man, observing the business on the Exchange, the studied impoliteness there, remarked that the gamble on the Exchange was like death in that it made all people equal. . . . It is a great error to assume that you can withdraw temporarily from the Exchange or that you can gain peace of mind when you cease to meet with the other speculators. If ill fate pursues you persistently, it can reach you just as well in the rocks and the forests, where lightning may strike you and wild beasts attack you. . . . Moreover, it is foolish to think that you can withdraw from the Exchange after you have tasted the sweetness of the honey. . . . He who has once entered the charmed circle of the Exchange is in eternal agitation and sits in a prison, the key of which lies in the ocean and the bars of which are never opened . . . [123]

At the end of the four dialogues, the merchant pragmatically chooses to say that he might eventually become a shareholder but never a speculator. The philosopher, in closing, states that he will keep his shares, not to gain wealth, but only until he "can get out of them in peace." He then concludes the book with this: "All schools of philosophy teach that the soul is nobler than the body, life nobler than death, and the existent nobler than the non-existent. But, as for the stock-exchange, I approve the paradoxical opinion of the Platonic musician that the non-existent is better than the existent. I think it much better not to be a speculator, and in making that statement I have in mind real speculation, not the honest business in shares, for what is fair in the latter is dubious in the former."[124]

The philosopher's attitude expresses a scepticism shared by many and summed up in a phrase used by Jews in the Inquisition and the literature following it: "No hay que nacer y morir" ("There is nothing more than to live and to die").[125] In other words, at least in one possible interpretation: wait and see, who knows what tommorrow may bring. Indeed, the shareholder's vision of the Exchange is an accurate portrayal of the inscrutable logic of terror initiated by the Inquisition, turning life itself into a prison, imposed from within and without.

For writers, in addition to the use of all kinds of other codes and subterfuges, translation was often the only mode ambiguous enough to work in. Curiously enough, Petrarch was restored as a model for *con-*

verso, Marrano, and New Christian intellectuals. In *The Spain of Fernando de Rojas*, Stephen Gilman notes just what made Petrarch so appealing to the forced converts: "While the traditional purveyors of consolation— Seneca, Job, and Boethius—were also read, they lacked one thing which Petrarch provided: a portrait of a man exposed to the world in all its aggressive immediacy."[126] The translation of his work by one of these converts, Solomon Usque, constitutes an unexamined episode in this chapter of Jewish culture in the Levant.

Aware of the dead end to which the courtly lyric as a disconnected entity led, Petrarch attempted, in a sense, a shift in linguistic units: the single word as conglomerate sign, and the single poem attaining the status of a word with greater semantic range within a sentence made up of the collection itself. The relatively simple romantic punning technique (compared to Semitic practice) used by Petrarch is given semantic breadth through time and the psychological pressures that shift through time. The reader's activity and intellect is called upon not to ascertain "meaning" in the usual sense, but primarily to contain and direct memory in the "crisis of choice" faced in locating references within the context of another time and place in the collection. This mode is very similar to the effects of embedding described earlier, but self-contained in a lyric book. The opacity of limited lexical counters—"old metaphors"—with their self-referentially enticing and seductive function, all givens of Petrarchan discourse, were already given clear articulation by theorists such as al-Jurjani in the eleventh century.

This is doubly ironic considering Petrarch's well-known opinion of the Arabs and Arabic poetry: "You know what kind of physicians the Arabs are. I know what kind of poets they are. Nobody has such winning ways; nobody, also, is more tender and lacking in vigor, and, to use the right words, meaner and more perverted. . . . To sum up: I will not be persuaded that any good can come from Arabia . . ."[127] Yet, it may precisely have been from Arabia, via the Hebrew poets of Andalusia, that some of the clearest articulations and most solid justifications for the kind of lyric poetics Petrarch practiced did come. Regardless of his opinion of the Arabs, Petrarch inherited many of the earlier Levantine assumptions concerning choice, range, limitation, effect, and intent in poetic composition. Though contemporary, the centerless conjunction of Petrarch's collected lyrics, the *Rerum vulgarium fragmenta*, would not, at first glance, seem to have much in common with works like al-Harizi's the *Tahkemoni* or the *Canterbury Tales*. Yet it is the apparent lack of precise structure in these works (as opposed to Dante's more obvious scheme) that accentuates the reader's own structural presuppositions and conjectures. The openness of these works is most adeptly illustrated by the range of "closed" partisan interpretations they can accommodate.

The figure Solomon Usque (Salusque Lusitano) encountered (or projected) in his 1567 translation of "*sonetos, mandriales y sextinas de gran POETA y orador Francisco Petrarca,*" is a far cry from the stereotypical image of Petrarch as a static, precious, and overly embellished keener. This view has been handed down partly through the dismissal of Petrarch's style as "fustian and ornamental" by Ezra Pound who bemoaned the loss of Cavalcanti's and Dante's "radiant world . . . untouched by the two maladies, the Hebrew disease, the Hindu disease, fanaticisms and excess."[128] While the course of Dante's bark is surely set, the opacity that permits substance to be transformed also bestows upon all who embark on Petrarch's vessel a turn to navigate. Subtly steering around points on the map of the literal, Usque locates the pain of his exile. In XXIII, instead of "com'io vissi in libertade," Usque condenses, merging his very self with liberty: "como yo libro antes era."[129] Later in the poem this transmutation:

> Spirto doglioso errante (mi rimembra)
> per spelunche deserte et pellegrine,
> piansi molt'anni il mio sfrenato ardire:
> et anchor poi trovai di quel mal fine,
> et ritornai ne le terrene membra,
> credo per pi dolore ivi sentire.[130]

is transformed into:

> M'acuerda espirto triste por agenos
> Lugares, y por cuevas, y abismo:
> Mi osadia llorar muy muchos anos.
> Del qual mal falle fin despues yo mismo,
> y tornado en los miembros fuy terrenos,
> creo para sentir mas mal y danos.[131]

Born in Lisbon in 1530 of a family that had fled the Inquisition in Spain only to face it again in Portugal before being forced to move on to Italy and Constantinople, Usque's use of "agenos lugares" for "pellegrine" is auspicious. The ambivalence of Petrarch's use of the word is already evident: if his pilgrimage is devoid of any sanctified destination, these wanderings may be aimless. The word "ageno" retains to this day an iconic resiliency in the symbolic consciousness of Spanish-speaking Jews, representing both the exile from Spain and the memorial recollection of the earlier Roman and Babylonian dispersions. By using it, Usque divests himself of any association with pilgrimage, no matter how ambivalent, and makes these peregrinations into a symbol of personal and communal catastrophe.

The use of "abismo" and "yo mismo" indicates more than a facile search for rhyme. The "abyss" Usque refers to is the day-to-day life *conversos* lived, reflected in such scathing expressions as the one mentioned earlier: "no hay que nacer y morir." Such final resolve in face of an executioner promising fulfillment in the world to come was also an act of extreme defiance, a bitter "denial of the immortality of the soul and divine reward and punishment" meted out under such conditions.[132] The bastardization of language so common in totalitarianism finds its modern origins in the Inquisition. For instance, the expression "relaxado en persona" (to weaken morally, be lax or relaxed "in person"), taken from an Inquisitorial record of 1538, simply means "burned at the stake."[133] It is another bit of pure irony that the poet whom modern critics have taken as the exemplar of a writer whose center is "the absence of intelligibility and, in that absence, the impossibility of maintaining the integrity of the signifiers,"[134] was wholly embraced as model and precedent by some of the first victims of this very breakdown. The bitter paradox of the last two lines refers back to "yo mismo." This "yo" is all Usque has left, and "miembros . . . terrenos" can easily imply something like "landed members of my people"; that is, those who have settled and found a new home. Yet turning to them in their own impermanence and instability would only be a cause to feel "mas mal y danos" ("more afflicted").

Perhaps the most poignant encounter in Usque's translation comes at the culmination of the canzone (CCLXIV) with which he chooses to end the poems of Laura's lifetime:

> En tal estado estoy, Cancion, y frio
> del miedo, mas che nieve,
> Sintiendome morir sin duda sedo.
> Qu'ya determinando, he embuelto al dedo
> muy mucha parte de mi tela breve.
> Ni peso creer si deve
> Fuesse, como el che yo sufro en tal estado,
> Che con la muerte al lado
> Busco de mi bivir consejo al cabo
> Y vieno lo mejor; lo peor alabo.[135]

> Canzon, qui sono, ed o'l cor via piu freddo
> de la paura che gelata neve,
> sentendomi perir senz'alcun dubbio:
> che pur deliberando o volto al subbio
> gran parte omai de la mia tela breve;
> ne mai peso fu greve

quanto quel ch'i' sostengo en tale stato:
che co la morte al lato
cerco del viver mio novo consiglio,
et veggio'l meglio, et al peggior m'appiglio.[136]

The rhetorical strategy differs just enough from Petrarch here to emphasize the personal and strip the "ornamental." This is my state, song, "y
frio / del miedo, mas che nieve." Rather than agglutinate, Usque
pauses—the oddity and incongruence of being "frozen with fear, more
than snow" (in relation to what?) refers back to Laura as sun diffusing
significance. Here, Usque insists that the sum of his fear is true petrifica-
tion, and will always be greater either in relation to any melting power or
any frozen substance. In the last two lines, Usque again avoids implication in any of the possible meanings "novo consiglio" might sustain by
shifting emphasis through word order and adding the ambiguous "al
cabo" ("at last," but retaining "cape, end, extremity"; "living on the
edge of the abyss"). If any doubts remain, Usque ends both the poem and
the collection with the word "alabo," the same word used in the Spanish
(Sephardic) prayer book for the Hebrew *hallel*, to praise. Following prophetic theology, Usque elects to praise whatever is left him to praise, the
remnant, "lo peor," "the worst" that can happen.

IX. Missing Pages: Women's Poetry in the Levant

Marking the effective start of the transparent walls/prism metaphor in
Dunash Ben Labrat's innovative act and gesture has given us only one
aspect of the "collective duration" outlined here as the "modern" Levantine period. A single *geniza* fragment existing in two versions, each with
its own circuitous and miraculous history, casts a very different light
through that prism. The incomplete version of this fragment, a four-line
poem that made its way from the local Cairo collection of Jacob Mossery
to Paris (through his widow) before reaching Jerusalem, was originally
thought to have been written by Dunash himself. The other complete
text, only discovered recently, presents another picture entirely:[137]

> Would the fair gazelle's / companion remember her
> the day they parted, / their only son in her arms,
> the day he set the seal / of his right arm upon her left
> and she, in his, / placed her bracelet,
> the day she, in memory, / took his mantle and he, her veil:
> given half the Prince's / kingdom, would he stay in Spain?

The customary introductory line in Arabic ("kitab le'zuga Dunash":
"Epistle of the Wife of Dunash") completely clarifies any questions about

the persona that had previously nagged the poem's explicators. The fact that its author remains nameless, identified only in relation to her celebrated husband, is only usual in "the republic of cousins," with its distinctive epicenter in the Mediterranean Levant, "where women, like fields, are part of the patrimony."[138] Yet, in a detailed and moving commentary, as exacting and cautious a scholar as Ezra Fleisher concludes that the very existence of such a perfectly accomplished and exquisite poem—at the *beginning* of the Andalusian period—should make it possible to rethink that history altogether. While traditional interpretations of Dunash, as in the wine song seen earlier, stressed the cracks in the seams of the new Hebrew poetry, Fleisher stresses the seamless, untainted quality of his wife's work:

> The poem's movement is striking in its beauty. The two clipped
> passages at the beginning and the end hold the middle in relief like some
> kind of inchoate sentimental ritual in which the acts, carried out as a
> metaphoric dialogue, express much more than words themselves can.
> The prolonged silence of the poem's center only emphasizes the sharp,
> near cry clasping both ends of the poem. . . . One way or another, this
> pearl has come down to us, the work of a mature and true poet who
> has managed to shed light on an explicitly singular, complex and fragile
> lyric situation, reenacting it through restraint, with a minimum of
> materials, using only the most indirect and economical means.[139]

Just how many women writers there were in the "modern"/Levantine period is difficult to say. Quite a few are already known. Others seem to have been "absorbed" into the oeuvres of their more famous (male) relatives. Certainly others remain hidden in unexamined manuscripts, concealed behind clues and leads never followed or lost altogether. The space created by Dunash's wife extends along the same parameters as initiated by him—only the conditions differ: of production, transmission, reception, opportunity.

Although the enormous range of forms created, adopted, and adapted within this space has been stressed, the need to cut across generic boundaries to assess whatever is available is an imperative even more urgent in the writing of Levantine women. The *geniza* letters of women, for instance, should be directly linked in formal terms to the correspondence of foreign secretaries to the Ottoman court, such as Esperanza Malki and Esther Kyra. Every period covered here provides evidence of just such "exceptional" women: that, though, should not be the point. Just as Goitein's examination of women in the *geniza* world does not attempt an apologetic of "accomplishment," that work should be taken as the basis for a parallel study that could more fully assess the writing and culture of women within the whole framework of the Levant.

Such an investigation would, first and foremost, have to consider conditions and their effect on the possible space of expression accessible to women. For instance, within the "universal Hebrew book culture" of the men, it is significant to note that all the Hebrew women writers whose work has survived (among them Dunash's wife, Kasmunah, Lady Maliha, Osnat Bat Barazani, Shama'ah Shabazi, and Rachel Morpurgo) were born into either prominent or very learned rabbinical families. Many others, those working in the mother tongue, such as the Italian renaissance poets Deborah Ascarelli and Sarah Coppia Sullam, or the many Spanish and Portuguese women writers (among them Estrella Lusitano, Manuela Nuñes de Almeida, Isabella Correa, and Bienvenida Cohen Belmonte) involved in the emigré literary life of seventeenth-century Amsterdam, were also born into favorable circumstances. Yet the so-called simple works created by the poor, those that have been relegated to the static realm of folklore, often both retain and comment on the culture of the "learned" in ways that can inform our knowledge of the whole social structure and the intertwining web of relations within it. Much of the rich Judeo-Spanish lyric and romance tradition (or, for that matter, the Yemenite and North African Arabic traditions), transmitted almost exclusively by women, should be seen in this light. Singers sometimes take the most deeply ingrained and oppressive values of "the republic of cousins," such as the code of virginity, and proudly turn it to their own favor. Accepting the decrees inevitably handed down to them, like Iphigenia going off to the pyre, they still preserve that minimal amount of space within which at least some choice can be made, some voice heard, as in this bitter jewel sung in Turkey, Greece, and the Balkans:

> Mother, if I am ill
> I don't want a doctor.
> If he gives me medicine
> I won't take it.
>
> Mother, if I should die
> I don't want a chorus paid
> off to lament my passing.
>
> I want twelve young men,
> my love at the head of them,
> all tossing candies,
> candies of every color.[140]

The custom of this singer's world dictated that the coffin of a young unmarried girl be draped with a bridal gown, with Jordan almonds strewn along the way to the cemetery, as they would have been on the way to the wedding canopy. Like the defiant joy of a New Orleans jazz funeral, the girl here knows what she wants: her illness is not just conventional lovesickness but willed resistance to an intolerable state of affairs in which the only "choice" left her is the order she can give to the "celebration" of her own suicide. Like the poem of parting written by Dunash's wife, this song uses only the sparest means, the fewest words to tell a whole untold world. By grasping the place of such works within their social and literary contexts, we can begin to appreciate the extremely intelligent and subtle rhetorical strategies employed by people whose means are circumscribed from without, the often very subversive role that a song can have, and the implications these missing pages hold for the validity of any books purporting to be complete, but compiled without them.

Chapter 3

History's Noise: The Beginning of the End

Error de los que entienden, que un mismo sueño se puede decifrar
del mismo modo a differentes sugetos, en differente tiempo.

(Those who believe the same dream can be interpreted the same
way by different subjects at different times are mistaken.)

> *Transformaciones de Morpheo ó Tractado de Sueños*
> Mosseh Almosnino, Amsterdam, Año 5494

los fonógrafos nos siegaron los garones

(phonographs have cut our throats)

> an elderly Sephardic woman to
> Maír José Benardete, New York City, 1922

Palestine is a land planted
by eyes
    refusing to be closed

> Etel Adnan

I. Colonialism and Literary Forms

In 1856, after traversing the frontiers of the New World past the Atlantic
to the Pacific, Herman Melville ventured back, into "the republic of
cousins," the Old World of the Mediterranean Levant. The trip to Cairo
and then Constantinople managed to stir something in him, a certain
"spontaneity":[1]

> To the Bazaar. A wilderness of traffic. Furniture, arms, silks,
> confectionary, shoes, sandals—everything. (Cairo). Crowded overhead
> with stone arches, with side openings.
>
> Immense crowds. Georgians, Armenians, Greeks, Jews, & Turks are
> the merchants. Magnificent embroidered silks & gilt sabres & caparisons
> for horses.
>
> You loose yourself & are bewildered & confounded with the
> labyrinth, the din, the barbaric confusion of the whole.
>
> The Propontis, the Bosphorus, the Golden Horn, the domes, the
> minarets, the bridges, the men of war, the cypresses. Indescribable.[2]

Given such "an absence of palpable woman in his works," it is striking that Asia and Europe are seen by Melville in the ancient figure of two women engaged in "a contest of beauty." The city of Constantinople itself appears through the metaphorical paraphernalia of the "harem": "The fog lifted from about the skirts of the city. . . . It was a coy disclosure, a kind of coquetting . . . like her Sultanas she was thus seen veiled in her ashmack."[3] Engaged in his own desparate search between water and stone, the sea and the desert, this vision was quite real for Melville, with a different hue and quality than the more exotic projections of flight and mastery then so prevalent in the European imagination. Yet, by the time Melville made his pilgrimage, the "East" already found itself in a subordinate position. This meant that perceivers from the "West" were locked into an "ideological superstructure with an apparatus of complicated assumptions, beliefs, images, literary productions, and rationalizations (not to mention the underlying foundation of commercial, economic and strategic vital interests)." This cumulative body of theory and practice has come to be known as "institutional orientalism," and finds itself situated squarely "within the context of the general historical expansion of modern bourgeois Europe beyond its traditional confines."[4]

This institutional phenomenon constituted only part of "the great Western Transmutation," a "world event" that marked a decisive break from the "relative evenness of historical development among all the societies" of the Old World since Sumer:

> The same generation that saw the Industrial and French Revolutions saw a third and almost equally unprecedented event: the establishment of European world hegemony. It was not merely, or perhaps even primarily, that the Europeans and their overseas settlers found themselves in a position to defeat militarily any powers they came in contact with. Their merchants were able to out-produce, out-travel, and out-sell anyone, their physicians were able to heal better than others, their scientists were able to put all others to shame. Only a limited part of the world's surface was actually occupied by European troops, at least at first. European hegemony did not mean direct European world rule. What mattered was that both occupied ("colonial" or "settled") areas and unoccupied ("independent") areas were fairly rapidly caught up in a world-wide political and commercial system, the rules of which were made by, and for the advantage of, the Europeans and their overseas settlers. Even "independent" areas could retain their local autonomy only to the extent that they provided European merchants, European missionaries, even European tourists, with a certain minimum of that type of international "law and order" which they had become accustomed to in Europe, so that the Europeans remained free to vaunt a privileged position and to display among all peoples the unexampled new physical and intellectual luxuries of Europe.[5]

For the Levant, the change in modes of production, which in turn had great impact on the old, familiar routes, brought about changes that were both pervasive and irreversible. Charles Issawi describes them:

> The nineteenth century witnessed dramatic changes in this secular pattern of production and trade. At different times, the various parts of the Middle East were integrated in the world system of commerce and transport. New routes were opened, notably the Suez Canal, and old ones were revived, like the Tabriz-Trabzon road, diverting trade away from certain areas and expanding it in others. Modern harbors were built in some ancient ports, like Alexandria, Izmir and Beirut, drawing to them the traffic that had previously been scattered in many small places. In a few regions railways replaced caravans, further concentrating trade. New crops were raised—or old ones expanded—in response to European demand, such as Egyptian cotton, Turkish tobacco, and Iranian opium, and other crops like madder and valonia lost their markets when chemical products took their place. Modern banks gradually expanded their business at the expense of traditional moneylenders. European factory goods competed with Middle Eastern handmade products, and drove many craftsmen out of business. Population grew almost everywhere, and certain cities saw a sevenfold increase in the number of their inhabitants. Needless to say, these developments were very unevenly spread over the Middle East, some areas advancing very rapidly and others stagnating or even declining.[6]

The effects of these changes on the great majority of the native populations of the region were often devastating. Timothy Mitchell describes its effects in Egypt, for example:

> Capitalist production also required the creation and management of large bodies of migrant workers, to build and maintain the new structures being laid in place across the Egyptian countryside—roads, railways, canals, dams, bridges, telegraphs and ports. Larger projects such as the digging of the Suez Canal required the movement and supervision of tens of thousands of men. Smaller gangs of labourers were brought from southern Egypt for seasonal employment in constructing and maintaining the new network of perennial irrigation canals in the north, on which the cultivation of cotton depended. The British placed such gangs under continuous police control. . . . Rural Egypt was to become, like the classroom and the city, a place wherever possible of continuous supervision and control, of tickets and registration papers, of policing and inspection. . . . From the nineteenth century for the first time political power sought to work in a manner that was continuous, meticulous and uniform. The method was no longer simply to take a share of what was produced and exchanged, but to enter into the process of production.[7]

These changes are very similar to those that took place somewhat later, in Saudia Arabia and the Gulf region, under the impact of the discovery and need for oil, and which are so vividly depicted in Abdelrahman Munif's brilliant novel *Cities of Salt*. There, we witness the "march of progress" as the new usurps the old through the development of "modern," very strictly regimented institutions: the stature of the self, based on complex modes of moral and ethical behavior, gives way to fingerprints and photo ID cards; tribal henchmen give way to uniformed soldiers and armies. Custom and justice are replaced by arbitrary decrees and the rule of "law"; land, with its cosmic and spiritual significance, becomes property, useful only for what can be extracted from it. As the old life recedes and a new class has been formed, a new sense of solidarity also emerges:

> The people of Harran looked at their faces and then at each other,
> thinking how unhappy and oppressed they were, and grew sad when
> they reflected that there must be terrible reasons for their depression.
> They felt afraid, but still dared to say things they would never have said
> had they not been so consumed with sorrow and anger. Why did they
> have to live like this, while the Americans lived so differently? Why
> were they barred from going near an American house, even from
> looking at the swimming pool or standing for a moment in the shade of
> one of their trees? Why did the Americans shout at them, telling them
> to move, to leave the place immediately, expelling them like dogs? Juma
> never hesitated to lash out with his whip when he found the workers in
> "restricted areas." The Americans had erected signposts warning them
> against loitering or going near most of the places, and they had even put
> barbed wire in the sea to keep them at a distance.[8]

Munif, perhaps more thoroughly and distinctively than any Arab writer before him, traces this collective wound in Arab memory, but without ever idealizing the extent to which the natives themselves collaborated in their own tranformation. It is unquestionably, however, the collective wound of this suppressed prehistory of colonialism that charged the often vehement outbursts aimed at minorities—the Jews among them—who identified or allied themselves with the European colonizers.

For Arab and Levantine Jews, the effects of this process of transmutation that came with the industrial and French revolutions were extensive, ultimately transforming in a fairly drastic way the nature and particular qualities of life within the ancient Jewish communities of the "old world." To emphasize the radical nature of this change, on the other hand, is not to imbue that life with the ahistorical, static, but enticingly nostalgic and mythic glow of "tradition" so often attributed to rabbinic society. "The speed of the new" that characterized the drastic "change in

the patterns of investment of time and money" in the "technical age"[9] —
the decisive turning point of which Marshall G. S. Hodgson puts in the
year 1800—struck each community and each class within those communities at a different velocity. For some, the encounter represented liberation from the fetters of an overtly repressive and coercive structure. For
others, it meant either a loss of the name of "native" altogether or a further retreat into the confines of an even more restrictive but no longer
autonomous religious culture in which ritual in and of itself began to take
up an increasingly disproportionate but less and less integrated part of an
individual's cultural space.[10]

Competition by the colonial powers for the allegiance of the "inter-
mediary" communities (particularly the Jews, Greeks, and Armenians
that Melville correctly identified as the merchant class), was fierce. At the
same time, though, it was directed at those who could be expected to
give something back in return, either commercially through the old network of trade connections rooted in the *geniza* world or as part of the
new administrative structure being built around the Mediterranean in the
decades following the Napoleonic invasion of Egypt. By the middle of
the nineteenth century, these structures had put down deep institutional
roots. In terms of ethnic/class roles and the relationship between urban
and rural people, the fact that in the nineteenth century Ottoman currency fell into a state of chaos was of great significance. As Charles Issawi
points out: "With such a confused currency, the *sarrafs* (moneychangers)
—in Syria at first mostly Jews, and later Christians, in Iraq mainly
Jews—flourished, from those in small provincial towns to the Galata
bankers of Istanbul. In addition to exchanging currencies, they transferred funds, advanced loans, and discounted bills. They also paid a leading part in tax farming, standing as surety for the farmer or taking the
farms themselves."[11]

This process was part of a trend toward the privatization of many sustenance services. In addition to money lending and banking, an insurance
industry also developed. While in 1854 no such service existed, by 1900,
as Issawi notes,

> twenty-five companies had offices in Beirut, providing life, fire, and
> maritime transport insurance. In 1910 there were 19 companies in
> Beirut, 5 French, 4 British, 3 German, 2 American, one Canadian, and
> one Italian. These developments helped merchants and other
> townspeople, but almost nothing was done for farmers. In 1837 there
> was talk of establishing a bank to lend to small landowners at 10-12
> percent, but the project did not materialize. In 1852 a decree fixed the
> rate for rural loans at 8 percent; the British consul pointed out that the
> usual rates were 20-24 percent, which—given the risks attached and the

fluctuation of exchange rates—represented real rates of about 14-18 percent. The decree was naturally ineffective, as was another attempt in 1861 to reduce rates to 8-12 percent, and farmers continued to borrow from townsmen at 20-24 percent, repaying at harvest time.[12]

In addition to this, small landowners and peasants were faced with a notoriously disproportionate system of taxation:

> Taken as a whole, Syria's tax burden was relatively light, but it was very unevenly distributed. First, the rural share was very large: tithes alone contributed some 40 percent of revenues, to which should be added the other taxes mentioned above and the duties on silk and tobacco production that were paid to the Public Debt Administration. Conditions became particularly bad when crops were poor. Aktan has calculated that in the 1890s farmers in Turkey (present borders) contributed 77 percent of total taxes more than proportionately, and this may also have been true of Syria. Moreover, customs were levied at a flat rate and no other tax was significantly progressive. Upper and middle urban incomes seem to have been very lightly taxed, and the incidence on large landowners' incomes was also low.[13]

Such conditions touched off and fueled the fires of resentment that burst forth periodically in lesser and greater conflagrations. In addition, such conditions led to popular uprisings and movements for social reform; these antifeudal movements, in turn, served to inspire many of the cultural and intellectual trends that had come to characterize the Levant's confrontation with a new world order.

Along with foreign capital and foreign-based financial institutions came foreign culture. French education, for example, came hand in hand with imperial ventures: the concession for the Suez Canal was granted in 1854 and completed in 1869 with the labor of 20,000 conscripted Egyptian peasants.[14] Meanwhile, the Alliance Israelite Universelle, established in Paris in 1860, opened its first school in Tetouan in 1862. From that point on, the gaze of the Jewish bourgeoisie was drawn more intently to the capitals of Europe: to Paris, Vienna, and London. By 1912 there were 71 Alliance schools for boys and 44 for girls all over the Levant, in Baghdad and Jerusalem, Tangier and Istanbul, Beirut and Cairo, Damascus and Salonika.[15] The net result of this was to progressively link "the Jewry of the Mediterranean Islamic countries to the movement of European expansion, detaching it from the fate of the Arab peoples."[16] For the masses of Arabic- and Spanish-speaking Jews, the stevedores of Salonika or the dyers of Fez, still largely living within the rabbinic domain but increasingly isolated from the "native" population and their anti-imperial concerns, there was less and less room to maneuver. And it was clearly they who would be most affected by the new reapportioning of power and the brutal dictates that went into the "reconstruction of historical geography" in and after the colonial period. As the conflict in Palestine completely collapsed into a confessional war between essentialized "Jews" and "Arabs," an appalling shade began to block the rays of light once clearly refracted through the Levantine prism.

This schematic review cannot hope to do justice to such a complex set of circumstances, nor can it account for the extent of Jewish participation in all facets of the burgeoning economic and cultural life of the late nineteenth- and early twentieth-century Levant. In the ideological tug of war that constitutes the writing of history, it is these aspects of modernity in the Levant—for obvious reasons—that have received the least attention. To put it simply: If the Jews of the Levant were "primitive" and came from "backward countries," then how could their accomplishments in so many fields have been so prominent? For the native Muslim population, the prominence of the Jews was simply a given; as Kassem, the communist son of a peasant, says in Shime'on Ballas's novel about Iraq, *The Other One*: "More than their own wanting to participate," he said, "the new government needed them because they were the most educated sector of the population, with the ability to serve as functionaries in the new administration. Faisal knew whom to choose. Sasson Yehezqel was the man who bolstered the Iraqi economy. Who else at the time was qualified to be the minister of finance?"[17] While the role of Jews in the modern economic development of countries like Egypt and Iraq is well documented, less attention has been paid to the Jewish role in the changing face of Arabic culture.

Sasson Somekh tells us that

> the first half of the twentieth century witnessed a clear trend whereby members of several Jewish communities in the Middle East strove to take part in the evolution of a modern Arabic culture. In Iraq, Syria, Lebanon, and elsewhere in the region, young Jews, whenever the political climate permitted it, became engaged in literary and journalistic pursuits in their respective countries. . . . Literature in the narrow sense of the term, however, is only one component of the cultural scene. Cultural life involves a variety of other activities, some of which, like the theater, are related to literature; others, like music, are essentially autonomous. In many of these manifestations of culture, the participation of Jews in the present century has been far from negligible.

Some of these manifestations would include, to mention only some examples, the contributions of major innovators like the musician Daud Husni (whose 1919 *Cleopatra's Night* was the first Egyptian full-length opera), the filmmaker Togo Mizrahi (whose films of the 1930s, *Cocaine* and *The Children of Egypt*, are considered landmarks of Arab cinema), or the many other composers, singers, actors, actresses, directors, producers, scriptwriters, and technicians who worked in the formative years of the Egyptian and Iraqi entertainment industries.[18]

In addition, the overly simplistic tendency to exclusively identify rabbinic culture with the regressive forces of a closed society must be tempered by the actual record of many Levantine authorities. Again, just a few examples can be cited to give some sense of this. A well-known instance of the tolerance of Levantine rabbinic culture can be seen in the bitter disputes that took place between Sephardi and Ashkenazi rabbis from the turn of the century through the 1930s as to whether nonreligious subjects or vocational training should constitute part of the standard curriculum. In Palestine, these differences of philosophy led to major rifts between the communities, with the Arab and Levantine rabbis consistently opting for broader, more integrated and practical pedagogic approaches. This also extended to the debate between the communities regarding the voting rights of women. Here, as well, Benzion Uziel, the chief Sephardic rabbi of Jaffa, formulated a highly original ruling that even overrode the misogynistic authority of Maimonides. This, it should be noted, was in 1920, at a time when only some European countries had granted voting rights to women and those only recently.[19]

Cultural involvement outside the community was not only common but expected. Rabbi Haim Nahum Effendi, for instance, besides being a member of the Egyptian senate, was also one of the founders of the Arabic Language Academy, appointed by a royal decree in 1933. As remarkable as his career was, the biography of Nahum Effendi is not that extraordinary among the elite of Levantine and Arab Jewry during this period. Born in 1872 in Magnesia, Turkey, he was sent at the age of eight to the yeshiva of Rabbi Abbo in Tiberias where he remained for over five years. From there he went to the college at Smyrna before studying Islamic jurisprudence at the faculty of law in Constantinople. After attaining a degree, he went on to Paris where, in 1879, he graduated from the rabbinical seminary as well as the College de France, where he specialized in Semitic languages. After directing the rabbinical seminary in Constantinople, he was appointed by the Ottoman government to be professor of languages at the Superior Academy of Artillery and Military Engineering. In 1907 he was delegated by the Alliance to take part in a mission to Abyssinia to study the early history, customs, and particular needs of the Falashas. This exploratory voyage resulted in a book that shed new light on the Jews of Ethiopia. During the audience granted him by Mendik II in Addis Ababa, he delivered a speech in Amharic. In 1908 he was appointed chief rabbi of the Ottoman Empire, a post he held until 1920. In 1923, he was asked to become the chief rabbi of Cairo before being appointed to the senate in 1931. The biographies of many other prominent nineteenth- and twentieth-century Jews in the Levant reveal similar peregrinations and involvements.

Again, besides the lack of a comprehensive intellectual history of this period,[20] it is also indicative to note that one needs to go to the *earlier* editions of Jewish encyclopedias to find data on many of these "minor" Levantine figures. Working from the *Jewish Encyclopedia* (1903-1916), through *The Universal Jewish Encyclopedia* (1942), to *The Encyclopedia Judaica* (1971) a very clear pattern emerges. As Zionist ideology consolidates its gains, both on the ground and ideologically, certain entries — archaeology, for instance — gain great prominence. Others, such as the deep and extensive involvement of Jews in Arabic secular culture, almost disappear completely. The "reconstruction of historical geography" and reapportionment of cultural space are all effected smoothly, "with no scars on the body at all."

All of these episodes were part and parcel of the diversification of social structure, opportunity, and aspiration brought about by the "great Western transmutation" initiated and fed by both the industrial and the French revolutions. Writing, naturally, inscribed and internalized all the issues dredged up by this new order. This happened both in generic terms and through the changing roles of authority. This process directly translated itself into new sets of choices, constraints, and possibilities for Levantine writers themselves. Older established printing centers like those of Livorno and Amsterdam, set up primarily to reprint classic texts, rabbinic works, and belles lettres, found themselves overwhelmed by the new publishing enterprises that began operating in the 1850s, which were geared toward a much wider audience. The emergence of a popular press throughout the Levant, in Hebrew, Arabic, Judeo-Spanish, and French, became a great catalyst in shifting the pace at which news traveled, as well as affecting the type of information exchanged.

As the governing powers of religious authorities began to erode, the learned class (or those aspiring to it) branched out into a whole new assortment of endeavors. Although certain genres persisted and even flourished (thousands of original plays were written and performed in Judeo-Spanish before and between the two world wars, for example),[21] those whose primary avenue of expression would have been in the "modern"/ Levantine Hebrew poetic or rabbinic mode could now pursue other kinds of writing. Some of the most important genres developed through this exchange were journalism, historical and scholarly writing, the novel, drama, and poetry in the modern languages. Yaqob Sanua, for instance, the Jewish Egyptian nationalist who had coined the phrase "Egypt for the Egyptians," opened a theater in Cairo in 1870 where his own enormously popular Arabic plays and satires were staged.

By the First World War, with the popular press already in operation for over fifty years, this generic and linguistic exchange had become prevalent. In the 1920s and 30s, Jewish writers in Iraq experimented with the new Arabic forms that had emerged from the free verse movement. As Samir Naqqash points out: "In modern Iraq, some of the most outstanding poets and writers were Jews. Studies in the development of contemporary Iraqi poetry and literature concluded that the first short story was written in the twenties by a Jewish youth—Murad Mikha'il."[22] In Tunisia and Algeria, alongside the traditional modes, a literature in French developed. The same holds true for Cairo where, one should not forget, Edmond Jabès published his first book in 1930. At that point he was only one of many Levantine writers—in Italy, southern France, North Africa, Greece, Turkey, the Balkans and the Fertile Crescent—struggling to forge new and different forms of expression out of the older cultures and traditions indelibly marked by the radical reordering of their world.

For Jews, participation in the creation of this new literature also marks a watershed in the less and less subtle shift in the very terms constituting Jewish identity. That process, set in motion during the Inquisition, saw the legal, covenantal, and communal bases of Jewish existence give way to the racial, the ethnic, and the national, something to which the new forms of written authority—often unintentionally—lent credence.

II. Traveling in Time: Mordekhai HaKohen and Nahum Slouschz

Mordekhai HaKohen, the Libyan encountered earlier through his *Book of Mordekhai* (that curious blend of rabbinic erudition and enlightenment/positivist scholarship), spent quite a bit of time assisting the well-known European scholar and traveler Nahum Slouschz. Slouschz had come to the Levant in 1906 to search "for traces of the biblical past and evidence of groups boasting an autonomous Jewish existence." This "national romanticism" was accompanied by another trait in Slouschz's own work and later accounts of that journey: "a unilineal, evolutionary view of cultural development" that led to a "penchant for building grand historical theories that overshadow the data on which they are based." HaKohen, on the other hand, combined the practical experience of a jurist with the firm knowledge of a scientist to reach a point where "no aspect of life was foreign" to him. By using "a wide range of tools," HaKohen's text exhibits a precision and logic that often collapses in Slouschz's grand designs.[23]

Eager to continue collegial relations after their work together, HaKohen corresponded with Slouschz for several years, from 1906 to 1910. Interestingly, many of the requests HaKohen made to Slouschz were of a "highly specific and technical nature. In one letter, for example, he asks Slouschz if there is some demographic law whereby a population equalizes its sex ratio if many men are killed in a war. In another letter, he discusses color terminology in Hebrew and Arabic and asks for reactions to his interpretation from Slouschz or his colleagues. He asks Slouschz to send him detailed maps of Libya. He seems to have received no replies to these various requests."[24] Later, there was talk of a French version of *The Book of Mordekhai*, yet in the ensuing letters the matter is dropped entirely. The relationship remained completely lopsided, with HaKohen's invaluable assistance barely noted in Slouschz's work: "The overall impression is that of a nineteenth-century explorer condescendingly appreciating his 'native guide.' "[25]

Slouschz's work, at least that part dealing with the Jewish presence in Libya and among the Berbers, ultimately remains more valuable for garnering information on European attitudes to the Orient than for its ethnographic or anthropological data. HaKohen's text, on the other hand, remains an open book. Fertile ground for further analysis, it is planted with the precise and minute details of ways of life forever past. The archaeological material gathered by Slouschz, however, does stand out and it is quite instructive to observe that Slouschz's "national romanticism" led him to the promised land. There, in 1919, he revived the Palestine Exploration Society, a venture responsible for many of the digs establishing the "material testimony" (to use the parlance of the *Blue Guide*) that could buttress, through a "militant archaeology," the later reconstruction of historical geography that would characterize Jewish settlement in the Holy Land.

HaKohen, at least from the evidence extant, does not seem to have been particularly attracted to Zionism even though he did make a trip to Jerusalem's close and familiar terrain to find a spot "in which his mother could eventually be buried."[26] He chose to remain in Tripoli where, "as his daughters said, he became more and more removed from daily affairs, and was primarily concerned with making an important contribution to science. He would sit and work with single-minded concentration, even ignoring the cat if it jumped on his shoulder as he sat at his desk. He had become preoccupied with a classic challenge of the physical world, the invention of a perpetual motion machine. In the midst of his work, on August 22, 1929, he died of a stroke."[27]

There is something profoundly ironic in this juxtaposition: Slouschz, the "Westerner," chose to dig into the ground for long-lost roots, hoping to rejoin the tribe in an idealized and romantic vision of the collective past. HaKohen, the "Easterner," firmly rooted in his own native space, remained where he had always been while aspiring to invent a machine that could defy the laws of both motion and gravity. The very date of HaKohen's death is also significant, for it marks another dim but precise point in the slow, steady revolution of the Levantine prism.

III. Yitzhaq Shami, Yehuda Burla, and the Hebrew Novel

The "disturbances" of 1929, in which 133 Jews were killed and several hundred more wounded in the old Arab Jewish communities of Hebron and Safed, came after eight years of relative tranquillity. The sheer brutality of the events, the fact that the victims were mainly traditional Jews with little or no interest in the machinations of the Zionist enterprise, masked the underlying political and economic factors leading to the violence and made clear just how convoluted the struggle in Palestine would become, at least on the surface. These urban Jews again found themselves caught between dispossessed peasants and an ever-widening sphere of power. The constituents of this sphere included absentee feudal landlords and ideological zealots as well as crumbling empires, each involved in both cool and desperate ploys to secure their precious, and often mutual, interests.

The publication of two works in Hebrew that have been taken to represent the best of "authentic" Sephardic writing in the prestate period also occurred in 1929. They were composed, as one Israeli critic put it, by "writers charmed to some extent by the exoticism of the Orient and inspired by the figure of the noble Arab horseman with his cartridge belt riding on his mare, or by that of the fellah whose way of life was similar to that of the Jews of the Biblical period."[28] These writers, however, rather than being seduced by the Orient, simply happened themselves to be native "Orientals." Yehuda Burla, author of *In Darkness Striving*, was born in the Old City of Jerusalem in 1886, descendant of a family that had settled in Palestine in the eighteenth century. Yitzhaq Shami, author of *The Vengeance of the Fathers*, was born in Hebron in 1888. Shami's mother was from the Kastel family, with its deeply rooted line of descent going back to the four cities of the Holy Land and Jewish settlement in them following the expulsion from Spain. His father, sage Eliyahu, was a small-time merchant from Damascus whose business—precisely like that of the protagonist of Burla's novel—took him from city to city and village to village throughout Palestine and Syria. Both Shami and Burla found themselves in that category of writers who remained within their native space but whose work, and its ultimate meaning and reception, was transformed through the altered circumstances brought about by the "reconstruction of historical geography" within that space.

Shami received a traditional religious education before attending a new school, attached to the Talmud Torah of Hebron, dedicated to introducing students to a wider range of Orientalist studies. It was only after this that Shami shed his native garb and donned the clothes of the *franj*, the European, in order to go to Jerusalem and continue studying at the Ezra school, an institution paralleling the Alliance. There he began writing and publishing his first stories, along with poems and descriptions of the workshops of the potters, glassblowers, and other craftsmen of Hebron. But before completing his studies, Shami left Jerusalem to teach Arabic in some of the new settlements of Judea. From there, retracing his father's steps, he went to Damascus. Between the two world wars he taught in Sofia before returning to Palestine and settling in Haifa. His collected works, as opposed to Burla's prolific output, can be found in one slim volume composed of six short stories and the novella he is most known for, *The Vengeance of the Fathers.*

On the surface, this work tells a tale in the classical sense, one ostensibly contained by the events it depicts. The story begins in the spring, describing the elaborate preparations made for the festival of pilgrimage to the tomb of Nebi Moussa, the Prophet Moses. The protagonist, Nimmer Abu Il-Shawarab, leader of the pilgrims from Nablus, "was the only man who scrupulously observed the customs of the fathers,"[29] but his pride drags him into battle with the leader of the pilgrims from Hebron. The death of Abu Faris at the hand of Abu Il-Shawarab leads to an irreconcilable blood feud with the Hebronites and Abu Il-Shawarab is forced to go into hiding. The fall of Abu Il-Shawarab is slow but steady. His decision to flee was not taken lightly, and soon the upright and robust figure begins to merge into darkness, "sorrowing and bent under the desperate suffering and agony of men exiled from the land of their birth."[30] After a trying journey through the desert, he arrives in Cairo and rents a

> room in a large *khan* consisting of a vast number of cubicles and crannies, like an anthill, in one of the poorer sections of the city. Here— in the whirlpool of the city, in the incessant noise of masses of refugees and exiles from different lands and of different races, among sad displaced peasants in broad blue gowns who had left a homeland not their own to oppressors and bloodsucking landlords to escape emptyhanded to the distant and enchanting city of promise and to try

their fortune there as porters and street-cleaners, doormen or
pickpockets—here his presence aroused no wonder or astonishment.[31]

This is precisely that part of Cairo that can be extrapolated from Umm
Kulthum's memoirs, from the narratives of Mahfouz or Idris. It is here
also that Abu Il-Shawarab is drawn to the taverns and coffeehouses, the
sweet voices of the famous songstresses and the soothing intoxication of
the narghile spiked with hashish. A period of progressive dissolution follows: Shami's use of time, so leisurely embroidered in the earlier part of
the book by the details of nature and custom, is masterful. After a night
of terrifying hallucinations and physical exhaustion ending in "white visions that cannot be expressed," in which "he rocked like a child relieved
of its suffering, who falls asleep, calmly and quietly, in his mother's lap,"
two years are consumed in a single sentence: "Autumn and winter
passed, and the summer and autumn after these, and nothing happened
to give Nimmer even a gleam of hope."[32]

After a mortifying vision of the Fathers (the patriarchs Abraham,
Isaac, and Jacob), Abu Il-Shawarab finds himself driven across the entire
length of Cairo, down to the Old City, on the other side of the Nile.
There he goes through the large iron gates of al-Azhar, the ancient complex housing the mosque and university, the seat of Islamic thought and
practice. A dervish immediately recognizes both the pain and the urgency
betrayed by Abu Il-Shawarab's expression and leads him directly to
Sheikh Al-Azhar, the reigning authority. After a full confession, reminiscent of both the healing sequence in Burla's novel and the methods of
psychoanalysis (a practice of which Shami was most certainly aware,
given his knowledge of German and his connections to A. S. Yahuda, the
Semitic scholar from Jerusalem who had befriended Freud in Vienna),[33]
the saintly sheikh proposes a repentance ritual. Fulfilling this means going back to Hebron, and it is there ("A winter Friday in Hebron. A day of
cold and drizzle. Low leaden skies, mud, slush"),[34] in an atmosphere
contrary in every way to the story's spring beginning, that the tale ends.
The bitter, vindictive Hebronites lie in wait at the Cave of Machpelah,
the Tomb of the Patriarchs, only to turn away in terror as they witness
Nimmer Abu Il-Shawarab collapse and sink into the ground, joining it
forever, as he himself is laid waste by "the vengeance of the Fathers."

As in much of Shami's work, Jews are barely mentioned or only noticed in passing. Here it is instructive to note that they appear at the very
beginning of the story, as the new *hawadjas*, the masters and landowners
who offer high wages for a day's work in their fields. The workers lured
by these wages are described as "the frivolous—the curse of Allah upon
them!—the young renegades who live in the Sahal [the coastal plain],

near the Jewish settlements, where they work as hired hands—only they have begun to reject the old tradition and to scoff at the sanctity of this pilgrimage."[35] The accuracy of Shami's local knowledge in this passage is remarkable and it has taken several generations of scholars to reach conclusions that were, for him, simply self-evident. According to Gershon Shafir, one of the new Israeli revisionist historians, "the preconditions for Zionist settlement in Palestine were the existence of a land market brought into being by the integration of the Ottoman Empire into the world capitalist market, and the sparseness of the Palestinian Arab population in the coastal plain and inland valleys."[36]

Shami's linking of the landowners to the changing mores of the young workers as a frame around Abu Il-Shawarab's desperate attempt to guard the honor of the old ways, along with the inevitable fall that lands him in the slums of Cairo where his fate is suddenly joined to that of all the other dispossessed peasants and exiles, provides as much particular knowledge about one of the pivotal dynamics of the conflict in Palestine as dozens of scholarly works. Yet contemporary critics—or at least the few who have dealt with Shami's work—often go to great lengths to present a "true naive," locked into a "traditional" world, aloof in the face of the great changes taking place at the time. But Shami's text, like the "native" discourse of Albert Antebbi's brief letter examined earlier, deals in irreducible specifics: the "Jews" are never such in any collective sense. Nor are the "Arabs" just quaint mirror images of an idealized "biblical" way of life: they remain, rather, both the guardians and conscience of the history inscribed in and enacted upon the land, live conduits through whom the sources of events elevated to site and ritual still flow.

Besides yielding this kind of detail, Shami's work can sustain a number of other readings. His few remaining letters reveal a tormented figure struggling for material sustenance, desperately coaxing the sparks needed to ignite and maintain the fires of creativity. This struggle was enacted on three fronts: the road away from home ("How on earth could a youngster from Hebron, whose very surroundings were so utterly permeated by awe of the Torah, even think of secular studies?"[37] as Shami's close friend David Avissar recalled); the difficulty of being recognized and finding his place as a writer, and finally his own temperament, that of an impulsive perfectionist. These contradictory qualities are reflected in the short note he left in his will regarding the seven works he felt might be worthy of further life:

My literary remains are meagre and sullen. The fountain of my
creativity, following all the disturbances and internments, was not a
blessed spring, abundant and refreshing to the soul, but a harsh stony

spring out of which no path could be paved. Enraged at its obligation, it dripped in spurts here and there, dampening the smooth wall before again consuming itself.

Must everyone with creative powers bear a heavy burden of parchment upon their very backs on the long path to the everlasting? My load is light and I surely shall not bow down under it every step I take.[38]

The steps away from home, the roaming, include home itself, and (without engaging in overly simplistic psychology) the depth and the structure of the written conflict—the fathers and the mothers of the text—also recall accounts of the clashing and irreconcilable spheres of Shami's parents. In a footnote to *The Vengeance of the Fathers*, Shami points out that a battle such as the one he has just depicted actually took place twenty-five years earlier. He would have been fifteen at the time and surely such an occurrence (not to mention the pageantry and spectacle of the pilgrimage itself) must have made a deep impression. All of these elements combined, then, can also lead to a reading of the work as a precise and consummate transformation of highly charged and very personal material. But the native is only allowed to sketch—with greater or lesser skill—the trappings of an exotic ambience, not intentionally transform experience into finely wrought and highly self-conscious art.

Yehuda Burla's short novel, *In Darkness Striving*, is somewhat more transparent than Shami's work. Yet its narrative structure belies the sometimes simplistic ideological thrust and tone of the book. Like the medieval *maqama* genre, this is a frame story. The complexities here, however, do not pertain to the identity of the narrator but the identity of the narration. The narrator of the frame is a Zionist from Palestine working as a Hebrew teacher in the Jewish community of Damascus. He finds himself drawn to Rahamo Hibb, a blind Jewish merchant described by some as "a shiftless loafer, a woman-chaser, a desecrator of the Sabbath, an eater of forbidden food." Others, however, "defended his odd behaviour and praised his virtues," saying that "the fellow isn't what he seems to be . . . there are moments when he can be a truly fine man . . . when he's in the mood, you may hear him speak words of wisdom."[39] The Hebrew teacher sees Rahamo in one of those moments, during a ritual vigil at the home of a woman who had just given birth to a son. Here the blind man takes on the role of the *rawi*, the traditional Arabic storyteller:

> The rhymed couplets were reminiscent of those of the classical Arab poets, charged with wisdom and linguistic brilliance, and he recited them with astonishing ease and eloquence, and with a calm, pleasing

intonation. He sang the melodic parts of the narrative tunefully despite his hoarse voice.[40]

The two befriend each other and, after much pleading, the Hebrew teacher, and the headmaster of the school finally convince Rahamo to tell his life story. Rahamo humbly submits, because "I have come to feel great affection and esteem for you; I see that you are Zionists, and your thoughts are pure, and your way of thinking is unlike that either of the Jews or non-Jews. I found you 'human', clear-sighted. I once knew a man like that, an honoured sheikh who could stare straight and deeply into a man's heart and into his inner life."[41]

The rest of the book, after this very brief introductory frame, consists of Rahamo telling the tale of his life, in "Arabic." The main thread of the story involves a kind of process of elimination of possible remedies for the impossible and ultimately tragic love affair between Rahamo the Jew and Shafikah the Muslim. Although Rahamo is already married, Shafikah counters his reservations with a proverb: "Let the stream water our land, and also all the other lands in the village. Would that make ours any the less fruitful?"[42] All avenues are considered, including conversion by either one to the other's faith. Deliberations in her family over this are suddenly interrupted by an attack on Rahamo in which he is blinded, carried out by members of a clan who had once bought Shafikah as a wife for one of its members; she, however, detesting this husband, had escaped back to her own family, eventually managing to obtain a divorce. After the blinding, both Shafikah and Rahamo succumb to different forms of madness and desperation. Rahamo tries everything, even attempting to confess all to the rabbi, the sage Zadok Abulafia. Failing this, he decides on suicide but, significantly, realizes that he can no longer find the door of his own room. Finally, the services of a certain "wise sheikh, called Abdul Karim a-Tunisi, who treated all kinds of mental diseases, disorders, melancholy and the like,"[43] are procured. His large house in a residential area of Damascus serves as a clinic, with separate facilities for men and women. It is here that Rahamo, and later Shafikah, begin treatment.

The sheikh finds that poetry is a particularly effective cure for Rahamo's malaise, especially the verses of the great blind poet Abu Ala al-Ma'arri. The choice of al-Ma'arri, often accused of heresy, along with the sheikh's discourses on Rahamo's need to leave off beseeching the favor of the "petty God of men" ("You knock in vain. There is no one here. The owner of the castle does not live here and there is no one to hear you. The house is empty!")[44] and begin meditating on "the Eternal God," fully reveal the book's not-so-hidden agenda. This agenda, the stormy journey away from the dictates of the tribe and onto the road of secular reason, is summed up—after Shafikah's suicide—by Rahamo's laconic conclusion: to make something of this life, one must be "the author, not of words, but of deeds."[45]

As a "native," however, Burla does not pronounce the new credo by denouncing the trappings of the old, the fetters of the tribe. Even as they fulfill their expected roles, the families of both characters are not unsympathetic to the plight of their wayward offspring. Even as the story lags here and there, two things beyond the more obvious theme of the love affair between a Jew and a Muslim remain significant. First, the role of the sheikh: an idealized figure, he embodies all the qualities implicit in a nostalgic vision of the height of classical Arabic culture and it is he, ultimately, who saves Rahamo from hopelessness and despair. In addition, at a number of points in the story, great emphasis is placed on Rahamo's superb and expressive spoken Arabic, something readers of this Hebrew text can only imagine or take at the author's word. This, particularly in a writer like Burla where the ideological bias is so open, subtly internalizes and emphasizes the extent to which appreciation of and allegiance to Arabic culture had become a conflict in figures of his standing. The internalizations of these conflicts are all the more explicit when looked at in relation to Eliachar's very bitter critique of Burla's political allegiances and unwillingness to give up his standing in the establishment in order to participate in the struggle for the equality of Sephardi and Oriental Jews:

> It was he who led some of the most stinging attacks against the Sephardic leaders who requested true representation at the election assemblies as well as the other Yishuv institutions in the cities and the agricultural settlements. He was instrumental in dissipating Sephardi representation at the assembly and stood at the head of the Sephardi list of the "Workers' Union" (*Histadrut Ha'Ovdeem*). More than once did he pave the way for the confrontations that began and then increased as the days went by with those same Sephardic representatives who became emissaries for various parties, both of the left and the right, as they exacerbated and degraded the general position of the Sephardic public without reaping any benefit whatsoever, other than to the dubious honor they gained for themselves. . . . Today, when I look back along the way to take a true reckoning of our actions and the steps with which we began as young Zionists in order to account for how we arrived at the humiliating and degrading position that non-Ashkenazis find themselves in their own country, I can affirm without any hesitation whatsoever that the factors leading to this gloomy situation are those very Sephardim and Orientals who bound their glory to the

parties and disregarded the fate of their brethren in the Land and in the diaspora.[46]

The more deeply embedded and firmly bound ties to music ("wounded kinship's last resort") seen in the unbroken tradition of liturgical poetry begin to unravel and scatter in a "high-culture" text such as Burla's. The "Jewish" world depicted becomes just that: subject matter, and not the very material of a way of life that is simply practiced from within. From this point on, the gap steadily widens between a more popular, generally working-class Arab Jewish or Judeo-Spanish culture, and the secular Hebrew culture of Zionism or one of the many versions of culture inherited by European colonialism. As the working-class Jews of the Levant found themselves more and more marginalized within this framework, with fewer and fewer avenues of expression open to them due to the undermining of rabbinic authority and popular culture, "authentic Orientals"—in a kind of Orientalism in reverse, celebrating the "exotic"—began to depict worlds they had long left behind. At the same time, the very real political conflict between Arabs and Jews, with its tremendous cost in human suffering, increasingly began to affect precisely those Jews most firmly rooted in Arabic culture, something that would ultimately result in the cultural schizophrenia of Levantine Jews in Israel.[47]

For a writer such as Burla, with unequivocal ties to the Zionist cause, the discord is internalized, woven into the tale. For those whose gaze had been directed beyond the minarets of home to the capitals of Europe, the ambivalence of their position often led to a bewilderment that resulted in a kind of existential short circuit, as this passage by the Tunisian-born novelist Andre Nahum so poignantly shows: "I turn and perceive, far back in the past, a young boy, partly Arab French and partly (more) Jew, a character who has no real place anywhere, colonized by others who are colonized themselves, awkwardly sitting on three chairs in a precarious equilibrium."[48] This very sense of "in-betweenness," however, was often turned into a positive attribute by women writers such as Jacqueline Kahanoff (who shaped a whole approach to culture from it) or the Egyptian-French novelist and poet Andrée Chedid. As she writes in *Return to Beirut*:

> What are roots? Distant ties or ties that are woven through life? The ties of a rarely visited ancestral land or those of a neighbouring land where one spent one's childhood, or are they those of a city where one has lived longest? And, indeed, had not Kalya chosen to uproot herself? Had she not wished to graft those different roots and sensibilities onto one

another? A hybrid, why not? She revelled in that crossbreeding which broadened her outlook and made her receptive to other cultures.[49]

IV. Keys to the Garden: Albert Cohen and the Levantine Novel

In 1930, just one year after the publication of these two works by Shami and Burla, Albert Cohen, a native of Corfu whose family emigrated to Marseilles, published his classic novel *Solal*. This was also the year the first book of Jabès appeared; links between the two writers, in the wider scheme of the new forms of Levantine writing then emerging, are not at all spurious. By his own admission, Jabès was then writing a kind of ethereal symbolist poetry aspiring, from the remove of Cairo, to enter the pantheon of an idealized French literary world. This work had neither overt nor covert reference to anything that could even vaguely be described as a "Jewish" thematic. But by 1921, Albert Cohen had already published his *Paroles juives*, a book of poems that must have seemed quite odd in the French scene of that time.

Cohen's advance party, made up of the Jew as writer and prophet within the terms of a newly interpreted law no longer bound to a concrete community, spied out and surveyed the terrain that would turn into that drifting abode, the homeland of the book, with its cult of absence. For Cohen, the tranquil space of a garden enclosed—so perfectly embodied by the very real Greek island he was born on and accentuated even further by the very particular language he was born into, the Venetian dialect of the Jews of Corfu—ruptured early on. His family moved to Marseilles when he was five and his first trip back to the island only came at the age of thirteen. The impressions of this magical world with its picaresque cast of characters, who would come to people Cohen's books, provided the impetus for a flight into memory indebted to and often worthy of Proust. But while the known itinerary from flight to absence, the prehistory of the Jew = writing = book equation, generally leads from Proust to Kafka, this flight (and the absences nurtured by it) maintains the distinct qualities of very different circumstances.

All of the writers discussed here grapple, in their own ways, with the angel who can no longer deliver; with seeing, as Walter Benjamin wrote, that "the gate to justice is learning," and knowing (like Kafka) that one "dare not attach to this learning the promises which tradition has attached to the study of the Torah." Here, the "assistants are sextons who have lost their house of prayer, the students are pupils who have lost the Holy Writ."[50] In Shami, the earthly codes of honor and vengeance are ironically usurped by the Patriarchs themselves. In Burla, the problematic of absence is articulated through Rahamo Hibb's inability to find the door to his own room and by the empty, ownerless castle spoken of by Abdul Karim a-Tunisi, the worldly philosopher/sheikh turned psychoanalyst. Cohen's castle, in *Solal*, is of an entirely different nature, not empty but full; yet, in the final analysis, this fullness might amount to the same thing.

Solal (heir to the tribe of the Solals of Cephalonia, in the direct line of the priestly class leading back to Aaron, the brother of Moses), after having completely rejected his family and become a high official in the French government, decides to buy a castle with huge underground halls, vaults, and chambers, and to move his entire native tribe into it. When his wife, not of the chosen tribe, catches sight of this astonishing scene, Solal confesses:

> I went and threw myself before the lord my father and the man of
> mercy pardoned me. He commanded me to build a secret dwelling
> within my European dwelling. I obeyed.—He is wise and understands I
> have my western life to live. —I brought the Solals together, those of
> Cephalonia and others. A Biblical city swarms under His Excellency's
> House. In the daytime, the Ministry, the Chamber, the party meetings.
> In the night, I return to my country. And day and night, I am sad, so
> sad.[51]

What ultimately differentiates these Levantine writers from the interiority informed by Kafka's rupture with the Law, and from the tradition emerging from that break, is their concrete and sensual attachment to the fact and memory of a native space. But even the terms in Cohen (the European dwelling, the Western life, the biblical city), come at a point when the autonomy of the Levant, the autonomous history of the Jews of the Levant, has already been overwhelmed by the "great Western transmutation." What does come through in these earlier writers, however, and later on in Jabès (despite his further burrowing into the interior book), are the vestiges of worlds forever gone, inscribed as cautious testimony to an enduring rift that ends in a cleavage, "where a cut separates different types of happening." These missing pages of time and place have since largely been filled by partisan histories of convenience that studiously reject, as Walter Benjamin put it, that "gift of fanning the spark of hope in the past" which exerts a "retroactive force that will constantly call in question every victory, past and present, of the rulers." What remains at stake, then, is the ability to "seize hold of a memory as it flashes up at a moment of danger; to wrest tradition away from a conformism that is about to overpower it."[52]

At the end of *Solal*, in a most remarkable retelling of the stories both of

Abraham and Isaac and of Adam and Eve, Solal takes his sleeping child away from the house of his estranged wife, and

> pulling on the wide black velvet trousers, the soft boots, the linen shirt girdled with golden braid, he thought of the horrible dead before him. The moon, mingled with the earliest dawn, was pouring out its bluish milk. He saw the Hebrew praying shawl, unfolded it, and put it over his shoulders. Now, he was a mad prince, covered in silk and fringes. . . . The pearls in one hand, the shining dagger in the other, he went down the stairs. He was Solal. At this hour who could stop him from being Solal?[53]

Although he takes his son with him, Solal's only intention is to kill himself. He enters a beautiful garden where he plays with his boy before eating a flower and a fruit and wounding himself. His wife wakes up and, realizing her son is missing, runs to the garden where she sees her child playing with his dying father's curly hair. "Then five old men, three brothers, other old men, beggars, visionaries and women emerge from the Commandery," the name of Solal's underground biblical city, his Eastern dwelling. At this

> Solal placed his hand on his wound, raised to his lips fingers dipped in the wine of the flesh, and blessed life. He no longer knew why he had sought death. His heart was beating. . . . They had thought him dead; he was not dead. Behold, from his bare chest gilded by the sun, the blood had ceased to flow! O race of the living![54]

For Solal, resurrection is nothing out of the ordinary. He sought oblivion, attempting to annihilate the past. Failing this, he tried leading a double life whose only compensation was sadness. When the biblical city emerges, when the family comes out of its Eastern dwelling into the full light of day, Solal is ready to look the sun in the face: his suicide had only been figurative, a desire to destroy part of himself. An infinite amount of such regenerative hope, to again paraphrase Benjamin quoting Kafka, may exist, "but not for us."[55]

V. The Alphabet of Nightmare

A death warrant on the world of Cephalonia (no matter how well concealed beneath or within the "European dwelling"), signed by indifference and sealed by power, was delivered through the auspices of efficiency and pragmatism. In another exile, in a language almost lost, Rachel Castelete, daughter of the wandering minstrel Yakov Yona of Salonika, inscribed a gentle, bittersweet testament, delivered in the 1950s:

When I Came to London

When I came to London
I was a girl on vacation.
I met this young man
And married him.

I had bad luck:
He left me in my old age.
And I, a fool,
Had never relished my youth.
I had brought him a good dowry,
Along with lots of Turkish liras.
I changed them into English money
And got nothing of it.

I came to this city
And have had to wage my own wars.
I thank my God
My children are all right.

If I had stayed in Salanik,
Hitler would have killed me
Just as he killed
All of my people.
Still, today in this city
I find myself
Miserable;
Today I find myself here,
And I cannot even buy a little bottle
of wine or raki.[56]

Unlike the Arabic side, slowly dimming but still scattering light throughout the spectrum, the Spanish facet of the Levantine prism shattered suddenly, with just a few isolated glints surviving the shock of annihilation. Only the barest skeleton of romance—the dashing figures of the Castilian epics, Urraca and the Cid, Roncevaux and Charlemagne, once scrupulously gathered, edited, and recast by Yakob Yona—remains in his daughter's verse. Born in Monastir in 1847, Yona already sensed the transient nature of his time, the precarious state of the 500-year-old songs and legends still binding the community together, and he spent the better part of his life trying to preserve that tradition. His daughter, though, was left to her own devices and the mechanics of her poem are self-generated, without either the trappings or the codes of chivalry so perfectly preserved in the Judeo-Spanish lyric and ballad. In this poem, it is *she* and not a maiden handed down through the years who comes to London, meets and marries a young man, brings a dowry, and changes liras into pounds. It is she, too, who finds herself miserable, plagued by both the guilt of survival and the ache of the unfamiliar. The loneliness of the poet in these lines; the singed photograph of her father's grave in Salonika (partially burned during the bombing of London, the grave itself destroyed by the Nazi occupation forces); the sadness of Solal, compromised in his European dwelling by the inadmissible and no longer extant biblical city of his heart and mind: all mark the enormous distances traversed by Levantine Jews since the "great transmutation."

Some prefigured the extent to which things would change. Close to the end of "Cassandra's Dream" (written between 1939 and 1940), a remarkable poem by Edouard Roditi (the prolific surrealist poet, historian, art critic, biographer, and translator whose family traces its Sephardi origins to the island of Rhodes), we are faced with a new landscape:

> I speak through lips no longer living
> But stiff with sorrow, stony with fear,
> A dead man in a world dead, to the dead
> I speak, not knowing who lives, who hears,
> Deaf to my words, shrill twitter of ghosts.
>
> I know not yet which friends are dead,
> Which maimed, whose mangled bodies
> Gape at the sky through yawning wounds
> And laugh in death's distorting mirror
> Which makes such mockery of life.
>
> The fringes of the blind night's cloak
> Are matted thick with dust and sweat
> Of other lands and times swept up
> As she staggers round the reeling world.
>
> She stops to whisper in our ears,
> Curled as a shell and always loud
> With echoes of her hoverings,
> Those dreams that are our other lives.[57]

Like his predecessor Solomon Bonafed, one of the last Hebrew poets in Christian Spain before the expulsion, Roditi writes of a world turned inside out. Using the conceits of a bard recounting "the turn of Fortune's wheels / Which grind when empires reach their peak,"[58] this wanderer charts a terrain between the living and the dead in which our very lives have become "other."

The final marker of this otherness, as Jacques Hassoun recalls, was "an alphabet of nightmare," not only unspeakable but somehow unpronounceable as well:

In the Near Eastern city of his childhood, the Jewish journals *La Tribune juive*, *L'Aurore*, *El-Chams*, in speaking of it, would evoke the place of nightmare. Later, he saw some Hungarian Jews, survivors, disembark in his congregation in Alexandria. He heard them pronounce the name in deathly silence. It was then that he learned some Yugoslav women were hospitalized in part of the Hôpital Israelite of his native city. The word of an experience undergone in that location of barbaric consonants had then already been enunciated.

He had heard his cousin weep, in Cairo, over the disappearance of his brother and his entire family in the morass of that unnameable country. They had departed from Vincennes toward The Place where they died unburied.

One day in Alexandria, he saw his aunt dancing a funeral dance, wailing her pain in Judeo-Spanish and Turkish—*Aman! Aman!*—to evoke the memory of her family, deported from Rhodes. She turned about in empty space. She turned on herself, describing an orbit around that dead star, that hole.

And he knew that space was a bottomless pit.

And he knew that foreign word—radically foreign—named that collapse of the earthly core.

He saw his country cousins from Mehallah al-Kobra sitting up straight and rigidly in their blue woolen robes, evoking the parting of their uncle from Bordeaux toward the unutterable, the unimaginable, with singular and awesome words. Some years later, he understood that those responsible for that destruction were the followers of Charon, the Parisian vulture, butcher of Arabs and workers.[59]

But as the magnitude of the horrors increased, the space left in which to define oneself autonomously—as a Jew—greatly shrank, as in the kabbalistic trope of God's appearance as a point. Ironically, the promise and the act of "redemption," in the official form of ascent to the promised land, often entailed another, often more bewildering suffering, precisely because it came at the hands of purported "saviors," members of the same tribe.

Chapter 4

Postscript: "To end, to begin again"

What utter folly to wish to name the promised land

Mony de Boully

Oh, what did you do, Ben-Gurion?
You smuggled us all in:

Because of the past we gave it all
up and came to Israel!

Oh, if only we'd ridden in on donkeys
and hadn't yet gotten here!

Alas, what a black hour it was—
To hell with the plane that brought us here!

popular Iraqi immigrant song
in Israel in the 1950s

And I also intend to speak of the Hamdi-Ali family. What is it, in
essence? Look, the Hamdi-Ali family is the joy of life, the
unvanquishable Mediterranean edge. Yes, Mediterranean. Really.
Maybe it's by right of that same Mediterranean that I sit here
unravelling this tale. Here, in the Land of Israel, bordering the
shores of the Baltic Sea. Sometimes you find yourself utterly
perplexed—is Vilna the Jerusalem of Lithuania or is Jerusalem
actually the Vilna of Eretz Israel? It's because of this I wanted so
much to tell the story of the Hamdi-Ali family, and the story of
the city of Alexandria.

Yitshaq Gormezano Goren

I. 1948: The End of an Era

The "miraculous cleansing of the land," in the form of the forced expulsion and flight of the Palestinian Arabs in 1948, left empty houses, de-
serted shops, abandoned villages, and untended orchards, which, lest the
refugees attempt to return, all needed "Jewish" bodies to fill them.[1] During and after the destruction of over 400 Palestinian villages, from 1949
to 1951, at a period when immigration was at its height, about 600,000
people, one way or another, came to the new state of Israel. Many were
survivors of the death camps in Europe. The majority, however, drawn
step by step into a tangled net of circumstances they could no longer find

220

a way out of, had been expelled—more or less brutally—from countries they and their families had lived in for thousands of years. Most of the ancient Levantine and Arab communities were completely uprooted.

The rich and the poor—seamstresses, filmmakers, rabbis, singers, actresses, artisans, merchants, dentists, journalists, lawyers, writers, people from every walk of life—all part of very particular societies still connected to the old network of the *geniza* world one day, found themselves dependent refugees the next. Once delivered, they also found themselves completely cut off from the textures and rhythm of a deeply ingrained and familiar way of life, not to mention from the houses, businesses, professions, neighbors, books, manuscripts, artworks, religious artifacts, and personal mementos left behind.

From here on in, memories of this old world would be banished. This banishment would also, to a great extent, be internalized, despite great resistance and the results of that resistance in the form of social movements, sporadic uprisings, music, writing, customs, ways of thinking and acting, or other forms of personal and collective struggle. The gradual exchange of the legal, communal, and cultural basis of Jewish existence for the racial, the ethnic, and the national (a process with a longer history and more dire consequences in Europe) assumed a final, physical form in the Levant. Official discourse spoke matter-of-factly of the "elimination of the Diaspora," a slogan that even slipped into the "elimination of the Jews."[2]

This discourse, however, did not only encompass the Jews of the Levant. As Tom Segev's pioneering new book, *The Seventh Million: Israelis and the Holocaust*, painstakingly and in great detail illustrates, the Zionists in Palestine remained preoccupied solely with their own affairs. As Ben-Gurion himself admitted, "In those awesome days at the beginning of the destruction threatening Europe's Jews, I was still worrying over the local elections in the MAPAI branch in Tel Aviv."[3] The narrow, party-based interests marked by ideological obsession and petty power struggles, which Eliachar had condemned so vehemently, took on macabre proportions. As Segev documents, nothing was more important than realizing the national project; a Jewish Agency memo, for example, stated, "If it is in our capacity to rescue only 10,000 out of 50,000 people who would be useful in building the land and reviving the nation, as against a million Jews who would only be a burden to us, we must exercise restraint and save the 10,000." Another memo stated: "Children must be rescued first and foremost, because they constitute the best material for settlement. The pioneer youth must be saved, and particularly those who have undergone agricultural and ideological training and who are mentally prepared for Zionist work. And the Zionist functionaries should also be rescued, since they deserve something from the Zionist movement in return for their efforts."[4] Such dictates often meant sending the elderly or infirm *back* to Nazi Germany, as Henrietta Szold, the legendary head of the division of social work at the Jewish Agency, ordered.

Political considerations and the consolidation of institutional structures remained paramount. During the height of the destruction, Ben-Gurion said, "The function of the Jewish Agency is to build the Land of Israel. Perhaps it might be important to rescue some child from Zagreb every now and then, but all in all the business of saving Jews or transferring them to other countries is a function of organizations like the World Jewish Congress or the Joint . . . " Another memo stated that "even the smallest result, however, must at all costs be made politically beneficial — the whole world should know that the only country willing to take in these rescued Jews is the Land of Israel." Not only was this the message that the Zionists wanted the world to hear, they also wanted to insure full control of any reparations that might be forthcoming. These issues were debated as early as 1940 and, as Segev writes, "The trend was to insure that the Jewish Agency would be authorized to represent the claims of the Jewish people before the great powers, and that most of the reparation money would not be directed to individuals but earmarked for the settlement of immigrants in the Land of Israel under the auspices of the Jewish Agency and, later, the government of Israel."[5] Again, as Eliachar had consistently emphasized, true consideration for the well-being of the Jewish people took a back seat to controlling the resources within the party-dominated structure. The more recent controversy regarding American loan guarantees to subsidize the immigration of Soviet Jews, without compromising on settlement activity, shows just how little this party-based mechanism has changed.

Even when the true horror and magnitude of the events came to light, official discourse retained its arrogance and inured itself to any feelings of sympathy; as *The Young Worker*, an official organ of MAPAI, put it in an editorial, "If the Nazi enemy succeeded in defeating us here in this place, the destruction would surely be much less in terms of quantity than the destruction of Jewish centers in Europe, but in the quality [of what would be destroyed] and historical significance, this would be the greater destruction."[6] As for the survivors, an emissary wrote, "Our relationship to the survivors cannot be determined by humanitarian motives alone, but first and foremost according to an assessment of the function that they could fulfill within our campaign."[7] But, as Ben-Gurion noted in December of 1942, "The destruction of European Jewry is the ruin of Zionism. We will not have with whom to build the Land."[8]

It was only with this grim realization that Zionism's cynical "rediscovery" of non-European Jews began in earnest. These potential new builders were spoken of, and dealt with, in the most dehumanizing terms: all were considered "human material," some "antisocial" and others "easily transportable." A Zionist emissary sent to Libya, for example, spoke of the "material" there in the following terms: "They are handsome as far as their physique and outward appearance are concerned, but I found it very difficult to tell them apart from the good quality Arab type."[9] An irony entirely lost within the context of this kind of cynical and pragmatic kinship can be found in Mordekhai HaKohen's account of the Italian occupation of Libya just a few decades earlier, where Muslims pretended to be Jews in order to slip through the clutches of the foreign invaders.[10]

The discourse of "deliverance" did not just operate on the bureaucratic level: it permeated all facets of public and private life. Side by side with the more openly slanderous and racist homiletics of politicians and journalists (such as the previously cited and infamous *Ashkenazi Revolution* by Kalman Katznelson), academics constructed elaborate theories to justify "re-education" schemes that could break the "primitive" mentality of these not-so-noble savages and introduce them to the glories of "civilization." Tom Segev describes such theories:

> Some time after the number of immigrants from the Arab countries began to exceed that from Europe, the quarterly *Megamot* approached five prominent scholars of the Hebrew University in Jerusalem, Ernst Simon, Natan Rotenstreich, Meshulam Groll, Yosef Ben-David (Gross) and Karl Frankenstein, all of Central or East European origin, and asked them to consider this new problem. They approached it with appropriate academic rigor, their articles bearing such titles as "Absolute Criteria" and "The Dignity of Man." Karl Frankenstein's article ended with the sentence: "We must recognize the primitive mentality of many of the immigrants from the backward countries." The others were of the same opinion. Frankenstein proposed that in order to understand the mentality of the immigrants it should be compared, among others, to the primitive expression of children, the retarded, or the mentally disturbed. Yosef Gross was of the opinion that the new immigrants from the Arab countries were suffering from "mental regression" and "a faulty development of the ego." His colleagues discussed "the nature of primitiveness" at great length. As a whole these articles project an Ashkenazi consensus, which was partly paternalistic and benevolent as well as being supercilious and contemptuous.[11]

In effect, such efforts only served to further justify the blatant economic exploitation of the new immigrants and to smother *any* truly effective alternative social organization or cultural expression. As hundreds of thousands of people were herded into the transit camps, families were deliberately broken up, children—as in the scandalous case of the Yemenites—were even "lost."[12] Then the factories opened and people were assigned to a routine of toil, with life measured out by the time clock and space calculated by the square meter, for maximum efficiency. The camps became tent cities, the tent cities huts, and the huts "development" towns or slums fixing a millennium of fluid Levantine urban culture fast within the very cement of their rectangular structures.

Nevertheless, this process was not simply accepted passively. Life in the transit camps was a constant cat-and-mouse game played out between the authorities and the residents, punctuated by concerted efforts at political organization, both independently and through the Ashkenazi-dominated party structure. The presentation of demands, strikes, and outbursts of frustration were not unusual occurrences but in fact set the tone for the whole period of the 1950s. The famous riots in the Haifa slum of Wadi Salib in 1959 were preceded by many other waves of protest, organization, and rejection of the conditions that the new immigrants were forced to accept.

Wherever there were large concentrations of people from the same city or country—as in Petah Tikva, with its Baghdadi population—political and cultural involvement was strong. Jewish actors performed in Arabic in musical and social clubs, along with musicians playing classical Arabic music. Many former members of the Iraqi communist party continued their activities in Israel. All of this ran contrary to the racist assumptions of an establishment that expected all these "primitive" Jews to be "traditional," with no experience in expressing themselves in secular terms. Despite the work of Segev and others in bringing some aspects of this period to light, little has been done toward a more detailed history of it. Very little that has appeared in print comes close to depicting the sense of this time conveyed through interviews given by people who participated in the social, intellectual, and political life of the period.

Following widespread efforts to suppress these modes of expression during the 1950s—through co-optation within the party system, bribery, physical intimidation by collaborators, the breakup of communities through geographic spread, and maintenance of a stranglehold on autonomy by denying the transit camps municipal status—a new wave of movements emerged in the 1970s. The most significant of these were the Black Panthers and the Ohalim (the Tents). These two movements, along with the events in Wadi Salib, were important markers in the consolidation of an Israeli Oriental identity, not based on memories of the past in the old Levantine world but purely on the often brutal reality of life in the promised land. In addition to these more well-known events and groups, the late 1970s also saw the growth of Ma'atz, a self-styled Oriental Israeli "Red Brigade" that carried out "extensive sabotage and arson operations."[13]

The attention and resources that the government put into either suppressing or co-opting such groups also confirms that the aims and popularity of these movements were perceived, at various times, as threats to the dominant structures. There is more than some speculation that one of the covert strategic aims of the 1973 war was to divert attention from the social fissures developing on the home front. Another indication of just how seriously breaches in the status quo are taken can be seen in the establishment's reaction to Oriental Jewish reformers working within the system, as in the cases of Rafi Suissa, former superintendent of prisons, and Ovadiah Yosef, former Sephardi chief rabbi. Prior to Suissa's reign as superintendent of prisons—well over 90 percent of the Jewish prison population are Oriental Jews—conditions within Israeli prisons were only considered on par or, in some cases, even below those of the neighboring countries. During Suissa's appointment, massive reforms were undertaken and prospects for true rehabilitation became a reality. Soon, however, Suissa was dismissed on account of minor infractions. Throughout, the media reveled in every piece of circumstantial evidence indicting Suissa, covering his case incessantly while other scandals involving long-standing Ashkenazi establishment figures were put on the back burner.

Rabbi Ovadiah Yosef, on the other hand, has been treated with selective media coverage. When he first proclaimed that Jewish law could accommodate trading land for peace, the story was all but ignored in Israel, receiving much broader coverage in France. When, however, he started the non-Zionist ultra-Orthodox Shas party (Sephardi Torah Guardians), he was prominently branded a separatist and scrutinized constantly for even the slightest hint of any financial mismanagement, for practices that are not only condoned but even considered normal in the present party structure of Israeli politics. The case of Ovadiah Yosef was particularly threatening because he could deliver a message of political and territorial compromise—in an acceptable language and style—to a population long considered "right-wing."

In both of these cases, the primary goal was not the discovery of evidence, or any eventual determination of guilt in order to weed out endemic corruption, but media assault that could effectively curtail a career. Such an assault, of course, plays into the stereotypes of both the dominant *and* the dominated. While the dominant group assumes that those from the dominated group must be guilty, the dominated *know*—from experience—that nothing can be accomplished by honest people within the system. In both cases, the old double standards still apply: everyone is supposed to work for the common good of "one people," as long as those considering themselves part of that "one people" are of the dominant group. As soon as someone from outside the dominant group begins to work for their own interests, they become stigmatized and discredited, considered a threat to the "unity" of the nation.

The deep cynicism of these policies, and the ideological attitudes that make carrying them out possible, has only been reaffirmed by the mass immigration of Soviet Jews. The old rhetoric of "East" and "West" has again reared its ugly head. While the new immigrants are hailed as saviors before Israel's frightening "descent" into the torpor of "Levantinization," much more significant institutional policies—on the economic, political, and educational levels—are shaping Israel's future for decades to come. One recent manifestation of this has been the phenomenon of young working-class Israelis being forced to move into tent cities sprouting up all over the country as the rental allowances for Soviet Jews have knocked them out of the housing market.[14] Another is the forcing of Oriental children into inferior schools due to increased enrollment and special programs set up for new Russian immigrants. Such policies insure that yet another generation of "Oriental" Jews (now third-generation Israelis) will either remain locked out of the power structure or be forced to leave the country, following the more than (by very conservative estimates) half-million people who already have left.

There is, though, at least some poetic justice in having the Yemenite Jews ("those most Jewish and most Arab of all Jews," as Goitein put it),[15] deliver the formal eulogy on the "modern" period of Jewish culture in the Levant. The Yemenite Laments, written by Rabbi Yehuda Arieh Durani and his son Avraham after the traumatic events in the transit camps, sadly seal off life in the old world and drive an unbreachable wedge between them and any other subsequent "traditional" Hebrew poetry of the Levantine period that does not take those events into account. These traumatic events include the shooting death of a young Yemenite boy, in 1951, at the hands of the police during a riot at the 'Ein Shemer camp protesting the policy of removing children from their parents in order to be educated in secular Israeli schools. In the Laments all the standard "old metaphors" used to mourn the burdens of exile and the destruction of the Temple are stood on their heads to confront this stunning new reality. In the following poem, for example, the very use of the word "Yemen"—in a thousand-year-old poetic mode in which places other than Jerusalem are rarely mentioned—emphasizes the shift into a "naturalism" that grapples with lived, and not inherited, experience:

> Why was justice, meted out with power
> and wisdom, a way of life in Yemen
>
> while now, here in our Holy Land—far, so far—
> the cry of the humble receives no just rejoinder
>
> nor, in times of need, is the widow
> answered: and still, there is no Savior.
>
> Why were the sages and the teachers
> in Yemen held in high esteem, the patrons
>
> and the leaders all revered, while here,
> in our Holy Land, grief's their only lot:
>
> the word of the wise is worthless, and no one
> grants these wretched souls the least respite.
>
> Why were we as one in Yemen, bound
> selflessly to the single God, while here,
>
> in our Holy Land, we're spread and
> shattered, our wall of faith is fallen—
>
> O who shall tend our wounds
> and who,
>   relieve the pain?
> Were my head water
> and my eyes
> a spring
> of tears
> I'd weep both night and day
> to lament my loss of glory.[16]

II. New Hebrew: Language and Ideology

With a few notable exceptions Hebrew writers—at least on the European side—identified with one or another of the representative political streams of national revival. This identification, of course, was in itself a rebellion against either Yiddish or rabbinic culture or the European culture of assimilation. It is within the network of these relations that some of the deepest contradictions characterizing the radical transformation of the Jewish people and Jewish culture in the "neomodern" Zionist period can be found. The results of these contradictions can be seen in some of the linguistic displacements under examination here, particularly in the development of non-Jewish Hebrew literature or the monolingualism of a generation of younger Oriental Jews. Kalman Katznelson, an acute critic of official Zionist ideology despite his deeply racist way of thinking, detailed some of these results in *The Ashkenazi Revolution*:

> The new Hebrew literature was never either a national literature
> or a literature of the masses. The linguistic tool that was employed
> created a natural division between it and the masses and turned it
> into the means of expression for a select intellectual group. At the
> very basis of this literature there rests duplicity, even hypocrisy. It
> spoke in the name of the people and about the people but, in actuality,
> it fought its own wars, because it sought to disassociate itself from
> the people. The Hebrew language was the result of a will towards
> disassociation and a remarkably effective tool with which to carry
> that disassociation out.[17]

As diverse as this "new Hebrew literature" is, involvement and participation in at least some form of the ideological and political project of Zionism imbued much of the work that emerged from this period, the "neomodern," with certain characteristics. These characteristics still mark much mainstream Hebrew writing coming out of the "neomodern" milieu, a literature that often still fights its own wars within its own contradictory tendencies for a select audience. At the same time, because this audience represents the interests of a dominant elite, the terms of its discourse have been translated into a general language of reference for the whole culture. Thus the success of this literature has to do with the fact that it has forged a larger audience for itself through its close correlation with the development of the state itself, simply by virtue of the state's encroachment upon more and more areas of life once under the jurisdiction of other systems, whether cultural, spiritual, or communal. The definitive philosophical critique of this encroachment has been given by Shmuel Trigano in his remarkable book *The New Jewish Question*. Regarding religion, for example, Trigano wrote:

> In Israel, Judaism has lost all autonomy in proportion to politics and
> ideology. Zionism only extolled Judaism as a safeguard for the nation
> during exile, just retaining some customs that could nourish an obliging
> national folklore. . . . Regarding God, the Land, the people and the
> nations, religion has become an exclusive referent of the State, the new
> Supreme Being: the quest for truth has become a means of political
> socialization.[18]

The significance of language in this process of transformation has always been paramount. Katznelson has written of it in his new book, *The Ash-kenazi Reckoning*:

> Modern Hebrew served as a remarkably effective therapeutic tool
> for the Second Aliya; by seizing hold of all intellectual and emotional
> concerns, and consigning to oblivion all associations with Eastern
> Europe, an open space was created to absorb the new reality. This
> is the power of modern Hebrew. But this is also its tragic weakness.
> The language is completely tied to the mechanisms of state life,
> with no significance beyond that, without the transcendental or
> eternal foundation that has always characterized Jewish culture.[19]

The all-encompassing nature of the Zionist project—to create a distinct national entity in a particular place with people from the four corners of the earth—deeply affected both the minutiae of linguistic particulars as well as the nature of its preferred "master narratives." Despite the almost unprecedented diversity of background and influence, this is not a literature that celebrates its heterogeneity. Writers who did—the late Avot Yeshurun, for example—had to wait for rediscovery through the more seasoned eyes, ears, and tongues of second- or third-generation readers, writers, and speakers. Many "neomodern" texts seem tinged with a sense of desolation, but it is not the desolation of exile, whose pain is acutely connected to a concrete place and its past. This desolation, rather, seems disembodied, constructed or inherited as the function of an ideological category.

An example of this can be seen in relationships to the land. While "love of the land" was an intensely nurtured and highly sanctioned ideological value, many found it an acquired taste. Those parts of the land that actually did have a past that wasn't simply conjured up were clearly the territory of outsiders to the Zionist sphere, the domain of either Palestinian Arabs, Levantine Jews, or the ultra-Orthodox Ashkenazi communities. The fact that so many people were new to the country and the region cut off vast areas of the kind of intimate local knowledge so readily available in a text like that of Yitshaq Shami. Descriptions of the land as "alien" and "harsh" became commonplace. The rich interstices of the Levant seem reduced to an "existential" space in which narrative only plays out the drama of representative characters attempting to negotiate the uninhabitable. In prose, this manifests itself most blatantly and obviously in the representation of "others," namely Arabs and non-European Jews, as already illustrated in the work of Yosef Haim Brenner. Brenner himself is only an early instance of this phenomenon; it can be seen, as well, in the work of a contemporary writer such as Amos Oz. Oz himself has also pointed out a major theme in Hebrew literature, the displacement of another dialectic of rupture that is primary to the eastern European-based Jewish and Zionist experience; as he put it: "Even the atheist writers were as obsessed by the absence of God as religious writers were obsessed by the presence of God."[20] This too courses throughout contemporary Hebrew writing, which, as Oz points out, finds its antecedents in the work and thematic of writers such as Brenner, Bialik, Agnon, and Berdyczewski. Interestingly enough, a case could be made charting the development of a truly secular Hebrew novel, which, on the other hand, never explicitly or polemically pronounces the absence of God, through regionally based writers like Shime'on Ballas, Sami Mikhael, Yitshak Gormezano Goren, and Anton Shammas. Here, religious systems or affiliations are neither emphasized or denied, they are simply part and parcel of the worlds depicted.

In terms of texture and the powers of description, the will toward either obliterating or valorizing the past places "neomodern" writing in an extremely precarious position. Since many of the "neomodern"/Zionist writers are first-generation native speakers of the language with no background in the culture of the region, the writing seems to emerge from nowhere. At the same time, given the gaps in local history, Hebrew texts of the past exert a disproportionate amount of pressure. The space left free for the reader confronted by "old metaphors" is often choked off by a more openly referential and functional approach to the things of the world. The open and autonomous nature of the text, such a seminal idea in the writing and reading of the biblical, rabbinic, and kabbalistic worlds—the "premodern" and "modern"/Levantine periods—is reduced to a subservient role, the means to an end.

Some linguistic evidence for this can be found more easily in poetry: there, "neomodern" reading often becomes a treasure hunt for references. This pursuit comes not because of the pleasures of recognition or the desire for the infinite production of new meaning found in the links between "old metaphors" and the recontextualized use of words witnessed in the "modern" period, but in order to verify the writer's knowledge of the Hebrew sources and, more significantly, his or her deep ambivalence about them. It is on this level of recognition, that of a common "existential" and social bond in relation to the use and interpretation of historical materials for the fulfillment of a specific project—national revival itself—that reader and writer connect. In some cases, as in Amalia Kahana-Carmon's very dense and textured work, this linkage and its connections to the national project are interrogated from within to provide a critical reading of conventional assumptions about language and its referents.

This double bind—the erasure of, inability to see, actual native culture, along with the zealous but equivocal search for the traces of "timeless" ancient roots—characterizes much of the writing of the "neomodern"/Zionist period. On one hand, this writing played an instrumental role in creating a new "imagined community" then in the process of formation.[21] On the other hand, the radical historical revisionism inherent in this very process of "recreating" the nation ultimately led to what Ilan Halevi has called "the mass production of false consciousness."[22] The consequences of this consensus can still be felt in much contemporary Hebrew literature and its alliance, whether more or less tenuous, with the covenant of consensus represented by officialdom's sanctioned versions of the past.

An excellent example of this could be seen in the Israeli reaction to a poem by Mahmoud Darwish written four months after the beginning of the *intifadah*. Debated in Parliament and explicated in the press, the poem caused an uproar. The poem itself seemed like a weather balloon, floated in to test the atmosphere of that time, when the world press converged on the scene and the seeds of a real antioccupation movement had begun to grow within Israel. Yet, with rare exceptions, the consensus was that, at least after this poem, Darwish could no longer be considered a partner for "dialogue." The crucial element involved, particularly for liberal discourse (which goes to great lengths to cover the tracks of the institutionalized brutality that is inevitably part of any power struggle), had to do with the question of responsibility. Writers such as Amos Kenan, Yoram Kaniuk, and Nathan Zach, all clearly identified with the "left," fell into line, refusing even the vaguest gesture in the direction of recognizing the Israeli role in the destruction of Palestine. Even more indicative of the parameters of this consensus is the fact that one of the most vocal dissenters from it happened to have been an Oriental Jewish actor and activist, Yossi Shiloah, who had recently completed a performance piece— the first of its kind initiated by an Israeli—based on the texts of Palestinian writers. In direct opposition to the prevailing climate, Shiloah stated that it was precisely the common bonds he felt with Darwish *as an Arab* that made him respect both Darwish's feelings and the legitimacy of his people's struggle:

> I am in search of my roots, my identity, and I cannot find it within
> Israeli culture; if I do, then it is only negatively. I went to Palestinian
> Arabic literature in search of my culture and, being Oriental, found that
> I feel much closer to certain Palestinian poets than to Israeli writers.
> Since the beginning of the conflict, no initiative has been taken in Israel,
> neither in the theater nor in the educational system, to bring the cultural
> and spiritual dimension of the Palestinian people to light. I reject the

common idea that the two peoples are "condemned" to live together.
This is a coercive, negative concept. There is nothing negative or
coercive about life in common. On the contrary, one contributes to the
equilibrium of the other.[23]

Naturally, as in any writing, the human, social, and ideological affiliations of the writer, the user of language, assume crucial priority in plac-
ing the work. The transition from the "neomodern"/Zionist to the
"postmodern"/new Levantine period in Hebrew writing remains highly
instructive, given the exacerbated circumstances of its history. These circumstances include the conception of a new national entity, the physical
creation of a new state, the collective adoption of a new tongue, and the
actual formation of a new culture. It is here that one can see just how
naked the affiliations are, and just how important it is to know *who* is
using the language in what context. This is particularly true when it
comes to translation and critical attention outside the realm of specialists.

Given this, it is important to note that it is not *only* writers from the
Levant who have been neglected outside of Israel's native readership,
but—to a lesser or greater degree—anyone who strays from the dominant ideological or "thematic" consensus. The construct, in this case, is
that of Labor Zionism, with its particular version of a "master narrative." Here, even the diversity and range of *mainstream* contemporary Israeli writing—and thus what is available to Jewish culture as a whole—
has been greatly "abbreviated." The existence of a certain mold, can
determine the range of possibilities open for writers who become difficult to place within the accepted terms of the discourse. The mold, both
self-created and externally constructed and promoted, is generally that of
the engaged liberal, exemplified by such writers as Amos Oz, Yehuda
Amichai, or David Grossman.

Despite their secure canonical position within Israel, particularly when
compared to Levantine writers, the works of many others are also difficult to place among a general readership. These include writers such as
David Shahar (many of whose novels deal with life in the heterogenous
old city of prestate Jerusalem); Uri Zvi Greenberg (an ultranationalist
who was a member of the Irgun); Pinhas Sadeh (whose work spans a
great variety of both formal and historical concerns); Binyamin Tammuz
(a novelist associated with the Canaanite movement); Aharon Amir (a
novelist, essayist, and translator, also associated with the Canaanites);
Amalia Kahane-Carmon (a writer whose work has carved out distinct
new areas of subject matter, including women as subjects in Hebrew
writing); Chaim Be'er (a younger writer whose novels are set in the Orthodox communities of Jerusalem; and Yoel Hoffman (a scholar of Japa-

nese whose work movingly describes states of internal exile within the promised land, particularly during the 1950s).

To reiterate: the Hebrew/Jewish context only presents a more highly concentrated instance of processes that are generally true in cultural formation, particularly regarding access and exchanges through translation. One can see this, for example, in a variety of trends prevailing in, to, and from different literatures. A good example is the ideological scaffolding that buttressed, at one point, the popularity of Eastern European "dissident" writing in America. Another is the prominence given to the invented and very general category of "magic realism" from Latin America, as opposed to more overtly political writing emerging from the resistance movements of particular countries such as Nicaragua, El Salvador, and Guatemala. An even larger construct would be the very category of America itself as an English continent, without its French north, Spanish south, or native past. The tone is always set by the prevailing ideology, and exceptions to it are not easily granted. They must be struggled for or they must come in the guise of "great white hopes" — that is, as the dominant group's effort at promoting one thing in place of another, little fires instead of a conflagration.

III. The New Order

Painful and harsh as the record of the complete breakdown of Arab and Levantine Jewish culture is, the co-optation of individuals and whole communities into an alien and alienating system is even more incomprehensible, as pointed out in Eliachar's critique of Yehuda Burla. Another example can be found in the life and work of Ya'aquob Yehoshua. While inscribing testimony that is both extremely poignant and of inestimable historical value, Yehoshua could at the same time silently fulfill the role of director of the Muslim division in the Israeli Ministry of Religious Affairs during a period when Islamic institutions, monuments, and landmarks were systematically neglected, desecrated, or seized.[24] Interestingly enough, Yehoshua's son, the novelist A. B. Yehoshua (who once characterized himself as an "assimilated Sephardi")[25] has gone back in his last two novels to fully re-examine the nature of the Sephardi-Ashkenazi encounter. This co-optation, however, was never total. While the "mass production of false consciousness" continued (particularly in the educational system and all forms of mainstream Israeli culture), prophetic and testimonial voices, albeit in the wilderness, remained. These voices, both hearkening back to another time and pointing ahead to a different order, comprise a formidable alternative tradition, but one that has always been considered entirely marginal.

One of the strongest and most persistent of these voices, as the passages quoted throughout testify, was that of Eliyahu Eliachar. His two books, *Living with Jews* and *Life Is with the Palestinians*, belong to a peculiar genre of Levantine writing, the autobiographical political memoir, with a good dose of conscious historical, sociological, and anthropological data added for the record. These books, like so many of the works produced by Levantine and Arab Jews in Israel, reflect the kind of genre displacement typical in the Levant since the 1860s, but with a more fiercely recuperative and polemic urgency. Outside the standard modern genres of poetry, the short story, the novel, and theater, this alternative canon includes works as varied as collections of liturgical poetry (such as *I Shall Arise at Dawn*, mentioned earlier, along with scores of others); autobiographical political memoirs (such as Eliachar's books or the Arabic work of the poets Anwar Shaul and Meir Basri); historical and sociological writing falling well outside the academic mainstream; community histories (such as Ya'aquob Yehoshua's monumental *Childhood in Old Jerusalem*); memoirs of childhood centered on cities or particular neighborhoods; combinations of a number of these genres (as in Nehorai Meir Chetrit's *Desert Djin* and *Terror of the Dream* or Shalom Medina's *The Messiah from Yemen*); and local, community-based newspapers and journals.[26] Almost none of this material is published by commercial or institutionally subsidized presses nor is it generally available except by word of mouth or through direct contact with the authors/publishers themselves. Although, if such material were thoroughly documented, a good case could be made for this alternative line *itself* constituting the primary culture of a good part of the population, it remains largely ignored and rarely referred to even in purportedly thorough historical accounts or studies of Israeli culture.

The production of false consciousness as an essential part of the mechanism in any such sweeping historical process ultimately serves to abrogate responsibility for the human price exacted by ideology and the precise logic of power. But the suppressed ghosts creep back into consciousness one way or another, whether in the form of rebellion, witness, art, or Baudrillard's "circular response of the polled," that phenomenon which, for "the analyzed, the natives, is all the same a challenge and a triumphant revenge."

The 1950s and 1960s remained a time of shock and deep trauma, not only for the *she'erith Yisra'el*, the "scattered remnant of Israel" reunited in the promised land, but for the native Palestinians who remained within the new order.[27] This order, besides hermetically sealing the country off from the Arabic culture of the surrounding environment, also meant scrupulous adherence to the invasive censorship code that went along with the repressive military rule of a civilian population. Efforts to create space for literature within this pressurized vacuum included the experience of exile, as in the case of Rashid Hussein (a writer persecuted by both Arabs and Israelis for his belief in coexistence), and the persistent wait of Emile Habiby, one of the most innovative contemporary Arab writers, whose first book of fiction only came out in 1969, when he had reached the age of fifty. The very title of Habiby's most characteristic work, *The Pessoptimist* (*al-Mutasha'il*), reflects the spirit of the times.

For Levantine and Arab Jews, the collective process of reclassification—from which they literally emerged as a new class, as proletariat "human material"—again redefined the space in which writing could be possible. Some of the immigrants—particularly Iraqis who had been associated with or influenced by the Communist Party there—arrived fully formed, with years of political involvement and literary activity behind them. The work of these writers during the 1950s remains one of the forgotten episodes of Jewish literary history. In one of the few articles (besides those of Sasson Somekh previously cited) available in English on this period, Reuven Snir describes the courses of action taken by these immigrant writers:

> The harsh material conditions, the difficulties of adapting to a new society and a lack of knowledge of Hebrew took their toll on a number of them. They underwent an "experience of shock and uprooting," as Somekh says, and under those conditions "it became difficult to think about literature." In spite of this, not a few continued to create in Arabic, while adhering to the poetics they had grown accustomed to in Iraq, which was suffused with English and French influence. A significant thematic change appeared in their work: alongside the conventional subjects which had preoccupied them in Iraq . . . subjects touching on the pressing social and political circumstances of Israel in the 1950s became dominant in their work. Furthermore, as far as concerned Arabic writing by Jews in Israel, those works which dealt with traditional themes were marginal . . . these writers and poets devoted all their literary energies to intellectual struggle, focusing their attention on three central concerns: the manner in which new immigrants were absorbed; the inequality between the Oriental Jews and the Ashkenazi residents; and the fate of the Arab minority. The manner in which new immigrants were absorbed was a searing insult to these writers. Even the passage of time would not let them forget how a new culture and values were imposed on them while their pasts were derided, and in this context their Party activity was a means to an end— a change in this condition . . .
>
> The impulse to their literary activism was not party politics, but rather, in Somekh's words, "a spontaneous inclination towards the

brotherhood of peoples," which in turn characterized the activity of the Communist Party, "the only party shared by both Arabs and Jews." Their work was a sensitive seismic register of Arab minority sentiment in Israel, and occasionally an expression of its collective conscience in the shadow of the military administration's restrictions and political censorship.[28]

David Semah, for instance, in a neglected but extremely moving episode, was the first poet to write about the infamous massacre of Palestinian civilians by Israeli soldiers at Kufr Qassem in 1956. In a poem constructed as a dialogue between the mother and the daughter of one of the men killed, the mother's only reassurances can come in the form of hopes for a better future won through struggle:

> The day of the final struggle is near
> The storm already blows
> Over the world, raging and sweeping
> Striking oppression and oppressors
> Those who steal the bread of the hungry
> The prison and the prisoners
> Those who steal milk from babies
> Those who spill blood
> To save their lust from oblivion
> Gather courage![29]

That a Jew could compose a work in Arabic about a completely suppressed incident at a time when every possible form of pressure, external and sometimes even internal, was exerted against it, makes the gesture more significant. The fact remains, however, that Semah stopped writing Arabic poetry, eventually finding a niche within academia, where many of the most impressive Arab Jewish intellectuals have been ghettoized. There they are allowed to be "experts" on classical or contemporary Arabic literature, but given little or no chance to either voice their thoughts on the contemporary Hebrew scene or contribute to its reformulation. A perfect case in point here is Sasson Somekh, one of the most respected scholars of Arabic literature and language in the world. While Somekh is given complete legitimacy within his own field, whenever he ventures into the realm of contemporary Israeli culture and Hebrew literature — an area in which his erudition is second to none — his influence is diverted into things that are of concern only to "Orientals."

Despite wide-ranging efforts and activities, eventually the implacable fate of the Jew writing Arabic in Israel was to remain unread. On one hand, the increasingly high and feverish pitch of official nationalist Arab culture cut off outside avenues of expression to anyone even remotely as-

sociated with "the Zionist entity." On the other hand, fewer and fewer
Jews found the means to maintain the level of Arabic needed to contend
with works of literature. One of the rare exceptions to this is Samir
Naqqash, a writer who somehow managed to persevere against great
odds. Naqqash not only continues to work in Arabic and have his books
published in the Arab world, but he sometimes blends the standard literary language of narrative with dialogue written in the peculiar Jewish
dialect of Baghdad, making his work even more demanding to an audience less and less familiar with the context that vanished world provided.
But Naqqash's work is not by any means nostalgic; in a recent interview,
he spoke of some of his influences and the unique position in which he
finds himself:

> Sartre and Mahfouz have been direct influences. Faulkner speaks to
> me, so does Albee. Pinter speaks to me. I am very fond of the French
> New Wave, not in its latest manifestation, but in its initial phase. It's
> also possible to be impressed by books written in India, in Turkey. . . .
> I feel discriminated against for a number of reasons: first, a Jew writing
> in Arabic is not read in Israel and gets no institutional support from
> the literary establishment. Alongside sales in the thousands by Israeli
> writers, I barely expect to sell over a hundred copies of those books of
> mine that appear in Israel. Secondly, the general attitude towards a
> writer like me is not positive. The question always looms in the
> background: why should a Jew write in Arabic? Thirdly, I would
> like to emphasize an absurd fact: I am much more well-known in the
> Arab states and abroad than in Israel. Doctoral theses have been written
> on my books in Italy, the United States, England, Arab countries
> including Iraq, Egypt and the West Bank. Fourth, I don't know why
> Israeli literature is translated into so many languages while my own
> work, so far, has not been translated into any of the European
> languages.[30]

Many other writers did make the transition to Hebrew, but they—
particularly two of the most important, Shime'on Ballas and Sami
Mikhael, both from Baghdad—have also faced great difficulty in finding
their way into other languages through translation. As noted in the introduction, one of Mikhael's novels, *Refuge*, has appeared in English,
while nothing by Ballas has yet appeared. Although their work is enormously popular in Israel, it has not yet found the receptive space and approval needed to be included in the list of genuinely exportable Israeli
"products."

Part of this, of course, has to do with the dual roles that establishment
critics such as Gershon Shaked play. As editor of the English-language
journal *Modern Hebrew Literature* and visiting professor at numerous

American universities, the influence of a critic such as Shaked in shaping what gets read by whom is enormous. An indication of the selectivity involved can be gotten from a look at two articles by Shaked, "The Arab in Israeli Fiction" and a survey piece called "Waves and Currents in Hebrew Fiction in the Past Forty Years."[31] In the first article, only Yitshaq Shami and Yehuda Burla are brought up, in the most superficial way, as part of a past in which Arabs formed a "natural" part of the landscape. There is no mention of Ballas, Mikhael, or any other contemporary Hebrew writer from the Arab world. Similarly, in the second article, not a single Oriental Jewish writer is mentioned (although Sami Mikhael is footnoted). For Shaked and others in the literary establishment, these writers simply do not exist.

IV. Shime'on Ballas, Sami Mikhael, and the New Israeli Novel

In Shime'on Ballas's first Hebrew novel, *The Transit Camp*, two of the characters, 'Eyni and Shaul, discuss their fate:

> "Even the name they came up with for these immigrant camps is as tragic as our fate. I asked them why they called these 'transit' camps and they told me they were a 'passage' to complete integration into the life of the state. I looked for the word in the Bible and found it in the Book of Samuel. You ever looked into the Bible?"
> "No."
> "I studied. With the Sage Yehezqel, Peace Be Upon Him, I studied. Maybe you've heard of him. There isn't anyone in al-'Amara who doesn't cherish his memory. He was a great master of the Torah. Even Muslims used to go up to his house to contend at the dust of his feet and seek his blessings. With awe and respect they called him the Sage of the Jews. So, I looked into the Bible and in the Book of Samuel I found a passage about Jonathan 'going between the passes,' and they had 'a sharp rock on the one side, and a sharp rock on the other side.' There's a 'transit' camp for you! A rock on one side and a rock on the other side. Go ahead and try to break those rocks! Isn't this just another way of saying exile?"[32]

Prior to writing this bitter but certain and unapologetic account of life in the tent cities in 1964, Ballas was a regular contributor—under the pen name Adib al-Qass—to the Arabic journals and newspapers of the Israeli Communist Party. Before his immigration to Israel, brought about through "necessity, not ideology," Ballas was active in the Iraqi Communist Party. In Iraq, he also served as an aide to the Iraqi Jewish senator Ezra Ben Menahem Daniel.[33] In many ways, Ballas has always found himself between a rock and a hard place. In terms of politics, culture, and the circumstances of his own career, the narrative strategies he has chosen to use foreground what Barbara Harlow has claimed is "central to resistance narratives. . . . The connection between knowledge and power, the awareness of the exploitation of knowledge by the interests of power to create a distorted historical record."[34]

Ballas has explored this connection in all of his work, directly and indirectly. Through the course of seven novels and two collections of short stories, Ballas has opened a window onto worlds uninhabited and unexplored by most of his Israeli contemporaries, creating counter-narratives that have tried to stay one step ahead of facile definition or categorization. In *Downtown*, a collection of stories published in 1979, Ballas creates representations of different stages of the self in a manner that recalls Joyce's *Dubliners*. In one very brief story examining the narrator's relationship to an old Armenian neighbor, we move from first memories ("I stared at the rising smoke and I picked up fragments of conversation that penetrated deeply into my consciousness. I was four . . . "), to childhood ("New worlds opened their gates to me and the more I discovered something new, the more my instinct for curiosity grew") and adolescence, with its early recognition of belonging and not belonging:

> It was something I simply assumed, that exiles would find joy in returning to their homeland. But Aunt Ghawni was not like the other Armenians. She was alone. The Turks had killed her family, seized her only daughter and expelled her and her husband from their land. I remembered all this and other things that I had heard from my parents and neighbors, but for some reason it was hard for me, at the time, to understand why she would be lonelier in her own homeland than in a foreign country.[35]

In what amounts to a profound but subtle meditation on growth, the development of different stages of consciousness, memory, and its meaning in the present, the stories go on to describe the narrator's political involvement as a young man. The earlier memories and relationships build upon each other to create the effect of a prism that can be turned and turned to reflect different facets of significance. Connections to a collective disrupt the boundaries of time ("I imagined that I was an old man leaning on his cane, staring at his world from the past"), while emphasizing the comings and goings of life in public ("From time to time a lone car passed or a wheezing bus dragged itself by. From the edge of the financial district came the clickety clack of carriages creeping off into the distance. From somewhere, the national anthem surfaced"), to the point at which the narrator realizes that "I am other."[36] This otherness is partly the retention of memories that only attain their full meaning retrospec-

tively; as the fear of arrest and possible expulsion loom, so does the fear
of exile:

> I told myself: here I am eating halvah for the last time, seeing this
> street corner for the last time, going to see the Tigris for the last
> time. Of course I knew this was all folly, that I would eat halvah
> again and pass this street corner again, but thinking about the Tigris
> quickened my pace and made my heart beat faster. . . . Where did
> this feeling of parting come from? I asked myself. I am not leaving
> any place. I'm bound to my own solitude, and I won't even part from
> that. It dwells within me, as a constant companion since childhood, it
> moves me from my world to day dreams and turns me into the hero of
> novels I've read and heroic historical events I've learned about. I
> swallowed and trembled. I was alone, opposite the river, and slowly the
> awareness that I was a free person began to sink in, that I could do
> whatever came into my head, disappear suddenly, jump into the river,
> even yell at the top of my lungs. The hours of emptiness no longer
> frightened me.[37]

Throughout the stories, much like Canetti in his autobiographical
works, particularly *The Tongue Set Free*, Ballas restrains himself from
commenting on the layers of irony implicit in the narrative. It is only at
the end of "Imaginary Childhood," a short epilogue, that we garner the
full weight of what has preceded:

> Are the two houses in which I grew up still standing intact? A young
> Iraqi friend in Paris could not answer my question, but he gave me a
> map of the city, one of those given out to tourists. I found there streets
> and gardens, squares and bridges and blocks of apartment buildings on
> its outskirts.
>
> "I have a different map," I said to him, "a map of alleys twisting
> and intertwining like an intricate cobweb. I can draw it on paper
> because I remember every single curve, every single niche, every single
> arch, every single window and every single side of a house that
> protrudes in a sharp angle near which men stood and pissed." "Many
> quarters have been pulled down," my friend replied promptly, "yours
> too, perhaps."
>
> Whether it has been pulled down or not, what is the difference? As
> far as I'm concerned, it will stand forever. The world of childhood is
> beyond Time, located in the imagination rather than reality. It is a
> complete experience that cannot be apprehended by mere words. We are
> used to telling stories in a logical way. The language we use is arranged
> according to fixed rules and it obeys Time. Every result has a cause, and
> causality is the guideline of the sentences we utter. Otherwise no one
> will understand. How should we retell a dream? How should we relate
> an experience that is beyond Time? Childhood experiences can only be

retold at the expense of locking them up in Time, of binding them in a
tight chain of cause and effect. Such are the childhood stories that we
read. They are stories, a faded shadow, or a polished reflection of an
imaginary experience. I do not put great trust in childhood stories, just
as I do not put great trust in dream stories. I particularly do not believe
writers' childhood stories — those whose main strength lies in writing
fiction are less trustworthy in telling things as they really were, not to
mention childhood events.

The house that I grew up in, the quarter, my childhood, are all a
wonderful dream, a fantasy, a marvellous vision. No, I cannot
apprehend them in words.[38]

By discrediting what he has just accomplished in the stories, in the world
he has created prior to the epilogue, Ballas creates another fiction. This
fiction, however, needs its own subterfuges to insure that it not be taken
for something other than what it is: that his "childhood," the expression
of that time in a particular place, not be reduced to a yearning that accepts
the dominant discourse, that simply wants to add another story to the
existing and accepted stories in order to find equality among them. Here,
the key to this other yearning, for autonomy and the use of the past
within the context of the present, is found in the narrator's friend, the
young Iraqi he met in Paris. For the average Israeli reader, the very presence of this young Iraqi would trigger a whole set of questions couched
in various levels of suspicion: who is he, why do you know him, can you
trust him?

It is this allegiance, in the present, that Ballas goes on to examine and
construct from a variety of angles. Narrated by a young architect from a
village in Galilee, *A Locked Room*, appearing in 1980, gave Israeli readers
one of the first complex Palestinian characters in Hebrew. Following that
came *Last Winter*, a major political novel centered around a group of Jewish and Arab exiles in Paris. His most recent novel, *The Other One*, is also
Ballas's most complex work to date. Based on a number of historical figures (the Iraqi Jewish poet and public figure Anwar Shaul as Assad Nissim and Ahmed Soussa, a Jew who converted to Islam in the 1930s, as
Haroun Soussan), the novel covers every crucial period and event in the
development of modern Iraq from the end of the Ottoman Empire to the
Iranian revolution. This is not done, however, through the use of annals
or historical sources. Rather, the novel consists of a diary kept by the narrator, a converted Jewish engineer and historian who has tied his fate to
that of his country and Islam, the region's dominant religion. Some of
the other options available are depicted through Soussan's relationship to
his closest friends Assad Nissim and Kassem Abd al-Baki. Nissim, although he remains in Iraq through the 1950s and 1960s before going to

Israel in the early 1970s, still identifies himself as a Jew. Kassem, the son of a peasant, is an active communist who ends up in exile in Czechoslovakia. The option that does exist, or has been created, for most Jews, is seen as the collision and collusion of opportunistic forces, historical circumstance, political expediency, class interests, and atavistic, narrowly defined identities:

> Nor did I expect life to be easy for the few thousand who chose to stay. Most of them were property owners, merchants, functionaries in public institutions, or retirees who had once served the state in higher positions. But to think of someone like Assad Nissim getting up and joining this crowd, to show him the way out, something like that just seemed to me contrary to any kind of logic. As I drove by on my way from al-Sa'adun Avenue, I would stop occasionally by the sidewalk opposite the Massouda Shemtob Synagogue and stare at the noisy crowds assembled at the gate. Israeli agents got what they wanted when they planted bombs in the synagogues, for they managed to sow panic among Jews who hadn't exactly rushed to sign on for immigration at first. They worked hand in hand with the authorities to realize the Zionist program, and Jewish money worked on the decision makers who had made a covenant with the enemy. In looking at those Jews, my heart sank thinking of my sisters and the rest of the family, probably standing among them. I wasn't worried about the immigrants, but I had this disdainful sense that they were pulling out; yet, it was impossible to remain indifferent to their wretched appearance, the miserable future awaiting them, their being used as a pawn in a game between Zionist emissaries and avaricious government officials. It was just then that I was told of the jolting speech given by the Jewish dignitary Ezra Daniel in a closed session of the Senate. I had known him when I was a child because my father was responsible for his family's property in al-Hila; if my memory serves me well, he died of a stroke just a year after this. He was a member of the Senate and one of the most prominent of the Jewish dignitaries who not only remained unsympathetic to the Zionists but even condemned them at different times. His speech at that session was not published because it included details incriminating the government, particularly Nuri Said who, already in the twenties, had given the Zionist emissaries free rein despite opposition by the leadership of the community.[39]

The trope of the now-elderly Haroun Soussan's failing memory (as he recounts his friendships, activities, conversion in Cairo, his first marriage to an American woman along with his years in America, the relationship to his daughter from his second marriage, all framed by historical events) is central to Ballas's engagement with the issues of power and knowledge. Here, memory serves to present an ironic and powerful commen-

tary on the legitimacy of forms. It is the very integrity of the split per-
sonality of the narrator, in the form of his recollections, that provides a
source antithetical to "public fictions" that have "created a distorted historical record" and foreclosed the possibility of imagining alternatives to
that record.

While the "master narrative" of so much mainstream Israeli fiction has
mimicked the dichotomies of Zionism (commitment to ideology as
against alienation from it; living out the "solution" to the Jewish "problem" or withdrawing from it, with the resultant guilt feelings of that
withdrawal), Ballas offers choices that have no clear borders. Choosing
one option does not necessarily cancel out the other. Assad Nissim, once
in Israel, conveys his feelings of exile from Iraq through recollections of
his town, al-Hila, broadcast over the Voice of Israel. Haroun, because of
the distance he has traveled through his conversion and the new allegiances it has engendered, offers a testimony of the dissolution of a community that is rendered even more poignant precisely because he is no
longer even a part of it. Each possibility encroaches upon another, but all
of them are rooted in cultural, political, and emotional ties—in a deep
allegiance to the languages, cultures, and common struggles of all the
peoples in the region.

It is only in the last few years, after having reached the age of 60, that
Ballas has begun to gain some grudging respect on the Israeli literary
scene. Even so, his political activities and politically informed opinions
have not exactly increased his popularity. In an interview that he gave,
for example, during the Gulf War, he had this to say regarding an open
letter in support of the war signed by prominent liberal writers such as
Amos Oz, A. B. Yehoshua, Yoram Kaniuk, Amos Elon, and others:

> I wouldn't sign a declaration like that, and I think that it was a mistake
> on their part to attack the peace movements of the world. What
> disturbed me is the tendency of writers [here] to be part of the
> consensus. And the consensus is a sacred cow. . . . I can understand
> the Palestinians. Those who were clapping when missiles fell on the
> Israelis, they did that after decades of repression. We destroy their
> houses, arrest them, torture them, kill them. And here, all of a sudden,
> the Jews are scared too, and their houses are being destroyed. Of course,
> I don't accept joy over affliction, but the Israeli peace camp felt
> "insulted." If they are for Sadaam, then we have nothing to talk about
> with such people. I don't agree with this position, and I think that it
> emerges from feelings of superiority over the Palestinians. A reaction
> like this is extremely grave, because it expresses a lack of will to
> maintain equality between the two sides. Of course we rule, and they are
> the ruled, but the struggle is a common one. And if we fight against the

government, the authorities, the right, we are not only doing this for
them but for our own good as well, and they are under no obligation to
thank us.[40]

Further on in this same interview, Ballas breaks one of the great taboos of
modern Jewish discourse about Jews from the Arab world:

> I have never denied my Arab origins or the Arabic language, despite
> also having had a French education. The Arab identity has always been a
> part of me. And I have said and I say: I am an Arab who has taken up
> an Israeli identity, but I am no less an Arab than any other Arab. That's
> a fact, and I have nothing to be ashamed of about it. If Arabs are
> perceived as being inferior, then it seems as if I am doing this as a
> provocation. But there are Arab Jews, just as there are French Jews:
> How come a Christian can be an Arab but a Jew cannot? Why should it
> arouse such amazement, then, when I say that I am an Arab Jew? I am
> always told that I am Iraqi. Where is Iraq—on the moon?"[41]

In a conference on Salman Rushdie, the British novelist Maggie Gee said:

> Literary fiction has come to be of special interest to twentieth-century
> academics with the growing recognition that all other types of
> discourse—scientific, historical, religious, political—are fictions too. In
> one sense, literary fiction is a model for the others, but in a much more
> important sense it challenges them. Of its nature (individualistic,
> eccentric, exploratory) the novel sets itself against public fictions.
> Unsurprising, then, if those who are protected by public fictions turn
> savagely on the novelist who dares to undermine them. In that sense, all
> serious novelists are subversive.[42]

The work of both Ballas and Sami Mikhael (whose biography is so similar: born in Baghdad, active in the Communist Party both there and
in Israel; switched from Arabic to Hebrew after many years of publication in the Israeli communist press) has run against the grain of many
prevalent Israeli "public fictions." After years of total neglect at the
hands of the critical establishment, the recognition they have begun to
win is due primarily to the inescapable fact of the popularity bestowed
upon them by dedicated readers, many of whom see parables and parallels of their own lives in Ballas's and Mikhael's books. Their work is
often hard to place in the Israeli context since it seems much more
intimately related—in terms of narrative structure, subject matter, and
intentional trajectory—to modern Arabic, North African francophone,
African-American, or contemporary "Third World" novels than the
last vestiges of "neomodern" trends still prevalent among many of their
own Israeli contemporaries. Ballas's immersion in the world of Arabic

literature through his academic work, including a steady output of articles as well as his highly original and compassionate study *Arabic Literature under the Shadow of War*, emphasizes this affiliation. Both writers gave Israeli Jewish readers their first complex Arab characters and it is only one of the anomalies of "the great transfer" that, in Mikhael's work for instance, one can find a more finely tuned account of the communist underground in Iraq during the 1940s — in a Hebrew novel published in Israel in the 1970s — than in any comparable Iraqi work.

In Mikhael's novels, the relentless demands of the narrative, of the story to be told, serves as an armature around which the personal and political get wrapped to the point of snapping. Stereotypes are constructed only to self-destruct through the complexity of their own human motives. Constructions of the self are subject to the tug and pull of competing and conflicting interests, as desires — be they political or sexual — attempt to spring free of binding ties to family, country, language, religion, and party. At the same time that his novels expose the cruelty these categorical definitions can inflict, their substance, power, and ability to entice, attract, and entrap is never denied.

In *Refuge*, the only novel of Mikhael's to appear in English, we are brought into the world of intimate relations between old friends in the Party during the October War of 1973. Mardukh, an Iraqi Jew who had been imprisoned and tortured as a communist in Iraq, is called into the reserves as the war starts. Meanwhile, the Party asks that his wife Shula provide refuge for Fathi, a vain but prominent Palestinian poet. At the end of the book, as Fathi believes the victory of the Arab forces to be imminent, he offers to take Shula and her son Ido into hiding. It is only at this point, among a tangle of ambivalence and mixed emotions tinged with desire, that they lose their autonomy and collapse back into the dictates of circumstance:

> "You hate me," she said.
> "Does that really matter to you now?"
> She kept quiet. He got up and his dry lips sought hers in the darkness. Her face snapped back, and he felt a chill, as if a wall had come between them, cold as death. At that point they stopped being a man and a woman. He was just an Arab and she was just a Jew.[43]

Here, clearly, the contrasts between "man" and "woman," "Arab" and "Jew" are both pointed and poignant. What is even more significant, though, is the fact that in Mikhael's relatively conventional and realistic narrative style, he is able to achieve a theoretical depth regarding the underlying "truths" and ideological underpinnings of representation that is quite rare in the contemporary Hebrew novel.

An instructive analogy can be drawn here between what Erica Hunt has described as the "speculative" and the "liberatory" approaches to writing:

> In literature—a highly stratified cultural domain—oppositional projects replicate the stratification of the culture at large. There are oppositional projects that engage language as social artifact, as art material, as powerfully transformative, which view themselves as distinct from projects that have as their explicit goal the use of language as a vehicle for the consciousness and liberation of oppressed communities. In general, the various communities, speculative and liberatory, do not think of each other as having much in common, or having much to show each other. In practice, each of their language uses is radically different—not in the cliched sense of one being more open-ended than the other, but in the levels of rhetoric they employ. More interesting is the limitations they share—limitations of the society as a whole which they reproduce, even as they resist. To articulate these intuitions, by no means mine alone, is to go down to the deepest roots of official culture and the state's role in preserving the status quo, and find how oppositional culture is both a wedge against domination, opening free space, and an object/material, absorbed by dominant culture.[44]

Imputing quantitative values (better or worse, higher or lower quality) to these different approaches to language and fetishizing technical innovation have led to the almost apartheidlike separation of races and styles that has until recently characterized the transmission of American literary history. Thus the academy can eventually absorb a Louis Zukofsky or a Charles Olson at the cost of ghettoizing a Langston Hughes or a Gwendolyn Brooks. The narrative work of writers such as Richard Wright, Ann Petry, Paule Marshall, Chester Himes, James Baldwin, or Toni Cade Bambara, to give just some examples, is somehow not considered as "theoretically" textured and complex as writers whose work is more overtly concerned with language and form (Gertrude Stein, Djuna Barnes, Dashiell Hammett, Jane Bowles, William Burroughs, and John Hawkes, among many others, come to mind). This elevation of the "speculative" over the "liberatory" cuts off an enormous range of material upon which theoretical and practical considerations of literary history can be based, as if work whose narrative techniques appear more conventional did not also contain the seeds and fruit of speculation. As Barbara Christian has pointed out:

> And I am inclined to say that our theorizing (and I intentionally use the verb rather than the noun) is often in narrative forms, in the stories we create, in riddles and proverbs, in the play with language, since dynamic

rather than fixed ideas seem more to our liking. How else have we managed to survive with such spiritedness the assault on our bodies, social institutions, countries, our very humanity. . . . My folk, in other words, have always been a race for theory—though more in the form of the hieroglyph, a written figure which is both sensual and abstract, both beautiful and communicative.[45]

Given the close institutional and ideological affiliations between Israel and the United States, it is instructive to note that the acceptance of theory within an academic context, as something new, essential, and "unconventional," coincided with the more vocal assertions and greater production of Oriental and Levantine culture. On the Israeli scene, the decontextualization of figures like Jabès and Derrida is even more radical than it is in America. At the same time, despite the efforts of figures like Michel Elial and the journal *Levant*, the further but related constellations of contemporary Arabic and North African francophone writing remain distant planets in a cultural solar system whose sun still rises in the West.

V. Israel/Palestine and the New Levant

Many signs marking the possibility of a new collective duration, of a new period, are discernible in trends and particular works of the 1970s, the 1980s, and the beginning of the 1990s. This generation—following such writers as Ballas and Mikhael, and the dozens of other lesser-known writers who formed the dense terrain out of which their work grew[46]— pointed toward both the revival and the fruition of a genuinely pluralistic Levantine culture. Filmmakers like Moshe Mizrahi, Haim Shiran, and Nissim Dayan offered more immediate visual paradigms of alternative representations. A younger filmmaker, Haim Buzaglio, went back to re-read the films of the enormously popular Iraqi/Iranian/Israeli director George (Gurgi) Ovadiah.[47] Such a gesture is extremely significant, for it has opened the way for a younger generation to engage itself meaningfully with the imagery of popular culture—an imagery not always very flattering—in a genre known as the "bourekas" film, which often features ethnic and class themes. Ella Shohat describes the form:

Mainstream critics used the term "bourekas" as a pejorative noun (and later adjective) while also expressing moral and aesthetic outrage in evaluative and judgmental language, condemning the films as "commercial," "vulgar," "cheap," "dumb," "Eastern," "Levantine," and even "anti-cinema."[48]

It has taken quite some time for the "bourekas" films to be reread with some sense of what Shohat goes on to call their "playful, carnivalesque aspects . . . and, at times, even their parodic and self-parodic reflexive quality, to which the audience in some ways was attracted."[49] This quality is reminiscent of the African-American painter Robert Colescott's stunning depiction of a black family attentively listening to the *Amos 'n' Andy Show*, at the same time spellbound and horror-struck at the notion of participating in their own degradation. Nor is it coincidence that the revisionary and restorative work of Shohat mirrors that of Donald Bogle who, in numerous books, has attempted to extract the humanity of generations of black entertainers forced to work within productions in which control over their representation was extremely limited.

Significantly for the "bourekas" film, the leitmotifs taken from Egyptian, Iranian, Turkish, and Indian popular cinema have begun to exert some pressure on younger filmmakers.[50] Beyond the thematic, the very use of language has come into question. The dialogue in a film like Raffi Bukai's *Avanti Populo*, for example, is almost entirely in Arabic. Over half the dialogue in Haim Buzaglio's remarkable film *Fictitious Marriage* is also in Arabic.

This film, perhaps more than any of the newer films by Oriental filmmakers, shows just how flat and superficial renderings of the Jewish experience in Israel that do not take the Oriental element fully into account have generally been. Buzaglio's film, compared to more well-known films such as Daniel Waxman's *Hamsin* or Uri Barabash's *Beyond the Walls*, adds depth, texture, and substance to what had heretofore been almost exclusively a two-term equation. Within that two-term equation (the Ashkenazi Israeli sabra / the Arab Jewish and Palestinian "other"), assumptions of identity were never, or only very rarely, brought into question. The world and its players—with their respective roles assigned to them—continued going around and around. In *Fictitious Marriage,* on the other hand, the roles and their identities are called into question in a fairly radical way, both comically and tragically, as no one is whom they seem to be. Eldi, the protagonist, fakes a trip to New York and, leaving his wife and children in Jerusalem, holes up in a cheap hotel in Tel Aviv. There he meets Judy, the manager who only dreams of going to America, and Bashir, the Palestinian waiter who cheers on the Tel Aviv Maccabi basketball team, watches Israeli literary television shows and speaks comical Hebrew, but who also, simply and matter-of-factly, says thathe cannot leave the homeland. Soon Eldi, sitting on a bench in Tel Aviv and eating an Arab *beigele*, is mistaken for a Palestinian worker. Although he speaks Arabic, he opts to present himself as mute as he enters intohis new role as a black worker in the Jewish state, a role that takes him as far as Gaza. Here the implication is that anyone—even a tourist—who *looks* like an Arab is immediately put to work building the Jewish homeland.

As the plot thickens the film deals with a dizzying set of issues, but they all seem to revolve around constructs of identity, and it is this, more than anything, that differentiates what might be called the beginnings of Israel's New Levantine discourse from that which preceded it. A work such as this also gives us an inkling of the human treasures buried behind flimsy categories and ideological masks. Ella Shohat suggests the possible richness of the cultures to be represented at the end of her *Israeli Cinema: East/West and the Politics of Representation*:

> In cultural terms, Israeli cinema has been relentlessly "Eurotropic" in the main, spurning any authentic dialogue with the East. . . . The filmmakers take for granted the Zionist rejection of the Diaspora without offering any deeper analysis of the Israeli Jew as a multidimensional precipitate of millennia of rich, labyrinthian syncretic history lived in scores of countries. One is struck by a kind of cultural superficiality in Israeli cinema, a lack of reflection concerning issues that have preoccupied Jews over the centuries, issues which often have cinematic resonances. . . . How might Jewish "textophilia" be inscribed via the deployment of written materials in the cinema, and how could perennial Jewish modes of textuality and exegesis be "translated" into cinematic modes of expression?
>
> Israeli cinema has also yet to become "polyphonic," not only in cinematic terms (the contrapuntal play of track against track and genre against genre), but also in cultural terms, of the interplay of socially generated voices. . . . The challenge now is to go beyond positive portraits of individual representatives of the diverse groups, to go beyond even a concern with positive and negative images in order to present diverse community perspectives, to stage, as it were, the polyphonic clash of what Bakhtin would call "socio-ideological languages and discourses."[51]

It is also during this period that forgotten figures have been reread and rediscovered: the essays of Jacqueline Kahanoff, for instance, the Egyptian who wrote in English, became available in a collection edited by Aharon Amir, the most active surviving member of the old Canaanite school. The work of Bracha Serri, one of the first to give formal expression to the possibilities of reconnecting to the world of banished memory, emerged following the 1967 war. While Naomi Shemer's "Jerusalem of Gold" became the official anthem of the "reunited" city, Serri expressed different feelings altogether. The city was not "empty" and "desolate," as in Shemer's song, inanimate until the Jewish presence breathed

life into it. For Serri, it was precisely the opposite. The great Arab city
was filled with a spirit either absent or suppressed in the "beautiful" but
hermetically sealed "little" Israel:

Jerusalem
on high

   and

      Sa'ana

         down

           below

are one. One is my city.
The same openness / the same majesty . . . I longed

to kiss "these strangers," "our enemies,"

to whisper my thanks

that they exist

as in days gone

by never to

return[52]

Even the visual presentation of this poem represented an assault on the
consensus. Besides the abstract drawings, sketches, and hieroglyphs scattered across the page (much like Etel Adnan's *Arab Apocalypse*), there is
Arabic writing the length of one side of the text and transliterated Yemenite dialect on the other. The urge to disrupt conventional modes of
presentation was taken up by others as well.

The North African-born poet Erez Bitton revived the practice of reciting poetry accompanied by music. His work eloquently limned the parameters of "another Hebrew," outlined in his poem "Shopping Song on
Dizengoff":

I bought a shop on Dizengoff
to strike some roots
to buy some roots
to find a spot at the Roval
but
the crowd at the Roval
I ask myself
who are these folks at the Roval,
what's with these people at the Roval,
what's going on with the people at the Roval,
I don't face the people at the Roval

but when the people at the Roval turn to me
I unsheathe my tongue
with clean words,
Yes, sir,
please, sir,
very up-to-date Hebrew,
and the buildings standing over me here
tower over me here,
and the openings open here
are impenetrable for me here.
At dusk
I pack my things
in the shop on Dizengoff
to head back to the outskirts
and another Hebrew.[53]

This "other Hebrew" is a language far from the fashionable phrasing of
Tel Aviv's Dizengoff Street and its slavishly imitative modes that set the
tone for the country as a whole. Bitton's idiom is the tongue taken home
by those closing shop and heading back to neighborhoods not included in
any tourist's itinerary, places where the common language remains music, "wounded kinship's last resort." Besides practicing this bond
through his recitals, Bitton's poetry paid tribute to some of the forgotten
and neglected greats, the once-famous singers and musicians now relegated to a life of obscurity:

Zohra al-Fasiya's song

Zohra al-Fasiya

singer at Muhammad the Fifth's court in Rabat, Morocco
they say when she sang
soldiers fought with knives
to clear a path through the crowd
to reach the hem of her skirt
to kiss the tips of her toes
to leave her a piece of silver as a sign of thanks

Zohra al-Fasiya

now you can find her
in Ashkelon
Antiquities 3
by the welfare office the smell
of leftover sardine cans on a wobbly three-legged table
the stunning royal carpets stained on the Jewish Agency cot
spending hours in a bathrobe
in front of the mirror

with cheap make-up—

when she says

> Muhammad Cinque
> apple of our eyes

you don't really get it at first

Zohra al-Fasiya's voice is hoarse
her heart is clear
her eyes are full of love

Zohra al-Fasiya[54]

Here naming and the use of almost formulaic epithets and images turn the present back to the fertile space of its own memory. While conjuring up an unbridgeable abyss, the very act and gesture of the poem spans the chasm. The poem cannot restore either Zohra's voice or her audience, only record the indelible fact of her life: even as memorial, the word regenerates. Bitton's own bitterly ironic experience informs this paradox. Playing with his friends at the age of ten in one of the abandoned orchards of Lod, he discovered an old grenade. Picking it up cost him his eyes and the partial use of an arm but it also brought him to one of the better institutions for the blind, where he received the kind of education that those he left behind could never even have dreamed of. For them, however, those of the neighborhoods speaking "another Hebrew," there was no real need to return to the voice of Zohra or the other great musicians for they remained an inseparable part of their vocabulary.

The distance of this "other Hebrew" from the mainstream is put in stark relief by an astonishing passage in *The Modern Hebrew Poem Itself*, a book that serves as the first introduction to contemporary Israeli culture for many American students. In an appendix to the new edition, several poems by Bitton are included and commented on by one of the volume's editors, Ezra Spicehandler:

> Erez Biton (b. Algiers, 1942), more than any other poet of this younger group, strongly reflects his Middle Eastern heritage. Much of his poetry springs from a childhood spent in the slum world of Moroccan immigrants in Israel. Typical is his ballad of "Zohorah Al-fasiah," a *fictive* [my emphasis] Jewish favorite of King Muhammad V of Morocco.[55]

Again, in distorting the circumstances of Bitton's life through racist assumptions (a major theme of Bitton's poetry is the "salvation" his blindness provided for him), Spicehandler goes so far as to simply eradicate even the possibility of a character like Zohra al-Fasiya's existence. Here, the average Middle Eastern Israeli—for whom Zohra al-Fasiya is simply a cultural fact—has a decided advantage over the scholars, copyeditors, and fact checkers trying to present this culture.

Nor is this, by any means, an isolated example. In another popular and authoritative presentation, *Israeli Poetry: A Contemporary Anthology*, edited by Warren Bargad and Stanley F. Chyet, we learn that

> Israel is geographically part of the Middle East—and indeed is a major factor in contemporary Middle Eastern consciousness. Yet as astute an Israeli intellectual as Shulamith Hareven defines literary Israel as a territory whose borders skirt present-day Manhattan and nineteenth-century Odessa, with Czernowitz somewhere in between. She would prefer a more Mediterranean Israel, though she surely knows that such an Israel is, in literary as well as political terms, still very much within the realm of utopian fantasy. Yoram Bronowski, too, is clear on this point: that Israeli literature moves willy-nilly on paths determined by European literature. It does seem that, for literary purposes, the Israeli sensibility is incontrovertably a Euro-American sensibility. Very little about Israeli belles-lettres can be called Levantine, even though a sizable proportion of the Israeli population (a segment that includes such authors as A. B. Yehoshua, Nissim Aloni, and Erez Bitonn) has Levantine or Oriental antecedents. From a Middle Eastern perspective, then, all Israelis, even those of Moroccan or Persian or Yemenite origin, are European; their literature is European; their outlook is alien or external to the Middle East.[56]

Needless to say, not one Israeli poet of Middle Eastern descent appears in this anthology. Nor are we given any clues as to the remarkable gymnastics performed in turning Moroccans, Persians, Yemenites, and, for that matter, *Israelis*, into "Europeans."

Such critics, translators, and academics, while deluding themselves into believing they form part of a pro-Israel fifth column on the American literary scene, are actually doing precisely the opposite. By inventing such absurdities as "Euro-American sensibility" and completely ignoring the pertinence of postcolonial discourse, they condemn *all* of Israeli literature to be viewed in the most parochial and patronizing terms, constantly quantifying its value through forced comparisons to well-known "Western" writers, other members of the club. Thus, Saul Bellow can classify A. B. Yehoshua as "one of Israel's world-class writers," as if the whole endeavor were a horse race or a prizefight.

Despite efforts to extricate Israel from the Middle East, along with all the technical and psychological obstacles, there is probably nowhere in the Levant where such a vast variety of music from the region can be found. Against great odds, each group of immigrants either preserved or, if at all possible, continued to follow the trajectory of their musical culture from afar. In the alleys of the open marketplaces, at the central bus stations, out of suitcases, kiosks, flimsy stalls, or tiny shops, virtual walking encyclopedias of popular culture sell cassettes and videos, in every dialect of Arabic, in Turkish, Greek, Persian, and Kurdish. Every imaginable form of the *piyut*, the Hebrew religious poem (either chanted according to the traditional rules of prosody or set to music in one of the ancient Arabic *maqam*), is available.

There is great admiration for the young Moshe Habusha, a cantor from Jerusalem whose lifelong dream had been to meet the venerable Muhammad Abdel Wahab, the late dean of Arabic music whose death in Egypt became a national day of mourning. Stories are told of Abdel Wahab's special effort to travel from Cairo to see the Tunisian Jew, Raoul Journo, at his appearance at the Olympia in Paris. Older Egyptians reminisce about Laila Mourad, the beautiful singer whose father was a rabbi and a cantor; they speak of how Farid al-Atrache went into seclusion and stopped singing after his sister Asmahan was killed; of the bitter feud between her and Umm Kulthum. The Moroccans speak of how famous orchestra leaders would come to Rabbi David Buzaglio to answer a musical query once they had exhausted all other sources. The Algerians tell of the singer and 'oud player Reinette, and how one of her accompanists was deported to Auschwitz by the Vichy regime. And then there is the constant gossip, about the new Israeli "cassette" singers; about the Persian, Turkish, and Moroccan musicians who come to play the nightclubs in Jaffa; about the sweet voice of Zohar Argov, his addiction and suicide.

But it is here, as well, where the very real political and cultural schism creates a true split. In this sense, the majority of Levantine and Arab Jews are still hostage to policies and hierarchies of power they did not institute: social, political, and economic structures and realities directly confront cultural limits, memories, affinities, and events. Like Zohra al-Fasiya, hundreds of old singers and musicians remain forgotten, living and dying in obscurity. The great 'oud player Brahim Souri, for instance, can be found selling shoelaces, razor blades, cheap perfumed soap, and other assorted odds and ends out of a cardboard suitcase on Jaffa Road in Jerusalem. Even more pointedly, one can hum the tunes of Farid al-Atrache, Umm Kulthum, or Muhammad Abdel Wahab one minute, and serve as an interrogator in which the Palestinian subject becomes an object of misplaced rage the next. Such is the nature of Israeli working-class dislocation and each turn of the screw in both the hegemonic cultural structure and the continuing occupation, always amply abetted by the industry of official imagery, only serves to further mutilate memory itself as an entirely new history and set of relations is constantly being produced.[57]

Younger artists, those in their thirties and forties, have come closer to confronting this dilemma: from the painter Pinhas Cohen-Gan to the musician Shlomo Bar, from the playwright Gabriel Ben Simhon to the filmmakers Haim Buzaglio, Benny Turati, and Eli Hamo, from the novelists Yitshaq Gormezano Goren and Albert Suissa to the poets Shlomo Avayou, Peretz Dror Banai, Shelley Elkayam, Amira Hess, Ronny Someck, Tikva Levi, and Sami Shalom Chetrit. Scholars such as Ephraim Hazzan, Yosef Halevi, and Yossi Chetrit have, as well, changed the landscape of cultural assumptions by unearthing and presenting vast areas of Hebrew literature that had been consistently marginalized. Due to the the presence and activity of such figures, older artists (the novelist Dan Baneya Seri, whose magnificent prose style is reminiscent of Agnon, for example) seem to have been granted a new sense of legitimacy. Of enormous significance, too, is the movement of a writer such as A. B. Yehoshua toward openly embracing issues and themes that had either been absent or just below the surface in his previous work. His latest novel, *Mister Mani*, is a tour de force that breaks into the interior of Sephardic life in the Levant. The interstices of this new thematic in Yehoshua's writing, the engagement with a complex identity, its construction and representation, simply make works or discourse that neglect this thematic seem flat and superficial in comparison. All of these artists have somehow struggled, in different ways, to transfix the splintered shards of the past's mirror into the available present before projecting them into an intelligible future, where memory can truly be free to invent and reinvent form.

In Eli Hamo's powerful documentary *New Direction*, for example, the subtle mix of music, image, text, and content elevates the film's relatively conventional mode into another realm. Shot in black and white (except for one shot of the Israeli flag and one shot of the yellow star worn by Jews during the Nazi period), Hamo's film manages to imbue timely debate with a timeless quality. Much of the material is taken from open discussions with various Israeli political and cultural figures at a club run by social activists in Tel Aviv's HaTikva quarter during the mid-1980s. This material is intercut with shots of the neighborhood, footage of the Ethiopian Jews demonstrating and speaking before the chief rabbinate in Jerusalem, stills and news clips. The stills and clips (of Eastern European shtetl life; Nazi Germany and the death camps; Israel during its "pioneering" period, wars and the intifadah) are spliced in with quotes from various Zionist leaders and Israeli figures about Oriental Jews. All the music during these shots is by Wagner. The film is framed by two long shots, one centering on the HaTikva quarter (moving from the roofs down into the street and the marketplace) and the other, disjointed, cutting back in staccato fashion before leveling off into a slow, steady fade. The neighborhood itself could be any number of places in the Middle East: Cairo, Gaza, the slums of Beirut. Throughout, the music comments on and interacts with the imagery. As we are flooded with images of Ethiopians in flowing robes greeting each other before their tents, set up to protest against their need to undergo a "conversion" ceremony, we hear the exhilarating rhythms of the North African group Nas el-Ghiwane. As all the elements of the film recede back into the neighborhood and the concluding comments of the activists regarding their future in the Middle East, we hear Mounir Bashir battling to tune his 'oud into the steady beat set up by his percussionist. An exact opposite of the lilting and leisurely Andalusian *petiha* (prelude), this ending works in reverse: as the shifting and clipped images (going to the beat of the drums) find a resolution in the retreating camera, so the 'oud settles into its theme. The sounds and the images seem to say that only with harmony, with all the elements tuning into each other and the space they inhabit, can life be viable.

This impulse also finds parallels among Palestinian writers, artists, filmmakers, and musicians. The musical group Sabrin, for instance, has been influenced by jazz, blues, African music, Algerian rai, and reggae, but all filtered through the traditional instruments of the Levant. The el-Hakawati theater has renewed old lines of communication by requesting a theme song for one of their plays from Sheikh Imam, a popular Egyptian singer whose work has often been banned in Egypt and other parts of the Arab world. As part of the general boycott of Israeli goods during the uprising, many Palestinian painters have given up manufactured art supplies in favor of indigenous, homemade materials.[58] The mix of informality and political militancy in the work of Sahar Khalife has struck a resounding chord among other writers of her generation throughout the Arab world. The consistent similarities, in fact, not only between younger Palestinian and Oriental Jewish artists but also among their other contemporaries in the Levant, far outweigh the distinct national, linguistic, and social differences that remain.

VI. Recreating Memory: Alexandria and Baghdad in Israel

While the integrity of memory as a form of oppositional knowledge remains a central motif in the work of Shime'on Ballas, the work of the younger Yitshaq Gormezano Goren revolves around the elusive vicissitudes of desire. His Alexandrian trilogy (only two volumes of which have appeared so far, *Alexandrian Summer* in 1978 and *Blanche* in 1986) is a narrative tour de force that presages a number of developments in Hebrew fiction. Framed by an omniscient narrator who both is and is not

the character Robbi, *Alexandrian Summer* and *Blanche* center on life in the
Jewish middle class of Alexandria in the pre- and post–Second World War
years, prior to the 1952 revolution. The last two chapters of *Blanche* shift
to Israel, after many of the characters inhabiting the novels have immigrated there:

> The temperature in Beersheba got up to 110 degrees. The boy Moshe,
> named after his grandfather Moshe Vital, killed in Jerusalem by a bomb
> in the Anglo-Palestine Bank, loved to roll around in the sand. His
> mother, a housewife about to give birth again, went out looking for
> him. Levana Vital cursed the imprisonment of her pregnancy.
>
> Three years had passed since they came to the capital of the Negev.
> With Vita Shime'on's small inheritance, they managed to buy an
> apartment in one of the two-family house blocks with small courtyards.
> Vita Shime'on rescued them from the burning tin huts of the transit
> camp. Close to the time of their arrival, Raphael was supposed to be
> drafted into the army. Blanche was already carrying little Morris in her
> womb, Moshe that is, and she threatened to cut her veins if Raphael
> went into the army. The IDF wasn't very impressed by the hysterical
> woman, but Raphael knew his wife was capable of doing it. A
> compromise was finally found and Raphael enlisted in the police force
> and was stationed in Beersheba, which is how they happened to end up
> in the desert city. In Egypt we fled from the desert to the openness of
> the coastal cities, and in Israel the desert blows its arid heat over our
> faces and the backs of our necks in this Beersheba of theirs, which is
> just a small-scale Cairo, without even the Nile for relief.
>
> Blanche-Levana's and her husband Raphael's years in the capital of
> the Negev were hard, hot and dry. It is difficult to write about them.
> The eastern winds seemed to dry up the ink in the pen, and nostalgia
> for hopeful youth smuggles the narrator back to the cool sea breeze of
> Alexandria.
>
> Blanche and Raphael, a good-looking, romantic couple. I see them
> sitting at the L'Auberge Belle of memory, but I know there is no
> avoiding the Beersheba story. It isn't just that the Land of Israel served
> as an incline for them to roll down. Everything already started there, in
> Alex, but the affliction was covered up, certainly from the sight of a
> boy like our Robbi, from whom anything unpleasant was hidden. But
> beneath the sun of the Negev it was difficult to hide anything, even
> from the eyes of a child.[59]

Like the shifting names and shifting identities of the characters and the
narrator, everything in Gormezano's novels is a metonym for the travails
of narration, for the impossibility of reaching the "promised land," for
the inability of the tale and the timeless to finally meet in union. Like Ballas, Gormezano fends off facile categorization through diverse narrative

strategies. But instead of exploring the construction of a self layer by layer, Gormezano simply opens Pandora's box by going back to the somewhere else that is the forbidden past, in his case, childhood in Alexandria, with its hypocrisy and cynicism, its Ladino and French and English, its Greeks and Jews and Arabs. His work is a far cry from nostalgia, even though there is real, albeit gentle, mourning in it. The forgotten, distorted world—willed into oblivion by the discourse of "deliverance" and the ideology of return's tunnel vision—is faced like an ecological disaster, as an inseparable part of the eroded self whose contours must at least be retraced to right and write the body and the mind's own damaged, unbalanced economy.

Constantly punctuated by indeterminacy, the novels are framed by very specific details. The title of the first chapter in *Alexandrian Summer* is "From a Distance of Twenty Years"; in chapter two, the narrator writes, "Alexandria from the time of King Farouk, with his curly mustache and dark glasses, that same Alexandria I knew in my childhood, the Alexandria that has fed my imagination more than twenty years, from the time I left on the 21st of December, 1951, when I was ten." The novel ends like this: "From then until today, the 10th of April, 1977, he hasn't seen the city of his childhood other than in his memories and his dreams." The first chapter of *Blanche*, "18 Years Old," also grounds us in time, as does the end of the book when Robbi and the narrator part ways again: "Today is the 10th of August, 1985." These details underline a part of Gormezano's agenda that is very well hidden, just as unpleasant things are kept hidden from Robbi's sight. This agenda lies somewhere in between these specifics and the narrator's constant ploys to make believable the difficulty of his project:

> The story of an Alexandrian summer is not easily written. See, it is wrapped in layers of nostalgia, of forgetfulness, of generalities. And I am trying to put my finger on the objective, the distinctive. Should I tell it in the first or the third person? Should I call people by their names, or perhaps just give them fictitious names and write that "Any resemblance etc. is purely coincidental"? Trivial details, but they hold you back.[60]

In the "story," the boy himself, Robbi, is obsessed with marking down license plates, fixing things in motion, just as he too is about to be propelled into an entirely new orbit. At the end of the first novel, his last day in Alexandria finds him determined to continue writing down the plate numbers: "Why is he so intent, today of all days, with stubborn determinacy, to write down the license plate numbers? Quickly he dips his pen into the inkwell on the ledge and writes and writes and writes." But the first rains come and "the notebook stayed on the ledge, and the rain came down on the numbers, blurring the ink, distorting the shapes, erasing everything."[61] The frame within which the erasure takes place is not presented from the point of view of "victims" and "victors," with roles etched in black and white. One of the main characters is a Muslim convert to Judaism. The Jewish community itself is clearly depicted within the context of colonialism, but not very sympathetically in terms of their relationship to the native population. The servants are a constant reference point for gauging the rapid movement, not only of Robbi—both as a child growing up and as someone about to embark on a new life in a new country—but of Egyptian society itself, tensely poised in wait for the revolution.

In one of the novel's climactic scenes, a near riot breaks out at the races when David Hamdi-Ali, the son of Joseph Hamdi-Ali (the convert) beats the Bedouin jockey Ahmed al-Talooni (who, it is implied, may *also* be Joseph Hamdi-Ali's son):

A hair-raising cry broke out from the bloodthirsty Bedouin's black throat. Even though it had all the signs of second-rate theater, it succeeded in shocking the crowd for an instant. Of course there were those who found this kind of vulgar behavior repulsive, seeing in it only an inability to lose with dignity, but the majority heard entirely different echoes in that cry. Later on, in court, someone said that in that scream he heard the agony of Egypt, trampled on by foreigners.[62]

The narrator's references to political events are given weight and substance by sympathetic portraits of the servants; this is enhanced by our privileged eavesdropping on gossip directed against them within the family circle. Even more pointedly, it becomes clear at certain junctures that Gormezano has transposed the experience of Oriental Jews in Israel during the 1950s onto his rendering of the Egyptian social fabric. When the narrator wryly comments that to succeed in Egypt "you only had to be a Jew or a European with minimal intelligence, and even that wasn't always a requirement," one cannot help but think of the rhetoric and the obstacles people like Robbi and his family would face in Israel. Again, as the novel ends, the narrator pauses to consider Salem, the doorman's son:

This Salem . . . he was a special kind of kid, alert, sharp, neither too industrious nor too lazy, amazingly adept at picking up languages by ear (French, some English and even Ladino), and on top of everything, he was in possession of a world of his own, one in which no stranger could intrude. If he was born into another class, at another time, he might have gone far. Maybe he did, even as it was. Maybe Salem was one for whom the Free Officers' revolt opened new horizons. For years and years Robbi wondered what ever happened to the kid who grew up in the same house with him.[63]

As in all of Gormezano's work, with its precise links between beginnings and endings, this passage too must be read in relation to the book's dedication: "To the memory of my father, who all his life nurtured the dream of writing, and did not attain it, but who passed on to me the love of creativity."[64] The irony here can certainly be sustained by both the text and the historical circumstances from which it emerged. Here, the reversal of fortunes and transformation of roles within generations is doubly mirrored. After all, Joseph Hamdi-Ali tries to pass on his dream of being a great jockey to his son David. These contingencies of circumstance are a constant function of the text as well. When Robbi and the narrator part ways and meet at the end of Blanche, after seeing her and her ex-husband Raphael Vital at the wedding party of their son Moshe (Morris), we are given the inspiration for the book we have just read:

> Here they are sitting at separate tables and looking on with great pride at their two children.
>
> That look of theirs is what prompted me, I who was also among the called, to set my heart upon the idea of writing within a book the story of Blanche and Raphael Vital.
>
> No, there cannot be any connection whatsoever between the two people sitting there like solitary islands, and the characters who will be created from a reflection of their sorrow.
>
> If they themselves read these things one day, maybe they won't recognize themselves.
>
> It's enough that I myself recognize them.[65]

The language in this passage lends it a quality that is very difficult to render in translation, but the overtones in the original Hebrew are unmistakable. While there is pride in creation, its meaning must somehow be not only ascertained but *recorded*. By using the word "summoned" and not "invited," the narrator ups the ante of his own function: when we learn that he is not going to write a book about their story, but write their story "within" a book, we are closer to grasping the nature of the riddle we have been given to solve. When the narrator writes of "creation from a reflection" (using the root *bar'a*—the same word used in Genesis to mean "creation"—and not *yatsar*), we have entered the realm of Hebrew thought engaged with definition through difference, a "creation myth" that is less mythical than grammatical and reflexive.

The poetry of Amira Hess also peers into the past's forbidden box, the relationship between language and its referents in creating and recreating living bonds between the consonants; her first book, *And the Moon Drips Madness*, came late, at the age of forty-one:

> I am Baghdad's daughter
> Yet could swear
> I were native to London
> Recall those gates of iron
> All that golden glitter
> Horse guards and cavalry
> What a wind nipped at my feet
> To remind me I belonged in spirit
> But take not the body
> So weak and trembling[66]

Baghdad's colonial architecture, the changing of its guards, is at once the deepest recess of childhood sight, and an imposition, chilling to the bone. Interestingly enough, when Amira Hess appeared on a literary talk show in Israel, the host—one of the primary arbiters of Israeli public taste— was completely bewildered at the reference to London in this poem, thinking it must have been some kind of fantasy or figment of childhood imagination. It took Sami Mikhael, also a guest on the show, to point out that the reference was to a particular square in Baghdad that had, in fact, been built as a copy of a square in London by the British colonial powers.

None of the poems in Hess's collection are titled and from the first lines ("I am Amira / Salima's daughter, / the daughter of Hayim Yitshak Yehuda, / son of the Lord Be Firm, Peace upon him.")[67] the ghosts push open the lid to establish their own geneology, rushing out wildly in an exquisite, sensual language that recalls the hallucinatory visions and paradoxes of the Hebrew prophets. Amira is also Maria, the golden-haired infant woman. She is a mermaid and the Moabite and "Astarte Moloch of ancient times." She is also the reincarnation of her own foremother, the renowned Osnat Bat Barazani, a seventeenth-century teacher and poet. As in a sister work, the Lebanese writer Hoda al-Namani's "I Remember I Was a Point, I Was a Circle," these figures kaleidoscopically merge and clash but never conclude, all caught within the confines of an irresolute space:

> There was a time
> when I'd have said:
> with this vile Orient,
> I won't defile myself,
> I won't go back home to
> my mother's owlish face
> weeping over the ruins,

my father's cabbage patch look—
the Lord—graced him not.
And I also said:
the West, for instance,
has no caress to its spirit,
cooked within, scorched to the shrouds.
East and West I'll set out in a strong beat
and there is no ark
to bestir myself, if another
brainchild passes away
to make eagles soar.[68]

VII. Reclaiming Nativity: The Poetry of Shelley Elkayam, Ronny Someck, Tikva Levi, and Sami Shalom Chetrit

Much "neomodern" writing is marked by a tendency to "demystify" the Hebrew language, to diminish, degrade, or suppress sections of its se-mantic, environmental, or historical strata in a breakneck effort to be "new." This was often accomplished, ironically, by putting rarely used words originating in a more obviously religious or ritual climate into contexts that stripped those words of their prior meanings and connec-tions. This process sometimes led to the absurd situation of odd words being resurrected, with new shifts in meaning, in order to appear up-to-date and colloquial. Such lexical enrichment sometimes came at the cost of a lapse in the attention paid to the possibilities of "plain" language. This kind of "plain" language, however, finds a more direct counterpart in the *tsahut* (purity of language) of the "modern"/Levantine period than in the colloquial Hebrew of the popular Israeli poets of the 1950s and 1960s. In Shelley Elkayam's work, particularly *From the Song of the Ar-chitect*, the nativity inherent in the topography of an earlier poem such as "The Crusader Man" finds an even surer and more measured response to the treasure-hunting poetics of the "neomodern." The vocabulary in these newer poems is basic but by no means simple. Instead of looking for obscure words, she chooses precisely those counters with the widest semantic space, the textual black holes of the biblical world, always pa-tiently waiting to again be accommodated to new realities, as in Gormezano's very pointed use of certain terms.

Elkayam's most accomplished poem, "Yes Indeed I'll Answer God," is written in a flat, declarative tone that is prophetic as well, but not in the hallucinatory style of Amira Hess. The ambiguity of person, expressed in Hess through naming, is developed by ringing changes on the limited lexicon of the Song of Songs. Here, the "woman" as "writer" stretches and oversteps the roles and boundaries of gender. As the poem opens, "I

will ever be what I now am inscribing letters in light," the verb "inscribing" appears in the feminine. In some stanzas "she" beckons the lover
who "finds himself in the garden" to come: "Come, my pleasantly tied,
/ unlace yourself in the palm / of my hand." But in another stanza,
"she," the "writer," declares: "I forgive my father for doing things without questioning my desire. / Look, after all, the ledger's open. / Cere-
monial testaments inscribed in the body. / A man and his covenant /
carved in his form."[69] The verb "forgive" appears in the masculine. Here
the return to the semantic breadth of biblical language and Semitic syntax
takes the reader to the fuzzy edges of determinacy and meaning itself, to
the "antithetical sense of primary words," in Freud's terms. At the same
time, this vocabulary plumbs the further recesses of "plain" language in
a poetry that is entirely readable without being either banal or simplistic.
The other spheres of activity and the social space of Elkayam's work also
signal a different context for writing than that framed by conventional
Israeli models; they parallel the very precise criteria given for one kind of
intellectual by the American poet Bruce Boone:

> Writing would not be separate from whatever one does as an
> intellectual—in the body of those who both think and act, and who
> stand in a certain tendential, final relation to the modern Prince. It is
> impossible to assume that this writing has not already begun in places
> one visits each day. Writers, in this view, are simply engaged in
> teaching, political organization, community work and liberation groups
> and so on—in fact in normal activities we are already engaged in. This
> is the opposite of modernism and ecriture. Above all, a writing like the
> one I am supposing accepts its relation to power. It knows it has no
> other choice. But in this it feels tremendously exuberant at the thought
> of the possibilities opening before it.[70]

This definition also distinguishes the climate in which such work
emerges from that of many "representative" Israeli writers. As full-
fledged members of the "official" opposition (which has actually exercised hegemonic control over the Israeli cultural formation for decades),
their market value is often predicated upon the ability to eloquently articulate precisely those facets of a "humane liberalism" that the powers
that be not only like, but must project and promote as a survival tactic, in
order to perpetuate the race and the order of the race.

Another tack is taken by Ronny Someck, one of the youngest poets
actually born in the old Levantine world. His immediate roots go back to
Baghdad, but the past informs only by negation:

> So what if I came
> from where the garden of Eden once passed.

My father never talked of Euphrates and Tigris
    or of muscles
padding his shrunken arms,
    but in the pictures eternal mountains
stood erect
    and gladiolas British officers planted
as mementos in their back yards.
At 3, in the dunes of Bat Yam,
    the world blanched from the washing,
hands of diligent women shook in the wind,
Ben-Gurion made a speech at every election
and broads ringed Maurice Chevalier
    in a white top hat
on the cinema-front billboard.
Maybe because of all this
    I loved Marilyn Monroe when I touched
an American girl spending another summer
    at Kfar Hayarok.[71]

This poetry obviously owes much more to Western pop culture than to
any ancient, indigenous tradition, but this debt is not simply accrued un-
wittingly. The reverse is true. Someck domesticates the pop culture that
is trying (successfully) to dominate the whole region by confronting it
with the peculiarly contradictory realia of the particular world of which
he finds himself a part. The negation of the past, in itself, remains infor-
mative: it contains information while circumscribing a certain space and
the relations within it. The Tigris and Euphrates are etched in *before* the
British officers, Bat Yam, Ben-Gurion, Maurice Chevalier, and Marilyn
Monroe. Thus an always negotiable breach is established. In such a
breach, even what ultimately counts — the here and now — is bordered by
what it can and cannot offer, as in "Seven Lines on the Miraculous
Yarkon," a poem whose irony domesticates and personalizes the poverty
of local myths:

Soon the city of Tel Aviv will be drawn like a pistol.
What'll come from the sea starts with the hot wind and
on the street you can already hear the kind of quiet talk
that follows a shooting. Too bad there's no circus in this
town, too bad there's no sword swallower, no magician, no
elephants, no dragon; too bad just one dinghy floats by right
as I show someone not from here the miraculous Yarkon.[72]

Again, what is *not* in this poem becomes another mode of description.
Like Etel Adnan's "absence of absence of garbage" in Beirut, the lack of
a circus, sword swallower, magician, elephants, and a dragon all dis-

tinctly characterize the city. The sense of this poem is far different from that of (to give one very representative example) Lea Goldberg's well-known "Tel Aviv 1935." In Goldberg's poem, the disembodiment is literal: "And the kit-bags of the travellers / walked down the streets, and the / language of an alien land was plunged / into the *hamsin*-days like the blade of / a cold knife." The poem ends with these two stanzas:

> Like pictures turning black inside a
> camera, they all turned inside out: pure
> winter nights, rainy summer nights of
> overseas, and shadowy mornings of
> great cities.

> And the sound of steps behind your
> back drummed marching songs of
> foreign troops;—so it seemed—if
> you but turn your head, there's your
> town's church floating in the sea.[73]

The feelings of displacement, nostalgia, and desolation in this poem blur the particulars of its location. In Someck's work, the "neomodern" landscape is tempered by the consciousness that this landscape is still home. By unobtrusively embedding local knowledge within the most commonplace counters—which themselves are accurate indicators of greater historical tendencies—Someck intimates the approach to a New Levantine space.

This approach is brought into even starker relief in two poems connected to music:

Embroidered rag. Poem on Umm Kulthum

> She had a black evening gown on
> and her voice hammered steel nails
> into the elbow leaning on the table
> in the cafe on Struma Square.
> "My eyes have gotten used to seeing you,
> and if you don't come one day
> I'll blot that day from my life."
> I came with a sponge to rub out
> a huge eagle drawn in chalk
> on the edge of a cloud.
> A embroidered rag that years later the cook at
> the base at Be'er Ora hooked to his belt loop
> fluttered under its wings.
> I asked him for a couple of oranges
> and on the cassette player her gown darkened again.

He shut his eyes to the steaming lunch and kept peeling potatoes.
Who's that singing, I started, Umm Kulthum?
He nodded.
For all he cared, I could have cleaned out the whole kitchen.[74]

The prosaic nature of the present, the drabness, is contrasted to the royal countenance of Umm Kulthum as the poem's title tries to hold these opposites in balance. The encounter with Umm Kulthum (and the promised union), held in recollection, is reminiscent of Etel Adnan's "beneficial trauma." Despite the distance, despite the efforts to rub out even temporal imagery leading beyond the confines of a dull interior (the "eagle drawn in chalk / on the edge of a cloud"), the power of Umm Kulthum to evoke flight and a sense of almost mystical devotion remains. Even more pointedly, as the young conscript hears her again, this time at an army base, her power literally disarms the soldier on duty, fully transporting him out of the here and now, to the point that his mess hall is left open to all takers.

This sense of transport toward utopia is depicted brilliantly in another short poem, "Jasmine. Poem on sandpaper":

Fairuz raises her lips
to heaven
to let jasmine rain down
on those who once met
without knowing they were in love.
I'm listening to her in Muhammad's
Fiat at noon on Ibn Gabirol St.
A Lebanese singer playing in an Italian car
that belongs to an Arab poet
from Baqa' al-Gharbiyye on a street named
after a Hebrew poet who lived in Spain.
And the jasmine?
If it falls from the sky at the end of days
it'll stay green for
just a second at
the next light.[75]

In this poem about poetry, poets, singers, and songs, the sense is that even sandpaper can sustain a poem. Here, earth and heaven intersect in the quotidian possibilities that have not yet been formalized but certainly exist: as Fairuz invokes heaven, Hebrew and Arab poets, riding in an Italian car on a Mediterranean street named after an Arab Jew, look to an earthly light that, if it not only turns but stays green, would signal the coming of the Messiah and a time of peace on earth.

The work of Tikva Levi grounds the descriptive counters comprising Someck's at times seedy and at times utopic Levant in a vision that is at once more personal and more explicitly political. Her remarkable series "Purim Sequence" traces the journey of its narrator from the eve of the holiday to its close. The first two poems already stake out the problematic she has chosen to work with:

1. At the Bus Station
   Purim Eve

   The woman in the red jacket
   at the next station
   looked like a mailbox
   I took the letters out of my bag
   invitations to a meeting of
   The Public Committee on Education
   in Neighborhoods and Development Towns
   and went to put them in
   only realizing up close
   how far away I was

2. At the Bus Station
   Purim Eve

   A girl on the other side of the street
   by the stations heading North
   dressed up like Alexis:
   I saw Mali,
   a friend from the neighborhood
   who does Alexis
   all year round.

The distance between the mailbox and the woman limns the narrator's own distance between her observations and her activities, her consciousness as an activist and her own position in a concrete world, among others. In the second poem, the pop culture making up the surface of Someck's world is internalized. In the world that Levi depicts, people assume these very images, not as costumes to be worn for a day and then discarded, as is the custom on Purim, but as replacements for a self that has been *defined* by others. The next poem, "In the Bus," specifically mentions a well-known and established Israeli poet, Meir Wieseltier, with a "girl wrapped up in each / other lyrically kissing." The spot of their embrace is a border, one that Wieseltier said he would defend if need be. For Levi, however, this border crossing "is now a cesspool / even romantics avoid / navigating / not to mention / Arabs." And even more to the point, "Defending a cesspool / is a joke." This, too, recalls the young soldier's defenselessness in Ronny Someck's poem, his internalization of the absurdity of maintaining a vigil in face of the magnetic attraction to Umm Kulthum.

The next poem immediately moves to further divide the city in a way that Wieseltier would be oblivious to: for Levi, for Mali from her neighborhood "who does Alexis all year round," the primary division in the city is not between Arabs and Jews but along class lines: "the kids get off at / Tel Kabir and Tel Giborim / and Jessie Cohen as it meets / the Cemetery / of the Central City / that's where they spend their time / and here's where they live." Only after having made these political and class distinctions and allegiances clear does the poet introduce herself as a writer, perplexed at the fate of her work, both mocking and cajoling the usual routes of acceptance and transmission: "what will become of them / and if only one person / reads them / will that make them poetry / and what if two / or even ten / will that make them poetry / 'Oh let not the LORD be angry' / literary critics / 'and I will speak, yet but this once' / may these poems find / favor in your eyes."

The colloquial tone of the earlier poems is suddenly disrupted by biblical citation: the critics should know that this poet is also capable of such language (echoing Abraham's questions to God about how many innocent people need to be found in order to save the city of Sodom from complete destruction), but it is a language that Levi will go on to subvert in her reading of the Scroll of Esther, the holiday's central ritual. Before this, however, there are two central events. In the eighth poem, "After Midnight," Levi imagines how she will join her family the following day. Here, other more specific allegiances are added to those already established:

> In the afternoon we'll eat off the grill
> the uncle, a professor from Haifa
> who's researching the history of the community
> that came from the village of 'Ana in Iraq
> along with all his research assistants:
> the aunt who can recite dozens of poems
> you'll never see on state tv
> and the uncle who sings the immortal *maqam*
> that the son, doing his doctorate in economics
> in Chicago and maybe going to work in Peru,
> won't hear, even from the distance
> of the poem before this one
> and my mother, who knows the family tree
> back nine generations,

in other words,
the name of the grandfather of the grandfather of
my grandfather
whose picture is now before me

this family tree
won't be computerized at the Museum of the Diaspora
and this tree,
I just want to make clear,
has nothing to do
with any poem

Here the stereotypes of the Oriental family at the grill are turned completely upside down. This family is both educated and cosmopolitan. Ironically, it is the doctoral student who doesn't have the knowledge of the "research assistants," who are not academics but who possess a culture excluded from official modes of transmission (state TV, the Museum of the Diaspora, or, for that matter, the academy). Moreover, the culture they possess is not fully assimilable to those forms. This is emphasized by Levi's absolute refusal to let even this poem serve as a vehicle for transmitting the "exotic" customs of "authentic" Orientals. This family tree is not an image conjured up to accommodate the communal roots of her "tribe." It is, rather, her own autonomous space. In defining it, and making her other allegiances specific, she also refuses the role that the critic of the fifth poem would want her to fulfill.

In poem nine, "Later than After the Midnight of the Last Poem," there is a return to the Persian music of poem seven. There are allusions to the Iran-Iraq War: "every melody is colonized / by the West / Homeini alone / holds the breach / but at the same time / arms deals / with Israel and the US / flourish / as long as Iraqis die / there is joy and jubilation in the Land." References to this war are startling for a contemporary Israeli work, in which the tendency is simply to ignore the surrounding world unless it is of immediate concern, as in the case of Lebanon. Levi places herself at a crucial junction: she is at once a neighbor, a person who clearly identifies as an Iraqi, and an involved political observer. This sequence is followed by a joke at a conference organized by "The International Education Fund." The upshot of the joke is that the more Iraqis and Iranians die, the better. A woman protests, shrieking "I don't get it / I don't get it like crazy," and the poem ends with these lines that further (and more fiercely) undermine the accepted constructs of "education" outlined in the family poem: "but who pays attention to loonies / especially in an ivory tower." In addition, the "local" joke of defending the cesspool in poem three is now globalized.

It is this joke that begins to resonate backward and forward through the poem as the sensitive meshing and intermingling of instruments in poem ten ("Cats Wailing Outside During the Second Watch of Purim") is contrasted to the relationship "between the conqueror and the conquered." Now the holiday itself, with its "happy ending" in which the evil Haman is hung "upon the highest tree in the Kingdom," seems like a "joke" that "has long ceased to be funny." The next poem, "Reflections on Purim," is a brilliant mock sermon analyzing the traditional interpretations of the story of Queen Esther. The language in the poem shifts rapidly from traditional phrasing and citation to a highly idiomatic and colloquial tone:

> Is Mordechai a righteous man?
> The wrath of Ahashverosh upon
> Vashti was appeased—parenthetically
> a word in favor of Vashti whose only sin was
> her refusal to be a sexual object
> heaven forfend she serve as model "to all the women,
> so as to make their husbands contemptible in their eyes"
> for their sake, "King Ahashverosh commanded
> Vashti the Queen to be brought before him,
> but she came not"—
> so he sought "fair young virgins"
> a golden opportunity, thought the righteous man,
> and brought Esther into the picture
> "Now when every girl's turn
> was come to go in to King Ahashverosh after she had been
> under the regulations for the women,"
> somewhere around the age of 11, 12, 13,
> "twelve months, for so were the days of their anointing,
> namely, six months with oil of myrrh, and six months
> with sweet odors, and with other ointments of the women,"
> and the King opened and returned the merchandise
> and Mordechai knew like everyone else
> except the piece
> warehoused for a year
> but who actually reads
> The Scroll of Esther
> they only wait for Haman
> to pound the noisemakers
> only wait for Purim
> to put on a costume
> and be whatever they want
> according to the rules
> but they just forgot or didn't read

in last month's paper
that at the end of *Dynasty*
Crystal turns into a vegetable
and Alexis fries in the hot seat
for bumping Blake Carrington off
in last week's paper
it said Israel was about
to take *Dynasty* off the air
my paranoia tells me
that someone's interest is at work here
that my friend from the neighborhood in poem two
will just go on doing Alexis
the whole year through

In the next to last poem, "Third Watch of the Holiday," the final allegiance is made explicit, through a quote from a song by the Palestinian group Sabrin:

Kamilia from Sabrin's on the tape:
"He who says—the homeland is only land—
is a traitor—
the homeland's human"
I turn down the volume
so only I can hear
my paranoia is transmitted
to the door or the window
someone might think that whoever listens
to Arabic is an Arab
and come to kill me
I hate to wake up early
but tomorrow I'll gladly
do it to water
my tree

This "tree," by the end of the series, becomes the act of steadfastness itself:

it's my paranoia again
drawing me back to poem thirteen
which is bound to raise the ire
of those from poem five
but I know nothing can make
me go back on the last one
I still have the strength to cleave to it
and remain steadfast right
to the end of the line[76]

The ire that will be raised by those in poem five has to do with the poet's solidarity with the "enemy." It also has to do with the steadfastness expressed on all fronts: a general refusal to accept the terms as they have been dictated, whether they relate to the purported role of a writer, the accepted wisdom of canonical texts, or the extent and kind of sympathies that one is allowed to express regarding other people or countries. But what is most threatening here is the fact that these sympathies—in and through embracing the "enemy," by remaining steadfast to the autonomy of one's "tree"—promise a way out of the perpetual costume party that can only lead to self-destruction.

Another young poet, Sami Shalom Chetrit, cited earlier in the introduction, takes on the discourse of consensus using its own language. Just as in the trajectory of Israeli education—which almost comically leaps from the creation of the world in the biblical text to the creation of the state—Chetrit plots the narrative of his own upbringing in the language only to subvert it. Using the parameters that have been given by the ideology of return's obliteration of space and memory, he repopulates them with righteous anger at a hypocrisy that has drained the sacred texts of all their humanity. His poem, "Hey, Jeep," certainly one of the strongest expressions by an Israeli on the uprising, is worth quoting in full:

1. Eight kids in an army jeep
   Eight soldiers, one major:
   eight kids and one minor

2. *Hey Jeep, Hey Jeep,*

3. And his son Ishmael was thirteen years old
   at the cutting of his uncircumcised flesh.

4. And eight of his sons in the army jeep
   and his son cries to the Lord but no one hears

5. And behold his father running:
   Run, Muhammad, run,
   your son's spirit is coming towards you

6. Lord, Lord, where is the lamb for a burnt offering?

7. Now these are the generations of Ishmael, Abraham's son,
   whom Hagar the Egyptian, Sarah's handmaid, bore unto
   Abraham: And these are the names of the sons of Ishmael,
   by their names, according to their generations: the first-
   born of Ishmael, Nebaioth; and Kedar, and Abdeel, and
   Mibsam, and Mishma, and Dumah, and Massa, Hadad,
   and Teman, Jetur, Naphish and Kedemah . . .
   and Muhammad Said Qarada and Said Qarada whose years
   numbered thirteen at his death.

8. And these are the generations of Isaac, Abraham's son:
   Abraham begot Isaac; and Isaac begot Esau and
   Jacob; now the sons of Jacob were twelve in number; the sons of
      Leah:
   Reuben—Jacob's first-born—Simeon, Levi, Judah, Issachar, and
      Zebulun;
   the sons of Rachel: Joseph and Benjamin; and the sons of Zilpah,
      Rachel's maid:
   Gad and Asher: these are the sons of Jacob who were born to him
      in Paddan-aram.

9. . . . And eight soldiers in an army Jeep.
   One has officer's stripes on his shoulder,
   a Hebrew officer to the Kingdom of Israel:
   maybe a bleeding-heart liberal
   or a down-and-out reactionary

10. *Hey Jeep, Hey Jeep,*
    what a night it is!

11. Maybe his name's Itsik

12. And the seven under him:
    one's an eagle eye
    another's bound to ritual
    the third has his feet on the ground
    the fourth's got his head in the clouds
    the fifth's got to do it all
    the sixth replies stoically
    the seventh can't wait for liberty

13. And there are "dovish intellectuals" among them
    and there are "militant hawks" among them
    and God is there among them
    and an officer is there among them

14. soon there's neither
    affection nor innocence

15. Black combat boots on their feet:
    "that oppress the poor and crush the destitute"

16. Subject displayed the following signs:
    pallor, bleeding from the nose and left ear.
    Internal hemorrhaging in the vicinity of the left temple.
    Compound fractures resulting from a blow
    (not a projectile) on the left temple.
    Break in the left knee.

17. He was thirteen the day of his murder.

18. Thirteen: the age of obligation.

19. Theater of the struggle:
    As one they arose and came from the
    combines and the collective farms
    from the shareholder's settlements
    and their surroundings, from the towns and from the cities.

20. *Take her to the left a bit,*
    take her to the right.

21. And the boy cried to his father: Father, I'm choking

22. Eight pairs of heavy-duty combat boots

23. Eight outstretched pairs
    and there were white among them
    and there were black among them

24. *Hey Jeep, Hey Jeep.*

25. Eight soldiers, one a Hebrew major:
    eight soldiers, and one Arab minor

26. *Hey, everyone agrees: with a jeep*
    the only thing you need is speed

27. They finally pitched him from the fleeting coach,
    cast their spirit to the blinding night

28. *Like wind up in the sky*
                we'll fly
                        right on by

29. but thou shalt love thy neighbor as thyself
    but thou shalt love thy neighbor as thyself
    but thou shalt love thy neighbor as thyself
    but thou shalt love thy neighbor as thyself
    but thou shalt love thy neighbor as thyself
    but thou shalt love thy neighbor as thyself
    but thou shalt love the neighbor as thyself
    but thou shalt love thy neighbor as thyself
    but thou shalt love thy neighbor as thyself
    but thou shalt love thy neighbor as thyself
    but thou shalt love thy neighbor as thyself
    but thou shalt love thy neighbor as thyself
    but thou shalt love thy neighbor as thyself[77]

As in Tikva Levi's work, or that of Bracha Serri quoted earlier, what characterizes this poem is its willingness both to identify with the "enemy" and to use "our" language to delineate the moral parameters of that relationship. As in all of his poetry, Chetrit brings many sacred images down to earth here. The lyrics of the song "Hey, Jeep" are from the "heroic" period of Israel's history, the Palmah generation of 1948. In addition, the figure of Isaac being led to sacrifice became a staple metaphor for a whole generation of poets reenacting a national ethos. In this poem, it is an actual son of Ishmael, thrown randomly into the genealogy, who is literally sacrificed by being thrown out of a speeding jeep. The jeep-riding heroes of the song, meanwhile, have become nothing but thugs in combat boots. The ethical symmetry of action and blindness is perfectly played out: everyone participates, no matter what aspect of the political or religious spectrum they come from. At the same time, every neighbor must be loved as oneself.

This ironic juxtaposition of language that points beyond irony to posit the biblical text as an ideal to be aspired to can also be seen in a more recent poem of Chetrit's, written after a number of years of living in America:

"And thou shalt teach them diligently to thy children"

I am teaching my son to play soccer
in a strange land
I diligently teach my son soccer
in the land of baseball
I bring up my son in soccer
the way we used to over there.

Me and my son
kick back and forth to each other in Hebrew
I'm cautious and weary
he's quick and tough on his feet

kicking a soccer ball
back and forth
as we remember Zion.[78]

VIII. Anton Shammas and Israeli Hebrew as the Language of Exile

Erez Bitton spoke of "another Hebrew." The writers seen here have all attempted to articulate both the desire for and the knowledge of something else, something other than the expected or accepted. Yet none of these writers has been able to attempt the kind of internal and external attack on received ideas that can radically realign the past, snap it back into an entirely different focus. This was accomplished by Juan Goytisolo in his trilogy—*Marks of Identity*, *Count Julian*, and *Juan the Landless*. Carlos Fuentes wrote of it:

It is a mockery no other writer has dared make of the hollow imperial gesture by which Spain defeated herself, fatally cut herself off from the human, cultural, and economic resources that fled with the expulsion of the Jews and the defeat of the Arabs. . . . . Goytisolo takes the totality of Spanish language and history, traps it, imprisons it, encapsulates it, digests it and then expels it. . . . His enterprise offers a dual aspect: attack the myths and do so by assailing the language on which the myths rest; it is, first and foremost, an adventure of language, a critical battle against the language appropriated by power in Spain. It is also a search for a new/old language that would offer an alternative for the future but also a fecund link with the outlawed Arab and Jewish strains.[79]

At the end of the last book of the trilogy, *Juan the Landless*, Goytisolo "breaks the habit of language" itself, "by writing it in accordance with simple phonetic intuitions."[80] From there, the text goes into a phonetically transliterated mixture of this new language and Arabic before finally shifting completely into Arabic. On the final page, Goytisolo even goes so far as to write in Arabic script, penning the five lines that close the book in hand: "Why don't the people understand me / Why don't they follow me / My relations are finished / I'm without doubt on the other side / With all the poor people always / They will find the knife."

For Hebrew literature, for the writing of Levantine and Arab Jews now in Israel, and for the place of both in a realigned set of Levantine allegiances in which differences could be recognized, the decisive move from the "modern" to the "postmodern" comes from a most unlikely source. Once one might have hoped that things could have been different, that Jews would continue as integral and innovative partners in the creation of Arabic culture—writing plays, poetry, and novels; making music, films, and art; publishing newspapers; reading and speaking and thinking and singing and dreaming in the mother tongue. Yet the extent to which ignorance of this possibility has been internalized as a truism within the discourse of consensus is truly remarkable. A precise indication of this can be found in David Grossman's *Yellow Wind*, hailed for its sensitivity to the nuances of the Israeli/Palestinian relationship. At one point in the book, during a conversation with Raja Shehadeh, the question of language comes up:

"You would think that, if the Hebrew language is part of a higher culture, it would be a strong influence on Arabic, right? But the only Hebrew words which have been absorbed into Palestinian Arabic are 'roadblock,' 'traffic light,' and, oh, right—'walkie-talkie.' And what has happened to Hebrew during the same period?"

I tried to remember. A large number of Arabic words had been naturalized by Hebrew even before '67, probably as a result of our acquaintance with another group of Arabs, those who live in and are citizens of Israel. But today you hear many more Arabic words in daily conversation, in all different contexts.[81]

In trying to locate the possible sources of Arabic influence, the very idea that a good portion of the *Jewish* population were native Arabic speakers remains completely unimaginable, even unspeakable. "Jews," after all, at least in the ideology of return's tunnel vision, can never be "Arabs." Rather than continuing and renewing the Arabic tradition or creating "another Hebrew," however, the Levant has been given an "other" *writing* Hebrew. There has been no frontal attack; rather, there is a compassionate opening into a possible future. This effort, by a true native son, Anton Shammas, a Palestinian Israeli, comes in a form (the arabesque) that is as much a part of the Levant as of the postmodern world.

By not only accepting but even celebrating his own exile within language, Shammas fully realizes the conditions and problematic of writing anywhere. He enters that infinite and mysterious void described by Blanchot as "the only space in which literature can exist," where the writer must "discover the language of literature" by searching "for the moment which precedes literature."[82] In many ways, Shammas's novel *Arabesques* is about finding this constantly recurring and elusive moment. It is about pulling differently colored threads through the labyrinth of form, divided in this novel into two parts, "The Tale" and "The Teller" or the narration and the narrator. Ostensibly, the narrator is looking for a lost relative, but the search ends up as an essay in recuperation. This becomes an attempt to at least gather the shards of the long-shattered primal vessel, if not to assemble it. The narrator is driven not by false nostalgia but by the need to make some sense of the delicate and layered existence that is the life of those Palestinians who stayed after the disaster of 1948. These layers include the now airtight world beyond, represented by Beirut, both as it was and is; the West Bank, with all the attendant ambivalence and confusion involved in that relationship; and Israel itself, with the incessant hope and disappointment it offers. By going back in time from the village of Fasuta, in a world where Beirut was still the urban reference point, and forward, past the carnage at Sabra and Shatila to Paris and Iowa, Shammas emerges as both teller of tales and narrator of texts. He includes the nineteenth-century novels many would have preferred he continue writing by interrupting, interrogating, and finally, through sheer bravado, outdoing them. Rather than rely on the ploy of the found manuscript, the long-lost relative himself (the character Michael/Michel

Abyad) offers the teller of tales the book of his own life when they finally meet in Iowa City, so far from everything that has separated them this long.

Form and language are not mere surrogates on this journey, but intimate partners. The first section of the book, along with the remaining sections that comprise the family chronicle dating from the mid-nineteenth century, embed their fable in words that are themselves part of the past: here, the archaic and the magical coincide. The eyes of the child (observer/narrator) process all the information—colors, sounds, smells, feelings—and release it through the art of a medieval storyteller. Yet just as the storyteller was seldom content to rest on the merits of the tale without at least suggesting its consequences, so Shammas employs various means to reprocess that primal information. By doing this, he rescues it from interment in the past, where, static and eloquent in its beauty, it is ultimately inapplicable to the only place where it can be of use—the present.

These themes mirror and fold in on themselves. The characters that belong to this primal past possess a kind of subterranean vision. Seeing from the underground up, they often take to the road, in both flight and search, to wander through the same displaced strata as the narrator. Other characters, those from the "afterworld" (Israelis and others the narrator meets along the journey), can only see in reverse. They have to try and reconstruct Anton the narrator by finding those parts of himself he is still in search of. Paris and Iowa City are just two of the further way stations in this search and, as Shime'on Ballas has pointed out, they link another of the book's underlying themes, that of the love story. This love story, though, is more the story of unrequited love, something that has always served to limn the difficulty of a final union, whether with oneself, one's past, or one's promised land. It is precisely this transition from the magical world of childhood to the composition of a mature identity that sounded the alarm for some readers. After all, the native—admired and even envied for an "authenticity" long lost by those whom the luxuries of civilization have "spoiled"—must remain innocent and childlike, in need of the guidance that aspiration to "higher" modes of life can offer.[83]

In a different context ("Algerian Literature Towards the Year 2000") Jamal Eddine Ben Cheikh wrote: "Our Palestine is within and the language we have to express it guards its secret voice."[84] By guarding the secret voice of his own language, Shammas counters complexity with complexity to reinforce the relentless lesson about what happens once a whole order of life has been shattered and fragmented, both politically and in nature. *Arabesques* is a book that should never have had to be written. As the narrator himself writes, "I am gripped by the feeling that it would have been better if the story had remained curled up like a caterpillar in the cocoon of silence forever. But now the cocoon has hatched and the butterfly of the story, with a magical flick of its wings, has shaken off the webs of years of forgetfulness and the way back is blocked, both for me and the butterfly."[85]

With the way back blocked, there is nowhere to go but forward: once circumstances dictated the very possibility of such a book, it is almost as if it had to be written. And once it is written, as in the wake of any truly innovative work, branches of affiliation are realigned, retrospective and prospective readings change, and new maps must be charted. In making Hebrew a lingua franca that just happens to dominate this particular region for the time being—and which can be used, due to political and cultural vicissitudes, by anyone who happens to be trapped within such circumstances—Shammas has pulled the proverbial finger out of the dike damming the basic contradiction within the definition of Israeli nationality and nationhood. Israel as a "democratic Jewish state," which is also the "homeland" of the "Jewish people," must now come to terms with the presence of a Christian Palestinian writing in Hebrew who also claims (along with another 20 percent of the population, the other 750,000 Palestinian Israelis, Christian, Muslim, and Druze) to form a distinct part of this nationality.

By blazing this path with such accomplished art, Shammas has also presented solid reason to reexamine, a little more thoroughly this time around, some of the ethnocentric assumptions that have so long and exasperatingly governed so many (un)critical readings of "Jewish" writing. At the same time, the aching political, social, sexual, and cultural problematic drawn so finely by this text snaps the frame of a Levant in which Israel clearly belongs sharply into focus. The specific terrain of Shammas's *Arabesques* refers us to the environment of other Levantine writers. These writers have either come to light only recently within Israel or else remain completely unknown. As such, they do not constitute a presence, in the form of a common referential axis or as an assumed part of the general literary vocabulary. Yet the context in which these Levantine works have been presented here—from whatever period—simply shows how much more sense all of these works make when looked at in relation to each other, reflecting and refracting their own light.

IX. Envisioning a Future: The Covenant of Sarah and Hagar

The Mediterranean, "by right of which," to paraphrase Yitshaq Gormezano Goren, "the tale unravels," is now a polluted sea crowned by an orderly, confident, and overdeveloped North slowly meeting and merging with a chaotic South. Parts of this South, Cairo and Beirut for example, test the limits of discourse itself, each in their own way. And Jerusalem, what George Seferis called the "ungovernable" city, remains as cut off as ever since its "reunification," divided even more distinctly within itself since the beginning of the *intifadah*, the Palestinian uprising. As in Lebanon, the blatant imbalance of power determines each concentric circle of oppression and violence. The occupation—with its constant surveillance, mass arrests, detentions, land seizures, random and sytematic violence—dictates the pressures brought to bear within the Palestinian community itself. Here, there is more violence: bereft of any legal recourse, the revolution metes out its own punishment as the insidious crime of collaboration is matched by increasingly frequent and brutal forms of retribution.

Since most of the men are either hiding in the mountains or in prison, the street is ruled by the boys who, besides their proclaimed and public role as the vanguard of the struggle, have another side to them. As Etel Adnan writes in *Sitt Marie Rose*: "I know the Chabab mafia, that gang of boys. They have a constant need to find themselves alone. They live as a function of their vanity. They are bound together as if with steel."[86]

Those bloated signifiers "Arab" and "Jew" have accrued a set of vile and ugly characteristics: terrorists, child-killers, primitives on one side; bloodsuckers, occupiers, fascists on the other. Even more depressing is the fact that these images and stereotypes have become institutionalized through children's literature. This is true both in Israel and throughout the Arab world, as each side shapes and colors its own respective demons with facile, terrifying, and extremely effective propaganda.[87] This demonization only diverts attention from common problems that get more urgent and pressing by the day.

Rather than basking in the sparkling sun and clarity of "Mediterranean" tourist brochures, the old Levantine world is beset by all the problems of modernity. Poor and crowded cities—many still marked by the devastation of war—are ringed by shanties filled with rural migrants hoping to make better lives for themselves. The lack of water and other resources is exacerbated by foreign debt. And there are other, more ancient and insidious forms of oppression, such as the subjection of women, unabated in this "republic of cousins" where, as the Algerian writer Assia Djebar writes, "the ancestral barriers are being rebuilt."[88] The changes brought about by industrialization, the "great Western transmutation," and colonialism are, in many cases, only compounded by more "progress." The Egyptian architect Hassan Fathy tells here of the corrosive effects mass production has created:

Energy-intensive mechanized tools have diminished the personal, cellular contribution to the fabrication of objects, the building of structures and the growing of food. Production of beauty, once the prerogative of millions, is replaced by industrialization—even of bread— under the control of a minority of owners. . . . Constant upheaval results when industrially developed societies weaken the craft-developed cultures through increased communications. As they interact, mutations create societal and ecological imbalance and economic inequities which are documented to be increasing in type and number. Profoundly affected is the mass of the population, which is pressured to consume industrially produced goods. The result is cultural, psychological, moral and material havoc.[89]

Yet the Levant is still a space of immense human richness, a space that can propose new models for a world rapidly losing sight of the dependence of each part upon every other part. As one of Fathy's prize students, the well-known Egyptian architect Abdul Wahed El-Wakil, remarked:

The people who speak of imitating the past are the people who are imitating the West. The people who are innovative and have made contributions to art and architecture, they have never abolished the past. They look to the past with reverence. Revival is not imitation because imitation is when you are clinging to your past. You show your poverty if you only go after something if it is new or different or imported. Only those people talk about imitating the past who know nothing about the past. . . . I am not imitating, I am recreating the past. And the only way you can avoid imitating or repeating the past is by keeping it alive. Once you forget it, you repeat it.[90]

By having the light from both ends of the spectrum—the highest accomplishments of the ancient world and the most convoluted problems of the modern—refract through its prism (like the pyramids in the distance at Giza dotting Cairo's dense cityscape), the Levant is in a unique position. As Yusef Chahine, the Egyptian film director, has remarked, "France, England, they are the Third World—I'm the First World, I've been here 7,000 years."[91] Yet to repossess these years, to peel off the layers of imposed and alien interpretation, means confrontation on all levels. Above all, it means a confrontation with memory, with both received and constructed images of the self. As Chahine put it:

Memory is confrontation, a confrontation with oneself. You must first confront yourself before confronting other people, or a whole country, or the whole Arab nation. That's also the political context of memory, as you look back at yourself caught in the American dream or the pseudo-socialist dream you gradually move forward. The final confrontation is when you ask if you accept yourself. Because if you can't communicate with yourself, how can you communicate with others?[92]

This submission, these lapses, letting events be defined and determined outside the self, is akin to what, in another context entirely, Andrea Dworkin has called "the initial complicity, the acts of self-mutilation, self-reconstruction," which recur "until there is no self, only the diminished, mutilated reconstruction."[93] The confrontation—to attack, perforate, and subvert various forms of hierarchical power and the institutionalized transmission of memory—can only be one stage on the way to a freedom in which memory and event discover their own forms. The Tunisian Nouri Bouzid, another film director, emphasizes repressed memory:

> What others call a defeat, I call a break in memory. The very word
> "defeat" is connected to events in our history, but I link it to our
> collective memory, to our education. We must seek explanations there:
> unless we start there, we can do nothing. We must unveil our memory
> and confront it. Change comes from knowledge. We dare not see
> ourselves in the mirror. We look for someone else. We're not proud of
> what we see. We're not used to seeing ourselves because we can't cope
> with the errors in our memory or the bad memories of an education
> based on repression, frustration, agression, in sum, all social
> prohibitions. Our history is bound by memory prohibitions and taboos.
> We must uncover what we keep hidden. Only then will we know who
> we are.[94]

The ancient fragments, sites, and images; the contemporary texts, paintings, and films—what can now in all frankness and without shame be called Levantine writing and Levantine art—are still the Levant's most treasured resource, but they must be reoriented within the terms of an altered, more plural and just political and cultural economy. Music, once again, persists. It is there, for instance, where perhaps kinship's deepest wound—for the category "women" is certainly more ancient than that of "Jews" or "Arabs"—can at least begin to heal. As Assia Djebar writes: "From the fragments of ancient songs I can see how we might search for the restoration of a real conversation among women."[95]

The attempt at such a conversation can be seen, for example, in the Palestinian videomaker Mona Hatoum's *Measures of Distance*. Using the latest medium to explore the Levant, one which is also particularly apt to its present circumstances, this work investigates the possibly futile attempt to reconstruct a certain state of intimacy. The tape addresses the relationship between the videomaker and her mother but extends its exploration into the realm of social life and the isolated, fragmented shards created by war. Images of Hatoum's mother form and reform themselves behind the veil of a letter, whose Arabic script serves as a screen through which all other images are filtered. More than a map, the text becomes the body: starting from the fingers grasping the page, the film moves to her face, then to her naked back and breasts as she comes out of the shower and dresses. These images are all accompanied by a background of familial voices chatting in Arabic. Here Hatoum creates her own language, one that accommodates the complex nature of relations while questioning both the validity and possibility of representing them. In doing this, she simultaneously pronounces the need for testimony and the fear that no image or art can do these issues justice.

Music also opens a new window on what has been of most concern here, the relations between *'eber* and *'arab*, Hebrew and Arab, those two unvoweled peoples whose estrangements and embraces make up just one chapter of the Levant's long book of memory. But putting the vowels back into each other's consonants is a mutual enterprise, and just as the Arabic needs to be read back into the Hebrew, the Hebrew must be read back into the Arabic. One of the strongest gestures pointing this way can be found in *The Man of Ashes*, a film by Nouri Bouzid that tenderly depicts the friendship between a young Arab and an old Jewish musician. It is fitting that precisely this part of the mirror, in which the Jew's image is refracted through the light of the Levantine prism, also be unveiled through a "new" medium. At one point in the story the two sit across from each other at a table in the Jew's home. The candles of a menorah, the ancient seven-branched candelabrum symbolizing both eternity and mortality, light and the life cycle, flicker behind the old man. As the Jew strums his 'oud, the young man recites this poem:

I came to see you / the doors were closed
I remember when / the streets were full

The old places / lose their magic
No more singing / no more parties

The doors don't dance, the locks are still
The roofs are in tears for the parting sparrows

The Jew then starts to sing, beginning with the first stanza:

I came to see you / the doors were closed
I remember when / the streets were full

before adding these lines:

> I strummed this song to recall your features
> Let joy run free and break down frontiers
> push back boundaries and break down frontiers[96]

The young man's words meld the sensuous diction and figures of the lover's plaint in the Song of Songs with the terse pain of the blues in a world where absence is present everywhere. The old man's part seems a role reversal: it is he who switches tense, pointing further, turning the texture of memory ahead.

To idealize and romanticize this memory seems as futile and bankrupt an endeavor as to appropriate and pervert it. But to not sift through its very particular qualities, in order to chart a map based on the contradictory knowledge that the flux of events can yield, is a complete abdication of responsibility. Jacqueline Kahanoff once suggested that

> we need not be bound forever by the terms set by our ancient myths and holy scriptures. While recognizing the crucial role they play in shaping us, we might interpret them within the context in which we now live. By objectively prodding those areas where our myths clash, we may become more rational in appraising the passionately irrational element at the core of most human actions, where the feeling of identity is concerned . . . Sarah and Hagar were rivals and victims within the framework of a patriarchal society, and while they are still among us, nothing prevents them from establishing a new covenant for themselves and their children.[97]

In this hopeful vein is a vision of what Shmuel Trigano called "The Great Return":

> When Isaiah announced: "In that day shall Israel be a third with Egypt and with Syria, a blessing in the midst of the land. . . . Blessed be Egypt my people, and Syria the work of my hands, and Israel my inheritance," he was certainly not thinking of a union or the fusion into a state, an empire(!), but the opening into a space for the three peoples, the passing beyond a stage of belligerency, of the state, the leaping beyond formal boundaries.[98]

Somewhere between visions based on the old prophecies and the need for a new covenant, between the closed doors and the full streets, the magic of the old places and the locks of rooms without song, a space remains, a space for a poetics and a politics of the possible.

Notes

Introduction: Charting the Terrain

1. Jacques Derrida, *Writing and Difference*, trans. Alan Bass (Chicago: University of Chicago Press, 1978), p. 65.

2. *Ethical Writings of Maimonides*, ed. Raymond L. Weiss with Charles E. Butterworth (New York: Dover, 1983), p. 62. The study of Maimonides, within the context of modern, primarily European Jewish thought, is a perfect example of the kinds of distances that have been traversed and the very different uses to which classical Mediterranean and Arab Jewish thinkers have been put. For one of the rare studies treating Maimonides within the whole scheme of Mediterranean and Arab culture and rabbinical practice, see José Faur, *Studies in the Mishne Torah* (Jerusalem: Mossad HaRav Kook, 1978)[Hebrew]; more accessibly, see Faur's *Golden Doves with Silver Dots: Semiotics and Textuality in the Rabbinic Tradition* (Bloomington: Indiana University Press, 1986), particularly chapter 3, "Freedom, Language and Negativity," pp. 59–83. For a very different approach to Maimonides, certainly the most accomplished of its kind but quite far removed from the practical cultural context in which Maimonides still operates as a familiar figure and authority, see Isadore Twersky, *Introduction to the Code of Maimonides: Mishneh Torah* (New Haven and London: Yale University Press, 1980).

3. For the most far-ranging, poetic, and historically grounded discussion of these issues in the context of Jewish thought, see (also quoted below) Yosef Hayim Yerushalmi's *Zakhor: Jewish History and Jewish Memory* (New York: Schocken, 1989). For an excellent critique of Yerushalmi's secular assumptions, see David Shasha's "Theories of Writing in Shem Tob Ardutiel's The Battle of the Pen and the Scissors," an unpublished master's thesis presented to the Faculty of the Graduate School of Cornell University (January, 1990). After a brilliant exegesis of instances of writing in the *Scroll of Esther*, Shasha points out that: "for Yerushalmi and most modern historiographers, there is an epistemological separation between what really happened and how it has been remembered. Due to the objectification of such a science, modern historiography believes that it can access the 'truth' of history and reconstruct a more 'authentic' version of the 'facts' than has heretofore been possible. . . . If we are to accept Yerushalmi's thesis (of history as the faith of fallen Jews), we will have allowed the modern scientific historian to usurp a quite significant portion of Jewish memory; as if history now belongs exclusively to those who are not what we would call traditionally observant"(pp. 142–44).

4. Mandelstam's lines are from "Theodosia" and section XII of "Armenia," found in Osip Mandelstam, *Selected Poems*, trans. David McDuff (New York: Farrar, Straus and Giroux, 1975), pp. 61 and 109. In *Hope Abandoned*, trans. Max Hayward (Harmondsworth: Penguin, 1976), Nadezhda Mandelstam traced her husband's sense of Jewish identity in the following terms: "M., who was Osip, not Joseph, in his birth certificate, never forgot he was a Jew, but his 'blood memory' was of a peculiar kind. It went right back to his biblical ancestors, to Spain, and to the Mediterranean, retaining nothing from the wanderings through Central Europe. In other words, he felt his affinity with the shepherds and kings of the Bible, with the Jewish poets and philosophers of Alexandria and Spain, and had even decided that one of them was his direct ancestor: a Spanish poet who was kept on a chain in a dungeon during the Inquisition. 'I must have just one drop of his blood,' he said in Vor-

onezh, reading the life of this Spanish Jew, who composed sonnets during his confinement ('You could not take away his moving lips') and wrote them down after he had been released for a brief period" (p. 563).

5. Janet L. Abu-Lughod, *Before European Hegemony: The World System A.D. 1250–1350* (New York, Oxford: Oxford University Press, 1989), p. 367.

6. Maria Rosa Menocal, *The Arabic Role in Medieval Literary History* (Philadelphia: University of Pennsylvania Press, 1987), p. 6. Menocal's book is the most comprehensive and accessible presentation for a radical shift in our perceptions of European literary history at this crucial, formative stage.

7. Yosef Hayim Yerushalmi, *Zakhor: Jewish History and Jewish Memory* (New York: Schocken, 1989), pp. 99–100.

8. Norman A. Stillman, *The Jews of Arab Lands in Modern Times* (Philadelphia: Jewish Publication Society, 1991), p. xxi.

9. Ibid., pp. 111–12.

10. Erica Hunt, "Notes for an Oppositional Poetics," in *The Politics of Poetic Form: Poetry and Public Policy*, ed. Charles Bernstein (New York: Roof, 1990), pp. 199–200.

11. Menocal, *Arabic Role*, p. 21.

12. Ibid., p. 139.

13. Although there are many others, the exemplary work of three scholars immediately comes to mind: Peter Dronke, Dan Pagis, and Maria Rosa Menocal. Dronke's most accessible work, *The Medieval Lyric* (New York: Harper and Row, 1964), is essential to any reading of medieval poetry. The work of the late Pagis, the most innovative scholar of nonreligious Hebrew poetry, unfortunately remains untranslated.

14. Menocal, *Arabic Role*, p. 139.

15. Ibid., p. 1.

16. For more on the terminology employed to separate cultures, see Menocal, *Arabic Role*, p. 23. While I have come to very similar conclusions, my own convictions and arguments have found extraordinarily erudite and well-considered support in Menocal's work; for the idea of "possibility," one I have stressed much more in the modern period, see chapter 1, "The Myth of Westernness in Medieval Literary Historiography," pp. 1–25.

17. Janet Abu-Lughod, *Before European Hegemony*, pp. 364–65.

18. See Jack Shaheen's *TV Arab* (Bowling Green, Ohio: Bowling Green State University Popular Press, 1984). Also see the excellent introduction by Ella Shohat to her *Israeli Cinema: East/West and the Politics of Representation* (Austin: University of Texas Press, 1989). In addition, the work of Edward S. Herman and Noam Chomsky, particularly *Manufacturing Consent* (New York: Pantheon, 1988), is enlightening. The role of Arab stereotyping and the media in the Gulf War is examined in *Beyond the Storm*, ed. Phyllis Bennis and Michel Moushabeck (New York: Olive Branch Press, 1991).

19. Quoted in my "Gulf States of Mind: Learning to Read Arabic Fiction," *Voice Literary Supplement*, June, 1991, p. 15.

20. This obituary appeared in the Saturday, August 3, 1991, edition of the *New York Times*.

21. One almost got the sense from the reception given *Arabesques* that the book fulfilled certain accepted projections of the Israeli social structure: a pluralistic, multicultural entity in which, with perseverance, anyone could come to expression. The fact that works by Israeli *Jewish* writers from the Levant and the Arab world have either not been translated or have taken longer to appear is indicative of the odd imbalance prevailing in Israeli society itself as well as in perceptions of it, particularly in the United States.

The question of language, and Shammas's extremely complex and subversive move to use Hebrew (discussed at length in chapter 4), was paid less attention than the narrative trajectory of village boy going to the city and becoming an artist. Ironically, it was Cynthia Ozick's almost hysterical reaction to Shammas's claim that he was attempting to "de-Jew" the language that came much closer to describing the ambition of the project that Shammas set himself.

22. See Barbara Harlow's excellent discussion of the social context of the young Algerian writer Mehdi Charef's *Le Thé au harem d'Archi Ahmed* (Paris: Mercure de France, 1983) in her illuminating and extremely useful *Resistance Literature* (New York and London: Methuen, 1987), pp. 25–28.

23. Menocal, *Arabic Role*, p. 149.

24. An unpublished paper given by Homi K. Bhabha at the "Critical Fictions" symposium held at the Dia Art Foundation in New York on May 11, 1990.

25. Trinh T. Minh-ha, *When the Moon Waxes Red: Representation, Gender and Cultural Politics* (New York and London: Routledge, 1991), pp. 107–8.

26. Charles Bernstein, "State of the Art / 1990," an unpublished paper presented at The St. Mark's Poetry Project 1990 Symposium "Poetry for the Next Society: Assertions of Power" in New York on May 5, 1990.

27. For an excellent examination of one of these particular instances, see Michelle Wallace's "Multiculturalism and Oppositionality" in *Afterimage*, October, 1991, pp. 6–9.

28. Zora Neale Hurston, *I Love Myself*, ed. Alice Walker (Old Westbury, N.Y.: Feminist Press, 1979), p. 153.

29. Tillie Olsen, *Silences* (New York: Dell, 1983), p. 46.

30. Sami Mikhael, "On Being an Iraqi-Jewish Writer in Israel," in *Prooftexts* 4 (1984), p. 32.

31. Trinh T. Minh-ha, *When the Moon Waxes Red*, pp. 80, 89.

32. James Scully, *Line Break: Poetry as Social Practice* (Seattle: Bay Press, 1988), pp. 105–6.

33. Erica Hunt, "Oppositional Poetics," pp. 199–200.

34. Ibid.

35. The quotes from Naqqash's article, originally appearing in Arabic in *Liqa* (July 3, 1987), are from G. N. Giladi's *Discord in Zion: Conflict Between Ashkenazi and Sephardi Jews in Israel* (London: Scorpion, 1990), p. 281.

36. Erica Hunt, "Oppositional Poetics," p. 200.

37. See Charles Bernstein's "Time Out of Motion: Looking Ahead to See Backward," in *American Poetry*, vol. 4, no. 1 (1986), pp. 78–90.

38. For more on this, see Benjamin Harshav's superb and detailed introduction to *American Yiddish Poetry* (Berkeley: University of California Press, 1986), particularly pp. 27–30.

39. Arturo Islas, unpublished paper given at the "Critical Fictions" symposium held at the Dia Art Foundation in New York on May 11, 1990.

40. Norman A. Stillman, "Contacts and Boundaries in the Domain of Language: The Case of Sefriwi Judeo-Arabic," in *Jews Among Arabs: Contacts and Boundaries*, ed. Mark R. Cohen and Abraham L. Udovitch (Princeton: Darwin Press, 1989), pp. 98–99.

41. That these debates are internal mean they mostly transpire in Arabic; for some hints at the issues involved, however, see the following: *Le Temps Modernes* (October, 1977; special issue devoted to francophone North African writing); chapter 1 ("The Theoretical-Historical Context") of Barbara Harlow's *Resistance Literature*; Miriam Cooke's *War's Other Voices: Women Writers on the Lebanese Civil War* (Cambridge: Cambridge University Press, 1988), particularly chapters 4 and 5 ("A Different Expression," and "Responsibility," pp. 69–119); and "Toward a World Literature? A Conversation with Tahar Ben Jelloun," in *Middle East Report*, 163 (March-April, 1990), pp. 30–33.

42. Zora Neale Hurston is a good case in point; one of the many reasons for the neglect and hostility her work faced had to do with the fact that she refused to depict characters according to what she perceived as the prevailing norm among "official" representatives of African-American culture, what she called "the sobbing school of Negrohood who hold that nature has somehow given them a dirty deal," in which "black lives are only defensive reactions to white actions." For more on this, see the Afterword by Henry Louis Gates, Jr., to Hurston's *Tell My Horse* (New York: Harper and Row, 1990), p. 293.

43. Barbara Harlow, *Resistance Literature*, p. 70.

44. James Scully, *Line Break*, p. 73.

45. Roque Dalton, *Poems*, trans. Richard Schaaf (Willimantic, Conn.: Curbstone Press, 1984), p. 58.

46. Quoted by Miriam Cooke in *War's Other Voices*, p. 65.

47. To use Erica Hunt's very acute phrase, in "Oppositional Poetics."

48. Abraham L. Udovitch and Lucette Valensi, *The Last Arab Jews: The Communities of Jerba, Tunisia* (Chur, London, Paris, New York: Harwood Academic Publishers, 1984), p. 117. Udovitch and Valensi's work is filled with insights about the particular qualities and strategies that have gone into maintaining a traditional Jewish life-style in the Islamic context; see also p. 118: "For the notions of reliability and honesty implied by the phrase haqq al-yahud have their counterpart in the value system internal to the Jewish community itself. The anecdotes and miracle stories of their rabbis and holy men highlight most prominently and most consistently their reliability and faith (Hebrew: *imun*) and absolute uprightness and integrity (Hebrew: *yashar*). It is not only personal honesty which these stories emphasize, but rather the quality of uncompromising, consistent adherence to moral and religious principles. It is to this unwavering, single-minded religious integrity—exemplified by their rabbis—that the Jews of Jerba attribute their success in resisting assimilation and communal decay. For them it is this quality which enabled them to maintain a community which was and, in view of many, still is the "Jerusalem of Africa." This dominant theme, rooted in their internal communal lives, transformed and applied to their economic life and commercial contacts with Muslims, became the haqq al-yahud. Internally, the values emanating from the inside serve to demarcate for them the moveable boundaries of their everyday relations with non-Jews, and provide the bridge between their complex, overlapping internal network and individual members of their neighbouring communities."

49. H. Schirmann, "Problems in the Study of Post-Biblical Hebrew Poetry," *Proceedings of the Israel Academy of Sciences and Humanities* 2 (1968), pp. 228–36.

50. Udovitch and Valensi, *Last Arab Jews*, pp. 84–85.

51. Menocal, *Arabic Role*, p. 151.

52. Eliyahu Eliachar, *Life Is with the Palestinians* (Jerusalem: Council of the Sephardic Communities, 1975), p. 279 (my translation).

53. Ibid., pp. 277, 236.

54. G. N. Giladi, *Discord in Zion*, pp. 188–89.

55. Erica Hunt, "Oppositional Poetics."

56. Shlomo Swirski, "Their Heart Is Not in the East," *News from Within*, November 14, 1988 (Jerusalem: Alternative Information Center).

57. Shlomo Swirski, *Israel: The Oriental Majority*, tran. Barbara Swirski (London: Zed Books, 1989), p. 26. Just as in the case of Sami Mickael's *Refuge*, the fact that Swirski's groundbreaking work took eight years to appear in English translation is indicative of the power relations at work in the transmission of material that is not ideologically fit for pre-conceived consumption.

58. Shlomo Swirski, *Israel: The Oriental Majority*, p. 45.

59. Albert Suissa, *The Bound* (Tel Aviv: Siman Kriya, 1990)[Hebrew], p. 19 (my translation).

60. Sami Shalom Chetrit, "Don't touch my wounds," my translation from manuscript received from the author.

61. David Ben-Gurion, *The Eternity of Israel* (Tel Aviv: 'Ayanot, 1964), see pp. 9, 14, 23, 34, and 37. Also see chapter 8 of G. N. Giladi's *Discord in Zion*, particularly p. 209.

62. Ella Shohat, *Israeli Cinema*, p. 115.

63. Ibid., pp. 116–18.

64. Kalman Katznelson, *The Ashkenazi Revolution* (Tel Aviv: 1964)[Hebrew], pp. 153–54, 206 (my translation).

65. See Elie Eliachar, *Living with Jews* (Jerusalem: Marcus, 1980)[Hebrew]; this quote is from p. 413 in a letter to Ben-Gurion dated April 27, 1964. For other references to Katznelson, see p. 568 (my translation).

66. See chapter 5 of Giladi's *Discord in Zion*, particularly p. 116. Unfortunately, very little nonpolemical research into the economics of the immigration of Arab Jews in the 1950s and their contribution to the literal construction of the state has been undertaken.

67. Walid Khazindar, "At Least," trans. Lena Jayyusi and W. S. Merwin, in *Paper Air*, vol. 4, no. 3 (Philadelphia: Singing Horse Press, 1990).

1. Discontinued Lines: Drafts for an Itinerary

1. Timothy Mitchell, *Colonizing Egypt* (Berkeley: University of California, 1991), p. 171.

2. Ilan Halevi, *A History of the Jews*, trans. A. M. Berrett (London, and Atlantic Highlands, N.J.: Zed Books, 1987), p. 71. Originally published as *Question juive: La tribu, la loi, l'espace* (Paris: Editions de Minuit, 1981). Whatever faults some may find with Halevi's work, he is one of the rare historians who has seriously taken into account what he calls the two "great transfers" (that of the native Palestinian Arab population away from Palestine and that of the native Levantine and Arab Jewish population into Israel/Palestine), and their implications for a rereading of the history—beginning from the present—of the Jews.

3. S. D. Goitein, *A Mediterranean Society* (Berkeley: University of California Press, 1967–83), vol. I, pp. 6–7.

4. These immigration figures are from the *Statistical Abstract of Israel* (Jerusalem: Central Bureau of Statistics, 1979), p. 137. The best available analysis of "the ethnic division of labor" during the formation of the Israeli industrial, agricultural, and economic infrastructure is in Shlomo Swirski's *Israel: The Oriental Majority*, trans. Barbara Swirski (London: Zed Books, 1989).

5. Halevi, *A History of the Jews*, pp. 208–9. Besides Swirski, one of the rare sociologists to explicitly put the "Oriental" question in economic and class terms, the standard sociological work (though already a bit out of date), is Sammy Smooha, *Israel: Pluralism and Conflict* (London and Henley: Routledge and Kegan Paul, 1978). Smooha's work supplanted the established old guard of Israeli sociology, particularly the approach of S. N. Eisenstadt, with its concept of the "integration" and "absorption" of non-Western Jews into a "Western" (read: Eastern European Ashkenazi) social, cultural, and political framework rather than the "absorption" of Israel as a whole into a pluralistic Levantine context. To get some sense of this Levantine approach, see Nissim Rejwan, "Israel's Communal Controversy: An Oriental Appraisal," *Midstream* (June, 1964), pp. 14–26; also his "The Two Israels: A Study in Europocentrism," *Judaism* 16 (Winter, 1967), pp. 97–108; and "Israel's Ethno-Political Cleavage," *Midstream* (June/July, 1983), pp. 18–22. Also see Avraham Shama and Mark Iris, *Immigration without Integration: Third-World Jews in Israel* (Cambridge: Schenk-

man, 1977). One of the most comprehensive alternative "native" approaches to the problem—in terms of both history and sociology—can be found in Nahum Menahem, *Ethnic Tension and Discrimination in Israel* (Tel Aviv: 1983); a French edition is available as *Israel: Tensions et discriminations communautaires*, trans. Michèle Bitton (Paris: Editions L'Harmattan, 1986). Two other interesting collections can be found in a special issue of *Les Temps Modernes*, no. 394 (1979), called "Le second Israel: La question Sepharade"; and *Khamsin* 5 (1978), "Oriental Jewry." Articles from this issue can also be found in *Forbidden Agendas: Intolerance and Defiance in the Middle East*, selected and introduced by Jon Rothschild (London: Al-Saqi, 1984), pp. 17–122.

6. Quoted by G. N. Giladi in *Discord in Zion: Conflict Between Ashkenazi and Sephardi Jews in Israel* (London: Scorpion, 1990), pp. 103–4.

7. In an extremely important study, Ya'akov Nahon has shown that the educational gap has *increased* for the Orientals each generation they have been in Israel. This means that second and sometimes even third generation Israelis have lower educational levels than their grandparents from Islamic countries. *The Nahon Report* (Jerusalem: Institute of Applied Social Research, 1988)[Hebrew].

8. For more on this period of socialization, see Tom Segev's groundbreaking *1949: The First Israelis* (New York: The Free Press, 1986).

9. Elie Eliachar, *Life Is with the Palestinians* (Jerusalem: Council of the Sephardic Communities, 1975)[Hebrew], pp. 23–24.

10. See Norman A. Stillman, *The Jews of Arab Lands in Modern Times* (Philadelphia: Jewish Publication Society, 1991), p. 341. Also see the letter of complaint by an Iraqi Jew on pp. 340–41. For figures on contributions by Middle Eastern Jews to various Zionist institutions, see Menahem, *Ethnic Tension and Discrimination in Israel* pp. 113–23.

11. Shlomo Swirski, *Education in Israel: Schooling for Inequality* (Tel Aviv: Breirot, 1990), p. 35. Swirski's landmark study is a masterpiece of archival research, analytical clarity, and visionary conclusions. One can only hope that an English translation of this book will take less than the eight years it took for Swirski's other book, *Israel: The Oriental Majority*, to appear.

12. Swirski, *Education*, p. 48.

13. Elie Eliachar, *Living with Jews* (Jerusalem: Marcus, 1980)[Hebrew], pp. 498–99 (my translation).

14. Ibid., p. 273 (my translation).

15. Ibid., p. 505 (my translation).

16. In Halevi's *A History of the Jews*, pp. 203–4.

17. Swirski, *Israel: The Oriental Majority*, p. 54.

18. These "classic" quotes are taken from Eli Hamo's powerful documentary film *New Direction* (1991), discussed further in chapter 4.

19. Swirski, *Education*, p. 55.

20. From the Prophet Obadiah, 1:20. *The Jerusalem Bible* (Jerusalem: Koren, 1977), p. 695.

21. See chapter 6, "Development Towns," in Swirski, *Israel: The Oriental Majority*. Also see Shlomo Swirski and Menachen Shoushan's *Development Towns of Israel* (Haifa: Breirot Publishers, 1986).

22. Halevi, *A History of the Jews*, p. 198.

23. Stillman, *Jews of Arab Lands*, pp. 178–79.

24. Ibid., p. 201. It is very difficult to find any survey works that critically question the assumptions of Zionist ideology regarding this mass exodus from the Islamic countries. The most accessible critical survey of this process is still Marion Woolfson, *Prophets in Babylon: Jews in the Arab World* (London: Faber and Faber, 1980).

25. Abbas Shiblak, *The Lure of Zion: The Case of the Iraqi Jews* (London: Al-Saqi, 1986), p. 23. This is the only work I am aware of that analyzes the modern displacement of one specific Arab Jewish community in its global sense, that is, in relation to the push and pull of Zion *and* the fate of the Palestinians. Shiblak is also one of the first scholars to work with British archival material that had heretofore been unavailable. Also see Nissim Rejwan's extremely cohesive account in part 3 ("A Century of Radical Change / 1850–1951") of his *The Jews of Iraq: 3000 Years of History and Culture* (London: Weidenfeld and Nicolson, 1985).

26. Nissim Rejwan, "Life Among Muslims: A Memoir," *Present Tense* (Autumn, 1981), pp. 43–46.

27. Nissim Rejwan, "Henry Miller: The Wandering American," *The Iraq Times*, August 6, 1947.

28. Nissim Rejwan, "The Plight of Europe," *The Iraq Times*, October 22, 1947.

29. The very rare photographs described here—which shed more than some light on a largely unknown world, particularly in the Israeli context—can be found in the Hebrew edition of Nahum Menahem's *Ethnic Tension and Discrimination in Israel* (Haifa, 1983), pp. 294, 264, 192, 184, 147, 227, 229, and 242. Three recent and very significant works providing access to the other "other," the Palestinian, through photographs are Sarah Graham Brown, *The Palestinians and Their Society, 1880–1946* (London: Quartet Books, 1980); Walid Khalidi, *Before Their Diaspora: A Photographic History of the Palestinians, 1876–1948* (Washington, D.C.: Institute for Palestine Studies, 1984); Edward Said and Jean Mohr, *After the Last Sky* (London: Faber and Faber, 1986). Although the Israeli Museum of the Diaspora in Tel Aviv has published a number of photographic essays on the Levantine and Arab Jewish communities, including *From Carthage to Jerusalem: The Jewish Community in Tunis* (Tel Aviv: Beit Hatefusoth, 1986), as well as an exhibition catalog on Libyan Jewry, these works remain within the framework of the "integration" and "absorption" models, stressing the uniqueness of each community in the past and their leaps into "modernity." In addition, the disruptive nature of the transfer and socialization process undergone in Israel is completely avoided. For projects that come much closer to the recuperative intent that distinguishes the books on the Palestinians, see *Juifs d'Egypte: Images et textes*, ed. Jacques Hassoun (Paris: Editions du Scribe, 1984), and *Les Juifs d'Algerie: Images et textes*, ed. Jean Laloum and Jean-Luc Allouche (Paris: Editions du Scribe, 1987). The fact that these two works appeared in France (while the books on the Palestinians appeared prior to them and in English) again points out the configuration of cultural assumptions, balances, and spaces of reception available now for works dealing with Levantine and Arab Jews.

30. For some of the implicit and explicit alliances of the Zionist movement during this period, see Lenni Brenner, *Zionism in the Age of the Dictators* (New York: Lawrence Hill, 1983).

31. Stillman; *Jews of Arab Lands*, pp. 331–33.

32. Shiblak, *The Lure of Zion*, p. 44.

33. Jacques Hassoun, "The Traditional Jewry of the Hara," in the excellent and diverse volume edited by Shimon Shamir, *The Jews of Egypt: A Mediterranean Society in Modern Times* (Boulder: Westview Press, 1987), p. 172.

The whole set of relations discussed here and further on can, so far, unfortunately only be gotten in bits and pieces. There is to my knowledge no comprehensive study dealing with the plethora of social relations both within the Jewish communities of the Levant and between them and the greater societies of which they formed a part. For some examples of works that at least suggest the complexities involved, see Shiblak's *Lure of Zion*; chapter 28, "Youth in Revolt," of Rejwan's *Jews of Iraq*; Renzo De Felice's superb *Jews in an Arab Land: Libya, 1835–1970*, trans. Judith Roumani (Austin: University of Texas, 1985); Maurice Mizrahi, *L'Egypte et ses juifs: Le Temps revolu—XIXe et XXe siecles* (Lausanne: Maurice

Mizrahi, 1977); *Juifs du Nil*, ed. Jacques Hassoun (Paris: Le Sycamore, 1981), particularly Gudrun Kramer and Alfred Morabia's "Face à la modernite: Les juifs d'Egypte aux xix⁰ et xx⁰ siècles"; also see Gudrun Kramer's "Political Participation of the Jews in Egypt Between World War I and the 1952 Revolution," in Shamir, *Jews of Egypt*; Michael M. Laskier, *The Alliance Israelite Universelle and the Jewish Communities of Morocco, 1862–1962* (Albany: State University of New York Press, 1983); Y. D. Eskandarany, "Egyptian Jewry: Why It Declined," in *Khamsin* 5 (1978).

For the most cohesive Marxist approach to Jewish society as a whole, see Abraham Leon, *The Jewish Question: A Marxist Interpretation* (New York: Pathfinder Press, 1970); this should be accompanied by Maxime Rodinson's critical introduction, "From the Jewish Nation to the Jewish Problem," in *Cult, Ghetto and State: The Persistence of the Jewish Question*, trans. Jon Rothschild (London: Al-Saqi, 1983).

For good background works, one general, the other particular, that help give some sense of the greater context within which Jewish communities existed in the Arab world, see Albert Hourani, *Minorities in the Arab World* (London: Oxford University Press, 1947); and H. Batatu, *The Old Social Classes and the Revolutionary Movement in Iraq: A Study of Iraq's Old Landed Commercial Classes and its Communists, Ba'athists and Free Officers* (Princeton: Princeton University Press, 1978).

34. Stillman, *Jews of Arab Lands*, pp. 150–51.

35. Jean Said Makdisi, *Beirut Fragments: A War Memoir* (New York: Persea, 1990), pp. 102; 105–7.

36. See, for example, Rejwan's *Jews of Iraq*, p. 232. Also see Nahum Menahem's original archival research analyzing correspondence between Levantine and Arab Jewish communities and the Zionist authorities in Palestine, pp. 163–333 [Hebrew edition]; pp. 155–326 [French edition]. Another extremely important source is Eliyahu Eliachar's *Life Is with the Palestinians* (Jerusalem: The Council of the Sephardic Communities, 1975), particularly pp. 168–290 [Hebrew]; also his "The Status of the Sephardic Jews Since the Balfour Declaration," *Shevet Ve'Am* 1 (Jerusalem: The Council of the Sephardic Communities, 1970), pp. 67–84 [Hebrew].

37. See Dr. Abraham Matalon's important study *The Hebrew Pronunciation in Its Struggle* (Tel Aviv: Hadar, 1979)[Hebrew]. Also see José Faur's "A Sense of Language," *The Sephardic World* (Summer, 1972), pp. 5–9. For this problematic in a different context, see Jacques Hassoun, *Fragments de langue maternelle* (Paris: Editions Payot, 1979), as well as his "Eloge de la dysharmonie," in *Actes Colloques sur le bilingisme à Rabat* (Paris: Editions Denoël, 1975).

38. See José Faur's *Golden Doves with Silver Dots*. Of particular relevance here are all of chapter 3 ("Freedom, Language and Negativity," pp. 59–83); chapter 4 ("Textuality in Rabbinic Tradition," pp. 84–113), and section 1 ("Semiotic and Semantic Reading," pp. 118–122) of chapter 5. For two examples of the ritualistic aspects of reading among Jews, see A. Stahl, "Ritualistic Reading Among Oriental Jews," *Anthropological Quarterly* 52 (1979), and S. Deshen, "Ritualization of Literacy: The Works of Tunisian Scholars in Israel," *American Ethnologist* 2.

39. Halevi, *A History of the Jews*, p. 222.

40. Cited by Ehud Ben-Ezer in "Brenner and the 'Arab Question,' " *Modern Hebrew Literature*, vol. 12, nos. 3–4 (Spring/Summer, 1987) (Tel Aviv: Institute for the Translation of Hebrew Literature), p. 20.

41. Yosef Chaim Brenner, "Nerves," in Allan Lelchuk and Gershon Shaked's *Eight Great Hebrew Short Novels* (New York: New American Library, 1983), p. 44. Also see p. 52: "From a courtyard opposite a voice that could have been either a man's or a woman's shouted in a mixture of Arabic and Yiddish through the night air: 'Rukh, rukh min hon!

S'tezikh tsugetsheppet?' The little colony's large synagogue looked down on us with its broad but dark windows. Beneath them some local citizens stood discussing their affairs. 'It's time I fired Ahmed,' one of them said. 'I've never seen such a thief in my life.' " The Arabic/Yiddish phrase can be translated as: "Scram, get out of here, why have you glued yourself to me?", a question that, it seems, could just as easily be reversed: "Why have you attached *yourselves* to me?"

42. Ibid., p. 43.

43. Dr. Michael M. Laskier, "Albert Antebi: On His Activity in Eretz Israel, 1897–1914," *Pe'amim* 21 (1984) (Jerusalem: Ben Zvi Institute)[Hebrew], p. 59 (my translation). Walid Khalidi also notes Antebbi's views in his *Before Their Diaspora*, p. 32.

44. Laskier, "Albert Antebbi," p. 77 (my translation).

45. Eliachar, *Life Is with the Palestinians*, p. 229 (my translation).

46. Laskier, "Albert Antebbi," p. 79.

47. Ibid., p. 76. Again, these attitudes are not just those of Antebbi; any of the sources cited above (see Stillman, *Jews of Arab Lands*) reveal identical positions.

48. Ben-Ezer in "Brenner and the 'Arab Question,' " p. 22.

49. Ibid., Ben-Ezer here just reflects the prevalent attitude of the contemporary Israeli literary establishment toward non-European prestate Hebrew writers. No matter what, they remain, in Swirski's phrase, "representatives of their 'race.' "

50. For some of the sources tracing this, see Lev Hakak, *Inferiors and Superiors: Oriental Jews in the Hebrew Short Story* (Jerusalem: Kiryat Sepher, 1981)[Hebrew]. To see just how ingrained such attitudes are, see the work done on the image of Arabs in Hebrew children's literature by Fouzi El-Asmar, *Through the Hebrew Looking Glass: Arab Stereotypes in Children's Literature* (London: Zed Press, 1986); Adir Cohen's *An Ugly Face in the Mirror* (Tel Aviv: Reshafim Publishers, 1985)[Hebrew], as well as Risa Domb's *The Arab in Hebrew Prose* (London: Valentine, Mitchell, 1982).

For a more recent controversy that essentially follows the same typology, see Amos Oz, *In the Land of Israel*, trans. Maurie Goldberg-Bartura (London: Fontana, 1983), pp. 25–48. This section of the book, perhaps the most "hopeless" in Oz's despairing journey, portrays a visit made by him to the working-class town of Beit Shemesh outside of Jerusalem and the rage of its residents that greeted him there. Oz's bewilderment and revulsion at this scene is quite apparent; moreover, the chapter is juxtaposed with a very earnest and searching visit to a group of young Palestinian intellectuals. The book itself, and particularly this juxtaposition—between brutal and enraged Orientals and sensitive, intelligent Palestinians—was vehemently attacked by Oriental Jewish intellectuals. Unfortunately, this whole exchange took place mostly in the Hebrew press. Except for the Rejwan articles cited above (see note 4), the best and most accessible piece available is Inge Lederer-Gibel's superb "Radical Chic in Israel," in *Christianity and Crisis*, vol. 44, no. 16 (October 15, 1984). The present mass immigration of Soviet Jews is bringing these sentiments and debates back to the forefront of Israeli culture; unfortunately, nothing has been written about it in English and the best source remains the ever-vigilant and remarkably diverse Hebrew press.

The extent to which class, ethnic, and cultural questions about Israel's "Middle-Easternness" are either totally ignored, suppressed, or distorted within Israeli liberal discourse—i.e., practically all of the literature and information that reaches the West—is truly remarkable, and one does not have to search farther than the nearest magazine (see, for example, the newest Jewish American liberal production, *Tikkun*). More remarkable is the fact that this erasure covers the spectrum of general discourse, regardless of political persuasion. Even a progressive journal like *Magazine Z* consistently ignores these issues in their Middle East coverage (see, for example, Moe Seager's "Israeli Opposition," May, 1990, pp. 52–62).

The best and most accessible works dealing with these issues are both by Ella Shohat; see her comprehensive essay "Sephardim in Israel: Zionism from the Standpoint of Its Jewish Victims," *Social Text* 19–20 (Fall, 1988); as well as chapter 3, "The 'Bourekas' and Sephardi Representation," in her *Israeli Cinema: East/West and the Politics of Representation* (Austin: University of Texas Press, 1989).

51. Besides Eliachar's autobiographical works, *Life Is with the Palestinians* (Jerusalem: Council of the Sephardic Community of Jerusalem, 1975)[Hebrew], and *Living with Jews* (Jerusalem: Marcus, 1980)[Hebrew], see Philip Gilon, *Israelis and Palestinians: Co-Existence or . . . The Credo of Elie Eliachar* (Tel Aviv: Gedalyah Cornfeld, 1977), where there are some references to the attitudes of the generation preceding him.

52. Aharon Cohen, *Israel and the Arab World* (Boston: Beacon Press, 1976), pp. 72–93, p. 81. For additional material on A. S. Yahuda, see his remarkable *Dr. Weizmann's Errors on Trial* (New York, 1952)[published privately by Ethel R. Yahuda]. A brief sketch of Rabbi Haim Nahum Effendi's career is given in chapter 3.

53. Moise Ventura, *Soupirs et espoirs: Echos de la Guerre 1939–45* (Paris: Librairie Durlacher, 1948), pp. 76 and 86 (my translation).

54. To get a sense of precisely how deep the "moderate" attitudes of Orientals are, see my "Reorienting: Sephardim in the Middle East," *New Outlook: Middle East Monthly* (Tel Aviv: January/February, 1987), pp. 51–54; and my "La communaute sepharade en Israel et le processus de paix," in *Perspectives Judeo-Arabes* 7 (Paris: August, 1987), pp. 47–85.

55. Shmuel Yoseph Agnon, excerpted from a letter: "To S. Z. Schocken after the 1929 Riots," in *The Jerusalem Quarterly* 9 (Fall, 1978), p. 54.

56. Halevi, *A History of the Jews*, p. 210. While Israeli liberal thought sees 1967 as the beginning of the end, Halevi is one of the few to make this important distinction about Israel's reemergence within the Arab and Levantine world only after 1967 in precisely these terms.

57. Raja Shehadeh, *The Third Way: A Journal of Life in the West Bank* (London: Quartet, 1982), p. 133.

58. David Grossman, *The Yellow Wind*, trans. Haim Watzman (New York: Delta, 1989). Given Grossman's skill in opening up some of the realities of the occupation to the Israeli and general public, it is quite remarkable how deeply set within the consensus his ways of approaching and depicting the problems are. Throughout, Grossman the narrator remains the hopeful innocent, the well-intentioned sojourner looking in on the misery and hard-heartedness of human nature. The consensus discourse of the state (that of the beleaguered bastion of humanist ideals in a sea of hostility) is reproduced on the interpersonal level, in Grossman's encounters with Palestinians. Although this might simply be a narrative strategy, the book is not informed by a political consciousness that would place the context for some of this misery within the historical arena. In fact, such a book—due to the very deep sensitivity it does display—can in some sense even be counterproductive to the work of more radical historical revision, since it fixes the consensus version of history within that very sensitivity, hiding as much as it reveals.

59. Charles Olson, "Billy the Kid," in *Human Universe and Other Essays*, ed. Donald Allen (New York: Grove Press, 1967), p. 137. Also see Olson's *The Special View of History*, ed. Ann Charters (Berkeley: Oyez, 1970), for an expanded treatment of this.

60. Mahmoud Darwish, "When the Martyrs Go to Sleep," in *Modern Poetry of the Arab World*, ed. and trans. Abdullah al-Udhari (Harmondsworth: Penguin Books, 1986), p. 139.

61. *Guides Bleus illustrés: Mediterranée Orientale, Egypte* (Paris: Librairie Hachette, 1938), p. 151 (my translation).

62. Ibid., p. 173.

63. Ibid., p. 176.

64. Ibid., p. 176.

65. Remarkably enough, in this seething cauldron of conflicting contentions, these figures are not really disputed; this particular instance is from Khalidi's *Before Their Diaspora*, p. 189. In general, the work to be consulted is *A Survey of Palestine*: Prepared in December 1945 and January 1946 for the Information of the Anglo-American Committee of Inquiry, 2 vols. and supp. (Jerusalem: Government of Palestine, 1946).

For the most comprehensive study now available on the early origins of the conflict, see Gershon Shafir's excellent revisionary work: *Land, Labor and the Origins of the Israeli-Palestinian Conflict, 1882–1914* (Cambridge: Cambridge University Press, 1989). An excellent synopsis of Shafir's findings is given in Joel Beinin's review, *MERIP Reports* 164–65 (May-August, 1990), pp. 69–71.

66. Jacques Derrida, *Glas* (Paris: Galilée, 1974), pp. 268–69. Cited also in Susan Handelman's *Slayers of Moses: The Emergence of Rabbinic Interpretation in Modern Literary Theory* (Albany: State University of New York Press, 1982), p. 165.

67. Handelman, *Slayers of Moses*, p. 166.

68. Two recent projects, the journals *Levant: Cahiers de l'espace mediterraneén* (edited and published in France and Israel), and *Mediterraneans* (edited and published in England), give some sense of this new Levantine culture.

69. Evelyne Accad, *Sexuality and War: Literary Masks of the Middle East* (New York: New York University Press, 1990), p. 6. This, along with Miriam Cooke's *War's Other Voices*, despite problematic aspects in both, serves as a more "internal" introduction to basic issues that comprise the formation of contemporary Arabic literature.

70. Halevi, *A History of the Jews*, p. 199. Also see Alistair Horne, *A Savage War of Peace: Algeria, 1954–1962* (Harmondsworth: Penguin, 1977), pp. 58–59, and this, on p. 36: "In 1870 the Crémieux Decrees had made the exception of conferring automatic French citizenship upon the whole Jewish community of Algeria. Here, for Muslims, was a constantly open wound: Why should the Jewish minority be open to political privileges denied to the indigenous majority?"

71. Yvette Chamache, "Contrepoint," in *Juifs du Nil*, ed. Jacques Hassoun (Paris: Editions Le Sycomore, 1981), pp. 198, 204 (my translation).

72. Hélène Cixous, *Dedans* (Paris: des femmes, 1986), p. 27 (my translation).

73. Denis Donoghue, *Ferocious Alphabets* (New York: Columbia University Press, 1984), see chapter 6, "Graphireading," pp. 149–202, particularly the section on Derrida, pp. 155–66, and the title chapter, pp. 203–11.

74. "An Interview with Edmond Jabès Conducted by Jason Wiess," *Conjunctions* 9 (New York, 1986), pp. 140–41.

75. Edward Said, *Orientalism* (New York: Vintage Books, 1979), pp. 158–62. Also see pp. 80–92. For a superb commentary on the analysis of photographs in the context of the "Orient," see "Photographs and History," Sarah Graham Brown's introduction to her *Palestinians and Their Society*, particularly pp. 1–19. Other works dealing with the use of photography and representation in this context include Graham Brown's *Images of Women: The Portrayal of Women in the Photography of the Middle East, 1860–1950* (New York: Columbia University Press, 1988); Malek Alloula's *Colonial Harem* (Minneapolis: University of Minnesota Press, 1985), and Nisan Peretz, *Focus East* (New York and Jerusalem: Abrams and Domino, 1988). Some of the most useful and thorough work on relations between the "Orient" and "Europe" is that of Norman Daniel; see his *Islam and the West: The Making of an Image* (Edinburgh: Edinburgh University Press, 1980), and *Islam, Europe and Empire* (Edinburgh: Edinburgh University Press, 1966).

76. Timothy Mitchell, *Colonising Egypt*, pp. 22–23.

77. Cited in Edward Said, *Orientalism*, p. 100; for more on Nerval, see also pp. 180–84.

78. Ibid., pp. 84–85. The part of this quote citing classical figures is actually by Jean-Baptiste-Joseph Fourier from the "preface historique" to the *Description de l'Egypte*.

79. Timothy Mitchell, *Colonising Egypt*, pp. 29–30.

80. Edmond Jabès, *The Book of Questions*, vols. 1–7, trans. Rosmarie Waldrop (Middletown, Conn.: Wesleyan University Press, 1972–87). The first passage is from vol. 4, *Yael*, p. 25; the second passage is from vol. 3, *Return to the Book*, p. 160.

81. Wiess, "Interview with Edmond Jabès," pp. 137–39. From "In Cairo, I felt . . . " is from Edmond Jabès, *From the Desert to the Book: Dialogues with Marcel Cohen*, trans. Pierre Joris (Tarrytown, N.Y.: Station Hill, 1990), pp. 13–14.

82. Jabès, *From the Desert to the Book*, pp. 16–17.

83. Jabès, *The Book of Questions*, vol. 3, p. 145.

84. Jabès, *From the Desert to the Book*, p. 51.

85. George Kubler, *The Shape of Time: Remarks on the History of Things* (New Haven and London: Yale University Press, 1962), p. 19. Kubler's unorthodox theories of segmentation inspired much of the thinking that went into my conception of the subject at hand. I was led to this line of thought by Ad Reinhardt's typically laconic but invaluable suggestions in "Art vs. History." Following nine rhetorical questions on Islamic art (whose answers would entail the rewriting of art history as we know it), Reinhardt asks, "What is there for artists in art historian George Kubler's book *The Shape of Time*, which has been called a 'manifesto' and described as having 'something of the quality of a work of art' itself and which is now out in paperback?" See pp. 224–27 of Ad Reinhardt, *Art as Art: Selected Writings*, ed. Barbara Rose (New York: Viking, 1975).

86. Kubler, *The Shape of Time*, pp. 129–30.

87. Jacqueline Kahanoff, *From the East the Sun*, manuscript of her collected essays obtained from her literary executor, Mrs. Eva Zeintraub of Tel Aviv; pp. 4–5 of the preface. Her work is available in a Hebrew translation bearing the same title and published in Tel Aviv by Yariv/Hadar Publishing in 1978.

88. Jabès, *The Book of Questions*, vol. 2, pp. 137–38.

89. Ibid., pp. 139–40.

90. *Du désert au livre: Entretiens avec Marcel Cohen* (Paris: Belfond, 1980), p. 49 (my translation).

91. Makdisi, *Beirut Fragments*, p. 111.

92. Etel Adnan, "Growing Up to be a Woman Writer in Lebanon," in *Opening the Gates: A Century of Arab Feminist Writing*, ed. Margot Badran and Miriam Cooke (Bloomington: Indiana University Press, 1990), p. 7. Adnan's account of Gabriel Bounoure follows on pp. 17–18: "The Ecole des Lettres was founded by an exceptional Frenchman who was for years the chief administrator of all the French schools in Lebanon and Syria. . . . Gabriel Bounoure was his name. He was an essayist and a major critic of French literature, sending papers on literature and poetry to the prestigious literary magazine called the NRF. He became, in addition to his official government functions, the director of the Ecole des Lettres and gathered in Beirut a small but exceptional staff of professors. . . . I was one of the ten or twelve first students of the Ecole. Gabriel Bounoure's classes were the equivalent of those mystic encounters one reads about either in the great sufis' writings of the Islamic past, or in the works of German Romantic writers such as Novalis or Herman Hesse. . . . The ten or twelve students of the Ecole des Lettres became thirty or forty, in a few years, but they did not dilute the intensity of the first years, rather they caught the fever, joined the paradise." In *From the Desert to the Book*, Jabès speaks of Bounoure's presence: "I was living in such an intellectual turmoil that Gabriel Bounoure became my life-raft. Today Bounoure is forgotten — an unforgivable injustice, I think. The reviews he published in the N.R.F. and elsewhere, like his major essays gathered under the title *Marelles sur le parvis*, bear witness to

unequaled critical acumen. He was considered a critic mainly focused on the past. This is wrong: his last essays, on Rene Char, on Henri Michaux, as well as the letters he wrote young philosophers such as Jacques Derrida, prove to the contrary his extraordinary openness to modernity.

"He read the manuscript of *The Book of Questions* in 1962. And he helped to make nearly acceptable to me what in those pages frightened me. He even went further by showing me that, my contradictions being the very substance of my books, trying to avoid them was pointless. A long correspondence ensued. It not only permitted me to come to terms with my chaotic experience, but helped to deepen it.

"Gabriel Bounoure's death in 1969, shortly before the publication of *Elya*, which was dedicated to him, affected me deeply. Ever since I have had the impression of writing under his gaze. I should add that Bounoure himself was split between Western culture and his passion for the culture of the Orient which he discovered through living there for more than thirty years, first in Lebanon, then in Cairo and finally in Morocco, as a teacher and cultural advisor.

"His influence in those countries was enormous, especially in Lebanon. In Beirut he founded 'L'Ecole des Lettres,' which made its mark on several generations of intellectuals. An avenue of that city is named after him" (p. 52).

93. From *The Umm Kulthum Nobody Knows*, originally published in Cairo in 1969; these excerpts appear in *Middle Eastern Muslim Women Speak*, ed. Elizabeth Warnock Fernea and Basima Qattan Bezirgan (Austin and London: University of Texas Press, 1977), pp. 146–47; translated from the Arabic by the editors.

94. Ibid., p. 153–54.

95. Ibid., p. 154.

96. Marshall G. S. Hodgson, *The Venture of Islam: Conscience and History in a World Civilization*, vol. 3, "The Gunpowder Empires and Modern Times" (Chicago: University of Chicago Press, 1974), p. 376.

97. This remarkable and recurring phrase was coined by the American poet Nathaniel Mackey; it appears in "Sound and Sentiment, Sound and Symbol," p. 88 of *The Politics of Poetic Form: Poetry and Public Policy*, ed. Charles Bernstein (New York: Roof Books, 1990).

98. Etel Adnan, "In the Heart of the Heart of Another Country," in *Mundus Artium*, vol. 10, no. 1 (1977), pp. 28–29.

99. Yahya Taher Abdullah, *The Mountain of Green Tea*, trans. Denys Johnson-Davies (London: Heinemann, 1984), pp. 72–74.

100. Ibid., pp. 80–81.

101. Ibid., pp. 82.

102. Paul Morley, *Ask: The Chatter of Pop* (London: Faber and Faber, 1986), p. 103.

103. Jean Baudrillard, *Simulations*, trans. P. Foss, P. Patton, and P. Beitchman (New York: Semiotext[e], 1983), pp. 130–31.

104. The quote here is from "The Discourse of Others: Feminists and Postmodernism" by Craig Owens in *The Anti-Aesthetic: Essays on Postmodern Culture*, ed. Hal Foster (Port Townsend, Wash.: Bay Press, 1983), p. 80. In coming to this sense of allegory, Owens cites Angus Fletcher; for more, see his definitive *Allegory: The Theory of a Symbolic Mode* (Ithaca: Cornell University Press, 1964).

105. Edward Said's foreword to *Little Mountain* by Elias Khoury (Minneapolis: University of Minnesota Press, 1989), p. xiii.

106. See *My Grandmother's Cactus* (London: Quartet, 1991), for example, a recent anthology of Egyptian women writers translated by Marilyn Booth.

107. Yusuf Idris, "The Dregs of the City," in *The Cheapest Nights*, trans. Wadida Wassef (Washington, D.C.: Three Continents Press, 1989), p. 109.

108. Ibid., p. 110.
109. Ibid., p. 111.
110. Miriam Cooke, *War's Other Voices: Women Writers on the Lebanese Civil War* (Cambridge and New York: Cambridge University Press, 1988), pp. 75, 85. The work of Lebanese women writers during the civil war constitutes one of the most remarkable but neglected instances of a deeply critical and extremely risky cultural history in the making. Miriam Cooke's book (along with the aforementioned book by Evelyn Accad, *Sexuality and War: Literary Masks of the Middle East*), by dealing with women's writing in particular, frames contemporary Arabic literature within that perspective.

Cooke points to Idris as one of the writers, along with Naguib Mahfouz in Egypt, Fuad al-Tikirli in Iraq, Mouloud Feraoun and Muhammad Dib in Algeria, Albert Memmi in Tunisia, Suhayl Idris in Lebanon, and the Palestinian Jabra Ibrahim Jabra, who "focused on women as prime objects of social injustice," and "offered searing indictments of values and of society itself." She goes on to note that "in many of his stories, Yusuf Idris shows that society's preoccupations with honor and shame are themselves as destructive as the acts that entail loss of honor. . . . For women, the greatest defilement of all is contact with society in its present form, usually through the agency of a weak man. Trapped by class and gender, men react in specific and expected ways; their conscience has been replaced by assumptions and social expectations." In addition, "there is something wrong, Idris tells his reader, when girls are educated but society is not prepared to accept them into the workplace without compromising their integrity." These quotes are from pp. 77–78. Chapter 4, "Women's Voices in Arabic Literature," and chapter 5, "Responsibility" (pp. 69–119) provide a good historical introduction to the subject as well as a theoretical examination of particular examples of women's writing.

111. Nawal El Saadawi, *Woman at Point Zero*, trans. Sherif Hetata (London: Zed Books, 1983), p. 96.
112. For just some of the diverse views surrounding the origins of Arabic free verse, see the following: Salma K. al-Jayyusi, *Trends and Movements in Modern Arabic Poetry* (Leiden: Brill, 1978); Shmuel Moreh, "Nazik al-Mala'ika and al-Shi'r al-Hurr in Modern Arabic Literature," *Asian and African Studies* 4 (1968), pp. 57–84, and his "Free Verse (*al-Shi'r al-Hurr*) in Modern Arabic Literature: Abu Shadi and His School, 1926–46," *Bulletin of the School of Oriental and African Studies*, vol. 30, no. 1 (1968), pp. 28–51. Also see pp. 14–17 of Mounah A. Khouri and Hamid Algar's introduction to *An Anthology of Modern Arabic Poetry* (Berkeley: University of California Press, 1974), as well as Nazik al-Mala'ika's own comments in "The Beginnings of the Free Verse Movement," pp. 231–49 of *Middle Eastern Muslim Women Speak*, ed. Fernea and Bezirgan.
113. Cooke, *War's Other Voices*, p. 3.
114. Booth, *Grandmother's Cactus*, pp. 116–17.
115. Michael Gilsenan, *Imagined Cities of the East* (Oxford: Clarendon Press, 1986), p. 20.
116. The Ibn Khaldun anecdote appears in Michael Haag's *Guide to Cairo* (London: Travelaid, 1985), p. 4. The Meshullam of Volterra quote can be found in Stillman's *The Jews of Arab Lands*, p. 264. Other accounts of the period testify to the impressive nature of the city; for example, Obadiah of Bertinoro, a Jewish pilgrim on his way to the Holy Land, wrote in 1488: "I shall not speak of the grandeur of Cairo and of the streams of traffic there, for many before me have described this, and all that has been said of the town is true. . . . The city is very animated, and one hears the different languages of the foreigners who inhabit it. It is situated between the Red Sea and the Mediterranean and all merchants come from India, Ethiopia, and the countries of Prester John [fabulous Christian monarch of Asia, whose seat from the fourteenth century onwards was located in Abyssinia] through

the Red Sea to Cairo to both sell their wares, which consist of spices, pearls, and precious stones, and to purchase commodities which come from France, Germany, Italy and Turkey across the Mediterranean Sea through Alexandria to Cairo." This text appears in Franz Kobler's *Letters of Jews Through the Ages* (New York: East and West Library, 1952), p. 299.

Literature on the Islamic city and urban culture within the Arab and Mediterranean world is vast; the following are works I have found particularly useful: L. C. Brown, ed., *From Medina to Metropolis: Heritage and Change in the Near Eastern City* (Princeton: Darwin Press, 1973); A. H. Hourani and S. M. Stern, eds., *The Islamic City* (Philadelphia: University of Pennsylvania Press, 1970); Ira M. Lapidus, ed., *Middle Eastern Cities: A Symposium on Ancient, Islamic and Contemporary Middle Eastern Urbanism* (Berkeley: University of California Press, 1969); H. A. B. Rivlin and Katherine Helmer, eds., *The Changing Middle East City* (Binghamton, N.Y.: Center for Social Analysis, 1980); Phillip K. Hitti, *Capital Cities of Arab Islam* (Minneapolis: University of Minnesota Press, 1973); Abdulazziz Y. Saqqaf, *The Middle East City: Ancient Traditions Confront a Modern World* (New York: Paragon, 1987); Ira Lapidus, *Muslim Cities in the Later Middle Ages* (Cambridge, Mass.: Harvard University Press, 1967); Andre Raymond, *The Great Arab Cities in the 16th–18th Centuries: An Introduction* (New York University Press, 1984); Janet Abu-Lughod, *Cairo: 1001 Years of the City Victorious* (Princeton: Princeton University Press, 1971); Janet Abu-Lughod and Richard Hays, Jr., eds., *Third World Urbanization* (Chicago: Maaroufa Press, 1977); Janet Abu-Lughod, *Rabat: Urban Apartheid in Morocco* (Princeton: Princeton University Press, 1980).

117. Morley, *Ask*, p. 103.

118. Michael Haag, *Guide to Cairo*, p. 53.

119. An instructive aside to this is that rural Egyptian tourists have the custom of asking Westerners to pose with them for a photograph that they take and keep!

120. Eric R. Wolf, *Europe and the People without History* (Berkeley: University of California Press, 1982), p. 9.

121. David Antin, *tuning* (New York: New Directions, 1984), pp. 137–39.

122. Michael Gilsenan, *Imagined Cities*, p. 20.

123. Makdisi, *Beirut Fragments*, pp. 20, 209–11. See chapter 3, "Beirut: A New Topography," for a beautiful physical and psychic description of the city; also see pp. 130–33 for descriptions of Beirut in the early 1970s, before the outbreak of the war.

124. Etel Adnan, *Sitt Marie Rose*, tran. by Georgina Kleege (Sausalito, Calif.: Post-Apollo Press, 1982), pp. 39–40.

125. Cooke, *War's Other Voices*, pp. 118–19.

126. Hana Abu Khadra, "A Pictorial Essay of the Reconstruction Process," chapter 16, p. 277 of A. Saqqaf, *The Middle East City*.

127. Albert Hourani, *A History of the Arab Peoples* (Cambridge, Mass.: Harvard University Press, 1991), pp. 303–4.

128. Ibid., pp. 303–4.

129. Charles Issawi, *The Fertile Crescent, 1800–1914: A Documentary Economic History* (New York: Oxford University Press, 1988), pp. 48–51.

130. Edward Said, *After the Last Sky* (London: Faber and Faber, 1986), p. 171.

131. Adonis, *Introduction à la poétique arabe*, trans. Bassam Tahan and Anne Wade Minkowski, preface by Yves Bonnefoy (Paris: Sindbad, 1985), p. 115 (my translation).

132. *Modern Poetry of the Arab World*, trans. and ed. Abdullah al-Udhari (Harmondsworth: Penguin, 1986), p. 119. Hawi's poetry has appeared in what may be the best critical edition of a contemporary Arab poet in English: *Naked in Exile: Khalil Hawi's "The Threshing Floors of Hunger,"* interpretation and translation by Adnan Haydar and Michael Beard (Washington, D.C.: Three Continents Press, 1984).

133. Etel Adnan, *The Arab Apocalypse* (Sausalito, Calif.: Post-Apollo Press, 1989), p. 51.

134. Cited in "Letter from Paris: Arab Cinema in Exile," Miriam Rosen in *MERIP Reports* 136/137 (October/December, 1985), p. 48.

135. This phrase was coined by Marjorie Perloff and defined in her *Poetics of Indeterminacy: Rimbaud to Cage* (Chicago: Northwestern University Press, 1983). The sense of it here should also be considered in the context in which Baudrillard places current discourse: "After the metaphysic of being and appearance, after that of energy and determination, comes that of indeterminacy and the code" (*Simulations*, p. 103). To get closer to the genesis of this kind of terminology, see John Cage's 1958 talk, "Indeterminacy," in *Silence* (Middletown, Conn.: Wesleyan University Press, 1973).

136. Taken from Jayyusi's foreword to a fascinating new biography of Gibran, *Kahlil Gibran: His Life and His World* (New York: Interlink, 1991), by Jean Gibran and Kahlil Gibran, p. iii. The case of Gibran and other Arab exiles active in North and South America, along with the Yiddish modernist movement mentioned earlier, presents as good an argument as any for a completely reconfigured literary history of modern "American" writing, one that would include the full range of influences encountered and poetries created in this hemisphere.

137. Al-Udhari, ed., *Modern Poetry of the Arab World*, p. 19.

138. Ibid., p. 19.

139. Ibid., p. 46.

140. Ibid., p. 98.

141. Quoted in Barbara Harlow's *Resistance Literature* (New York and London: Methuen, 1987), pp. 111–12.

142. Al-Udhari, ed., *Modern Poetry of the Arab World*, pp. 103–4.

143. Mahmoud Darwish, *Complete Works of Mahmoud Darwish* (Beirut: Dar el-Awda, 1977), vol. II, p. 243; trans. Kamal Boullata.

144. Elias Khoury, *Little Mountain*, trans. Maia Tabet (Minneapolis: University of Minnesota Press, 1989), p. 41.

145. Darwish, *Complete Works*, pp. 249–50.

146. My decision not to delve further into the Canaanites as a viable alternative to predominant Zionist ideology along the very similar Levantine lines that I have proposed was simply one of practicality: as it is, there is simply too much to cover. For an excellent study on this group, see James S. Diamond, *Homeland or Holy Land? The "Canaanite" Critique of Israel* (Bloomington: Indiana University Press, 1986). Less accessible, but of great interest as well, is Boaz Evron's *A National Reckoning* (Tel Aviv: Dvir, 1988)[Hebrew]. For a review more concerned with the political aspects of Canaanism, see "We Are Not One: A Post-Zionist Perspective," by James S. Diamond in *Tikkun*, vol. 5, no. 2 (March/April, 1990), pp. 106–10.

147. See Joseph Zeidan's excellent article "Myth and Symbol in the Poetry of Adunis and Yusuf Al-Khal," *Journal of Arabic Literature* 10 (Leiden: Brill), p. 71.

148. Abdullah Schleiffer, *The Fall of Jerusalem* (New York and London: Monthly Review Press, 1972), p. 5.

149. Cooke, *War's Other Voices*, p. 87. The previous phrase, "naming the enemy," is a paraphrase from Miriam Cooke; on p. 98, she writes: "In men's writings, to name the enemy politically, as fascist, communist, Zionist, etc., or religiously or economically, exonerates the narrator. By naming the other, he situates himself as morally right, above and against those who are wrong."

With the defeat in 1967, and ensuing involvement with actual Palestinians on the part of individuals, the emptiness of much of the rhetoric became more tangible. This can be seen in the following passage from Etel Adnan's *Sitt Marie Rose*. The story—based on a true incident—tells of a Christian woman who was kidnapped and finally executed for her "traitorous" allegiances to the Palestinians: "After the defeat of June '67, I founded the Association of the Friends of Jerusalem. I thought that in this country where Christians hold the power, many people would feel cut off with the loss of the Holy City. But Jerusalem has no friends in this city. I thought that this feeling of frustration could be channeled into material aid for the Palestinian refugees. We were just a handful of women, putting up posters, writing letters to the newspapers that were rarely published, soliciting funds, going to foreign embassies to alert the public to the moral and material misery that reigned in the camps. They treated us like madwomen. For them, Palestine was a myth without substance" (pp. 50–51). For more on this novel, see pp. 111–14 of Harlow's *Resistance Literature*, and pp. 31–33 and 98–100 of Cooke's *War's Other Voices*.

150. Cooke, *War's Other Voices*, p. 87.

151. See the title story, "A Space Ship of Tenderness to the Moon," along with "An Account of Her Trial on Charges of Obscenity and Endangering Public Morality," in Fernea and Bezirgan, *Middle Eastern Muslim Women Speak*, pp. 273–90.

152. Etel Adnan, "In the Heart of the Heart of Another Country," *Mundus Artium*, vol. 10, no. 1, pp. 24–25.

153. Cooke, *War's Other Voices*, p. 87.

154. Al-Udhari, ed., *Modern Poetry of the Arab World*, p. 64.

155. As above, see note 147; p. 80. Zeidan analyzes the early poetry of Adonis, particularly "Resurrection and Ashes," in terms of its conceptual, ideological, and metaphorical relationship to the thought of Antun Sa'ada.

156. Zeidan, "Myth and Symbol," p. 86.

157. Adonis, *Poetique arabe*, p. 112 (my translation).

158. Ibid., p. 108.

159. Edward Said and Jean Mohr, *After the Last Sky* (London: Faber and Faber, 1986), p. 150.

160. Gilbert Sorrentino, "Language—Lying and Treacherous," in *New York Times Book Review*, May 25, 1986, p. 23.

161. Adonis, "The Desert," in *Modern Poetry of the Arab World*, ed. al-Udhari, p. 70.

162. *Birds Through a Ceiling of Alabaster: Three Abbasid Poets*, trans. G. B. H. Wightman and Y. A. al-Udhari (Harmondsworth: Penguin, 1975), p. 122.

163. For just one example, see Umberto Cassuto, *A Commentary on the Book of Genesis*, trans. Israel Abrahams (Jerusalem: The Magnes Press, 1961), p. 91: "When the Torah described man's creation (twice), the one in brief, general outline as an account of the making of one of the creatures of the material world and the second at length and in detail as the story of the creation of the central being of the moral world—it had no reason to refrain from duplicating the theme, since such a repetition was consonant with the stylistic principle of presenting first a general statement and thereafter the detailed elaboration, which is commonly found not only in Biblical literature but also in the literary works of the ancient east."

164. Adonis, "The Desert," in al-Udhari, ed., *Modern Poetry of the Arab World*, pp. 74–75.

165. Al-Udhari, ed., *Modern Poetry of the Arab World*, p. 139.

166. Cooke, *War's Other Voices*, p. 12.

167. Al-Udhari, ed. *Modern Poetry of the Arab World*, p. 142.

168. In *War's Other Voices* (p. 173), Miriam Cooke notes that "the Beirut Decentrists, like most Arab women writers, are rarely anthologized." A growing body of critical work, though, has helped to begin rectifying this.

169. Cooke, *War's Other Voices*, pp. 11–12.

170. Ghada al-Samman, *Beirut Nightmares*; quoted in Cooke, *War's Other Voices*, p. 44.

171. Ibid., p. 48.

172. Cooke, *War's Other Voices*, pp. 64–65.

173. Ibid., p. 42.

174. Hanan al-Shaykh, *The Story of Zahra* (London: Pan Books, 1986), p. 138.

175. Ibid., p. 182.

176. Hoda al-Namani, "I Remember I Was a Point, I Was a Circle," trans. Tim Mitchell, in *Women and the Family in the Middle East: New Voices of Change*, ed. Elizabeth Warnock Fernea (Austin: University of Texas, 1985), pp. 305–6.

177. Perloff, *Poetics of Indeterminacy*, p. 86. Also see p. 324.

178. Ibid., p. 316. Cited by Perloff from David Antin's *talking at the boundaries* (New York: New Directions, 1976).

179. The Darwish text is from al-Udhari, ed., *Modern Poetry of the Arab World*, p. 139; for Adonis see the same book, p. 75; for the al-Namani text, see Fernea, ed., *Women and the Family*, p. 307. For Etel Adnan, p. 78 in *The Arab Apocalypse*.

180. Craig Owens, "The Allegorical Impulse: Toward a Theory of Postmodernism," *October* 12 and 13 (1980); this quote is from Part II of the article, pp. 79–80.

181. John Cage, *Empty Words: Writings '73–'78* (Middletown, Conn.: Wesleyan University Press, 1979), p. 11. The second part is a paraphrase from David Antin cited in Perloff, *Poetics of Indeterminacy*, p. 302.

182. Cooke, *War's Other Voices*, p. 173.

183. Ron Silliman, "IF BY 'WRITING' WE MEAN LITERATURE (if by "literature" we mean poetry (if . . .)) . . . " in *The L=A=N=G=U=A=G=E Book*, ed. Bruce Andrews and Charles Bernstein (Carbondale and Edwardsville: Southern Illinois University Press, 1984), pp. 167–68. Also see Silliman's *New Sentence* (New York: Roof, 1987), particularly Part I, pp. 7–56.

184. Edward Said, "Opponents, Audiences, Constituencies," in Foster, ed., *The Anti-Aesthetic*, p. 150.

185. Gilsenan, *Imagined Cities*, p. 20.

186. Ya'aqob Yehoshua, *Childhood in Old Jerusalem* (Jerusalem: Reuben Mass, 1966)[Hebrew], vol. 2, pp. 228–29 (my translation).

187. Kubler, *The Shape of Time*, p. 2.

188. Kahanoff, *From the East the Sun*, "A Letter from Mama Camouna," p. 1.

189. Raymonda Hawa Tawil, *My Home, My Prison* (London: Zed Press, 1983), pp. 45–46.

190. Makdisi, *Beirut Fragments*, pp. 101–2.

191. For a survey of the more ancient aspects of Jerusalem, with references to the appropriate sources, see Henry Cattan, "The Repercussion of Israel's Occupation of Jerusalem," in *The Middle East City*, ed. A. Saqqaf, chapter 8, pp. 149–51.

192. My translation from Shelley Elkayam, *Song of the Architect* (Tel Aviv: Zmora Bitan, 1987)[Hebrew], p. 48. It has also appeared in my "Israel and the Levant: 'Wounded Kinship's Last Resort,' " in *MERIP Reports* 159 (July/August, 1989), p. 21.

193. Amin Maalouf, *The Crusades through Arab Eyes*, trans. Jon Rothschild (London: Al-Saqi, 1984), pp. 265–66. Also see Francesco Gabrieli, *Arabic Historians of the Crusades* (London: Routledge and Kegan Paul, 1969).

194. Guy Le Strange, *History of Jerusalem Under the Moslems* (no place of publication, publisher, or date), p. 5.

195. Jabra Ibrahim Jabra, *The Ship*, trans. Adnan Haydar and Roger Allen (Washington, D.C.: Three Continents Press, 1985), pp. 20–24.

196. Oleg Grabar, "Cities and Citizens," in *The World Of Islam*, ed. Bernard Lewis (London: Thames and Hudson, 1976).

Also see chapter 2, "Enframing," of Timothy Mitchell's *Colonising Egypt* (pp. 34–62): "What this anomalous urban life lacked in particular, we are sometimes told, is formal institutions—the 'inner structure' of the 'material' city. When we speak of an institution, somewhere in our thinking there often lurks the picture of a building or a street. The building stands for an institution, giving a visible exterior to the invisible 'inner structure', and it is remarkably difficult to think of a public institution without thinking of the building or street that represents it. Middle Eastern cities that 'lacked institutions' lacked more especially the imposing public buildings which might contain an institution, and represent it. It is perhaps worth thinking of our assumptions about urban structure in terms of this simple question. Further help can be sought in the writings of Ibn Khaldun and other Arab historians and geographers. In such works, and even in the everyday documents and correspondence that have survived from the pre-modern past of a city such as Cairo, official activities are never indicated by reference to or in terms of an imposing building; in manuscript illustrations, we are told, 'there does not seem to be an identifiable architectural vision of the publicly accessible official building.' Urban life was understood and referred to in written sources 'by function, never by location.' Or rather, since we saw in the model village that the notion of function itself depends on the partition of a system of frameworks, the life of the city was understood in terms of the occurrence and reoccurrence of practices, rather than in terms of an 'architecture'—material or institutional—that stands apart from life itself, containing and representing the meaning of what was done" (p. 59).

197. Abdullah Schleiffer, "Islamic Jerusalem as Archetype of a Harmonious Environment," in A. Saqqaf, *The Middle East City*, pp. 164–65.

198. Nardel Ardalan and Laleh Bakhtiar, *The Sense of Unity: The Sufi Tradition in Persian Architecture* (Chicago and London: University of Chicago Press, 1973), from the foreword by Seyyed Hossein Nasr, p. xii.

199. Kenneth Frampton, "Towards a Critical Regionalism: Six Points for an Architecture of Resistance," in Foster, ed., *The Anti-Aesthetic*, p. 26.

200. Said and Mohr, *After the Last Sky*, pp. 147–49.

201. A Benjamin mélange, see "On Some Motifs in Baudelaire," in *Illuminations*, trans. Harry Zohn (New York: Schocken, 1969), p. 188, and "The Work of Art in the Age of Mechanical Reproduction" from the same volume, p. 221. For the sense of "aura" referred to here, see Ron Silliman's "Benjamin's Aura" in *The New Sentence* (New York: Roof Books, 1987), pp. 32–54.

202. Halevi, *A History of the Jews*, p. 252.

203. Etel Adnan, "In the Heart of the Heart of Another Country."

204. This text appears in *A Big Jewish Book*, ed. Jerome Rothenberg with Harris Lenowitz and Charles Doria (Garden City, N.Y.: Anchor Doubleday, 1978), p. 307.

2. A Garden Enclosed: The Geography of Time

1. *The Itinerary of Benjamin of Tudela*, critical text, commentary, and translation by Marcus Nathan Adler (New York: Feldheim)[no date: reprint of first edition, published in London, 1907], p. 30.

2. Jacqueline Kahanoff, *From the East the Sun*, manuscript of collected essays, p. 5 of preface.

3. Ilan Halevi, *A History of the Jews*, trans. A. M. Berrett (London and Atlantic Highlands, N.J.: Zed Books, 1987), pp. 70–75. Also see Eliahu Ashtor, *A Social and Economical History of the Near East in the Middle Ages* (London, 1976); Walter J. Fischel, *Jews in the Eco-*

nomic and Political Life of Medieval Islam (New York: Ktav, 1969), and vol. 1, "Economic Foundations," of Goitein's *A Mediterranean Society* (Berkeley: University of California Press, 1967–83).

4. F. E. Peters, *Allah's Commonwealth: A History of Islam in the Near East, 600–1100 A.D.* (New York: Simon and Schuster, 1973), pp. 143–44.

5. Maria Rosa Menocal, *The Arabic Role in Medieval Literary History* (Philadelphia: University of Pennsylvania Press, 1987), p. 28.

6. For an excellent summary of this, see Eugene A. Meyers, *Arabic Thought and the Western World* (New York: Ungar, 1964). For a colorful look at Baghdad during the Abbasid period, see André Clot, *Haroun al-Rashid and the World of the Thousand and One Nights* (London: Al-Saqi, 1988). For the standard work on the "golden age" of the Jews during this period, see Eliahu Ashtor, *The Jews of Moslem Spain* in 3 vols. (Philadelphia: Jewish Publication Society, 1973–84).

7. Menocal, *Arabic Role*, pp. 148–49.

8. Oleg Grabar, *The Formation of Islamic Art* (New Haven: Yale University Press), p. 11. For a neglected but quite insightful look at particularly "Jewish" art within the Islamic context, see L. A. Mayer, *L'Art juif en terre de l'Islam* (Geneva: A. Kundig, 1959).

9. *The Itinerary of Benjamin of Tudela*, p. 40.

10. F. E. Peters, *Allah's Commonwealth*, p. 144.

11. See George F. Hourani's important work, *Arab Seafaring in the Indian Ocean in Ancient and Early Medieval Times* (Princeton: Princeton University Press, 1951), p. 61.

12. Janet L. Abu-Lughod, *Before European Hegemony: The World System A.D. 1250–1350* (New York: Oxford University Press, 1989), p. 199.

13. Germaine Tillion, *The Republic of Cousins: Women's Oppression in Mediterranean Society*, trans. Quintin Hoare (London: Al-Saqi, 1983), p. 156.

14. Janet L. Abu-Lughod, *Before European Hegemony*, pp. 361–62.

15. Germaine Tillion, *The Republic of Cousins*, p. 155.

16. For Abravanel on cities, see pp. 256–59 in *Medieval Political Philosophy: A Sourcebook*, ed. Muhsin Mahdi and Ralph Lerner (New York: The Free Press, 1963).

17. Germaine Tillion, *The Republic of Cousins*, p. 154.

18. Mordekhai HaKohen, *The Book of Mordekhai*, ed. Harvey Goldberg (Philadelphia: Institute for the Study of Human Issues, 1980), p. 81.

19. Ibid., p. 69.

20. Ibid., p. 79.

21. See, for instance, the introduction to Richard Gottheil and William H. Worrell's early *Fragments from the Cairo Geniza in the Freer Collection* (New York: Macmillan, 1927). "But the Geniza was known in 1750 and 1864 as we have seen and hence could not be 'discovered.' Also, if 'all the contents' were dumped into the courtyard, they must have been restored, in part at least, to the Geniza before Schechter's visit in 1897 for he found them there. In view of all the statements, perhaps the contents of the Geniza and the entrance to it were always known to the Synagogue authorities. They deceived Adler upon his first visit, in 1888, with a conventional answer: The Contents of a Geniza are regularly buried." For more specifics, see the general introduction to the first volume of Goitein's *A Mediterranean Society*. For an interesting usage of *geniza* sources by a Levantine rabbinical authority see Zvi Zohar's extremely interesting *A Great Sephardic Posek Champions Women's Rights* (Rabbi Uziel's responsum on Women's Sufferage, 1920) (Jerusalem: Shalom Hartman Institute, 1985).

22. Gershom Scholem, *From Berlin to Jerusalem*, trans. Harry Zohn (New York: Schocken, 1980), p. 158.

23. S. D. Goitein, *A Mediterranean Society*, vol. 4, p. 32. For more on the Fatimid period, see Jacob Mann's pioneering *The Jews in Egypt and Palestine Under the Fatimid Caliphs*, in 2 vols. (Oxford: Oxford University Press, 1920–22).

24. Ibid., vol. 2, p. 180.

25. Ibid., pp. viii, ix.

26. Abu-Lughod, *Beyond European Hegemony*, p. 186.

27. Menocal, *Arabic Role*, p. 46. See pp. 31–33 for an excellent sketch of William of Aquitaine's cultural background, and pp. 48–51 for an extremely suggestive interpretation of Eleanor of Aquitaine's career and reputation; for more on Frederick, see pp. 61–63. Norman Daniel's *The Arabs and Medieval Europe* remains a standard and important work in the field; the work of Richard Lemay, though often dealing with highly technical material, is superb: see, for example, "A propos de l'origine arabe de l'art des troubadours," *Annales: Economies, Sociétés, Civilisations* 21, pp. 990–1011 (1966), and "The Hispanic Origin of Our Present Numerical Forms," *Viator* 8, pp. 435–59 (1977). For a very interesting study that ventures on Arabic culture beyond the sphere of the Levant, see Dorothee Metlitzki, *The Matter of Araby in Medieval England* (New Haven: Yale University Press, 1977). The work of George Makdisi is also of great importance in tracing the institutional connections within the educational system; see his *The Rise of Colleges: Institutions of Learning in Islam and the West* (Edinburgh: Edinburgh University Press, 1981).

28. S. D. Goitein, *Letters of Medieval Jewish Traders* (Princeton: Princeton University Press, 1973), p. 141.

29. Ibid., p. 167.

30. Ibid., p. 78.

31. Ibid., vol. 2., p. 292; also see p. 289 of the same volume, and vol. 4, p. 21.

32. S. D. Goitein, *Studies in Islamic History and Institutions* (Leiden: Brill, 1966), pp. 246–47.

33. Ghassan Kanafani, *Palestine's Children*, trans. Barbara Harlow (Washington, D.C.: Three Continents Press, 1984), p. 32.

34. Jean Said Makdisi, *Beirut Fragments: A War Memoir* (New York: Persea, 1990), pp. 113–14.

35. Ya'aqob Yehoshua, *Childhood in Old Jerusalem* (Jerusalem: Reuben Mass, 1966–79)[Hebrew], vol. 1, pp. 215–16 (my translation).

36. Ibid., pp. 58–66 in vol. 3 and pp. 204–14 in vol. 1.

37. Naim Kattan, *Farewell, Babylon*, trans. Sheila Fishman (New York: Taplinger, 1980), pp. 47–48. For a survey of some examples of this genre of memoir, see Jacob M. Landau's "Bittersweet Nostalgia: Memoirs of Jewish Immigrants from the Arab Countries," in *Middle East Journal*, vol. 35, no. 2 (Spring, 1981).

38. Goitein, *A Mediterranean Society*, vol. 2, p. 42.

39. Ibid., pp. 44–45.

40. Ibid., p. 274.

41. Ibid., vol. 4, p. 8.

42. Ibid., p. 315. Also see the section on naming, pp. 314–19.

43. Ibid., p. 326.

44. Ibid., p. 332.

45. Ibid., p. 353. See the whole chapter "The World of Women," pp. 312–59. The literature on women in the Levant, spanning the whole indivisible spectrum — ancient, medieval, and contemporary — is continually growing. For references to the present scene, see chapter 4. For the ancient and medieval period, some of the works I have found most useful in the context of this study are Tillion, *Republic of Cousins*; Sarah B. Pomeroy, *Goddesses, Whores, Wives and Slaves: Women in Classical Antiquity* (New York: Schocken, 1975); J. G.

Persistiany, ed., *Mediterranean Family Structures* (Cambridge: Cambridge University Press, 1976), and his *Honour and Shame: The Values of Mediterranean Society* (London: Weidenfeld and Nicolson, 1966); Part I, "Tradition," of *Middle Eastern Muslim Women Speak*, ed. Elizabeth Warnock Fernea and Basima Qattan Bezirgan (Austin and London: University of Texas Press, 1977), pp. 3–86; Fatima Mernissi, *Beyond the Veil: Male-Female Dynamics in Muslim Society* (London: Al-Saqi, 1984); Margaret Smith, *Rabi'a the Mystic and Her Fellow Saints* (Amsterdam: Philo Press, 1974); Nabia Abbott, *Aisha: The Beloved of Mohammed* (London: Al-Saqi, 1986), and *Two Queens of Baghdad* (Chicago: University of Chicago Press, 1974); and *Written Out of History: Our Jewish Foremothers*, ed. Sondra Henry and Emily Taitz (Fresh Meadows: Biblio Press, 1983).

46. Goitein, *Letters of Medieval Jewish Traders*, p. 77.

47. Goitein, *A Mediterranean Society*, vol. 2, p. 191.

48. Oleg Grabar, "Cities and Citizens," in *The World of Islam*, ed. Bernard Lewis, p. 96.

49. See Goitein, *A Meditteranean Society*, vol. 1, pp. 200–201.

50. Ibid., p. 154.

51. Ibid., vol. 2, p. 48. Also see Hassan Fathy, *Natural Energy and Vernacular Architecture* (Chicago: University of Chicago Press, 1986), particularly the preface and Part 1, "Environment and Architecture." Also see K. A. C. Creswell's *Early Muslim Architecture* (London: Penguin, 1958); Oleg Grabar, *Islamic Architecture and Its Decoration, A.D. 800–1500* (London: Faber and Faber; 1964); and L. A. Mayer, *Islamic Architects and Their Works* (Geneva: Albert Kundig, 1956).

52. Goitein, *A Mediterranean Society*, vol. 2, p. 339.

53. Menocal, p. 75.

54. Ibid., p. 117.

55. Ibid., pp. 116, 127.

56. Ibid., p. 131. The whole chapter, "Italy, Dante, and the Anxieties of Influence" (pp. 115–35), is a model of the added depth that a canonical text like Dante's can gain through a contextual reading of the Arabic cultural presence in Europe.

57. Ibid., pp. 81–83.

58. A. S. Yahuda, *The Language of the Pentateuch in Its Relation to Egyptian* (Oxford University Press/London: Humphrey Milford, 1933), p. xxvii.

59. Jacques Derrida, *Writing and Difference*, p. 9.

60. David Shasha, "Theories of Writing in Shem Tob Ardutiel's *The Battle of the Pen and the Scissors*," unpublished master's thesis presented to the Faculty of the Graduate School of Cornell University, p. 144. Also see pp. 141–51, where Shasha presents a remarkably cogent argument subverting the positivist ideological assumptions underlying much modern Jewish historiography, including schools of thought claiming greater theoretical complexity than that of standard narrative history.

61. My translation, from the original text in Haim Schirmann, *Hebrew Poetry in Spain and Provence* (Jerusalem: The Bialik Institute, 1979)[Hebrew], vol. 2, p. 512.

62. Jacques Derrida, *Writing and Difference*, pp. 76–77. Some works on the importance of grammar and linguistics in this context include Khalil T. Semaan, *Linguistics in the Middle Ages* (Leiden: Brill, 1968); R. Arnaldez, *Grammaire et théologie chez Ibn Hazm de Cordoue: Essai sur la structure et les conditions de la pensée musulmane* (Paris: Vrin, 1956); Hartwig Hirschfield, *Literary History of Hebrew Grammarians and Lexicographers* (London: Oxford University Press, 1926). Also see José Faur's remarkable tour de force, "The Hebrew Personal Pronouns," in *Perspectives on Jews and Judaism*, ed. Arthur A. Chiel (New York: The Rabbinical Assembly, 1978).

63. This, again, is Nathaniel Mackey's phrase. See his "Sound and Sentiment, Sound and Symbol," *The Politics of Poetic Form*, ed. Charles Bernstein.

For information on the Egyptian custom described above, see Jacques Hassoun's "The Traditional Jewry of the Hara," in *The Jews of Egypt: A Mediterranean Society in Modern Times*, ed. Shimon Shamir (Boulder: Westview, 1987), pp. 169–73. For further details, the following Hebrew works can be consulted: Refa'el Aharon ben-Shim'on, *Nehar Mitzrayim* (Alexandria: 1906/1907); Yom-Tov Yisrael, *Minhagey Mitzrayim* (Jerusalem: 1871/1872); and Eliyahu Hazan, *Neve Shalom, Minhagey No-Amon ve-Eretz Mitzrayim* (Alexandria: 1892/1893).

For some works on music in the Hebrew/Arabic context that I have found particularly helpful, see the following by Henry George Farmer: *Saadyia Gaon and Music* (London, 1943); *The Oriental Musical Influence and Jewish Geniza Fragments on Music* (New York: Hinrichsen Edition, 1964); *A History of Arabian Music to the XIII Century* (London: Luzae, 1929); *Historical Facts for the Arabian Musical Influence* (London: William Reeves, 1930); *The Sources of Arabian Music* (Leiden: Brill, 1965); "The Music of Islam," in *The New Oxford History of Music*, vol. 1 (London: Oxford University Press, 1957), pp. 421–77. In addition, see E. Werner and I. Sonne's extremely important article "The Philosophy and Theory of Music in Judeo-Arabic Literature," in *HUCA* (Hebrew Union College Annual) 16 (1941), pp. 251–319, and 17 (1942/43), pp. 511–72. The numerous Hebrew articles of the Syrian-born Israeli scholar Amnon Shiloah have also been immensely useful; for one of the best bibliographies on the whole subject, in a book that is itself of great value, see Dalia Cohen, *East and West in Music* (Jerusalem: Magnes Press, 1986)[Hebrew].

64. R. Hayyim Raphael Shoshannah, *I Shall Arise at Dawn* (Beersheba, 1986)[Hebrew], p. 22. For more on the North African tradition, see Haim Zafrani, *Poésie juive en occident musulman* (Paris: P. Geuthner, 1977).

65. Goitein, *A Mediterranean Society*, vol. 2, p. 195. For comparisons and influences, see Bayard Dodge's excellent *Muslim Education in Medieval Times* (Washington, D.C.: Middle East Institute, 1962).

66. Moses Ibn Ezra as cited by Dan Pagis, *Change and Tradition in Secular Poetry: Spain and Italy* (Jerusalem: Keter, 1976) [Hebrew], p. 43.

67. Goitein, *A Mediterranean Society*, vol. 2, p. 221.

68. Shasha, "Theories of Writing," pp. 146–47.

69. Cited by Nahum Menahem in *Ethnic Tension and Discrimination in Israel*, p. 83; p. 86 in the French edition.

70. Ross Brann, *The Compunctious Poet: Cultural Ambiguity and Hebrew Poetry in Muslim Spain* (Baltimore: Johns Hopkins University Press, 1991), p. 26. Also see pp. 25–28, 70.

71. Ibid., pp. 25–26.

72. See my "The Quill's Embroidery," *Parnassus: Poetry in Review* (Spring/Summer, 1983), pp. 85–115. The translation is from a composite of sources: the original Arabic, and two Hebrew versions, one by Ben Zion Halper and the other by Dan Pagis. The Arabic text, *The Book of Conversations and Memories*, is available on microfilm in the National Library at Hebrew University; a Hebrew version appeared as *Shirat Yisrael*, trans. B. Z. Halper (Leipzig, 1924). For the most accessible version, see M. Schreiner, "Le Kitab al-Mouhadara wa-l-Moudakara de Moise ibn Ezra et ses sources," *Revue des études juives* 21, pp. 98–117, and 22, pp. 230–40 (Paris, 1890–1891).

For the importance of language, both Hebrew and Arabic, see A. S. Halkin's "The Medieval Attitude Toward Hebrew," in *Biblical and Other Studies*, ed. A. Altmann (Cambridge, Mass.: Harvard University Press, 1963), and Anwar G. Chejne's definitive "Arabic: Its Significance and Place in the Arab Muslim Society," *The Middle Eastern Journal* 19 (1965), pp. 447–70.

More accessible than these is chapter 2 of Ross Brann's *The Compunctious Poet*, pp. 23–58.

73. "An Interview with Edmond Jabès Conducted by Jason Weiss," in *Conjunctions* 9 (1986), pp. 137–39.

74. This phrase of Victor Zuckerkandl's is quoted by Nathaniel Mackey in his "Sound and Sentiment, Sound and Symbol." For the original reference, see Victor Zuckerkandl, *Sound and Symbol: Music and the External World* (Princeton: Bollingen Foundation and Princeton University Press, 1956), p. 371.

75. Andras Hamori, *On the Art of Medieval Arabic Literature* (Princeton: Princeton University Press, 1974), p. 38. There is nothing even remotely comparable except Fedwa Malti Douglas's recent *Woman's Body, Woman's Word* (Princeton: Princeton University Press, 1991), received too late for inclusion here.

76. Adonis, *Introduction à la poetique arabe*, trans. Bassam Tahan and Anne Minkowski (Paris: Sindbad, 1985), p. 80 (my translation). Since writing this, an English version, translated by Catherine Cobham, has become available: Adonis, *An Introduction to Arab Poetics* (Austin: University of Texas, 1990), p. 60.

77. *Birds through a Ceiling of Alabaster: Three Abbasid Poets*, trans. G. B. H. Wightman and Y. A. al-Udhari (Harmondsworth: Penguin, 1975), p. 20.

78. Cooke; *War's Other Voices: Women Writers on the Lebanese Civil War* (Cambridge: Cambridge University Press, 1988), p. 43.

79. *Modern Poetry of the Arab World*, trans. and ed. Abdullah al-Udhari (Harmondsworth: Penguin, 1986), p. 73.

80. My translation; for the original text see Schirmann, *Hebrew Poetry in Spain and Provence*, vol. 1, pp. 34–35.

81. *The Penguin Book of Hebrew Verse*, ed. and trans. T. Carmi (New York and Harmondsworth: Viking Press and Penguin Books, 1981), p. 25. This remains the most accessible source of "modern" Levantine Hebrew poetry for the nonspecialist.

82. Jorge Luis Borges, *Labyrinths* (New York: New Directions, 1964), p. 149.

83. See Shmuel Moreh, "Live Theater in Medieval Islam," in *Studies in Islamic History and Civilization in Honour of Prof. David Ayalon* (Leiden: Brill, 1985), as well as Metin And, *A History of Theater and Popular Entertainment in Turkey* (Ankara, 1963–64), referred to by Bernard Lewis in *The Jews of Islam* (Princeton: Princeton University Press, 1984), p. 131.

84. Borges, *Labyrinths*, pp. 153–54.

85. Shasha, "Theories of Writing," pp. 74–75.

86. Judah al-Harizi, *The Tahkemoni*, trans. Victor Emanuel Reichert (Jerusalem: Raphael Haim Cohen Press, 1965–73), p. 32. As mentioned earlier, the popular Hebrew edition, *Sefer Tahkemoni*, edited by Y. Toporovsky (Tel Aviv, 1952), remains out of print. The equivalent of this, in terms of a national literature, would be if *The Canterbury Tales* remained out of print in English, *Don Quixote* out of print in Spanish, or *Eugene Onegin* out of print in Russian. While the fact that the *Tahkemoni* remains out of print is both shameful and ultimately inexplicable, it is to be hoped that the schema of cultural biases and power shifts outlined in this study goes some of the way toward contextualizing it.

87. Al-Harizi, *Tahkemoni*, pp. 35, 36–39.

88. Carmi, *Penguin Book of Hebrew Verse*, p. 309.

89. Al-Harizi, *Tahkemoni*, pp. 39–40.

90. Ibid., p. 38.

91. Ibid., p. 36.

92. Dan Pagis, "Variety in Medieval Rhymed Narratives," *Scripta Hierosolymitana*, vol. 27 (Jerusalem: Magnes, 1978), p. 86. This article by Pagis is one of the rare pieces of criticism to take the rhymed prose collections seriously as intentional narrative structures. For other examples of the rhymed narrative, see the superb translation by Raymond P. Scheindlin of Isaac Ibn Sahula's "The Sorcerer," in *Fiction*, vol. 7, nos. 1 and 2 (New York,

1983), as well as a version of Meir Ibn Zabara's *The Book of Delight* rendered by Moses Hadas (New York: Columbia University Press, 1932).

93. Shasha, "Theories of Writing," p. 83.

94. Al-Harizi, *Tahkemoni*, vol. 2, p. 186.

95. Ibid., p. 69.

96. David Yellin, *Introduction to the Hebrew Poetry of the Spanish Period* (Jerusalem: Magnes, 1978)[Hebrew], p. 120. For the most accessible catalog/compendium of Hebrew rhetorical figures — the Hebrew equivalent of Quintilian — see Judah Messer Leon, *The Book of the Honeycomb's Flow*, ed. and trans. by Isaac Rabinowitz (Ithaca: Cornell University Press, 1983).

97. M. Gertner, "On Translating Medieval Hebrew Writing," *Journal of the Royal Asiatic Society* 3/4 (1962–63), p. 178. This excellent but neglected article is one of the most suggestive available on the poetics of translation from Hebrew, with a particular emphasis on the practice and problematic of biblical citation.

98. Al-Harizi, *Tahkemoni*, p. 32.

99. *Arabic Poetics in the Golden Age*, ed. Vincente Cantarino (Leiden: Brill, 1975), p. 73.

100. Sanford Shepard, *Shem Tov: His World and His Words* (Miami: Ediciones Universal, 1978), p. 72. Shepard's fine distinctions between the romance practice of punning and the Semitic idea of participatory semantic paranomosia open areas of comparative poetics rarely touched upon. See pp. 67–78, "Poetics and Translation."

101. Cantarino, *Arabic Poetics in the Golden Age*, p. 82. For another, more theoretically complex and "up-to-date" view on Arabic poetics, see Jamal Eddine Ben Cheikh, *Poétique Arabe* (Paris: Editions Anthropos, 1975).

102. Kamal Abu Deeb, *Al-Jurjani's Theory of Poetic Imagery* (London: Aris and Phillips, 1979), pp. 280–81. Also see chapter 7, "The Psychological Approach to the Image," pp. 257–302. I am not aware of a more accessible work that suggests and traces the vast conceptual and theoretical riches of medieval Arabic poetics. In addition to Abu Deeb, G. J. H. van Gelder's *Beyond the Line: Classical Arabic Literary Critics on the Coherence and Unity of the Poem* (Leiden: Brill, 1982) is an important work.

103. My translation from H. Schirmann, *Hebrew Poetry in Spain and Provence*, vol. 2, p. 489.

104. Ibid., p. 489.

105. Al-Harizi, *Tahkemoni*, pp. 146–49. For some of the specific historical background to this, see S. D. Goitein's "Contemporary Letters on the Capture of Jerusalem by the Crusaders," *Journal of Jewish Studies* 3 (1952), pp. 162–77.

106. Carmi, *Penguin Book of Hebrew Verse*, p. 327.

107. Ibid., p. 297.

108. Ibid., p. 295.

109. Andras Hamori, *On the Art of Medieval Arabic Literature*, p. 98.

110. My translation from H. Schirmann, *Hebrew Poetry in Spain and Provence*, vol. 4, p. 446. Also see Carmi's fine translation in *The Penguin Book of Hebrew Verse*, p. 416.

For more on Todros Abulafia, unquestionably one of the most interesting and theoretically complex poets of the period, see chapter 5 of Ross Brann's *The Compunctious Poet*, pp. 119–157.

111. The ground-breaking work on the *khardjas* was done by Samuel Stern, *Hispano-Arabic Strophic Poetry*, ed. L. P. Harvey (Oxford: Clarendon Press, 1974). For a very brief but good presentation of some of the texts, see Dronke's *The Medieval Lyric*, pp. 86–90. On pp. 83–113 of *The Arabic Role in Medieval Literary History*, Menocal presents an overview of both the poems themselves and the various scholarly and ideological battles that have characterized almost all the writing on them.

An excellent introduction to the whole subject can be found in Susan Einbinder's "The Current Debate on the Muwashshah," *Prooftexts* 9 (1989), pp. 161–94. Her conclusion is particularly noteworthy and is one of the few instances where a medieval scholar has attempted to inject theoretical issues into the debate for the ends of accessibility: "The issues concerning the muwashshah are, in essence, 'large,' complex and even ideological issues, which have come to expression on exceedingly stratified ground and at stratospheric heights. Indeed, what may perhaps emerge as the most striking feature of muwashshah scholarship is not so much the 'obsessive interest' it currently generates as the obsessive lines of expression it has assumed. It has become virtually impossible to enter the field without a committed position on a series of questions posed in an absolute form of binary opposition. This rigid array of antitheses means more than that only certain questions are possible: certain others are equally impossible, given the current parameters . . . a subject which ideally and uniquely lends itself to the shared and open cooperation of multidisciplinary effort is instead characterized by scholastic contentiousness and fierce territoriality. . . . It may be that the most fascinating and portentous aspects of the muwashshah for us today are their refusal to comply with historically delimited categories of knowledge, genre and 'reading.' A kind of platypus of poetry, the muwashshah deserves the integrated efforts of interdisciplinary analysis" (pp. 172–74).

112. Carmi, *Penguin Book of Hebrew Verse*, p. 407.

113. Shmuel Trigano, *La nouvelle question juive* (Paris: Gallimard, 1979), p. 208.

114. See Shasha, "Theories of Writing," for an excellent translation, introduction, and analysis of Shem Tov.

115. Carmi, *Penguin Book of Hebrew Verse*, pp. 430–31.

116. Ibid., p. 477. For an excellent survey giving some sense of the enormous range of writing produced through this period, see M. Steinschneider's standard work, *Jewish Literature from the Eighth to the Eighteenth Century* (London, 1857).

117. Yehezqel Hai Albeg, from *Kenaf Renanim: Verses, Poems and Lyrics* (New York, no date), pp. 7–8. The text used here is from an unpublished English translation by David Shasha.

118. Miguel Cervantes, *Don Quixote*, trans. J. M. Cohen (Harmondsworth: Penguin, 1950), p. 76. For remarkable but much neglected material on the Jews in Spain, see the work of Raphael Cansinos-Assens, the brilliant polymath who was an early influence on Borges: *Los judios en la litératura española* (Buenos Aires: Columna, 1937); *Los judios en Sefarad: Episodios y simbolos* (Buenos Aires, 1950), and "Cervantes y los Israelitas españoles," *Los Quijotes*, vol. 2, no. 27 (Madrid, 1963), pp. 3–11.

119. Henry Kamen, *The Spanish Inquisition* (New York: New American Library, 1965), p. 14.

120. See Allan H. Cutler, *The Jew as an Ally of the Muslim* (Notre Dame, Ind.: Notre Dame University Press, 1986). For some of the figures and dates of the Moorish expulsion, see J. H. Elliott, *Imperial Spain, 1469–1716* (Harmondsworth: Penguin, 1970), pp. 305–8; and R. Trevor Davies, *The Golden Century of Spain, 1501–1621* (New York and Evanston: Harper Torchbooks, 1961), pp. 109, 169.

121. For a biography and assessment of Amatus Lusitano's medical career, as well as this text, see Harry Friedenwald, *The Jews and Medicine* (New York: Ktav, 1967), pp. 332–81.

122. Joseph Penso de la Vega, *Confusion de Confusiones 1688, Portions Descriptive of the Amsterdam Stock Exchange*, sel. and trans. Professor Hermann Kellenbenz (Boston: Baker Library / Harvard Graduate School of Business Administration, 1957), p. xvii.

123. Ibid., p. 18.

124. Ibid., p. 42.

125. Sanford Shepard, *Lost Lexicon: Secret Meanings in the Vocabulary of Spanish Literature During the Inquisition* (Miami: Ediciones Universal, 1982), p. 91. This book is an invaluable aid to any reading of Spanish golden age literature; in fact, after having read it, one is amazed at just how hermetic and cryptic that writing is and how all its myriad and twisted implications can possibly be grasped without the use of such a lexicon.

126. Stephen Gilman, *The Spain of Fernando de Rojas* (Princeton: Princeton University Press, 1972), p. 177. For the most accessible anthology of Marrano poetry, see Timothy Oelman, ed., *Marrano Poets of the Seventeenth Century* (Rutherford, N.J.: Farleigh Dickinson University Press, 1982).

127. In *The Renaissance Philosophy of Man*, ed. Ernst Cassirer, Paul Oskar Kristeller, and John H. Randall, Jr. (Chicago: Phoenix, 1948), p. 142.

128. See "Cavalcanti" in *The Literary Essays of Ezra Pound* (London: Faber and Faber, 1954), pp. 149–201.

129. The Petrarchan text is from the *Canzoniere*, Gianfranco Contini (Turin: Einaudi, 1964), XXIII, line 5. The Usque text is available in the Hispanic Society of America or, on microfilm, from the Weidner Library at Harvard University, as Salomon Usque, *Sonetos canciones, mandriales sextinas de gran POETA y orador Francisco Petrarca*, traduzidos de Toscano por Salomon Usque, Hebreo (Venezia: Nicolao Bevilaqua, 1567), p. 127.

130. Petrarch, *Canzoniere*, XXIII, lines 141–46.

131. Usque, *Sonetos*, p. 129.

132. Shepard, *Lost Lexicon*, p. 91.

133. Ibid., p. 142.

134. Marguerite Waller, *Petrarch's Poetics and Literary History* (Amherst: University of Massachusetts Press, 1980), p. 4.

135. Usque, *Sonetos*, p. 161.

136. Petrarch, *Canzoniere*, CCLXIV, lines 127–36.

137. My translation based on the text in Ezra Fleisher, "On Dunash Ben Labrat, His Wife and Son: New Light on the Beginnings of the Hebrew/Spanish School," *JSHL* (Jerusalem Studies in Hebrew Literature) 5 (1984), pp. 189–202 [Hebrew]. Also see Tova Rosen Moked's "On Tongues Being Bound and Let Loose: Women in Medieval Hebrew Literature," in *Prooftexts* 8 (1988), pp. 67–87.

138. Tillion, *The Republic of Cousins*, p. 103.

139. Fleischer, "On Dunash Ben Labrat."

140. My translation from a text found on the jacket notes of *Ladino Folk Songs* sung by Raphael Yair Elnadav (New York: Collectors Guild, 1961). For an excellent presentation of "folk-poetry" by women, see Mishael Maswari Caspi, *Daughters of Yemen* (Berkeley: University of California Press, 1985).

3. History's Noise: The Beginning of the End

1. See Charles Olson on Melville's trip to the Levant in *Call Me Ishmael* (San Francisco: City Lights, 1971), pp. 89–96.

2. Quoted in Olson, ibid., p. 95.

3. Ibid., p. 94.

4. Sadiq Jalal al-'Azm, "Orientalism and Orientalism in Reverse," in *Forbidden Agendas: Intolerance and Defiance in the Middle East*, selected and introduced by Jon Rothschild (London: Al-Saqi, 1984), pp. 349. This article constitutes part of the Arab critique of Edward Said's *Orientalism* and offers a much more interesting counterpart to the usual partisan objections one is used to getting in the United States from figures such as Bernard Lewis. Unfortunately, there is very little material available on this debate in English. For an intro-

ductory survey, see Emmanuel Sivan's "Edward Said and His Arab Reviewers," in *The Jerusalem Quarterly* 35 (Spring, 1985), pp. 11–23. While clearly working out of the revisionist discourse that Said pioneered, Maria Rosa Menocal offers some extremely subtle and important insights regarding the whole question of Arabs on European soil, an area not covered by Said; see pp. 21–22 of *The Arabic Role in Medieval Literary History* (Philadelphia: University of Pennsylvania Press, 1987).

In his *The Jews of Islam* (Princeton: Princeton University Press, 1984), considered by many to be an authoritative work, Lewis seems too ready to accept the traditional curve of light to darkness in the history of the Jews of the Levant; he incorporates only minor revisions to it. This approach gets more and more uncritical the closer he comes to the modern period. Accounts of the conditions of Jews in Arab countries are given almost exclusively through the writings of foreign visitors and are not related specifically to other local and global developments. Compare, for instance, Lewis's interpretation of the infamous Damascus blood libel of 1840 (pp. 156–58) with Nahum Menahem's in *Ethnic Tension and Discrimination in Israel* (Tel Aviv: 1983; Paris: Editions L'Harmattan, 1986) (pp. 243–51 in the Hebrew edition, pp. 212-20 in the French edition). The major differences between these two interpretations stem from Lewis's polemical versus Menahem's nonpolemical stance regarding the "intentions" of the "other," specifically here the Arab "other." The deeper implication of this is that Lewis seems to accept the existence of "anti-Semitism" as an immutable and eternal phenomenon that only appears at different times in different guises. These prejudices are more clearly delineated in his very uncritical reading of Arab "anti-Semitism." One could just as easily (as Nissim Rejwan has done on different occasions) compile a record of official "philo-Semitic" statements issued by various Arab leaders and bodies. Even more important, however, is the lack of attention Lewis pays to autonomous and native Jewish culture in the Levant. In other words, if life was as grim as the accounts of Westerners would have us believe, how was it possible for thousands of books to be written, for artisans to continue producing a wide variety of beautiful objects, or for Jews to attain positions of wealth and power in every Arab country they lived in right up until the dissolution of those communities in the 1940s and 1950s? These are realities that cannot easily be dealt with given the ideological biases that seem to overshadow Lewis's much more sympathetic reading of that period of Jewish/Arab symbiosis—the golden age of Spain—that *has* been culturally sanctioned as a period of "good" relations.

5. Marshall G. S. Hodgson, *The Venture of Islam: Conscience and History in a World Civilization. Volume Three, The Gunpowder Empires and Modern Times* (Chicago and London: University of Chicago Press, 1974), p. 177. Chapters 1 and 2 of book 6 ("The Impact of the Great Western Transmutation: The Generation of 1789" and "European World Hegemony," pp. 176–248) are models of informed and "sympathetic" scholarship that never cross the border into polemics or partisan reporting. For the basic source on the economic history of the period in the Levant, see Charles Issawi, ed., *The Economic History of the Middle East, 1800–1914: A Book of Readings* (Chicago: University of Chicago Press, 1966).

6. Charles Issawi, *The Fertile Crescent, 1800–1914: A Documentary Economic History* (New York: Oxford University Press, 1988), p. 5. This remarkable book is invaluable in gaining an understanding of the changing global context that went into shaping the modern Middle East.

7. Timothy Mitchell, *Colonising Egypt* (Berkeley: University of California Press, 1991), pp. 96, 34–35.

8. Abdelrahman Munif, *Cities of Salt* (New York: Vintage, 1989), pp. 594–95.

9. Hodgson, *Venture of Islam*, Vol. 5, pp. 179–205 (for an extensive discussion and definition of the "technical age," as Hodgson describes it).

10. This can be attested to most recently in the phenomenon of Levantine and Arab Jews in Israel adopting the religious customs and rites of the most intolerant and orthodox Eastern European Jews more as a defense mechanism than a genuine spiritual or cultural bent. This process has not yet been adequately documented even though it constitutes one of the most significant processes in the dissolution and marginalization of Judaism as a practical way of life and its transformation into an increasingly self-referential "religion," something that traditional Levantine and Arab rabbinic practice has always tried to avoid by a variety of means, particularly through an integrative approach to education. See José Faur, "Introducing the Materials of Sephardic Culture to Contemporary Jewish Studies," *American Jewish Historical Quarterly* 63 (1974).

11. Issawi, *Fertile Crescent*, p. 410.

12. Ibid., p. 411.

13. Ibid., p. 419.

14. Eric R. Wolf, *Europe and the People without History* (Berkeley: University of California Press, 1982), p. 294.

15. Haim Vidal Sephiha, *L'Agonie des judeo-espagnols* (Paris: Editions Entente, 1979), p. 43. For an excellent case study, see Michael M. Laskier's *The Alliance Israelite Universelle and the Jewish Communities of Morocco, 1862–1962* (Albany: SUNY Press, 1983).

16. Ilan Halevi, *A History of the Jews*, trans. A. M. Berrett (London, and Atlantic Highlands, N.J.: Zed Books, 1987), p. 201.

17. Shime'on Ballas, *The Other One* (Tel Aviv: Zmora-Bitan, 1991)[Hebrew], p. 19 (my translation).

18. Very little is available in English on this aspect of Levantine Jewish culture; to get some sense of it, see two of Sasson Somekh's excellent articles, "Lost Voices: Jewish Authors in Modern Arabic Literature," in Mark R. Cohen and Abraham L. Udovitch's *Jews among Arabs: Contacts and Boundaries* (Princeton: Darwin Press, 1989), pp. 9–20; and "Participation of Egyptian Jews in Modern Arabic Culture, and the Case of Murad Faraj," in Shimon Shamir, ed., *The Jews of Egypt: A Mediterranean Society in Modern Times* (Boulder: Westview Press, 1987), pp. 130–39. The quote preceding is also from this last article, p. 130.

19. See Zvi Zohar's translation of and very fine commentary on Rabbi Uziel's decision in *A Great Sephardic Posek Champions Women's Rights* (Jerusalem: Shalom Hartman Institute, 1985).

20. For one of the few efforts, see the last chapters of Rabbi Marc Angel's valiant attempt at explicating in a coherent way the parameters of post-exilic Sephardic thought, *Voices in Exile: A Study in Sephardic Intellectual History* (Hoboken, N.J.: Ktav), 1991; this book was not received in time to be fully used in writing this section.

21. See Elena Romero's meticulously documented and extremely important work in three volumes: *El teatro de los sefardíes orientales* (Madrid: Instituto "Arias Montano," 1979). A good overview of the French and Judeo-Spanish press can be found in chapter 9 (pp. 97–106) of Sephiha's *L'Agonie des judeo-espagnols*. For the Egyptian climate, see Irene L. Gendzier, *The Practical Visions of Yaqub Sanu* (Cambridge, Mass.: Harvard University Press, 1966). For general bibliographic information, see Shmuel Moreh, *Arabic Works by Jewish Writers, 1863–1973* (Jerusalem: Ben Zvi Institute for Research on Jewish Communities in the Middle East, 1973)[Arabic]; *The Writings of Sephardi and Oriental Jewish Authors in Languages Other than Hebrew: A Bibliographical Survey of Belles Lettres in the Twentieth Century*, vol. I, ed. with an introduction by Itzhak Betsalel (Tel Aviv: Tel Aviv University and the Center for the Integration of the Oriental Jewish Heritage, 1982); *Asian and African Jews in the Middle East, 1860–1971: Annotated Bibliography*, ed. by Hayyim J. Cohen and Zvi Yehuda (Jerusalem: Ben Zvi Institute, 1976) [Hebrew and English].

22. Quoted in G. N. Giladi, *Discord in Zion: Conflict between Ashkenazi and Sephardi Jews in Israel* (London: Scarpion, 1990), p. 281.

23. From Harvey Goldberg's introduction to *The Book of Mordekhai*, p. 25. The whole introduction is well worth referring to as an example of a highly sensitive reading of neglected material. For Slouschz, see his *My Travels in Libya*, 2 vols. (Tel Aviv: Va'ad Ha-Yovel, 1938–1943)[Hebrew], along with *Travels in North Africa* (Philadelphia: The Jewish Publication Society, 1927).

24. Harvey Goldberg in *Book of Mordekhai*, p. 24.

25. Ibid., p. 23. Here, Goldberg mentions another relationship between guide and native: "In a similar fashion, Slouschz' teacher at the Sorbonne, Joseph Halevi, did not even mention his guide, Habshush, in his reports on his travels in Yemen." Even more interesting is the fact that it was Goitein, in a similarly sensitive act of recuperation, who edited the extremely valuable Arabic texts of this very guide, Habshush. See his introduction to *Travels in Yemen as Related by Hayyim Habshush* (Jerusalem: The Ben Zvi Institute, 1983)[Hebrew and Arabic].

26. HaKohen, *Book of Mordekhai*, p. 24.

27. Ibid., pp. 13–14.

28. See Ehud Ben Ezer's "Brenner and the Arab Question," in *Modern Hebrew Literature*, vol. 12, nos. 3–4 (Spring/Summer, 1987), p. 22.

29. Yitzhaq Shami, "The Vengeance of the Fathers," trans. Richard Flantz, in *Eight Great Hebrew Short Novels*, ed. Alan Lelchuk and Gershon Shaked (New York: New American Library, 1983), p. 65.

30. Shami "Vengeance of the Fathers," p. 123.

31. Ibid., p. 126.

32. Ibid., p. 136.

33. For the relationship between Freud and Yahuda, see Ernest Jones, *The Life and Work of Sigmund Freud*, 3 vols. (New York: Basic Books, 1953), pp. 234, 370, and 373. In the abridged version, Yahuda is reduced to a footnote. His idiosyncratic critique of *Moses and Monotheism*, written from the point of view of both a traditional Levantine Jew and a pioneering scholar of the Egyptian language, appears as "Sigmund Freud on Moses and His Torah," in *'Eber ve 'Arab* (New York: Hebrew Union of America, 1946)[Hebrew], pp. 37–73.

34. Shami, "Vengeance of the Fathers," p. 157.

35. Ibid., pp. 61–62.

36. See Gershon Shafir's truly remarkable work, *Land, Labor and the Origins of the Israeli-Palestinian Conflict, 1882–1914* (Cambridge: Cambridge University Press, 1989), pp. 41–43. For another good work on the complex process of land dispossession in Palestine and the subsequent class transformation of peasants into workers, see Ylana M. Miller, *Government and Society in Rural Palestine, 1920–1948* (Austin: University of Texas Press, 1985). Shafir's book, however, by starting as early as it does and dealing in very specific data, presents a completely new picture that should substantially deflate many of the less concrete and more ideological theories regarding the origins of the conflict.

37. Avraham Haim Elhanani, *Literary Conversations* (Jerusalem: Reuben Mass, 1960) [Hebrew], p. 198.

38. Ibid., p. 196. This text also appears in Asher Barash's preface to Shami's collected stories, *The Stories of Yitzhaq Shami* (Tel Aviv: M. Neuman, 1971)[Hebrew, my translation].

39. Yehuda Burla, *In Darkness Striving*, trans. Joseph Schachter (Jerusalem: Institute for the Translation of Hebrew Literature and Israel Universities Press, 1968), p. 11.

40. Ibid., p. 12.

41. Ibid., p. 17.
42. Ibid., p. 33.
43. Ibid., p. 95.
44. Ibid., p. 107.
45. Ibid., p. 135.
46. Eliachar, *Living with Jews*, p. 519 (my translation).
47. See Ella Shohat, *Israeli Cinema: East/West and the Politics of Representation* (Austin: University of Texas Press, 1989), chapter 3.
48. Andre Nahum, *Partir en Kappara* (Paris: Piranhas Editions, 1977), p. 15.
49. Andrée Chedid, *The Return to Beirut* (London: Serpent's Tail, 1989), p. 46. Also see Evelyn Accad's *Sexuality and War*, p. 84.
50. Walter Benjamin, *Illuminations*, trans. Harry Zohn (New York: Schocken Books, 1969), p. 139.
51. Albert Cohen, *Solal*, trans. Wilfrid Benson (New York: E. P. Dutton, 1933), p. 242.
52. Benjamin, *Illuminations*, p. 255.
53. Cohen, *Solal*, pp. 316–17.
54. Ibid., p. 321.
55. Benjamin, *Illuminations*, p. 144.
56. Translation by Stephen Levy in *Voices within the Ark*, ed. Howard Schwartz and Anthony Rudolf (New York: Avon, 1980), p. 1046. Levy, interestingly enough, is an American poet who grew up speaking Judeo-Spanish; he was one of the founders of *Adelantre* (The Judezmo Society), which attempted to revive and preserve this embattled language. His own work has included a collection of translations from Judeo-Spanish. The original text appeared in *Esta Gimka es el Tresoro de Rachael Casteleta Ija de Jacov Yona*, published in London in 1959. For information on Yakob Yona, see Samuel G. Armistead and Joseph H. Silverman's excellent and extensively documented study, *The Judeo-Spanish Ballad Chapbooks of Yacob Abraham Yona* (Berkeley: University of California Press, 1971).
57. Edouard Roditi, *Thrice Chosen* (Santa Barbara: Black Sparrow, 1981), p. 78.
58. Ibid., p. 67.
59. Jacques Hassoun, with Mireille Nathan-Murat and Annie Radzynski, *Non lieu de la memoire: La cassure d'Auschwitz* (Paris: Bibliophane, 1990), pp. 20-21. The end of this passage, and the mention of Charon, involves an elaborate play on words as well as a historical reference to an incident at the end of the Algerian war that occurred during protests at the Charonne Metro station in Paris. The day after bombings by the O.A.S. aimed at leftist leaders and writers (including Sartre and Malraux) blinded the 4-year-old Delphine Renard, large demonstrations broke out. Eight people were killed and hundreds injured at the Metro station. A week after, an estimated half-million people joined the funeral procession of these victims and the days of France's role in Algeria were numbered. For a description of these events, see Alistair Horne's *A Savage War of Peace* (New York: Penguin, 1977), p. 504.

4. Postscript: "To end, to begin again"

1. The literature on the 1948 expulsion/flight is vast. For an extremely significant and new revisionist overview using only recently available archival sources see: Benny Morris, *The Birth of the Palestinian Refugee Problem, 1947–49* (Cambridge: Cambridge University Press, 1988). A pioneering work that still remains immensely useful is Don Peretz, *Israel and the Palestine Arabs* (Washington, D.C.: Middle East Institute, 1958). For a rather shocking graphic account that, unfortunately, has no equivalent in English, see Kostandi Nikola Abu-Hammud, *Directory of Geographical Names in Palestine* (Jerusalem: The Arab Studies Society, 1984)[Arabic]; this book simply lists, along with a brief descriptive note on each, the

place names of some 400 destroyed Palestinian villages. Most recently, see Walid Khalidi, *All That Remains* (Washington: Institute for Palestine Studies, 1992). Ibrahim Abu-Lughod's *The Transformation of Palestine* (Evanston: Northwestern University Press, 1971) is a basic source. For specific accounts see: Walid Khalidi's "The Fall of Haifa," *Middle East Forum* 35 (Dec., 1959); and Nafez Nazzal's "The Zionist Occupation of Western Galilee, 1948," *Journal of Palestine Studies*, vol. 3, no. 3, (Spring, 1974). On politics, a major contribution is Simha Flapan, *The Birth of Israel: Myths and Realities* (New York: Pantheon, 1987).

Not enough has been written on the specific instances of property "exchange" in the global sense, in which the Jewish refugees from Middle Eastern countries—whose property and goods had been expropriated—were assigned "absentee" property in Israel. The one work that gives at least some sense of the implications of this is Abbas Shiblak's *The Lure of Zion: The Case of the Iraqi Jews* (London: Al-Saqi, 1986). Also see chapters 2 and 3 of Tom Segev's groundbreaking *1949: The First Israelis* (New York: The Free Press, 1986). For the Palestinian side, see Sami Hadawi's comprehensive *Palestinian Rights and Losses in 1948* (London: Al-Saqi, 1987).

2. "The attitude of the first Israelis toward the newcomers was complex and self-contradictory, charged with emotions and infused with prejudices, reflecting their self-images as Jews and Israelis. The key to their attitudes toward the immigrants lies in their contemptuous attitude toward the Diaspora. Most tended to regard themselves as Israelis first and Jews second. Israel was above all. . . . They discarded ancient Jewish cultures and did so without compunction, for they believed that they were making the only relevant history; the State of Israel meant more to them than the preservation of Jewish culture abroad." See pp. 117–18 in Segev, *1949: The First Israelis*.

3. Quoted in Rolli Rozen's article on Tom Segev's new book, "Us and Them," *Kol Ha'Ir* (September 20, 1991)[Hebrew], pp. 29–30.

4. Ibid.

5. Ibid., p. 30.

6. Ibid.

7. Ibid., p. 31.

8. Ibid., pp. 30–31.

9. Segev, *1949: The First Israelis*, p. 170.

10. Mordekhai HaKohen's description of the Italian invasion of Libya in *The Book of Mordekhai*, p. 185: "The remaining Moslems, who were unable to escape by the skin of their teeth, did so by denying they were Moslems. Hitherto, it had been a terrible disgrace for a Mohammedan to say "I am a Jew" or "I am a Christian," but on that day the tables were turned. In order to save his life, the Moslem found it expedient to say, "I am a Jew," to fool the Italians, who could not differentiate between the two."

11. Segev, *1949: The First Israelis*, pp. 157–58.

12. The tragic fate of the "lost" Yemenite children, an unknown number of children taken from their parents and put up for adoption to middle and upper-class Ashkenazi families during the transit camp period, keeps resurfacing in Israel. Most of the material on this is either from the Hebrew press or in works that are very difficult to get hold of, written within the Yemenite community itself in Israel. The only work in English that I am aware of that has accurate references to the Hebrew press as well as to other sources is Rabbi Moshe Schonfeld's *Genocide in the Holy Land* (Brooklyn: Bnei Yeshivos, 1980). For references to the Hebrew press and archival material, see notes 22 and 23 in Giladi's *Discord in Zion: Conflict between Ashkenazi and Sephardi Jews in Israel* (London: Scorpion, 1990), p. 110, where he refers to the following: "State Archives, Prime Minister's Office, Immigrant Camps 5558C: 11 April 1950, 18 April 1950 and 8 May 1950," also *Ma'ariv* of April 1, 1966, and "March 1968, State Archives, 1/968/1."

13. See G. N. Giladi, *Discord in Zion*, pp. 304–5. Also see the coverage in *Ha'Aretz*, October 13, 1978, of the in-camera trials of organization members for 13 acts of arson carried out between 1975 and 1978 in the Tel Aviv area.

14. Joel Brinkley, "In Emigre Crush, Tent Towns Sprout for Israelis," *New York Times* (Friday, June 22, 1990), p. A10.

15. In the preface to vol. 1 of Goitein's *Mediterranean Society* (Berkeley: University of California Press, 1967–83), p. viii.

16. The original Hebrew text can be found in Rabbi Moshe Schonfeld's *Genocide in the Holy Land* (my translation). For some background on the Yemenite arrival in Israel, see Segev, *1949*, pp. 178–94. For a more specialized and comprehensive work, see Niza Droyan, *And Not with a Magic Carpet* (Jerusalem: Ben Zvi Institute, 1982)[Hebrew].

17. Kalman Katznelson, *The Ashkenazi Revolution* (Tel Aviv, 1964), p. 83.

18. Shmuel Trigano, *La nouvelle question juive* (Paris: Gallimard, 1979), pp. 30–31.

19. Kalman Katznelson, *The Ashkenazi Reckoning* (Tel Aviv: Anakh, 1989)[Hebrew], p. 54.

20. From an interview with Joseph Cohen in *Voices of Israel* (Albany: SUNY Press, 1990), p. 181.

21. This term is used in the sense delineated by Benedict Anderson in his *Imagined Communities: Reflections on the Origin and Spread of Nationalism* (London: Verso, 1983). See pp. 14–16.

22. See pp. 164–65 in Ilan Halevi, *A History of the Jews*, trans. A. M. Berrett (London, and Atlantic Highlands, N.J.: Zed Books, 1987): "The attempt to consider, as Ben–Gurion did, the Jewish nation as a single entity all through history, from the exodus from Egypt to modern Israel, with the same identity, was bound to lead Zionist theoreticians to an apologetic and essentialist falsification of the history of the Jews, with which the whole Israeli educational system is deeply impregnated: the mass production of false consciousness." This consciousness has become so ingrained that those historians who stray from the consensus, not treating the Jews as a "single entity," are considered radical revisionists.

23. For more on the controversy surrounding this poem, see my "Who's Afraid of Mahmoud Darwish?" in *MERIP Reports* 154 (Sept./Oct. 1988), pp. 26–28; the passage from Shiloah is quoted from p. 28. Also see Mahmoud Darwish, *Palestine mon pays* (Paris: Editions de Minuit, 1988), with articles by Simone Bitton, Matityahu Peled, and Uri Avneri surveying the Israeli reactions to the poem.

24. See the bulletin of which Yehoshua served as editor, *Majallat al-Ahbar il-Islamiyyah* (Journal of Islamic News), published in Jerusalem by the Israeli Ministry of Religious Affairs from 1949 to 1974 [Arabic]. Further information on the function of this ministry was taken from David Neuhaus, "Politics and Islam in Israel 1948–1987," an unpublished master's thesis for the Department of Political Science at the Hebrew University.

25. Joseph Cohen interview, *Voices of Israel*, pp. 69–71, where Yehoshua describes his family background. Also see Eliachar, *Living with Jews*, p. 519, following the passages on Yehuda Burla: "The last manifestation that confirms my claims against the Sephardic intelligentsia is A. B. Yehoshua's confession that he is uninterested in the ethnic problem."

26. Some significant examples include the previously mentioned book by Nahum Menahem, *Ethnic Tension and Discrimination in Israel* (Tel Aviv: 1983, also available in French as *Israel: tensions et discriminations communautaires*), and Mordekhai Gabbai, *Whom Does the Israeli Establishment Serve* (Kfar Kadima, 1984). Both of these books are ostensibly "sociological" approaches, yet they provide true alternative histories with quite unorthodox conceptual assumptions and a good amount of original archival research. Another important book, Dr. Abraham Matalon's *The Hebrew Pronunciation in Its Struggle* (Tel Aviv: Hadar, 1979)[Hebrew], shows to just what extent the "subject" of such works is interconnected to

the aims and approaches of their authors. Through elaborate and exacting linguistic proofs and arguments, Matalon explicates a very succint thesis, namely, that only when Israelis pronounce Hebrew correctly (i.e., closer to the Arabic pronunciation), will there be a possibility for them to creatively and autonomously interact with their natural geographic, political, and cultural environment.

Afiqim (Tel Aviv), and *BeMa'arakha* (published by the Council of the Sephardic Communities in Jerusalem), are among the significant, more traditional "Oriental" journals that have been around for a number of years; *'Iton Aher* (a forum for social and political criticism edited by David Hamo in Haifa), *Aperion* (a journal of Mediterranean literature and arts edited by the poet Erez Bitton), and *Pa'amon* (a Tel Aviv neighborhood newspaper centered on local social and cultural issues), are among the more important newer projects to have appeared in the past five years. To document all this material systematically would require a separate study in itself.

As far as historiography is concerned, the tradition of history writing among Levantine and Arab Jews goes back to the beginnings of Jewish historiography itself. For a highly sensitive reading that probes the concerns of those writers who first worked in fifteenth and sixteenth century Spain, see Yosef H. Yerushalmi's *Zakhor: Jewish History and Jewish Memory* (Seattle: University of Washington Press, 1982). Yerushalmi defines memory as the central element shaping the forms used by these early writers and counters it to the development of modern Jewish history writing — more analytical but somehow outside of memory, constantly attempting to recuperate the collective experience of an imagined community — which commences with the Enlightenment. My own sense of this is that the tradition of memory writing does continue unabated within the Levantine and Arab context despite the considerable inroads made by European education along with Enlightenment models and conceptual structures. Thus the work of many late nineteenth and early twentieth century "local" historians such as Abraham Elmaleh, Moise Franco, Abraham Galante, Joseph Nehama, Salomon Rosanes, and Jacob Toledano seems much more an outgrowth of the rabbinic culture preceding it than a radically new and European implantation. The fact that many of these writers took to the chronicle form is naturally related to the kinds of vast and sweeping changes occurring throughout the Levant, as discussed in chapter 3. In addition, their work simply seems to make more sense when placed in the context of both their predecessors (rabbinic writers and the fifteenth and sixteenth century Spanish historiographers, such as Joseph HaKohen and Solomon Ibn Verga, discussed by Yerushalmi) and their contemporary followers, such as Menahem, Gabbai, or Matalon.

27. For some of the basic works on the Palestinians who remained within Israel after 1948, see Sabri Jiryis, *The Arabs in Israel* (New York: Monthly Review Press, 1976); Elia Zureik, *The Palestinians in Israel: A Study in Internal Colonialism* (London: Routledge and Kegan Paul, 1979); and Ian Lustick, *Arabs in the Jewish State: Israel's Control of a National Minority* (Austin: University of Texas Press, 1980).

28. Reuven Snir, " 'We Were Like Those Who Dream': Iraqi-Jewish Writers in Israel in the 1950s," in *Prooftexts* 11 (1991), pp. 156, 163–64.

29. Ibid., 165; trans. Susan Einbinder.

30. Interview with Samir Naqqash, in the Hebrew literary journal *Moznayim* 3/4 (November-December, 1989), p. 34.

31. Gershon Shaked, "Waves and Currents in Hebrew Fiction in the Past Forty Years," in *Modern Hebrew Literature* (new series) 1 (Fall/Winter, 1988), pp. 4–12; and "The Arab in Israeli Fiction," in *Modern Hebrew Literature* (new series) 3 (Fall, 1989), pp. 17–20.

32. Shime'on Ballas, *The Transit Camp* (Tel Aviv: 'Am 'Oved, 1964)[Hebrew], p. 51 (my translation).

33. Snir, " 'Like Those Who Dream,' " p. 162.

34. Barbara Harlow, *Resistance Literature* (New York: Methuen, 1987), p. 116.

35. Shime'on Ballas, *Downtown* (Tel Aviv: Sifriyat Tarmil, 1979)[Hebrew], pp. 13, 15, 17 (my translation).

36. Ibid., pp. 24, 31.

37. Ibid., p. 48.

38. Shime'on Ballas, "Imaginary Childhood," *The Jerusalem Quarterly* 21 (Fall, 1981), p. 60.

39. Shime'on Ballas, *The Other One* (Tel Aviv: Zmora Bitan, 1991), pp. 150–51.

40. Orly Toren, "I Am an Arab Jew" (an interview with Shime'on Ballas), *Kol Ha'Ir* (March 15, 1991)[Hebrew], p. 78 (my translation).

41. Ibid., p. 83.

42. Maggie Gee, in *The Rushdie File*, ed. Lisa Appignanesi and Sara Maitland (Syracuse: Syracuse University Press, 1990), p. 182.

43. Sami Mikhael, *Refuge* (Tel Aviv: 'Am 'Oved, 1977)[Hebrew], p. 372 (my translation). The English translation (Philadelphia: Jewish Publication Society, 1988) provides a different stress on the last sentence by choosing not to translate the Hebrew word *stam* (just), and it reads like this: "He was an Arab. She was a Jew" (p. 382).

44. Erica Hunt, "Notes for an Oppositional Poetics," in Charles Bernstein, ed., *The Politics of Poetic Form: Poetry and Public Policy* (New York: Roof Books, 1990), p. 203.

45. Barbara Christian, "The Race for Theory," in Gloria Anzaldúa, ed., *Making Face, Making Soul: Haciendo Caras* (San Francisco: Aunt Lute Foundation, 1990), p. 336.

46. For a detailed description of these writers and their works, see Shmuel Moreh and Lev Hakak's *Contemporary Literary and Academic Works by Iraqi Jews in Iraq and Israel* (Or Yehuda: Center for the Tradition of Babylonian Jewry, 1981) [Hebrew].

47. See Buzaglio's interview with Ovadia, "There isn't anyone who won't cry at this movie," in *Yidi'ot Ahronot* (September 17, 1991) [Hebrew], p. 22.

48. Ella Shohat, *Israeli Cinema: East/West and the Politics of Representation* (Austin: University of Texas Press, 1989), p. 126.

49. Ibid., p. 127.

50. Ibid., see p. 127 in particular and the whole chapter "The 'Bourekas' and Sephardi Representation," pp. 115–78.

51. Ibid., pp. 272–73. For more definitive statements on the nature of the movies referred to, see chapter 5, "The Return of the Repressed: The Palestinian Wave in Recent Israeli Cinema," pp. 236–73. Specifically, for *Beyond the Walls*, see pp. 252–53 and pp. 268–71; references to *Hamsin* are also scattered throughout the chapter.

52. My translation from Bracha Serri, *Seventy Wandering Poems* (Jerusalem: Bracha Serri, 1982), pp. 144–45.

53. Erez Bitton, *A Bird Between Continents* (Tel Aviv: Ha Kibbutz HaMeyuhad, 1990)[Hebrew], p. 38 (my translation).

54. Erez Bitton, *Minha Marokayit* (Tel Aviv: 'Eqed, 1976)[Hebrew], p. 29 (my translation). For biographical information on Bitton, see Dr. Shlomo Elbaz, *Revendication ou éveil culturel?* (Departement des Communautes Sepharades Organisation Sioniste Mondiale, Petite Collection Sepharade) [no date or place of publication], p. 18.

55. *The Modern Hebrew Poem Itself*, ed. Stanley Burnshaw, T. Carmi, and Ezra Spicehandler (Cambridge, Mass.: Harvard University Press, 1989), p. 220.

56. *Israeli Poetry: A Contemporary Anthology*, sel. and trans. Warren Bargad and Stanley F. Chyet (Bloomington: Indiana University Press, 1988), p. 3.

57. For more on this cultural schizophrenia, see chapter 3 of Ella Shohat's book *Israeli Cinema*; also see her article "Sephardim in Israel: Zionism from the Standpoint of Its Jewish Victims," in *Social Text* 19/20 (Fall, 1988), pp. 1–35.

58. For some interesting material on this phenomenon, see Jay Murphy's "Palestinian Art Under Occupation," in *Paper Air*, vol. 4, no. 3 (Philadelphia: Singing Horse Press, 1990), pp. 69–72.

59. Yitshaq Gormezano Goren, *Blanche* (Tel Aviv: 'Am 'Oved, 1986)[Hebrew], pp. 206–7 (my translation).

60. Yitshaq Gormezano Goren, *Alexandrian Summer* (Tel Aviv: 'Am 'Oved, 1979), pp. 8–9.

61. Ibid., p. 198.

62. Ibid., p. 147.

63. Ibid., pp. 197–198.

64. Ibid., p. 5.

65. Goren, *Blanche*, p. 212 (my translation).

66. Translated by Rebecca Toueg in *Modern Hebrew Literature*, vol. 12, nos. 3–4 (Tel Aviv: Institute for Hebrew Translation, 1987), p. 45.

67. Ibid., p. 44.

68. My translation from *And the Moon Drips Madness* (Tel Aviv: 'Am 'Oved, 1984) [Hebrew], p. 9.

69. My translation in *Ariel* (Jerusalem: Jerusalem Post Publications, no. 67, 1987), pp. 88–90. For Freud's sense of antithetical words mentioned below, see "The Antithetical Sense of Primal Words" in his *On Creativity and the Unconscious* (New York: Harper and Row, 1958).

70. Bruce Boone, "Writing, Power and Activity," in *The L=A=N=G=U=A=G=E Book*, ed. Bruce Andrews and Charles Bernstein (Carbondale and Edwardsville: Southern Illinois University, 1984), p. 145.

71. Translated by Gabriel Levin in *Modern Hebrew Literature*, vol. 12, nos. 3–4, (Tel Aviv: Institute for Hebrew Translation, 1987), p. 26.

72. My translation from Ronny Someck, *7 Lines on the Wonder of the Yarkon* (Tel Aviv: Opatowski, 1987), p. 5.

73. Lea Goldberg, "Tel Aviv 1935," trans. T. Carmi in *The Penguin Book of Hebrew Verse* (Harmondsworth: Penguin, 1981), pp. 553–54.

74. Ronny Someck, *Panther* (Tel Aviv: Zmora Bitan, 1989)[Hebrew], p. 18 (my translation).

75. Ibid., p. 19.

76. My translation from manuscript by Tikva Levi.

77. My translation; the original text appeared in *'Iton Aher* (An Other Newspaper), published in Haifa, 1989. This translation also appears in *MERIP Reports* 159 (July/August, 1989), pp. 20–21.

78. This poem is from an upcoming collection of Chetrit's, received in manuscript.

79. Juan Goytisolo, *Count Julian*, trans. Helen R. Lane (New York: Viking, 1974). See pp. ix, x, and xi of Carlos Fuentes's preface.

80. Juan Goytisolo, *Juan the Landless*, trans. Helen R. Lane (New York: Viking, 1977), p. 268.

81. David Grossman, *The Yellow Wind* (New York: Delta, 1989), trans. Haim Watzman, p. 153.

82. Gilbert Sorrentino, "Language: Lying and Treacherous," in *New York Times Book Review* (May 25, 1986), p. 23.

83. For example, the leading Israeli literary critic Dan Miron praised Shammas's portrayal of "the behavior of people and animals," attributing it to the "intuitive understanding of a villager," while claiming that the parts of the book taking place outside the village are unsuccessful because "Shammas has not yet reconciled himself intellectually and emo-

tionally with his past." See the *Jerusalem Post Magazine* (December 12, 1986), p. 18. In "The Double Bind: Anton Shammas' Arabesques" (unpublished paper), David Shasha notes: "It comes as a tremendous shock to Israelis that this noble savage, this enfant terrible, has inserted a narrative of his journeys from Jerusalem to Paris to Iowa. In the words of translator and critic Hillel Halkin: 'I felt cheated. No longer was I reading a magical novel about an ordinary and wondrous Palestinian village, but rather a flat exercise in literary modernism, with its airplane flights and cocktail parties, its self-conscious artifice and look-at-me-ness, its multiple narrators, split identities and writers writing about writing.' This, of course, is to simply ignore the very artifice that allows the metamorphoses of the "tale" to un-cocoon themselves."

84. Jamal Eddine Ben Cheikh, "Ecriture et ideologie (la littérature algérienne horizon 2000)," in *Les Temps Modernes* (Paris: October, 1977), p. 377.

85. Anton Shammas, *Arabesques*, trans. Vivian Eden (New York: Harper and Row, 1988), p. 241.

86. Etel Adnan, *Sitt Marie Rose*, trans. Georgina Kleege (Sausalito, Calif.: Post-Apollo Press, 1982), p. 39.

87. For some very current material on this phenomenon, see the article on Hawla Abu Baker, an Israeli Palestinian researcher of children's literature in the Arab world: "Little Red Riding Hood: Once Upon a Time There Was a Palestinian Child . . . " *Yidi'ot Aharonot* (June 22, 1990) pp. 47–48. For the Israeli side, see "Caution: Poison for Children?" in *Ha'Olam HaZe* (June 13, 1990), pp. 32–35.

88. Assia Djebar, "A Forbidden Glimpse, A Broken Sound," trans. J. M. McDougal, in *Women and Family in the Middle East: New Voices of Change*, ed. Elizabeth Warnock Fernea (Austin: University of Texas, 1985), p. 350. Originally in Assia Djebar, *Femmes d'Alger dans leur appartement* (Paris: des femmes, 1980), pp. 167–89.

In addition to the Fernea volume cited above (and the works listed in chapter 2, note 37), the following are some of the books I have found most useful on women in the contemporary Mediterranean and Arab world: Sarah Graham Brown, *Images of Women: The Portrayal of Women in Photography of the Middle East, 1860–1950* (New York: Columbia University Press, 1988); Malek Alloula, *The Colonial Harem* (Minneapolis: University of Minnesota Press, 1985); Judith Tucker, *Women in 19th Century Egypt* (London and New York: Cambridge University Press, 1985); Huda Shaarawi, *Harem Years: The Memoirs of an Egyptian Feminist*, trans. Margot Badran (London: Virago Press, 1986); *Women in the Muslim World*, ed. Lois Beck and Nikki Keddie (Cambridge, Mass.: Harvard University Press, 1978); *Scholars, Saints and Sufis: Muslim Religious Institutions in the Middle East Since 1500*, ed. Nikki R. Keddie (Berkeley: University of California Press, 1972); *Middle Eastern Muslim Women Speak*, ed. Elizabeth Warnock Fernea and Basima Qattan Bezirgan (Austin and London: University of Texas Press, 1977); Nawal El-Saadawi, *The Hidden Face of Eve: Women in the Arab World*, trans. Sherif Hetata with a foreword by Irene L. Gendzier (Boston: Beacon Press, 1982); Elizabeth Warnock Fernea, *Guests of the Sheik* (Garden City, N.Y.: Anchor Doubleday, 1969), and *A Street in Marrakech* (Garden City, N.Y.: Anchor Doubleday, 1975); Nayra Atiya, *Khul-Khaal: Five Egyptian Women Tell Their Stories* (Cairo: American University Press, 1984); *Women of the Mediterranean*, ed. Monique Gadant (London: Zed Press, 1986); *Women of the Fertile Crescent: Modern Poetry by Arab Women*, ed. Kamal Boullata (Washington, D.C.: Three Continents Press, 1981), and Foroogh Forrokhzaad, *A Rebirth*, trans. David Martin (Lexington: Mazda, 1985).

A very important and more recent book is Margot Badran and Miriam Cooke's *Opening the Gates: A Century of Arab Feminist Writing* (Bloomington: Indiana University, 1990).

Also, the following periodicals: *Khamsin 6*, a special issue on "Women in the Arab World," and *MERIP Reports* 58 ("Women in Egypt"), 82 ("Egypt's Working Women"), 95

("Women and Work"), 124 ("Women and Labor Migration"), and 138 ("Women and Politics").

89. Hassan Fathy, *Natural Energy and Vernacular Architecture*, ed. Walter Shearer and Abd-el-rahman Ahmed Sultan (Chicago: University of Chicago Press, 1986), pp. xix, xx.

90. Saleem Shahed, "Profile: Abdul Wahed El Wakil—Interpreter of a Living Tradition," in *Arts: The Islamic World*, vol. 1, no. 4 (Winter 1983/84), p. 64.

91. Interview from Ferid Boudjedir's 1987 film *Camera Arabe*.

92. Ibid.

93. Andrea Dworkin, *Intercourse* (London: Arrow Books, 1987), p. 167.

94. From Boudjedir, *Camera Arabe*.

95. Djebar, "Forbidden Glimpse."

96. From Nouri Bouzid's film *The Man of Ashes*, Tunisia, 1987.

97. Manuscript received from Eva Zeintraub, Kahanoff's literary executor.

98. Shmuel Trigano, *La nouvelle question juive* (Paris: Gallimard, 1979), p. 264 (my translation).

Index

Abbasid poetry, 93-94, 101, 113
Abdallah, Yahya Taher, 79-80
Abraham, 116, 150, 216, 268; in
    contemporary Israeli poetry, 272-73
Abravanel, Isaac, 126
Abravanel, Judah, 185
Abu Deeb, Kamal, 309 n. 102
Abulafia, Todros: "Poem from Prison,"
    178
Abu-Lughod, Ibrahim, 315-16 n. 1
Abu-Lughod, Janet, 3, 8, 123-25, 132
Accad, Evelyn, 62-63
Adler, Elkan, 129
Adnan, Etel, 82, 92, 97-98, 103-4, 106-7,
    118, 195, 250, 264, 266, 280; Beirut,
    civil war in Lebanon, 88-89; language
    and colonial education, 74; and Umm
    Kulthum, 77-79
Adonis, 12, 96, 113; on Mutanabbi, 176;
    on Abu Nuwas, 159; poetics of,
    99-108; translation into Hebrew, 109
Agnon, S. Y., 230, 255; on Arabs, 56
Akhmatova, Anna, 149
Albeg, Yehezkel Hai, 182-83
Alexandria, 120, 123; in works of Y. H.
    Brenner, 52-53; in Israeli narrative,
    256-60
Alliance schools, 40, 44-45, 200, 207
Alloula, Malek, 295 n. 75, 321 n. 88
Almanzi, Giusseppe, 153, 182
Almeida, Manuela Nuñes de, 193
Almosnino, Moses, 184, 195
Aloni, Nissim, 253
Amichai, Yehuda, 232
Amir, Aharon, 232, 249
Amrouche, Taos, 12
Andalusian Group, 93
Andalusian poetry, 155-83
Anderson, Benedict, 317 n. 21
Angel, Rabbi Marc, 313 n. 20
Antebbi, Albert: as an example of a native
    Jew, 52-55, 60-61, 209
Antin, David, 86-87
Arabia, southern, 120
Arabic: and Beirut, 90-91; Bible,
    translation into by Sa'adiah Gaon, 156;
    contemporary novel, 62-63; Europe,

transmission of poetics to, 188-89; and
    European literature, 5-7, 144-46; and
    exile, 91-99; use of by Juan Goytisolo,
    276; growth of, 120-22; Hebrew,
    relationship to, 283; Yusuf Idris, and
    use of colloquial, 81-83; Iraq, writing
    of by Jews in, 204; Israel, Palestinian
    Arabic culture in, 234-35; Israeli
    Hebrew, influence on, 276-77; Israel
    writing of Jews in, 234-35; Jews, loss
    of as native language, 51; Koran,
    inimitability of, 157-58; medieval
    poetics, 163-64, 172-73; oral and
    written traditions, 158-59; pre-Islamic
    Jewish poetry in, 156; pre-Islamic
    poetry, 150-51, 158-59; translations of,
    8-9
Arab Jews, 235-45; cultural activities of,
    201-2, 313 n. 18, 313 n. 21, 319 n. 46;
    legitimacy of Arab Jewish intellectuals
    in Israel, 235-39, 293 n. 50
Arabs: and Europe, 3-4, 11-13, 305 n. 27;
    and expansion of Islam, 36, 120-23;
    and expulsion from Spain, 184-85; and
    Jews, 4-5, 27, 57-59, 310 n. 120, 316
    n. 10; and minorities, 44-51, 122-23
Arayde, Naim, 57
Ardutiel, Sem Tob, 180
Argov, Zohar, 254
Aristotle, 168, 172; position in Hellenic
    world, 167
Arlosoroff, Haim, 55
Ascarelli, Deborah, 193
Ashkenazim, 25; and Arabs, 24-25; and
    Oriental Jews, 30-33, 39-44; party
    system of, 39-42
Ashtor, Eliahu, 303 n. 3, 304 n. 6
Asmahan, 254
Atrache, Farid al-, 254
Auschwitz, 254
Avayou, Shlomo, 255
Averroës (Ibn Rushd), 5, 172; cultural/
    historical fate of in West, 12-13; and
    "old metaphors," 163-64
Avicenna (Ibn Sina), 6, 121, 172
Avissar, David, 209
Azulai, Hayyim David, 153

323

Permissions

Hebrew Literature; Norman A. Stillman, *The Jews of Arab Lands in Modern Times,* © 1991 Jewish Publication Society.

Every effort has been made to obtain permission to reproduce copyright material in this book. The publishers ask copyright holders to contact them if permission to reprint has inadvertently not been sought or if proper acknowledgment has not been made.

Ammiel Alcalay is a writer, translator, and poet who lives in New York City. Currently an assistant professor of Hebrew literature in the Department of Classical and Oriental Literatures at Queens College (CUNY), he has written numerous articles on literary and history politics in the cultures of the Mediterranean.